THE MAGIC BOX

by the same author

ELECTRIC EDEN: UNEARTHING BRITAIN'S VISIONARY MUSIC
ALL GATES OPEN: THE STORY OF CAN (with Irmin Schmidt)

THE MAGIC BOX

Viewing Britain
Through the Rectangular Window

Presented by
Rob Young

faber
MMXXI

First published in the UK and the USA in 2021
by Faber & Faber Limited
Bloomsbury House
74–77 Great Russell Street
London WC1B 3DA

Typeset by Ian Bahrami
Printed and bound by CPI Group (UK) Ltd, Croydon, CR0 4YY

A CIP record for this book
is available from the British Library

ISBN 978–0–571–28459–7

MIX
Paper from
responsible sources
FSC® C020471

10 9 8 7 6 5 4 3 2 1

Contents

THE VINTAGE LENS

DIVIDED KINGDOM

THE WEIRD OLD ALBION

I've dreamt in my life dreams that have stayed with me ever after, and changed my ideas; they've gone through and through me, like wine through water, and altered the colour of my mind.

Emily Brontë, *Wuthering Heights*

When the waterholes were dry, people sought to drink at the mirage.

Evelyn Waugh, *Brideshead Revisited*

Sooner or later, everything turns into television.

J. G. Ballard, *The Day of Creation*

The eyeless screen of dawn. No cock is crowing. Instead, a clock's serrated circle materialises on a blue sky.

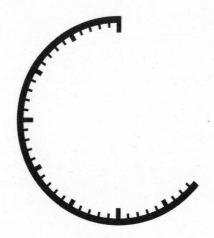

Second by second, time counts down like berries plucked from a branch. The scale eats itself away; the circle dwindles to the last few seconds and vanishes. Valves heat up and burn off the night's dust. Ghost ions float towards the inner surface of the glass.

The watchers are out there, ready to receive.

Fanfare.

Introduction

The Test Card

Long ago, in the corner of Eileen and Joe's living room, there stood a magic box.

The magic box lived next to the fireplace with its decorative brass poker and tongs, symmetrically guarded by a pair of porcelain spaniels.

Whenever it was time to look into the magic box, my grandparents would grasp the grooved Bakelite handles, carefully fold back the walnut doors, and reveal the dull, grey, convex window set into its brown veneer casing. The box awoke when a circular knob was twisted clockwise. Rolling its ridged surface between thumb and forefinger, you felt a mechanical thunk as you switched on. The window remained blank for several seconds, while a faint whine silvered the air. Then, painfully slowly, ghosts of movement materialised in the window.

Turning a special dial would decompose the picture into a hissing void, a blizzard of whirring white dots. When the box had 'warmed up', this snowstorm would resolve precariously into recognisable images as you rotated the dial. Knock it ever so slightly, and the image – Andy Pandy, a long-nosed Edward Heath, a bearded lecturer droning on about trigonometry – would distend and wobble in the middle, like a trick mirror at a funfair. The sound would be replaced with a vicious hiss, swallowing up your own sibilants, signalling the end of the familiar language and moving off again into alien interference.

■

At home in my parents' living room, I crawl to the box and place my face up close against the screen, feeling an invisible

layer of fine fluff prickling against my nose and lips, sensing
cobwebs forming a lump in my throat. Refocusing my eyes on
the curvature of the glass screen, I see into and beyond the
pictures; they magnify, dissolve, explode into a parade of dots
in red, blue and green – the primary-colour trinity of the tube.
A cowlick of static electricity tingles my eyebrows and lashes;
my eyes feel like they want to cry, but the ducts are dry.

Aged around three or four, I fantasise that my eyes contain
tiny cameras, transmitting a non-stop live feed to some
channel I could never tune into on my own TV. I hope it's
interesting for those remote viewers, wherever they are.
If I blink really fast, I can put the world into slow-motion
replay. That's a fun thing to do when we're out in the school
playground, playing games inspired by things we've seen on
TV – *Doctor Who*, *The Six Million Dollar Man* or *Colditz*.

Our house has a separate room purely for the television set.
The room is known as 'the study' and is on the ground floor,
just inside the front door, with windows looking out onto the
park opposite. The fireplace howls with the wind in autumn
and contains a three-bar electric fire with fibreglass coals
that glow orange if you flick the appropriate switch. In the
summer, sunbeams pick out the dust specks in the air and fall
blindingly across the glass TV screen, so we close the curtains
against the light.

There are three chairs for a family of four, so when we are
all gathered to watch something like *The Dick Emery Show*,
Planet of the Apes or *The Two Ronnies*, someone always has
to sit on the floor. On larger family occasions, like Christmas,
extra chairs are crammed in and the set is swivelled around
to provide the optimum viewing angle for all in the room.
Faces occasionally peer around the door, inquire 'What's this
rubbish?', watch for a few minutes, mutter something about
'square eyes', then depart.

During a redecoration, or just for a change, the TV – a
British-made Bush CTV 1122 model – is rolled on its
integrated wheels into the much larger living room with the
sofas, upholstered armchairs and French windows. On a hot
June afternoon, coming up the path on the way home from
school, I hear the thwock of racquets at Wimbledon from the
television's single speaker, hear the clink of my mother's cup
of Earl Grey. This is summer.

■

Joe and Eileen never opened their magic box on weekday afternoons,
but always made an effort to keep up with *Coronation Street*, *The
Generation Game* and the weekly 'Saturday Night at the Movies' slot.
This always felt like a treat and was heralded by a title sequence of
animated neon film reels, sparkling cowboys and zooming aircraft.
Invariably, it would be a blockbuster movie from the past couple

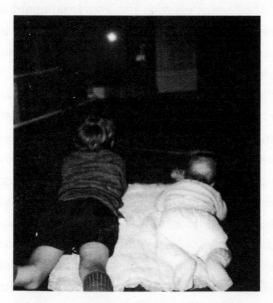

'Square eyes': the author (left) and his baby
brother, glued to the Bush CTV1122, 1974.

of decades: a John Wayne western or a thriller such as *The Satan Bug* or *Ice Station Zebra* (never James Bond: those films were held back for Easter, Christmas or Bank Holidays). My grandpa Joe rarely brought himself to reminisce about his teenage years fighting in the trenches of Ypres and Passchendaele, but he would never miss one of the many Second World War movies screened on Saturdays, such as *The Longest Day*, *The Bridge on the River Kwai* or *The Great Escape*. *Dad's Army*, another teatime favourite, occasionally drew out memories of his stint in the Home Guard. When I was a little older and occasionally stayed over at my grandparents' house, I looked forward to an episode of *Tales of the Unexpected*, *All Creatures Great and Small* or *Bergerac*, while eating lamb chops from a tray.

My grandparents' magic box inside its wooden cabinet, I realise now, was the first television set I clapped eyes on in my life. In the beginning it seemed to be a monsters' lair. The first screen memory I can dredge up dates back to when I was around three years old. For some reason, I must have been parked alone in front of the box for a few hours one Sunday afternoon, unable to take my eyes from the screen as spacemen brought a giant egg back from a distant planet. The egg hatched into a raptor-like baby dinosaur that quickly swelled into a giant monster, rampaging around a city. By the time it came to 'The End', I was terrified, but also strangely exhilarated.[1]

Another movie I recall was in very grainy monochrome, perhaps even sepia, and seemed to be about nothing more than an interminable walking race. What sticks in the mind is the recurring image of a lone man breaking away from the pack and cheating by running along a dusty, deserted track, only to collapse in a ditch or be otherwise waylaid. Then, while he was distracted, the rest of the walkers would march en masse round a corner and stomp past him, a trudging chorus of conformity set against his heroic existential helplessness. This scenario, its Sisyphean futility, impressed itself strongly on my mind. My memory was that it was called *The Walking Race*, but

I could not find a record of such a film anywhere. Eventually, a protracted googling session turned up a 1926 silent movie directed by Harry Edwards called *Tramp, Tramp, Tramp*. The synopsis explained that it was about a down-on-his-luck bum whose sweetheart encourages him to improve himself by entering a cross-country hiking contest – prize $25,000. That sounded like the one, and eventually I even managed to obtain a copy of the film. If I look back at the TV schedules, I can see exactly when *Tramp, Tramp, Tramp* was transmitted: Saturday 25 August 1973 at 5.45 p.m. I can pinpoint, then, exactly where I was and what I was doing at that distant moment in my childhood. Somehow, knowing this makes my vanished past that tiny bit more recoverable, reconnects me with the reality of that time. And perhaps it's for that reason that I haven't yet dared to rewatch *Tramp, Tramp, Tramp* as an adult. I don't want the reality of the movie to wipe my long-ingrained memory of it – to squash the mythic hold it has over my imagination.

There are many opportunities now to reconnect with these old moving images, courtesy of DVDs and Blu-ray discs, YouTube, commercial streaming services and a sluice of subterranean downloads. Watching television before the age of the video recorder – any time up to around the early 1980s – was a totally different experience. You had to tune your circadian rhythm to the broadcasters' scheduling. You switched on, you sat back, and you watched. There were no pause or fast-forward buttons. If you needed to nip out, you hurried back to miss as little as possible. The screen was magnetic, and you paid it close attention because, most likely, you would never have the chance of seeing this sight again. Screens may have quadrupled in size since then, but viewing was still more immersive, so much less casual. Alarm bells are occasionally raised about children's attention spans being diminished as a result of watching too much TV. In my experience, it was precisely the opposite.

■

I was trained from an early age to watch the ticking of an analogue timepiece as it laboured on its revolution around the clock face, measuring the minutes before the children's programmes would begin. I have spent hours of my childhood gawping at drizzling racecourses, Fanny Craddock's kitchen, the interminable legal inquisitions of *Crown Court* and the twitching palette knife of 'Paint Along with' Nancy Kominsky. Like a rodent hypnotised by the cobra's stare, I have sat immobilised by Trades Union debates and party conferences. I was undaunted by Open University lectures in all their flared-trousered, chunky-sweatered, formulae-on-chalkboard tedium, and can confirm the authenticity of Peter Serafinowicz's series *Look Around You* (2002–5), which perfectly spoofed the eerie patrician ambience of the academic and science programming of the 1970s.

There is no way to measure the length of my childhood exposure to one of the most enigmatic images in the history of human culture: the test card. In the days when daytime programming took an afternoon siesta, and when broadcasting shut down totally for the night, the test card and its accompanying musical wallpaper was a safety curtain that descended whenever there was a gap in the schedule.

'Test Card F' is a modern-day icon of British culture. If you walked into a television retail showroom in the 1970s, most of the sets would be displaying it simultaneously. I still find it hard to visually decode the image. A brunette girl hemmed in by her cuddly toys: a saggy clown and an odd, discomfiting green balloon head with no visible features. Around her is a thick frame of colours, lines, angles, moiré patterns. I now see, for the first time, that the green 'head' is actually the body of the clown, whose name was Bubbles, with two yellow buttons. The young lady, in real life Carole Hersee, as scrubbed and brushed as a birthday girl in a Ladybird book,

wears a *Mona Lisa* smile as she chalks noughts and crosses
on a blackboard. One of her 'X's marks the dead centre of the
screen. She looks out past the camera lens – the photo was
taken by her father George, an engineer at the BBC – into
the distance. Into her future.

There were other test cards and alternative ways of filling
the void. The ITV test card was more minimalist: thick
vertical bands of colour and a piercing whine. Sometimes
the engineers would pick from a vast library of trade test
transmissions – short information films from the archives
of Shell, ICI, the British Travel Association and the Central
Office of Information. These could be documentaries from
the edges of Empire or tours of Britain, with names like
*Rural Areas, A Journey into the Weald of Kent, The Heart Is
Highland, Machines on the Farm* or *Severn Westward.*

■

I grew up during the 1970s, a period often nostalgically reminisced
about as a time when kids still played with toys and spent time out
of doors. Well, we did – but we still found time to watch an awful lot
of television. Returning home from school on weekdays, the ninety-
minute 'children's hour' would just be starting on BBC1, an extension of an afternoon slot which my parents still referred to as 'Watch
with Mother'. In real-world usage, it was more like 'Watch While
Mother Does Grown-Up Stuff'. I was usually entertained by the TV,
until the sequence came to an end with a typical short animation
like *The Wombles, Roobarb and Custard* or *The Magic Roundabout*,
after which, at around half past five, worry-lined newscasters started
reporting on strikes and energy crises.

It's so easy to slip into this kind of rose-tinted nostalgic mode when
recalling childhood TV experiences, and there is already a mini-genre
of books dedicated to TV's 'golden age'.[2] What interests me more,

writing now in the middle of what is often referred to as another golden age of television (in the form of on-demand streaming series and box-set binge-watching), is what I have taken away from those hours and hours in front of the box, and how different was the experience of watching, and the nature of the content, compared to today. In every way TV has undergone a wholesale mutation. Simply taken as a physical object, the set my family and I watch today is more like a computer, with a flat digital liquid-crystal screen of the same kind of dimensions as a picture you could hang on your wall. It does not receive signals through the air via a roof-mounted aerial, nor is it even connected to a cable service. The images arrive via wi-fi, linking it to the internet, which arrives in the house through fibre-optic underground cables. Instead of clicking buttons, I choose what I want to watch by calling up various apps installed on the TV's hard drive. That word 'choose' is crucial too: I almost never need to get myself in front of the screen at a prescribed time. I used to scour my parents' newspapers for the TV listings; in the last twenty years I have never once looked at a TV page. Instead, I select what I want, when I want it, from the range available within various apps, or via the YouTube interface that can also appear on my television. I curate my own viewing, assemble my own schedule, and never idle away an evening channel-hopping or sitting through an insufferable chat show, flavourless cookery programme or exploitative documentary on some human perversion or deformity. Analogue TV screens bulged outwards with desire and potential. An LCD is a flat surface on which I project my own desire.

The television I grew up with, as I've already said, was not flat, but a three-dimensional box. It took up space in the room, it wasn't generally moved around, and you could arrange ornaments on top of it. But when someone asked, 'What's on the box?' they didn't mean, 'What are those glass paperweights with brightly coloured corals encrusted inside?' What they meant was, 'What will appear *in* the box tonight?' I can't have been the only child of that era who asked their parents whether the people in the television could see me as I could see them. Every day, some external authority planted something new in the box that was activated every time you turned it on. It was a channel, a conduit, a wormhole through which certain entities seemed to wish to plant ideas and stories in my mind. Nowadays, people 'watch' YouTube, iPlayer or Netflix. Or they'll watch a 'box set', meaning a series of digital episodes. In my youth, we watched *television*.

There are two types of magic box in the story that follows. One is a box that sits inside your room. The other is a room that you sit inside.

■

'Have you got the time?' The boy whispering into my ear from the cinema seat next to me looks to be around my age – eight or so – and appears to have come alone. My dad, sitting next to me on the other side, is the only one of us wearing a watch. 'What's the time?' I murmur. Distracted from the film – it might have been Disney's *Robin Hood*, or Dick Lester's *The Four Musketeers*, or the latest *Herbie* – he makes a show of peeling back his shirt cuff and looking at his watch. I relay the time to the lone boy, who proceeds to ask the same question a couple more times, with my father becoming increasingly irritated. The third time I find myself dutifully passing on the injunction: 'Time you went away.'

A trip to the cinema was often the occasion for displays of irritation with 'other people's behaviour'. A vastly different code of conduct was expected in this public ritual that was utterly unlike the private, therefore unregulated, experience of watching the domestic TV. Whispering, rustling sweet packets and slurping with a straw during the main feature were all tutted at. These were Odeons, Gaumonts and

ABC Regals, venues redolent of an earlier age of theatrical
cinema, with lethal folding seats upholstered in red velvet
and edged in wood. Before these grand halls were carved up
into living-room-sized 'studios', there were stalls and a grand
circle. Films came to life in spaces larger than reality. Inside
the cinema doors, familiar items assumed unfamiliar form.
Today's surround sound is no doubt pinprick-clear, but my
acoustic memory is indelibly marked by the sound space of
those 1970s cinemas. Everything was hazed in reverberation,
with a slight echo, drawing the seats into the lurid glow of the
screen. Fruit Gums and Fruit Pastilles weren't sold in their
usual tubes but in specially designed boxes only available in
the auditorium. Between features, usherettes with moulded
white plastic trays slung round their necks appeared in the
aisles dispensing ice cream in circular cartons, Jungle Fresh
peanuts salty enough to flay your lips, and Kia-Ora, an acidic
(agent) orange beverage served in square tubs, speared with
a sharpened plastic straw through a hole in the centre of the
lid. Blue smoke curled ceiling-wards from the 'designated
smoking area' on the left-hand side of the stalls, which was
announced in a crackly screen advertisement starring a fag –
or rather, an ash cylinder attached to a filter – smouldering at
forty-five degrees, as if held by some comatose uncle dozing in
front of the wrestling.

■

In the years to come I would spend thousands of hours in cinemas all
over the world, too. But it's important to note that until I left home,
the domestic television set, with its bowed, distorted 4:3 ratio, was
also the cinema. Terrestrial broadcasting included many more feature films than it does in the early twenty-first century, and themed
seasons were often curated with the assiduity of an independent arts

cinema. From Friday-night Hammer horror films to Channel 4's infamous 'red triangle' season of taboo-breaking movies in the mid-1980s, it's surprising how much quality cinema was available at a flick of the 'on' button. By the time I had reached an age when I was starting to take an interest in cinema as an art form, you could still be exposed to stuff like Masaki Kobayashi's tragic wartime trilogy *The Human Condition*, Robert Ellis Miller's *The Heart Is a Lonely Hunter*, or perhaps a season of Alain Resnais or Luis Buñuel. Many of these were watched on a bulbous fourteen-inch black-and-white portable up in my bedroom, after my parents had retreated to bed, with one hand constantly twisting the loop of aerial to stop the picture dissolving into a snowstorm, the other trying to keep a mono Bakelite earpiece from falling out. Maintaining a signal on this set was an existential battle with the void.

But there was equally strange stuff coming from closer to home. Television drama threw up all kinds of scenarios, some funny, some serious, some downright baffling. On Boxing Day 1981 I sat through all three hours of *Artemis 81* with my mother in our little TV room. Scripted by the playwright David Rudkin and starring Sting, the singer in my favourite band at the time, the Police, the piece remains largely incomprehensible many years later – a far more self-indulgent affair than the masterpiece Rudkin had written seven years before for the BBC, *Penda's Fen* (1974). The Thatcher years brought many telling indictments of the political system and social inequalities to the small screen, from Alan Bleasdale's *Boys from the Blackstuff* (1982) to a once-screened, never-forgotten Welsh TV drama, *The Happy Alcoholic* (1984), on S4C, whose transmissions we could pick up across the Bristol Channel.

It was so easy to take the television for granted. The BBC, currently under the threat of deregulation and competition from various multinational entertainment corporations, and with a Conservative government making noises about defunding it, seemed like a cultural edifice, immovable and inexorable. Adverts on 'the other side' (ITV, or commercial television) brainwashed me with slogans and phrases I still can't help but channel when I see or hear the names of certain products, decades later. Only in later years did I begin to think about the extraordinary nature of so much of the material that got caught in the dreamcatcher aerial bolted to the chimney pots, piped down into the house through the mud-brown cable and fed into the box in the corner. After I investigated the origins and meaning of folk in the British imagination in my book *Electric Eden*, I found myself thinking more and more about how, for the post-war generation, the television had replaced the village storyteller. In those far-off days of two or, at best, three channels, everyone had the same stories to discuss at work, at school; television contributed to the national conversation and collective memory.

With this book I wanted to examine many of the programmes and films that seemed to be preoccupied with similar issues as much of the folk and folk-inspired music of the same period. The bulk of it covers a period from roughly the mid-1950s to the mid-1980s, but I have cross-cut to recent productions for the small screen and cinema in which these preoccupations are starting to be reprised – both thematically and stylistically. I wanted to zoom in, past all the traditional nostalgic television of yore – the *Morecambe and Wise/Are You Being Served?* angle – and gorge on a huge cross-genre feast of moving pictures that in different ways express something about the nature and character of Britain, its uncategorisable people and its buried histories. Among the salient features and persistent themes are tensions between the past and the present; fractures and injustices in society; magical and occult notions; and presences and buried memories released from the earth.

That diversity ranges across the nation's science fiction, horror, drama, period pieces, literary adaptations and even its comedy. What's unique in Britain's case, though, is the way these genres slip and smear into one another. Sci-fi is more often about the past returning to haunt us than about gleaming visions of the future. Horror

frequently implicates itself tightly with the British landscape and its
eerie, unsettling atmospheres. History invoked via period drama may
be scattered with ghostly apparitions. Stories set in the realist present
can acquire a mythological underlay. Britain's self-image as a moated,
'sceptred isle' recurs time and again in fascist dystopias and speculative invasions. Class, social inequality and colonialism drive historical and period dramas, from genteel literary adaptations to muddy
rural sagas. As I seek to 'bruise a lane on the grass' of all this untamed
material, in Virginia Woolf's exquisite phrase, my lens sweeps in a
deliberately wide arc, seeking a telemetric folklore of the British Isles.

The Magic Box is neither a complete, conventional nor an academic history of British film and television; rather, it's a survey and
recontextualisation of some perennial cult favourites, some obscure
gems and some genuine oddities from several decades of British cinema and television. I can guarantee some readers will wonder why
film *X* or series *Y* was left out, but I have tried to include a mix of
'blockbusters' and obscurities.

■

In July 2012 I was holidaying on the coastal waters near Norway's
southernmost tip. One night, on the television in the small seaside
cabin where, in summer, the sun barely set, the screen showed the
opening ceremony of the 2012 Olympic Games, live from London.
A film-maker, Danny Boyle, had designed and produced it.

Unlike the Millennium Dome, which felt more like a trade fair,
Boyle's ceremony (which was scripted by the writer Frank Cottrell-
Boyce) at least had some vision, some historical perspective, attempted
to communicate a national story. This was Britain in a nutshell, a
potted kingdom's tale. From Stonehenge to waves of occupation,
to mistress of the seas and pioneer in trade and colonialism; later,
reaping the consequences of that colonialism in an expansive and
inclusive multiculturalism. The vibrant tableaux were indisputably

show-stopping, from the metamorphosis of fields into factories in the Industrial Revolution to Queen Elizabeth II's froideur-free cameo alongside Daniel Craig's James Bond – a royal dropping-of-the-guard unthinkable even ten years before.

The Olympic ceremony was one possible summation of many of the stories the British have been telling themselves about who they are for the past three hundred years. But how well do we know those stories? Have we really told them in full? That national timeline is rarely the one focused on in history lessons. The loss of access to the land, and to open space, after the enclosures of the late eighteenth century is not one of the core facts taught in schools. Britain's figures of power, monarchs and victorious battles are well known; its domestic armies of the defeated and oppressed are spoken of more rarely. Tales of the dispossession of the land – enforced urbanisation and impoverishment – have emerged via less official channels: through folklore, music, post-Romantic literature and, in the period since the Second World War, its home-produced film and television output.

The cross-section of films and televisual art in *The Magic Box* is part of the picture the nation has painted of itself, reaching into visions of Albion, Utopia, Camelot, Prospero's island, New Jerusalem. It emerges from the nation's subconscious via the technologies of the camera and the lens, and the artists and performers who write, direct or stand in front of them. Some of them are grand imaginings; others are nothing more than illusions – will-o'-the-wisps, tricking us into the marshes of self-delusion. Do we need to be diverted by these illusions any longer? Can these phantoms have any meaning for those who never glimpsed them in older times? I think they can. Like the tale pieced together in a dusty cathedral library of Barchester in the BBC's Christmas ghost story of 1971, the hidden threads can be reconnected, the subliminal messages decoded, and the shards of the magic box can be pieced together on the digital screen.

1

Two Great Leaps Forward
(1953 and 1963)

*Village of the Damned, Children of the Damned, The
Damned, This Sporting Life, Doctor Who, World in Action,
Billy Liar, Tom Jones*

People often say the 1950s was a decade in black and white, while
the 1960s exploded into colour. The reality was a great deal more
nuanced than that. Take the coronation of Elizabeth II on 2 June
1953, a day when every stop on the royal pomp-organ was pulled
out, the whole event being transmitted live on television. In fact,
the coronation was considered not only a triumph for the BBC's
outside broadcasting division, but a significant driver for households to acquire their first TV set. Cameras were allowed into
Westminster Abbey for the first time – at the Queen's insistence,
but against the wishes of most of the political establishment – but
this was a nation in the wake of the Festival of Britain, with its popular democratisation of culture. The public must be allowed to feel
they were participating, not just watching from afar. Thanks to its
televisation, the coronation can be said to have had a unifying effect
on the country, and could be visualised in a way that the conquest
of Everest, which occurred almost simultaneously, could not (Sir
Edmund Hillary ditched his expedition's camera equipment before
his final push to the summit).

Nineteen fifty-three was not the first time a royal coronation had
been televised. George VI's investiture of 1937 was also filmed, or
at least the parades leading up to it, by the BBC's fledgling outside
broadcast unit. But even if the public were not granted such an intimate seat at the ceremony itself, the fact that it was on television at

all seems to have struck a chord. 'When the state coach with the King and Queen appeared,' wrote a contemporary newspaper, 'the picture was so vivid that one felt that this magical television is going to be one of the greatest of all modern inventions.'[1]

The event brought discussion of the options for media coverage into the purview of the Coronation Commission, chaired by the Duke of Edinburgh. Geoffrey Fisher, Archbishop of Canterbury, made the Canute-like pronouncement that 'the world would have been a happier place if television had never been discovered'. Although Queen Elizabeth II's investiture has been called 'television's Coronation',[2] television ownership was nevertheless already on the rise in the early 1950s. Just over two million licences were issued in 1953, up from the previous year's 1.4 million. This was a steady curve rather than a spike, but the numbers were still impressive given that licensing had begun only six years earlier. Nineteen fifty-three saw a general boosting of resources and improved network coverage – new transmitters at Pontop Pike, in Durham, and Glencairn, overlooking Belfast – giving increased accessibility to previously 'blacked-out' regions. Special collective licences to watch the coronation were granted to large public gathering places, such as hospitals, churches, town halls, holiday camps, cinemas and theatres. Only 12 per cent of the British population, it has been claimed, did not watch the ceremony.[3] 'An epilogue sublime,' intoned Sir Richard Dimbleby, surveying the darkened, emptied Abbey just before the nightly closedown, 'touching and human as had been the great day itself.' The next time the Abbey's interior would be seen on the screen would be a few months later, in the final episode of the pioneering sci-fi horror series *The Quatermass Experiment* – about which more later.

And yet, despite the success of the coronation's colour pageantry, a decade later a significant amount of British films were still being released in monochrome. Nevertheless, as well as famously being the year of the Beatles' superstar breakthrough, the Kennedy assassination and Harold Wilson's 'white heat of technology' speech, 1963 appears to mark a sea change in the style and quality of British films and television productions – a clear progression from theatricality and kitchen-sink realism towards fantastical horror, sci-fi/speculative fictions and naturalistic representations of the past, with real outdoor location work taking over from studio sets.

■

There are four children in this painting. Behind them, in the distance, a marble sea meets an oil-grey sky. A ghastly tree, a semi-ruined building and a drystone wall delineate a garden where these youths stand, receding into the picture plane, in unnatural poses. The faces are broad, melon-slice crescents; their arms and hands throw awkward shapes, as if they have been ordered to freeze in position. Only one, a schoolboy in cap and blazer, with mismatched eyes and a hostile pout, holds the viewer's gaze. His arms hang by his sides as if at attention. The children in John Minton's painting *Children by the Sea*, made in 1945 and now in the Tate collection, are forever unknowable, but they clearly do not live in the halcyon childhood dreamworld celebrated in so much English children's fiction. These are children prepared to turn feral in order to survive the future.

Minton was one of the art world's more colourful personalities during the Second World War and immediate post-war period, a contemporary of Francis Bacon, John Piper and Graham Sutherland. His life, involving illustrating book jackets for Elizabeth David's cookery books and the Penguin edition of Alain-Fournier's *Le Grand Meaulnes*, dancing like a madman to the jukebox in Soho's bohemian bars and his suicide in the year of James Dean's demise, right after painting a picture of the tragic film idol, is a story in itself. In the late 1950s Minton lived in a flat in the same Kensington building as the novelist John Wyndham, whose dystopian fictions of the late 1950s and early '60s, including *Day of the Triffids* and *The Kraken Wakes*, provided rich fodder for science-fiction movies. The two-film franchise *Village of the Damned* (1960) and *Children of the Damned* (1963) took Wyndham's novel *The Midwich Cuckoos* (1957) as its departure point. The novel describes a 'Dayout' in a tranquil English village in which the entire population falls into a mysterious sleep. Later, every woman in the village is found to be pregnant and around sixty children are born, with none of their parents' genetic characteristics. They display supernormal powers and capabilities, little empathy and a form of psychic control or extrasensory perception. The story has resonances with the real-life baby-boomer generation. Although they could not know it yet, a significant fraction of children born just after the war would be responsible for the permissive society, the counter-culture, the embrace of rock'n'roll and feminism, for a liberalism unknown to their parents and a distaste for austerity. It's surely an early vision of Midwich's cold-eyed prodigies that we see in Minton's *Children by the Sea*.

The earlier film, *Village of the Damned* (Wolf Rilla, 1960), is a more faithful adaptation.[4] Still in black and white, its early minutes shatter a tranquil country harmony. Adults fall mysteriously asleep and a comatose tractor driver sits athwart his Massey Ferguson as it goes round and round in a field, eventually crashing into a tree. The comfortable pastoral of post-war agricultural documentaries – even the opening music resembles the soundtrack of a GPO Public Information Film – is destroyed. The world stands still; normal service is interrupted. Steam irons singe clothes, untended taps gush water, a stuck record twitches and runs down on a gramophone. A clear line, horizontal and into the airspace, defines the zone of collapse. After a few hours the population awakes, sensing something strange has occurred but none the wiser. The army moves in with trucks, motorcycles and metal detectors.

Every fertile woman in the village suddenly discovers she is pregnant. Joy is swiftly replaced with fear and mutual suspicion, perplexity. 'I 'ope that none of 'em lives,' utters one husband into his ale. Something is definitely awry here. As one couple celebrate the birth, a dog snarls and bares its teeth. As is gradually revealed, this is an alien invasion by covert impregnation.

The children are quick developers, becoming instantly familiar with technology and complex objects, such as a Chinese box puzzle. Blond, healthy, and with intense, unblinking eyes, they assemble in their own clique in the village when they grow older. They can read minds and influence actions in others. Adults sense there's something amiss, and that these children are impervious to 'the brake of morals'. It emerges that other remote regions around the world are experiencing a similar phenomenon. Government and military advisers get nervous, suspect dangerous influence, demand the children be locked up. 'Take a look at our world: have we made a good job of it? Who's to say that these children are not the answer?' asks Gordon Zellaby, the film's hero and 'Quatermass' figure – the rational, dependable moral centre – whose wife has had one of the children.

■

Was I – am I – one of these youngsters, born among a strange race of alien beings, where doctors smoke cigarettes, wives fawn adoringly on the arms of condescending husbands, men spend evenings together in pubs while their womenfolk stay indoors behind net curtains? A new being in a world of new opportunity, looking forward to one imaginary future while those who gave birth to me have never quite got over winning a war and are content to allow successive governments to impose the self-handicap of austerity in the name of sovereignty and self-determination? Are my eyes brightened and blanked out by the white-hot glinting of machines and screens? In 1979 I was an eleven-year-old schoolboy in a uniform. Pink Floyd's 'Another Brick in the Wall' was constantly on the radio, a powerfully nihilistic rock hit for the times. Accompanied by cartoonist Gerald Scarfe's gruelling animations of a deranged professor churning kids through the education system's meat-grinder, a wall of white bricks springs up and marches across the English countryside. In the full-length feature *Pink Floyd: The Wall* (Alan Parker, 1982), the wall is the psychological state implanted by post-war Britain on the mind of one individual, 'Pink' (Bob Geldof), based on the memories of the group's Roger Waters. The unconscious roots of this image are visible at the close of *Village of the Damned*, as Zellaby visualises a brick wall as a psychic shield against the blond nippers' mind-controlling abilities. The wall, superimposed on his face, strains and crumbles under their combined onslaught, but holds out long enough for a suicide bomb to be detonated. Winged eyes appear to fly from the burning house over the final frame.

Hyper-intelligent, possessing ESP, and with the power to influence material objects and dominate puny humans, it was hardly the kids who could be called 'the damned' in this scenario. Nevertheless, three years later the googly eyes took human form once more, in a sequel directed by Anton M. Leader and scripted by the American John Briley.[5] The title of the follow-up, *Children of the Damned*, makes no sense at all, as the premise is that the youngsters are somehow a freak genetic mutation showing what the human race will evolve into in around a million years' time. Perhaps the most trenchant point in the whole film, though, is that the children themselves, when asked who they are and what is their purpose, merely reply, 'We don't know.' This is definitely not the covert intrusion of some alien race, as in *Village of the Damned*; instead, the 'children of the damned' are a warning from the future, demonstrating the innate destructiveness of 1963-vintage humanity. Both films end with the explosive destruction of the children; the later film triggers it via a butter-fingered human error. In that sense it is the present day that's damned – a trenchant warning in the year of the Cuban missile crisis, the ongoing Vietnam War and the assassination of President Kennedy. (A similar fear was expressed in the 1963 Stanley Kubrick movie *Dr Strangelove*.)

In the sequel it's the children who represent a cosmic altruism in the face of a diminished human race, and yet they sacrifice themselves for the good of mankind in a quasi-Christian denouement. While not as successful as its creepy predecessor, *Children of the Damned* nevertheless feels prophetic in its celebration of youth/ alienation as the intellectual and moral centre rather than the adult/ conventional. Within five years that high ground would indeed be occupied by altruistic hippie hordes, self-righteous pop stars and outsider artists – the 'children of the revolution', as one glam hit of the early 1970s put it.

In *Children of the Damned* the youths encroach with pupils dilated, eyeballs glittering. It's the hollow glare of the ruthlessly driven, but it's also the absent stare attributed to the square-eyed consumption of television. This should have acted as a warning that the children's projected future would not offer the comforts implied by official children's television programming. On the contrary: if you were selective enough in your viewing, you could be mistaken for thinking that children were being perceived as threats, singled out as enemies of the people or dangerous emissaries of some foreign or alien power.

In both *Midwich Cuckoos* spin-offs, the children are segregated and confined, either at the behest of the local authorities or on their own initiative. Another film from 1963, simply and somewhat exploitatively called *The Damned* (occasionally *These Are the Damned*), also featured a small group of children with highly developed intellects who are sequestered away from an outside world that is rapidly heading towards self-destruction. Directed by Joseph Losey, an expat American living in exile in Britain since 1954, it was one of the strangest films Hammer had released up to that point. Hammer Films' background will be explored more fully later; suffice to say that by 1963, the company had become a byword for macabre horror movies that drew on a legacy of English Gothic: vampires, werewolves, Frankenstein's monster, murders and terrors from the tomb. They were rarely set in the present day, which makes *The Damned* all the more anomalous. It begins as a biker/youth gang movie set

The Damned (1963), an unprecedented hybrid of biker gangs, approaching apocalypse and avant-garde sculpture.

in the Dorset resort of Weymouth, with Oliver Reed as King, the leather-jacketed leader of a bunch of local toughs whose girlfriend Joan becomes involved with a visiting American, Simon Wells. At the same time as showing an increasingly common phenomenon in Britain – disenfranchised youth gangs, tearing up the peace of rural communities with loud motorbikes, mob violence and rock'n'roll – the film's second half introduces a disconcerting sci-fi element involving children reared in a subterranean cavern as insurance for the human race against an impending global holocaust.

Like the demon seed supra-geniuses in *Children of the Damned*, the pre-pubescent children in *The Damned* are barely characterised, and they act almost like automata. Raised to show utter obedience, academic excellence and a distinctly chipper private-school demeanour, one wonders what a future, post-apocalyptic world would have been like had these youngsters ever been unleashed from their cave-ark to repopulate the human race. The rugged coastline and the sculptures of Elizabeth Frink are deployed to good effect in this black-and-white cross-genre suspense piece, which deals with the British desire for the preservation of values, at the same time as graphically illustrating the breakdown of the ambience of local life through the impact of transatlantic pop culture. American influence, it's implied, is the real threat, with the lives of the children sacrificed to preserve an age-old decorum that's shown here to be lacking in compassion and acting on pure survivalist expediency. Yes, the pampered kids down in the cavern had never had it so good. But then again, they knew nothing else.

■

Kids in white T-shirts, sitting around in what looked like a giant wooden cabin or treehouse, just doing whatever grabs them at any given moment. Making stuff out of odds and ends, telling jokes with hand puppets made out of socks, playing tricks, singing songs, playing games, making snacks, generally dicking around as kids do. There are no visible adults on the set of the early-morning programme *Why Don't You Just Switch Off Your Television Set and Go and Do Something Less Boring Instead?* – usually shortened to *Why Don't You . . .?* – although presumably the grown-ups are not far away, telling them which marks to stand on, operating the cameras, manipulating the lighting, feeding them the script and supplying timely snacks.

Why Don't You . . .? fills the mornings of the school holidays, always on, apparently, apart from other kiddie fixtures, such as *Rainbow* and *Mr Benn*. The contradictory premise of this youth programme, enhanced by the fact that it seems to last for hours at a time, is to create a utopian atmosphere in which children seem to be dictating the terms of their own entertainment, in a kind of rarefied space of creativity and free play. But, of course, the more diverting the activities they propose are, the longer you want to keep watching.

■

Two 1963 movies in particular signalled a great turning point in the nation's film industry. Their respective settings were two centuries apart, but they handled remarkably similar themes. Both featured a charismatic misfit/orphan as hero; both dealt with growing permissiveness and blatant sexual advances by women on male characters; both dealt with marital commitment (or lack of it); both featured a backdrop of vested male power, which held the youthful main characters' fortunes in check. One film represented the end of an era; the other – paradoxically, set in the mid-eighteenth century – announced the imminent arrival of the permissive society. They were *This Sporting Life* and *Tom Jones*.

Lindsay Anderson's *This Sporting Life* can be seen as the culmination of the 'kitchen sink' tendency of the previous few years – a new wave of social-realist films dealing with the tribulations of the British working class that included *Room at the Top* (1959), *Look Back in Anger* (1959), *Saturday Night and Sunday Morning* (1960), *A Taste of Honey* (1961) and *The Loneliness of the Long Distance Runner* (1962). Anderson himself had been closely associated with the 'Free Cinema' movement of the early 1950s, which had picked up the mantle of the 1930s John Grierson-generation documentarists and applied its realist aesthetic and low-budget approach to a variety of subjects, from housing to the emerging youth culture of the 1950s.

Anderson's film titles hint at an ironic stance: that he was not just chronicling specific places and people, but that they are standing in as symbols of a wider malaise in the nation. *O Dreamland* (1953) is a barrage of imagery shot at a Margate funfair, Hogarthian in its depiction of sordidness and abjection, while *Every Day Except Christmas* (1957) is a thirty-seven-minute observation of London's

Covent Garden market, from its small-hours awakening to the full-stretch bustle of a typical day. Here Anderson came closest to the film-making of Humphrey Jennings and the socialist interwar documentary movement in managing to chronicle real lives and elevate them to something poetic and emblematic.

With that in mind, it's difficult not to read Anderson's first fiction feature, *This Sporting Life* (adapted from a novel by playwright and author David Storey), in the same light. Central to the narrative is the game of rugby, a sport which had trickled down from the playing fields of Eton, Harrow and (of all places) Rugby to the working classes. Wakefield, the city in the film, prides itself on its rugby team, with its board of directors made up of some of the richest businessmen and factory owners in the area. The weekly match acts as a lightning rod for the fortunes of the town and its inhabitants, providing a social and civic focus and a sense of loyalty and respect among the young males. However, Anderson portrays the game itself as an atavistic ritual, a malodorous mud bath in which rules are made to be broken and the most violent team wins. The hero, Frank Machin (a pugnacious Richard Harris), spends much of the film in a coma after being sedated following a nasty punch thrown by an opponent, and the film evolves in delirious flashbacks. Even in these he's often seen nursing injuries and bandaged-up. The binding element of civic life is founded in brute force.

The black-and-white *This Sporting Life* came in the wake of other films set in the north of England that showed an anything but cosy image of Britain, barely ten years after the end of the Second World War. In *Room at the Top* (Jack Clayton, 1959), the confused, James Dean-like Joe Lampton (Laurence Harvey) is forced to choose between exciting, alluring, older femme fatale Alice (Simone Signoret) and the jolly-hockey-sticks innocence of his boss's daughter, Susan Brown (Heather Sears). In a film that went further than most in the 1950s in showing sexual activity, Joe beds them both, but after finding happiness with Alice, learns that Susan is pregnant.

His father-in-law-to-be, the local tycoon, first tries to banish him by posting him elsewhere, but changes his mind when he hears of the pregnancy. The conclusion sees Joe cut up with guilt about Alice's apparent suicide and – with some cynicism – about to accept his social elevation.

The definitive kitchen sink drama was *Look Back in Anger*, John Osborne's angry young man play of 1956. Remarkably, the writer who redrafted Osborne's script for the big screen (in the 1959 version directed by Tony Richardson), and who even won a BAFTA for best British screenplay of that year, was the man most responsible for moving Britain's television and cinematic output away from realism and towards an uncanny cauldron of science fiction, superstition and ghostly presences, interrogating and shaking up the nation's deepest-seated sources of unease for at least the next two decades. His name was Nigel Kneale, and we will be hearing much more of him throughout this book.

But back to 1963, and already the winds of change were howling down the corridors of Broadcasting House, headquarters of the BBC. 'No more plays about kitchen sinks,' warned an internal memo distributed by Sydney Newman, a Canadian producer who had left his senior role at the Canadian Broadcasting Corporation to come to Britain in 1958. After introducing *Armchair Theatre* and *The Avengers* during his four-year stint working for ABC (the Associated British Corporation, which eventually became Thames Television) in Manchester, Newman took up a new post as head of BBC drama, and revealed himself as a visionary who flew the flag for a more creative and challenging drama strand on the small screen. Sympathetic to new developments in science fiction and horror – he had commissioned a series of sci-fi shorts called *Out of This World* in 1962 – Newman immediately hired producer Verity Lambert and set about developing a new series that would augment fanciful and otherworldly plotlines with believable, rounded characters rather than wooden stereotypes or archetypes. Bug-eyed monsters were right out.

'Human beings in general', declared the commissioning document, summing up his view of the role of contemporary sci-fi, 'are incapable of controlling the forces they set free.' The intended 'fastmoving, shocking episodes' would address moral dilemmas and raise ethical questions; at the same time, they demanded strong roles for women.

The result, transmitted at 5.15 p.m. on 23 November 1963 (the day after Kennedy's assassination), was a twenty-five-minute opening episode entitled 'The Unearthly Child', the first of a four-part series starring William Hartnell as the time-travelling magus Doctor Who. Nearly six decades later, the *Doctor Who* franchise had run to eight hundred and sixty-one episodes over twenty-six seasons and (since 2005) twelve series, plus spin-off specials, feature films, novelisations, fan conventions, merchandise, computer games and innumerable cultural references to hiding behind sofas. The Doctor – a shape-shifting folk hero in an age of space travel, quantum physics and imaginary numbers – underwent thirteen regenerations, sailing through the oceans of time and space in the TARDIS, a deceptively small police box that was a 'cross between Wells's Time Machine and a space-age Old Curiosity Shop', as one contemporary audience feedback report described it.[6] As originally conceived, the appearance of this mobile headquarters would exhibit perfectly the conflicted nature of British science fiction: that it should look like 'a small lab fitted with way out equipment, including some wondrous things acquired in previous investigations', but at the same time 'homely, fusty, comfortable, dustily elegant: it would not have been out of place in Holmes's Baker Street'.[7]

The TARDIS was conceived by Sydney Newman himself. 'I love [science fiction stories]', he once said, 'because they're a marvellous way – and a safe way, I might add – of saying nasty things about our own society.'[8] But Newman's brief ranged far wider than Daleks and Cybermen. In 1963 he instigated the BBC's regular 'First Night' slot, which marked the beginning of a commitment to new and innovative television drama that would remain a keystone of the corporation's scheduling until at least the mid-1980s. 'Nowadays, to satisfy grown women, Father-Figures are introduced into loyalty programmes at such a rate that TV begins to look like an Old People's Home,' complained BBC script consultant Cecil Webber in 1963.[9] Under Newman's steerage, TV drama was hauled into a modern and more inclusive age. 'First Night' soon became 'The Wednesday Play' and eventually 'Play for Today', exposing a broad spectrum of viewers to a host of new ideas and scenarios featuring the young, the working class, the underprivileged and the compromised, as well as the elderly and the educated. These plays made few concessions to populism, acted as a hothouse for emerging auteur directors and covered a bewildering range of subjects, from nuclear attack (*The War Game*, Peter Watkins, 1966 – banned until the 1980s) to social realism (*Cathy Come Home*, Ken Loach, 1969), wyrd English mythos (*Penda's Fen*, Alan Clarke, 1974) and Borstal brutalism (*Scum*, Clarke, 1977).

Nineteen sixty-three also saw other long-running television staples being broadcast for the first time, including Granada Television's *World in Action*, an investigative current affairs documentary series that went further than the Fourth Estate had ever managed before in exposing corruption, campaigned on issues of the day and held government and institutions to account. Hand-held cameras, innovations in recording and eavesdropping technology and a crew whose job was to make trouble added up to television with a conscience. *Ready Steady Go!*, launched on Friday 9 August 1963 ('The weekend starts here!'), paraded the new global pop phenomenon in its true colours. The show presented artists miming chart hits, marrying glamour and functionality. The cramped studios in Kingsway, London, made it impossible to hide the cameras, so the studio technology became part of the spectacle. Even children's television was given something new in 1963: overlapping with *Doctor Who* was *Emerald Soup*, a little-seen adventure series, now apparently wiped from the library, involving an intriguing-sounding rural setting in which thieves attempt to steal the formula for a radioactive isotope distilled from seaweed, and filmed largely among seaside coves and caves. As we'll see, the conflation of countryside settings – traditionally the locus of innocent children's play – and the horrors of science went on to underpin some of the most enduring and weird junior television masterpieces.

Time travel, pop ecstasy, governmental accountability, sexual liberation – were all of these glimpses of Ambrosia, the faraway land ruled by the over-imaginative Billy Fisher (Tom Courtenay) in *Billy Liar* (John Schlesinger, 1963)? In the gap between Billy's utopian visions of a new tomorrow and the grimier realities and social obligations of lower-middle-class Sheffield lie the contradictions of modern Britain, a nation looking to restore old certainties after the ruptures of war, while caught in the headlong rush towards an uncertain future. Billy's Sheffield is a city heaving with reconstruction; bombed-out houses are collapsing even as he passes by. Modern, clean lines are replacing older traditional decor – even in the funeral industry. He may live an internalised fantasy life, in which social mobility is an imaginative construct, but actually taking a confident step in reality is a wholly other, inconceivable action. Courtenay's co-star Julie Christie – the tigress to his fawn – mirrored her character Liz's escape to London, where Schlesinger cast her in *Darling* (1965), a movie that epitomised the permissive society and the louche morality of a newly swinging London. Schlesinger's 1967 adaptation of Thomas Hardy's *Far from the Madding Crowd*, also starring Christie, was a Mod-stained Dorset pastoral. There had been surprisingly few adaptations of classic English literature in British cinema of the 1960s, with one key exception earlier in the decade (1963, to be precise): *Tom Jones*. As Tony Richardson's rule-breaking film would demonstrate, mental liberation in Britain could occur only by renegotiating the relationship with history.

■

Tom Jones, produced by Richardson's Woodfall Films, is not only an unusual production from the team involved, it is also one of the most unconventional historical dramas in the British canon. Everything from the production design to the *mise en scène*, from its experimental filming techniques and occasional breaking of the fourth wall to its layers of metatext (it includes both intertitles and a narrator), went against the grain of literary adaptation thus far. With direction by Tony Richardson and a screenplay by John Osborne, all the hallmarks were in place for another realist drama. But, being an adaptation of Henry Fielding's 1749 novel *The History of Tom Jones, a Foundling*, it actually stepped back in time from the kitchen sink to the water-pitcher and basin.

The famous sequence where Tom and Mrs Waters, a woman he has just saved from being raped, sit in an inn devouring each other sexually over a fetishistic supper applied to the state of British culture too. After years of austerity and self-denial, it was now at last ready for an awakening, to gobble up all that the 1960s had to offer. Viewed back-to-back with *This Sporting Life*, the pictures of Britain on show could not have been more dramatically different. *This Sporting Life* appears almost catatonically bleak, with its central characters locked into cycles of self-denial and self-inflicted misery, with the only pressure valve a rugby bloodbath that takes on the appearance of a mini-Somme. *Tom Jones*, on the other hand, fizzes with vitality and insatiable appetites, for sex, food and romantic love. At the same time, it castigates the Methodist puritanism of Blifil, Tom's half-brother, and lambasts the hypocrisy of the teacher Thwackum, whose stern morals are undermined by the revelation of his own womanising.

The film also *looked* different from any costume drama made before 1963, and completely revitalised the genre. Hitherto, period films of the time tended to feel like stage plays observed by cameras, acted out on airless studio sets. In *Tom Jones*, history was brought several degrees closer, thanks to Richardson's decision to shoot the film outdoors and in colour.

Many years later, the director wrote in his autobiography that black and white 'seems to draw some life off the screen' and declared that he would have preferred to have made all his films in colour. 'We had determined to make the English countryside look as if it was unchanged from the eighteenth century and the people as real as today,' he wrote.[10]

Not only did it appear in colour, but Richardson's cinematographer Walter Lassally liked to rub wax on the lenses of his Arriflex camera or drape them with thin veils of gauze, which added extra nostalgic, aquarelle softness to the images. The newly released Eastmancolor film stock brought out the best of the West Country's natural light. Very little of the film was shot in the studio; instead, Richardson and his crew shuttled around a succession of real villages, towns and stately homes in Somerset and Dorset, including the medieval manor house at Cerne Abbas. Up on the fern-covered Quantock Hills there was barely a trace of modernity in the villages glimpsed down below (even London was represented by a strip of terraced seventeenth-century houses in Bridgwater). Richardson recalled the strange, forgotten worlds and bizarre eccentrics that location shoots unveiled: 'a vast overgrown seventeenth century manor house, with windows rotting and ceilings falling, inhabited by an old crone whom I met one day gathering twigs for her stove, dressed in a witch's hat and cloak, a straight-line descendant of the Plantagenets'.[11] At one point he and the crew were billeted in 'a sad eighteenth-century pile in Wiltshire, with a dining-room hung with rotting military banners and at one end a lectern with a family Bible full of the deaths of unnamed infants, per-ishing from whooping-cough or fever from the 1780s to the 1810s. Portraits on the walls showed tortured-looking eighteenth-century children whose groans and cries seemed forever recorded in the creaks and sighs of the wainscoting at night so that, for the first and only time in my life, I believed completely in a place being haunted.'[12]

Such encounters may partly explain the peculiar force of the film's immersion in the past. Lassally's hand-held camera captured the

Filming the past from revelatory angles: *Tom Jones* (1963).

intoxicating, steamy energies of the hunt, while no one had shot such scenes from a bumping vehicle or overhead helicopter before. This was the past viewed from astonishing and revelatory angles. All the more remarkable, as in Richardson's own account the making of the movie was beset with difficulties – hostile weather, a constrained budget, hot-tempered actors and plenty of overcooking in post-production. While he was dissatisfied with the natural conditions – occasionally the weather noticeably changes from sunlight to overcast from shot to shot, especially in the prolonged hunting sequence – the environmental slippages actually contribute to the film's faint air of detachment and unreality. It is a curious movie, with its subject and characters held at arm's length, as if studied as part of a seething colony of historical microbes.

Around 1958–9 the British film industry had been in dire straits, with studios closing (television was much to blame for the loss of revenue). With a budget of £350,000, *Tom Jones* somehow reaped the third-biggest box-office take of 1963 (up against the likes of *From*

Russia with Love, Cleopatra and *The Great Escape*) and plucked Academy Awards for Best Picture, Best Director, Best Music Score and Best Adapted Screenplay. The sheer audacity and energy of Richardson's formula had found a way to break the English historical picture out of its formerly parochial frame. But beyond these achievements – or perhaps explaining them – *Tom Jones*'s ribald sexual antics were in the process of filtering into society at large. In the week the film went on release, at the end of June 1963, the Beatles' *Please Please Me* LP was enjoying its seventh week at number one; the night before it opened, John Lennon and Paul McCartney composed 'She Loves You'. Several weeks earlier, Tory MP John Profumo had resigned under a cloud of scandal, admitting to 'misleading the House' about his inappropriate relationship with the model Christine Keeler. Three years earlier, a court had pronounced the uncensored *Lady Chatterley's Lover*, with its class-transgressive raciness, fit for public consumption. Notions of decency, and the boundaries of the permissible, were becoming far more fluid than at any time since Queen Victoria ascended the throne. The dining-room scene with Mrs Waters suggested a comic lasciviousness that had rarely been seen on British screens before, and yet it worked so well precisely because it was not set in the present day but was licensed by its eighteenth-century setting.

The only option thereafter was to tip the sequence in a comical direction. Bloated with oysters (which gave the actors a dose of off-set food poisoning) and other rich foodstuffs, the couple jauntily creep to the bedroom, accompanied by the kind of sprightly, saucy music you'd soon be hearing in the *Carry On* films. *Tom Jones* might have had an invigorating, almost aphrodisiac effect upon the flaccid UK film industry of 1963, but its antic hay-making also unconsciously signalled a slump on the horizon, for it contained the seeds of Benny Hill and the tawdry chauvinism of the *Confessions of a Window Cleaner* series. The erotic charge of history would dissipate its energies into crude displays of cocksmanship and tabloid-style voyeurism – sex as slapstick farce.

The literary prism, of course, was only one way to refract history. The years spent coming to terms with the outcome of the Second World War were full of fictions and dystopias speculating on what might have been, or what might yet be to come, for a nation not quite as self-assured as it would like to project itself.

AN ENGLISH DYSTOPIARY

2

The Creeping Menace

*The Changes, The Quatermass Experiment, X the Unknown,
Quatermass II, Daleks – Invasion Earth 2150 A.D.,
Quatermass and the Pit, The Machine Stops,
The Year of the Sex Olympics, Quatermass*

I am seven years old, and I know how civilisation will end.
There will come a day when the heat will grow sticky, sultry
and unbearable. A high-pitched whine will materialise out of
the air, and my mother will grasp her Kenwood Chefette and
her Tandberg radio, rip them out of the wall and dash them
to the ground. My father will smash the Bush 1122 colour TV
with the Hoover, hurl the Flymo against the garden wall and,
with the aid of our good neighbours, overturn his Triumph
2000, before returning the favour to their own parked vehicles.
Our street will soon be overrun with rioting, panicking citizens
demanding the destruction of all machinery, and I will become
permanently separated from my parents in the lemming-
like rush. I will become a vagrant, a nomad in my own land,
slipping furtively from farmstead to barn, sleeping among
the rusting hulks of dilapidated tractors, as the rest of society
reverts to a pre-industrial agrarian society.

I know this because I saw it happen on TV, just after coming
home from school, munching a crumpet. I even recognised the
street where it all happened: Alma Road in Clifton, a district
of Bristol where my mum often takes me shopping. *The
Changes*, on BBC1 in the afternoons, between *Jackanory* and
The Magic Roundabout, seemed like a documentary to me. My
own youthful memories of this series are woven together with

the power cuts and candlelit evenings of the Heath era and
the government-sponsored TV ads rubber-stamping the slogan
'SAVE IT!' (electricity, gas, etc.) onto the screen.

■

From the end times narratives of the English Civil War to the science
fiction that mushroomed during the Cold War, fearful fantasies of
the world being turned upside down, the nation being invaded and
conquered, infiltrated by alien colonists or usurped by totalitarian
regimes, have run riot in the British imagination. In literature, pulp
fiction, TV and cinema, science fiction escalated dramatically as a
genre immediately after the Second World War, making its presence
felt even in works for children. In the British take on sci-fi, a very
thin membrane often separates future from past. As a result of some
catastrophe, the country is plunged backwards and forced to adjust
to conditions more redolent of the pre-industrial age – *The Changes*
being the perfect example.

Adapted from a trilogy of dystopian young adult novels by Peter
Dickinson published at the end of the 1960s, *The Changes* was apparently broadcast only once on the BBC, and few of my peers shared
my recall of it at all. In more recent years, though, its themes of paranoid techno-fear, violent return to pre-industrial bucolia, and supernatural forces, not to mention its modish Radiophonic Workshop
soundtrack, have made it something of a grail to aficionados of the
large intersection of cultish interests that includes evocations of 'weird
Albion' in television, speculative fiction and music of a certain vintage.
Even though Dickinson's novels were published a few years before the
energy crisis of the early 1970s, the TV adaptation was made while
memories of winter 1973–4 were still fresh, when Britons experienced power cuts, blackouts and candlelit, oil-heated nights. The
national chaos that resulted from a global slump in oil prices revealed
the precariousness of a modern economy so reliant on fossil fuels and

electricity, which in turn fanned the dwindling embers of the idealistic, Ruritanian dreams of getting back to the pre-industrial garden.

British television studios are blessed with rustic names like
Shepherd's Bush, Pebble Mill, Maida Vale, Lime Grove. Out of this
secret geography of pastoral Arcadia, children's TV in the 1970s
brimmed with rustics with 'z's in their names (Worzel Gummidge,
Kizzy, Lizzie Dripping, or time-travelling Catweazle with his suspicion of 'electrickery') and uncanny fusions of geomancy, mythology
and science fiction (*The Owl Service, Children of the Stones, Sky*). *The
Changes* combined all these elements, but Anna Home's adaptation
presented it in a convincing realist style.

Episode one is as good as anything the BBC Children's department ever produced. A brief opening credit sequence features a bus-
tling soundtrack by Paddy Kingsland, including an early example of
Roland TR-808 'acid' squidge, and stock footage of factory production lines, traffic streaming over the old Severn Bridge and InterCity
diesels hurtling out of tunnels. The music is interrupted by dissonant
clangs over explosions and earth upheavals. The opening minutes are
nightmarish. A roaring electroacoustic shiver sweeps over an indolent
urban household, and the TV fizzles. The parents of Nicky Gore are
convulsed with a rage against the machine, mindlessly smashing the
television, lamps and household appliances. Outside in the streets,
rioters are overturning cars, trashing bikes and dumping electrical
goods. Nicky gets separated from her parents in the panic. With food
supplies running out and the water cut off, she is forced to go it alone.

Her journey through the hinterlands of rural England begins
when an old man in a doorway warns her of approaching disease. 'It's
like when I was a kid, nicer really, more peaceful,' he observes of the
empty city, but fleeing with a band of roving Sikhs, Nicky encounters
an England pitched back into a new dark age of agrarian subsistence
and gullible superstition, where brute force and racist xenophobia
hold sway and women are relegated to domestic roles. As she comments, 'We're going back to a time we don't belong in.'

The early sequences of society breaking down gradually give way to environmental meltdown and 'necromancer's weather', and it becomes clear the Changes are being directed by some mysterious entity. To an extent the mystery is preserved even to the end, but the Arthurian tinge to the finale, deep in an underground chamber, and the fact that only indigenous Anglo-Saxons are affected by the Noise, confirms that *The Changes* is an essay on the condition of England, warning of the dangers of isolationism and the tarnished dream of pre-industrial Arcadia, washed down with a draught of Gaianism. The countryside is full of dangers and pitfalls, while its inhabitants are submissive Little Englanders held hostage to brutal leaders and brigands. In episode five, 'Witchcraft', Nicky travels on a horse-drawn cart through Cotswolds trackways where farmhands toil impotently with bent pitchforks.

The footage shows its age, with the sandiness typical of archive mid-1970s news reports. But the roughness feels right, as if it's a documentary made on equipment furtively salvaged from the wreckage of civilisation. Factors alien to the CBeebies age include long passages of unsubtitled Hindu dialogue, pathetic swordfights, accents seesawing between Somerset and Glamorgan, and characters unashamedly enjoying a beer during teatime scheduling. But such anachronisms are all part of the entertainment in revisiting such an old series. Apart from the Luddite machine-breaking, what stands out today is the overt treatment of racism and the suggestion of the thin line between civilisation and barbarity. This was strong meat to place before a teatime audience, but Anna Home was committed to creating a canon of youth television to compare with the great works of children's literature, and *The Changes* deserves that comparison.

Moreover, its portrayal of everyday normality breaking down and re-forming as something new and yet old, enticing yet dogmatic, liberating but tyrannical, has been played out in many other films and programmes, which this section of the book will explore. This English Dystopiary catalogues the recurrence of alternative histories and paranoid fantasies that have hit the screen since the late 1940s. The current chapter examines how these ideas were knitted to the emergence of a British-flavoured science fiction. The two chapters that follow will look at various alternative histories, involving fears of invasion, imaginary fascist takeovers, societal breakdowns, environmental threats and that dreaded 1980s genre, the nuclear holocaust drama.

■

The insidious influence of foreign or alien powers was a recurring theme in the screenplays written by one of the most significant personalities in British television history: Nigel Kneale. Born in 1922, Kneale was raised on the Isle of Man, an anomalous body of land even within Britain, a partly self-determining society with its own government (dating back to Viking times) and currency. Over five decades, Kneale's screenwriting – which variously embraced alternative history, the supernatural and the near-future of science fiction – betrays an anxiety about what the present has to say about things to come; how memories persist to take control of the present; how the past refuses to be forgotten. At a deeper level his work is about overt and covert systems of power and control; who gets to control information, and thereby society; how such systems are open for abuse; and to what extent power is steered by historic events. In this way he is one of the great prophetic writers of twentieth-century Britain, somewhere between Orwell, Huxley and Ballard.

The 'yesternow' of Kneale's fictions is frequently associated with events that have taken place aeons earlier in time. Corpses walled into ancient brickwork, or sounds inscribed into stone foundations, have become embedded in the physical fabric of reality, doomed to repeat themselves for ever. In the case of his 1963 TV drama *The Road*, now apparently wiped from the BBC archives, premonition works in reverse: eighteenth-century travellers receive an intimation of the screams of humanity in a future holocaust, anguished voices simply drifting in the atmosphere of a particular geographic location in England.

Kneale never saw a television set while he was growing up on the Isle of Man, but he discovered a natural affinity for writing teleplays. Although he began as a staff screenwriter at the BBC in 1951, Kneale did not confine himself to science fiction, and even in those early days his relationship with the BBC was tarnished by what he perceived as a lack of financial commitment. He earned much of his keep in the 1960s and '70s adapting all manner of items for film, from *Look Back in Anger* (1959) to *The First Men in the Moon* (1964), and even *Halloween III* (1982) and *The Woman in Black* (ITV, 1989). He was also involved in the adaptation of his own *Quatermass* series for Hammer's big screen trilogy, culminating in the universally acclaimed best of them, *Quatermass and the Pit* (1967).

Between 1953 and 1979 the altruistic scientist Professor Bernard Quatermass appeared in four separate television series scripted by Kneale (as well as three cinema remakes). Even though he is indubitably human, it could be argued that Quatermass was the model for the popular and enduring Time Lord Doctor Who. Kneale himself described his *Quatermass* stories as trying to imagine 'life-threatening encounters with alien life forms' – the recurring phobia of conservative Britons trying to protect their sovereign shores, from the Second World War to the era of Brexit. Quatermass's unusual surname, lifted from the London phone book (an East End fruit-merchant family), sounds exotically futuristic but dates from William the Conqueror's day, a millennium ago (it denotes a hereditary division of land, like the more common name Middlemass). The choice encapsulates Kneale's ability to install a lightning rod between deep past and uncanny present in his fictions. His childhood in Douglas brought him into contact with a semi-autonomous region, both of and apart from the British Isles. As in Iceland, the island mentality has bred enduring belief in fairies and folklore; superstition pervades the everyday. Celtic lore, for instance, speaks of the Isle of Man once being ruled and defended by a wizard who could summon a defence force of eighty warriors. Kneale's young imagination was fed and watered by such vivid mythologies, and he translated tales of folkloric survival into the language of apocalyptic post-war science fiction. From Domesday to Doomsday in a single dramatic swoop.

At the time of the Festival of Britain in 1951 Kneale was still a floating script editor, adapting literary classics and B-film short stories in a bomb-damaged BBC shack, but soaking up the zeitgeist presented at the South Bank, where visions of the coming English brutalism and Albion space programme mingled with folksy fabrics and graphic patterns. By the time of the coronation in 1953 he was as much of a fixture as anyone could be on successive three-month contracts, volunteering to plug a six-week hole in the summer Saturday-evening slot, which had been overlooked by the scheduling committee. *Bring Something Back!* was the working title, a jokey reference to the serious business at hand: three astronauts out, only one back, with strange growths and mutations and a distracted manner to boot. Kneale soon retitled it *The Quatermass Experiment*. The England which gained global power in the first Elizabethan age, when it faced a seaborne invasion, now braced itself against more insidious hidden invaders as the reign of the second Elizabeth got under way. Kneale's early scripts are deeply infused with this creeping menace; science fiction provided the metaphoric language to express it, while the TV screen acted as the frame.

The BBC productions of *The Quatermass Experiment* (1953), *Quatermass II* (1955) and *Quatermass and the Pit* (1958) might be seen as early precursors of *Doctor Who*, but the series had its own identity. The surviving tapes underwhelm the pixels of twenty-first-century LCD screens, restoring the granules and snowstorms of the early black-and-white tube in a way that only adds to the confused state of national emergency taking shape over the six half-hour episodes. Hammer Films shadowed the television versions with their own adaptations, as well as a *Quatermass*-inspired *X the Unknown*

(1956, jointly directed by Leslie Norman and 'Joe Walton', a pseudonym for Joseph Losey). This proved to be the franchise that lifted Hammer, formerly a minor and failing player in the production of historical drama and low-budget thrillers, into a league of its own making, both stylistically and economically. Tapping into the anxieties of the age – the films appeared in the midst of the Suez crisis, H-bomb tests and a stepping-up of Cold War tensions – the enigmas unravelled by Professor Quatermass involve the gradual discovery of various forms of secret invasion, whether from without, as in the alien takeover of the British Parliament in *Quatermass II*, or from below, in the case of the extraterrestrial spacecraft buried for five million years underneath a London Tube station in *Quatermass and the Pit*.

Something wicked this way comes. Is it a doodlebug? Is it a jet? Is it the Skylon, cut loose from its moorings at the Festival of Britain? Or is it the noise of the future approaching? A courting couple, about to enjoy a tumble in the hay, are surprised by a sudden roar from the heavens and make a mad dash for the nearest farmhouse. 'Get inside!' screams the farmer, waving them into a parlour where pewter plates are stacked neatly on a mahogany sideboard, teatime white bread, ketchup and marmalade standing ready on the kitchen table. The rushing reaches eardrum-rupture levels, the floral curtains billow and the ceiling crumples. In the future, these opening seconds of Hammer's *The Quatermass Xperiment* (1955) declare, your cosy English tourist board imagery will no longer be safe. The horrors have arrived, and they are tipped with nuclear warheads. A slim, arrow-like rocket spiked in the earth of Oakley Green – heartland of the nation.

Compared to the surviving lo-fi, black-and-white, studio-bound episodes of the BBC original, Hammer's version is a hi-def miracle, with more emphasis on action. The fire engine is a handbell-ringing

jalopy straight outta Trumpton. These narrow streets actually belong
to the village of Bray in Berkshire, with the Hind's Head Hotel and
Bray Garage Ltd clearly visible in the scenes of panic. Here the police
car gently urges the townspeople to return to their homes, in the
soothing tones of a Light Programme announcer.

Right after this unexplained crash, Professor Quatermass and
his crew rock up in a Ministry of Defence Volkswagen camper van.
The unfolding film recalls and anticipates future horror and sci-fi
tropes in numerous ways. Kubrick's zero-gravity walk in the opening of *2001: A Space Odyssey* had its first try-out here, seen in the
footage retrieved from the rocket's black box recorder. The surviving astronaut, Victor Carroon (actor Richard Wordsworth, great-
great-grandson of the Romantic poet), soon to succumb to reptilian
mutations, sits unblinking in the laboratory, a test-tubed precursor
to the scientific dungeons Hammer would soon be building for
Peter Cushing's Baron Victor Frankenstein. Is Carroon's first name
a coincidence? There's also a replay of the famous *Frankenstein* scene
as monster meets innocence, next to the Thames at Deptford. Jane
Asher is the young girl with a doll, eight years before she would
become the girlfriend of Paul McCartney and appear in films such as
Corman's *Masque of the Red Death*.

Carroon's deformity worsens, while his pursuit becomes more desperate. He takes refuge in the clerestory of Westminster Abbey, where
a TV presenter is discussing the medieval murals, direct to camera:
'Hidden under layers of paint, and aged by the dust of time . . .'
Beneath the surface of this deceptively offhand commentary, Kneale
speaks of the direction of travel of British science fiction. Unable to
coherently imagine a future, it's dragged relentlessly, remorselessly
back to things older than memory. In real life, just a few months
earlier the Abbey had been the site of the biggest televisual event in
British history – the coronation of Queen Elizabeth II. The Royal
Peculiar, this most precious heritage building, site of the crownings of
every monarch since William the Conqueror, was now the spawning

ground for a gargoyle from deep space. This oozing mass of writhing tentacles and bulging eyes is caught by the TV cameras high up on a scaffolding gantry and is destroyed by the application of a massive electric jolt, the entire output of Battersea Power Station discharged into the creature's metal perch. The nation's jewels are saved, but a stoical Quatermass marches out, announcing that as for his rocket programme, he's going to keep on keeping on.

The double-bill release with historical horror film *The Black Sleep* made *The Quatermass Xperiment* that year's joint highest-grossing film. Released in the US the following year as *The Creeping Unknown*, it gained a *Guinness Book of Records* entry as the only horror film ever to have an audience member die during a screening.

'MAN MASTERS SPACE', screams the *Daily Mail* – or, at least, the generic tabloid front page mocked up by the Hammer props department for a brief newsflash shot during *The Quatermass Xperiment*. It's the day after the rocket crashes into the Berkshire countryside, and the newspapers have made it front-page news. Freeze the frames and a couple of interesting continuity details emerge. For a start, while both papers refer to the incident happening the previous night, the '*News Chronicle*' is dated 'Saturday October 23 1954', while the '*Daily Mail*' is headed 'Friday November 12 1954'. In both examples, only the opening lines of the reports are linked to the fictional story; the rest of the column inches are clipped from real newspapers. But if you look even further down the column in the '*Daily Mail*' front page, someone has included an anti-censor joke. A section of another story has been stripped in, calling for the BBFC (the British Board of Film Classification) to revise its 'X' (over eighteen) classification. It refers to the practice of submitting a script in advance of shooting, only for the censor's initial verdict of an 'X' rating to hamper production. This is the practice Hammer adopted and used repeatedly during the 1950s and '60s, and changing the original spelling to *The Quatermass Xperiment* clearly sought titillation value among hardened horror audiences. Hammer wanted to deliberately go after an 'X' rating with this movie – of all of them the one that convinced the company to prioritise horror after a couple of decades cranking out mediocre B-movies. The cross-head for the story reads 'British daring'. It's impressive that they bothered to hide such a tiny detail in a sequence lasting barely more than two seconds. They may have been able to envision space travel and alien contact, but the film-makers never foresaw the age of the digital freeze-frame.

■

With its Jimmy Sangster screenplay, pulpy Hammer treatment, mystery space invaders and scientist saviour figure, *X the Unknown* was a Quatermass picture in all but name. Its opening shot, a featureless wasteland, churned mud and iced puddles under the credits, could have been a First World War no-man's-land. From behind the cameraman's left shoulder steps a muddied boot: an army sapper brandishing a gurgling Geiger counter. Out of the mud comes a featureless metal cylinder. It's only an exercise – until it's not. A rookie in the squad takes another scan, which reveals a stronger presence than the dummy lump elsewhere, and he nearly falls down the crack that opens up in the earth.

In American invasion fantasies, danger generally comes from the skies. In Britain, by contrast, the intrusion is frequently buried under the earth and is either unleashed accidentally or erupts of its own volition. The mud of the nation is both the soil in which its hardy oaks are rooted and a carapace concealing latent horrors and ancient dark secrets. It's a trope that occurs across the generic board, from sci-fi to folk horror to comedy, from *Quatermass and the Pit* to *The Blood on Satan's Claw* to *Detectorists*.

At the research centre, we're still in a garden-shed test zone. Miniature radars herky-jerk on Meccano frames. It's a short step from here, the heart of British weapons research, to Bruce Lacey's steam-engine delivery of breakfast tea, eggs and bacon in *Chitty Chitty Bang*

Bang. Here 'security' equals 'Safe to come in, sir?' Meanwhile, there's an 'awfy creepy' presence in the ruined Gothic tower in the woods. Dr Royston, an American, theorises that the energy compressed into the Earth's core at the dawn of time might have developed an intelligent life of its own, having existed far longer than humankind. 'Their world is being slowly compressed out of existence, therefore survival must be uppermost in their thoughts.' It's the essence of Cold War geopolitics: dormant forces are now feeding more voraciously off the increased radiation emitted on the Earth's surface.

Bodies melt and smoke as a doughball of irradiated mud oozes around the Scottish landscape. The next time we would see such grim, charred corpses would be in nuclear holocaust shows like *Threads*. The 'Unknown' – an abstraction registered largely via actors' reaction shots – is less of a drain on movie budgets. This abstract horror stood in for all the existential threats believed to be building up out of sight behind the Iron Curtain, such as the Soviet Union's nuclear stockpiles and the rising tide of communism in South-East Asia.

The local phone lines become riddled with Geiger counter crackling and communication is interrupted. The church is people's last sanctuary. As they 'pile in where it's nice and warm inside', we see a brief view of a tumbled cemetery, with a Celtic cross prominent. The scene cuts to a mountain-scape of two electricity pylons, the lines flaring and severing under the sludgy onslaught. The mud then surges down the village high street. A toddler, abandoned outside the church, stands and watches as a drystone wall is toppled. Deepest Britain, swamped by irradiated goo. The final fightback is played out in a nocturnal, almost lunar landscape, with a horizon of blackest-ever black. The mulch that emerges from the fissure now glows with radiation and, filling the screen, resembles photos of atomic bomb tests at the instant of detonation. Although the thing seems to be blown up, the ending – Royston tentatively advancing towards the smoking pit – leaves it unclear as to whether the threat has been finally resolved.

■

In *Quatermass 2*, whose 1957 Hammer version, directed by Val Guest, is among the best of the studio's output in that decade, with its dismal northern landscapes, creeping dread and tensely cranked-up music by James Bernard, we glimpse a police state in operation on English soil, in league with unseen extraterrestrial colonists. It's subversive stuff, especially when you remember this alien body-snatching invasion is being envisioned just a few years into the new Elizabethan age. Much of it is shot as day-for-night, lending tenebrous menace to the outdoor scenes, including the dramatic car accident that opens the film.

Guest's film dispenses with several crucial and evocative details found in the original BBC version. The corporation's more politicised Quatermass tale amplified the decline of the rural. Poking about among the wreckage of Winnerden Flats, a village that's been evacuated and wiped off the map to make way for an alien food production plant and a new town for its human slave labourers (filmed in the real-life satellite town of Hemel Hempstead), Quatermass picks out a hand-painted sign reading 'Ivy Cottage'. It's a fleeting remnant, crunched between the silver domes and pipework of the rapidly encroaching hi-tech 'synthetic food' processing plant on one side and the newbuild, prefab housing estate on the other: both exaggerated but telling symbols of the new Britain erasing the old under Anthony Eden's Conservative government.

Information about Porton Down, the secret military research centre used for testing poison gases on human and animal subjects in the 1950s, and Imber, the village on Salisbury Plain that was evacuated during the war and retained as a ghost town for Cold War military exercises, occasionally filtered out to the public in the 1950s but was often a mystery even to Members of Parliament. The notion of a classified experimental plant, privately policed and operating independently of government, recurs in science fiction and even makes an appearance in Lindsay Anderson's *O Lucky Man!* (1973), where, as in *Quatermass II*, a rough track fizzles out at a perimeter and brutal guards are called out to deal with intruders. At Winnerden Flats the industrial installation is a Trojan horse for an alien invasion which has infiltrated the highest level of government and secured the local population's silence with propaganda and threats.

Episode one of the BBC production features a farmer described as a 'ploughman' unearthing a strange object in a field: one of the aliens' 'overshots', capsules containing the spawn of their breed which pop open to infect human finders with a 'satanic' mark. Quatermass calls the process a 'mental sting' – a complete takeover of the human nervous system. A 'funny smell – like old stables' is emitted when these pods explode. The last ageing survivor in the annihilated village, hanging on like a future extra in Richard Lester's post-holocaust black comedy *The Bed Sitting Room* (1969), is a Catweazle type

Nigel Kneale's *Quatermass* series heralded a new era of British science fiction. Here, Quatermass (Brian Donlevy) is strong-armed by the state in *Quatermass 2* (1957).

who warns Quatermass of the 'newbuild' town that is springing up
to house the aliens' zombie workforce – a plot element that links
Quatermass II to soon-to-come horrors such as *The Plague of the
Zombies*, another narrative of villagers whose minds and bodies are
coerced into slave labour. In the local pub, where there's still some
salt-of-the-earth resistance to progress, they talk of the illness from
the pods as 'country superstitions' and complain that the government only 'despoil and destroy' with bulldozers. Twenty years later, a
similar mix of imagery and hostility would inform David Gladwell's
essay film *Requiem for a Village*, with its bulldozers, village traditions
usurped by estate housing, and zombie uprising of history's departed
souls. The countryside at Winnerden Flats is in constant peril, with
none of the reassurance it typically supplies in English fiction. It is
the beginning of a long tradition of the usurped landscape, the rural
turned strange and forbidding.

This organism is an arch-coloniser. But aren't the humans guilty of
exactly the same ambitions? Quatermass is struck – and Hammer's
film makes this explicit in the opening minutes – by the similarity of
the Winnerden Flats complex (filmed at the real-life Shell refinery in
Shell Haven, Essex, on the Thames estuary) to his own blueprint for
a moon base (the latest jewel in the crown of the British Empire?).
Quatermass 2 is reduced in this reading to a simple struggle for survival between rival imperiums. But it's also one of Kneale's most
politicised works, with Orwellian overtones of secret government
and workers colluding with leaders in a conspiracy of silence. Not
surprising, perhaps, since (as we'll see in the next chapter) Kneale had
adapted George Orwell's most famous novel, *Nineteen Eighty-Four*,
for the BBC in 1954.

■

X the Unknown, *The Quatermass Experiment* and *Quatermass II*: these
storylines, all filmed over a space of three years, featured insidious

ideologies and unseen enemies taking over the nest. There were others too – many of them wiped, lost or stored in the bottomless archive – like *The Big Pull* (invisible extraterrestrials taking over humans one pair at a time, dir. Terence Dudley, BBC, 1962) and *Dimensions of Fear* (beings from the fourth dimension attack research station in remote English village, dir. Don Leaver, ABC/ITV, 1963). Kneale's third outing for Professor Bernard Quatermass, *Quatermass and the Pit* (BBC, 1958–9; Roy Ward Baker, 1967), physically digs into the soil of England, the loamy excavations unleashing primeval knowledge of humankind's origins, as well as the destruction of large areas of London. *Quatermass and the Pit* is rife with folk memories of the Blitz nightmare (especially emphasised in the black-and-white BBC series) and the pervasive presence of unexploded German bombs occasionally turning up in cellars and building sites.

In the late-1960s Hammer Films version directed by Roy Ward Baker, the opening shot could be a scene from wartime London. The streets are deserted save for a police constable strolling across the cobbles into a cul-de-sac, the fictional 'Hobbs Lane'. How effective the law and its officers will be when faced with extraterrestrial forces is one of the film's central questions. Meanwhile, just three shots in and the camera's lens is probing the mud. Drilling deep in the shutdown Underground station at Hobbs End, workmen strike a seam that contains deformed humanoid skulls, then a smooth metallic surface that seems impervious to blows or steel cutting equipment. The first half of the film's drama comes from the gradual uncovering of all the pieces of this gigantic puzzle as they are slowly regurgitated from the earth and the dawning of the idea that they are connected, in a five-million-year-old narrative of colonisation and inter-species exploitation by former Martians.

Immigration and racial purging were very much on Kneale's mind, reinforced by experiences within his own family circle. His wife, the children's book author Judith Kerr (creator of *The Tiger Who Came to Tea*, the *Mog* stories and more), was the daughter of

German Jews who grew up in Hitler's Germany and fled to live as naturalised exiles in Britain. The *Quatermass and the Pit* script was partly a response to her experiences, as well as to attitudes to rising immigration – the Notting Hill Carnival of August 1958 had ended in racially motivated riots. It also smartly combines science fiction with a connection to the prehistoric past, as well as adding in supernatural and ghostly elements around the slow-building revelation of the truth. One of the finest sequences happens in a derelict terraced house near the building site. These dwellings were abandoned before the war, and strange marks clawed into the walls reveal the reason why: the place was haunted by disconcerting noises. Researching local history, the investigators discover reports – dating as far back as the 1700s – that every 'disturbance of the ground' in the area has coincided with sightings of imps and demons. Police Sergeant Ellis's clammy breakdown in the haunted house – he acts as the lightning rod between the community and the authorities – is one of the film's best performances, embodying the threat to law and order from these lingering presences. Quatermass remains typically calm during the process of uncovering the full contents of the buried chamber, but he is still excited and horrified by its implications.

Why, Kneale was forced to ask, does human nature appear to harbour so much latent violence and fear/hatred of the Other? How did aggression and warlike instincts become so ingrained? For much of the film's duration, conflicts occur between human investigators who are supposed to be on the same side: the rationalists and scientists working for positive and altruistic reasons, such as palaeontologist Dr Roney and Quatermass himself, versus defensive, suspicious military men like Colonel Breen; their eagerness to fight is a trait directly inherited from the barbaric Martian insectoids, who are eventually uncovered in a sealed crystal pod inside the spacecraft. Then there is a third type, represented by Roney's assistant Barbara Judd, who takes on mediumistic attributes – someone who, in a sense, has outgrown the Martian progenitor. It's she who becomes aware of the significance of the name 'Hobbs Lane' and reminds Quatermass that 'Hob' is an ancient name for the devil. It's her brain which can be tapped, in a kind of electronic séance, for its primordial racial memories, which reveal to the investigators the full story of what happened. Despite Hammer's cheaply animated special effects, the imagery of massed Martian hordes on the march is clearly intended to be read as an extraterrestrial *Triumph of the Will*. Quatermass's interpretation – not entirely trusted by the politicians, who are more concerned with quelling public panic – is that the Martians wanted to transfer their brutal control methods genetically to humans ('their substitutes on Earth') and perpetuate their regime, and that technologies concealed in the crashed ship may reanimate this dormant violence. Kneale's conclusion, in lines spoken by Barbara, is: 'We are the Martians now.' Violence and division have been hard-wired into the human genome for five million years.

The spaceship starts its organo-technological pulsation, veins glowing against the hull, and it emits waves that drive nearby humans to embark on a riotous killing spree. Even Quatermass is briefly affected; knocked back to sense by Roney in the haven of a pub, he describes having had his mental faculties blocked so that 'you can't see this world any more'. It's the kind of mass hypnosis that occurred among Hitler's supporters in Nazi Germany, and Quatermass's sobering-up illustrates the mastering of the warlike impulse, as he remembers his humanity and rationality. The achievement of *Quatermass and the Pit* is the way it aligns this recent popular experience of war with the warning that no nation is immune from the fascist impulse. Its sombre final shot – Quatermass and Barbara, exhausted, in a burning street – graphically depicts the sacrifices that must be made. With the sound of sirens in the distance, the authority shown in the film's opening shots can be heard being restored.

■

Look, through the rectangular window, to where the actors'
feet tread. In the television studio, especially in the dramas of
the 1960s and '70s, you can often see the same flooring, like
no natural interior. The black vinyl membrane dully reflects
the studio lighting, streaked by myriad shoe-scuffs, dragged
cables, shunted prop furniture and scenery flats. Sometimes,
as in the *Blue Peter* studio, it is a wintry white, apparently
pristine, except when a rogue baby elephant guest evacuates
its bowels over it. At times like this, or when a marching
band muscles in off the streets of Shepherd's Bush, the Oz-
curtain of Television Centre's Emerald City is lifted. The
cameras turn on themselves and the mechanics of television
production are unveiled, in all its mess of coaxial cabling, sun-
starred lighting, assistant directors with clipboards and giant
headsets, electricians and stagehands, lighting technicians
and boom operators.

The cameras. You catch a glimpse of them in the darkness
at the start of TV quizzes or late-night chat shows, gliding
silently across those mopped floors, with operators bobbing
on hydraulic perches. You wouldn't want one rolling over your
foot. These are heavy, heavy beasts with Triassic faculties.
They don't zoom in and out; their single eye has a rotating
plate of lenses that can be dialled through a range of wide-
angle, normal and telephoto focal lengths. At the BBC, trainee
directors are introduced to studio plan templates, with plastic
triangles representing each lens's field of vision. The biggest
issue is the cables, which are plugged into fixed power points
on the studio walls. They are too thick for the wheels to pass
over, and it takes three technicians to lift a cable up and
over a tracking camera on the move. So the cameras must be
choreographed, martialled like a general with his infantry
and cavalry divisions (folks in the trade call them 'schools', as
in groups of fish). Their spatial relationships are controlled

to avoid tangling, while keeping to unwritten rules of film-making, such as reverse cuts, and at the same time, responding to the director's desire to invent new visual languages.

Unlike film, the television studio is not usually a place for creative cameramen or cinematographers. He or she is a mere operator receiving instructions from the control-room brain. Video technology in the 1960s comes with *Doctor Who*-like names such as 'orthicon' and 'vidicon'. After all, nothing is more like a television camera than a Dalek. Neither can negotiate a flight of stairs; both take their commands from a hive mind. In certain *Doctor Who* episodes the camera's point of view defers to what the Dalek can see through its head-mounted scope, whose movements seem cripplingly limited to up–down, left–right. Daleks trundle across smooth floors, admittedly liberated from coaxial chaos, but with limbs of limited function that resemble a bathroom plunger and an egg whisk. The form of the Daleks follows the function of television cameras, reflecting them back, darkly. Extermination versus illumination.

■

As in Philip K. Dick's novel from 1962, *The Man in the High Castle* (televised by Netflix in 2015), which also imagined a German victory in Europe, alternative history has often found science fiction to be a useful host for carrying its speculations. From the 1960s onwards the stand-ins for stormtroopers and SS *Oberleutnants* have been those lovable tinpot despots of the *Doctor Who* franchise, the Daleks, who appeared in two British Lion-produced feature-length films, both directed by Gordon Flemyng[1] and starring Peter Cushing as the Doctor. Hard on the heels of *Doctor Who and the Daleks* (1965) came *Daleks – Invasion Earth 2150 A.D.* (1966), in which London finds itself overrun by fascistic beings bent on extermination, blindly carrying out a master plan for global domination and in thrall to a terrorising leader. Admittedly, the leader in *Daleks – Invasion Earth 2150 A.D.* is fabricated from aluminium and finds it impossible to go up and down staircases, but in all other respects this is an act of speculative fiction clearly driven by the same impulses as those behind *It Happened Here* (which will be covered in the next chapter). Instead of the latter's German staff cars on London's thoroughfares, we have a painted Dalek flying saucer and rubber-suited human agents acting as law enforcers for their mechanical masters. Once more the bombed capital acts as a backdrop. Whether in the past or the future, the Blitz seemed to have become ingrained in the mental landscape.

'It's all different!' gasps Bernard Cribbins's hapless police constable, transported two centuries into the future against his will. All different, that is, aside from the poster advertising Sugar Puffs, the breakfast cereal that sponsored the movie in exchange for some inappropriate product placement all over the post-apocalyptic set.

Imprisoned within their metallic casings, the Daleks have embraced technology, but in the process they have become somewhat vulnerable to being pushed around and manhandled. Thus, they harness electronics to brainwash humans into unquestioning obedience. When the guards advance in lockstep – a squad of four extras was all that the budget could stretch to – the gas emissions from the Daleks' exterminators provoked all-too-recent memories of Panzer tanks and stormtroopers with flame-throwers.

With its hep jazz soundtrack, painted theatrical backdrops and pound-stretcher budget proudly on display, this Doctor Who offering ranks at the more preposterous end of the invasion-paranoia movies. That two of its heroes were future stars of children's TV, Bernard Cribbins and Ray Brooks (who voiced the time-travelling, shape-shifting Mr Benn), hardly helps later generations to take it seriously. But it did present, in the popular domain, the notion of hidden manipulations by self-appointed authorities, and when it is revealed that the Daleks' ulterior motive is to extract the Earth's magnetic core so that they can pilot the planet – a kind of evil reverse of Buckminster Fuller's *Operating Manual for Spaceship Earth* utopianism – and occupy it completely, the analogy with the Third Reich/ global takeover strategy is complete. (In case you didn't get the message, a control panel operated by one of the Daleks reads, 'TOTAL POWER'.)

The capacity to destroy them is right beneath our feet – Mother Earth's magnetic field. Or perhaps that was just Mother Britannia. 'There's always an answer to be found, if you only dig deep enough,' says the Doctor.

■

In the home-grown British variant of science fiction, there is an alternative vision of the future, the counterpoint to Orwell's 'boot stamping on a human face – forever'. That is when societies are portrayed as having *voluntarily* capitulated to control, their resistance weakened by narcotising mass entertainment. In the second half of the 1960s this was strapped to a raft of growing intergenerational concerns about youth delinquency, pop culture and the rise of the permissive society. With the emergence of the teenager as a distinct demographic category came a contradictory mix of student protest and dropout indolence, drug use and 'free love'. Hippies and gender-ambiguous folk with long hair were viewed in Establishment circles, and frequently by their own parents, as lacking physical and moral backbone. For many kids in the 1960s, emulating their conformist parents was no longer the cool option. Meanwhile, the real-life equivalents of Huxley's pacifying soma narcotic were affecting both sides of the generation gap: the elders with their mainstream television, valium and consumer durables; their offspring via marijuana and LSD. Which side of this generational divide was the more susceptible to dumbing down, apathy and cultish obeisance to higher powers?

This 'soft fascism' of leisure and pornography, a concept found in the writings of Aldous Huxley, J. G. Ballard and others, has found its place in film and television too. The original prophet of this version of mankind's future was, of all people, the novelist E. M. Forster. His short story of 1909, *The Machine Stops*, was a rare venture into science fiction by Forster, who was responding perhaps to the writing of his contemporary H. G. Wells, a fellow mover in socialist cultural circles at the time. In the film milieu, Forster is most strongly associated with literary adaptions by Merchant–Ivory (*A Room with a View, Maurice, Howards End*) and David Lean (*A Passage to India*), films that have become bywords for sumptuous costume drama and oodles of English reserve. When the thirty-year-old Forster was dipping his nib in his inkstand in 1909, the age of flight had barely got off the ground. The brittle TV adaptation of *The Machine Stops* from 1966, part of BBC2's 'Out of the Unknown' strand, was conceived in the age of space travel.

In the future leisure-based society of *The Machine Stops*, humans spend so much time in their personal pods, lounging in chairs or sleeping on beds that automatically fold out from the wall, absorbing information through screens, that they have practically lost the strength and motor skills to actually walk upright. This is also a technologically advanced society that is largely based in underground metropolises. It takes a mere two hours to travel from Australia to Devon.

Actress Yvonne Mitchell (Julia in Nigel Kneale's 1954 version of *Nineteen Eighty-Four*) is here metamorphosed into Vashti, hairless mother of the young Kuno (Michael Gothard). Vashti lives a life purely of the mind, shuddering with disgust at the idea of 'direct experience'. Kuno, meanwhile, is rebelling, in his own sweet way: he's thinking of what lies outside, though his depleted physical condition makes it devilishly difficult to walk more than a few steps. Normally a respirator and an 'egression permit' is required to exit the city, but even these privileges are now being withdrawn by the nameless, invisible authorities. After much staggering, he rips open the fabric of the plastic city and wriggles out to find himself in the 'hills of Wessex', a ridged semi-circular valley that appears to be shot in Uffington Vale. 'Happy the man, or happy the woman, that wakes the hills of Wessex,' he declares. The soundtrack swells with canned birdsong, the camera tracks low to the ground through waving wild-flowers and long grasses, and Kuno squints against the unfamiliar sun. A girl is glimpsed through the foliage, before gangling mech-anoid snakes clutch at him from the exit valve and he is dragged kicking and screaming back inside.

This version of the story bears no trace of its pre-First World War source. It's shot on what looks like an abandoned *Doctor Who* set, incorporating disorientating quick-cut montages straight out of Bergman's *Persona* and electronic music by the Radiophonic Workshop's Brian Hodgson. Forster, who lived until 1970, was still alive to see it.

■

Nigel Kneale's project of 1968 took a giant step further, going from depicting Orwell's Big Brother to predicting the reality television of *Big Brother*. The controlling function of the two-way 'telescreen' in Orwell's novel – described as 'an oblong metal plaque like a dulled mirror which formed part of the surface of the . . . wall' – appears to have lingered in Kneale's imagination. Broadcast on BBC Two's 'Theatre 625' strand in 1968, and repeated only once, as a 'Wednesday Play' in 1970, *The Year of the Sex Olympics* (Michael Elliott) is one of the great lost classics of British dystopian television. Its speculations about where permissiveness and the sexualisation of mass entertain-ment might end up appeared just as the 1960s counter-culture was peaking. In the 'sooner than you think' future depicted in *The Year of the Sex Olympics*, mass entertainment has merged competitive sports with sexual prowess. Grinning couples compete against each other on circular beds in a debauched travesty of *Strictly Come Dancing* or *The Great British Bake Off*. In a crude foreshadowing of *X-Factor*-style public voting, or the bellwether of social media 'likes', real-time audience feedback is monitored in the 'production pod', under the guidance of a team led by Ugo Priest – a brilliantly cynical performance by Leonard Rossiter – a member of the educated elite conscious of the populist processes at work even as he espouses the TV station's 'cool the audience, cool the world' philosophy.

By now, Kneale's long experience of working within the television industry had clearly made him dubious about the power of the medium and aware of its steadily degrading quality. Written in a climate of increased explicitness in controversial stage musicals like *Hair* and *Oh! Calcutta*, and coinciding with the globally televised 1968 Olympic Games in Mexico, *Sex Olympics* reflected an insider's distrust of the mass entertainment industry, as well as being an early example of the culture of television exhibiting a growing self-awareness.

In addition to the Orwellian echoes, Kneale synthesised Aldous Huxley's soma-tranquillised future with the more contemporary speculations of J. G. Ballard in depicting an enervated society whose desires and rebellious instincts are held in check ('apathy control') by a surfeit of sensationalist entertainment. The character played by Brian Cox (who half a century later would take a major role in HBO's *Succession*, a series that also deals with the deadened souls running a multimedia conglomerate) is named Lasar Opie. This rising studio hotshot gets off on zapping opium to the people via the cathode-ray tube.

As in Orwell's vision of Airstrip One, societal fault lines in *Sex Olympics* are appearing between proles and the educated elite, labelled as 'low-drives' and 'high-drives'. In this world – sanitised, dumbed-down and insulated from the outdoors (as in *The Machine Stops*) – the greatest distaste is reserved for the concept of 'tension', a word that stands in for memories of war. Anticipating the early twenty-first century's obsession with 'safe spaces' and the banning of 'triggers' in public life, here anything suggestive of upset or trauma – and even horrific images such as expressionist paintings of contorted human screams – ignite wailing and a gnashing of teeth in the closely monitored audiences.

The only surviving tapes are in black and white, but *Sex Olympics* was originally one of the BBC's first forays into colour. The actors playing the high-drives had their skin painted gold and their costumes were Carnaby Street on steroids – psychedelic swirls of purple, red and green. The extrovert Misch, with her mirrored hair extensions, is the epitome of this gaudy decadence, but Vickery Turner's performance harbours hidden reserves of melancholy. None of Kneale's characters fall into easy stereotypes or caricature. Liberated from the aggression of former generations, they come across as adult children playing power games with their fellow humans' impulse control. Kneale's fear of a trivialised and infantilised culture had already found expression in an unfilmed script, 'The Big, Big Giggle', from 1965, about youthful suicide cults. In *The Year of the Sex Olympics*, he planted seeds of dissatisfaction among the proponents of the cult of television. Square-jawed Nat Mender, whom Kneale summed up as a 'decahedral peg in a nonahedral hole', is beginning to believe the medium should be used to educate, rather than sedate, the masses.

The entire first half of the film is confined to the extraordinary interior sets representing 'Output 27', the TV studio and the junior facility where parents store any inadvertently produced children. We have no idea whether this brittle architecture of steel, glass and plastic exists in a tower block, a giant media centre or even an underground bunker, but it is the only environment they appear to know. As they monitor their TV output or hang about in the recreation areas with their nipple-substitute protein lollies and robotic chess machine, the characters, shot in spangly facial close-ups, reveal the moral parameters of this future world and hint that it emerged in the aftermath of a devastating global conflict. Kneale's linguistic inventiveness is given free rein with their mode of speech – a mid-Atlantic hipster patois, condensed by missing pronouns and evocative synonyms that unconsciously reveal a richness of life that has been lost.

Just after the halfway mark, an unforeseen tragedy signals a gear shift in the action. Just as viewers' sensibilities are becoming blunted by ever more explicit porn and moronic cream-pie fights, the brooding Kin Hodder, a troubled high-drive with a visionary new concept of art ('pictures' that last for ever), falls to his death while attempting to hijack a live broadcast and flash some of his disturbing paintings on national television. The monitored audience think it's hilarious, breaking the cycle of boredom and inertia and boosting the ratings. The controller and his team come up with a plan for a new series, *The Live-Life Show*, placing a couple on a remote uninhabited island and observing their attempts to survive in the wilderness. As many commentators have noted, this fly-on-the-wall format predicted the reality television hits of thirty years later, such as *Big Brother*, *Castaway* and *I'm a Celebrity . . . Get Me Out of Here!* Its outdoor scenes were filmed on the rugged, sea-lashed clifftops of Kneale's birthplace, the Isle of Man.

Nat and his colleague/former partner Deanie Webb have taken the unusual step of having a child together and feel unarticulated yearnings for a better quality of life ('We'd be something called a family'). They volunteer as the first subjects, despite obviously never having spent a second in the open air. Dispatched to the island bundled up in thick coats, and barely knowing how to strike a match or prepare food, they live out the Digger dreams of the hippie counter-culture, pitching up in a draughty crofter's cottage, just as Paul McCartney, at his Scottish farmhouse, or folk musicians like the Incredible String Band and Vashti Bunyan were doing around the same time. Anyone who has ever searched out practical instruction videos on YouTube will recognise Nat's desperate resort to his tape-recorded guide on how to make fire or bury a body.

In this windswept Garden of Eden, Nat, Deanie and their daughter Keten experience a sense of vitality and self-sufficiency they have never felt before. The strangeness of the cottage and the wilderness forces them to confront their previous state of blindness. 'We found our place,' says Deanie, and they have found happiness in spite of the cameras' perpetually vigilant eye – out on the moors, chasing sheep, laughing at dangers, gadding about in a prehistoric stone circle down by the cliff edge. The process of an urban, technological elite rediscovering the landscape, handmade furniture and running water is superbly acted by Suzanne Neve and Tony Vogel, like aliens discovering an unfamiliar planet. The wonder finds visible expression in Vogel's wide-aperture eyes, at times recalling a face out of the silent era. These are eyes large enough to gobble up the contents of his monitors back home, but also wide enough to take in the immense landscapes of the Isle of Man.

This later turn in the story brilliantly inverts the prevalent 'get ourselves back to the garden' mentality. This society may have lost some of its 'old-days' hang-ups and inhibitions, but out with the bath water has gone much of what made us human – love, parental attachment, privacy, permanence. In *The Live-Life Show*, television unconsciously begins to point the way back to some of what this future has rejected or forgotten.

Dumped in the wild in their fur-lined anoraks, they are reduced to the state of Stone Age primitives – then they meet a real fur-clad wild man. Grels tells appealing stories, understands the cyclical and tidal rhythms of nature, and most importantly, knows how to hunt and forage for food. When Keten develops a fever and dies, it feels like Nat and Deanie have crossed a threshold, no longer insulated from death or its emotional fallout.

The nasty, brutish and short ending, with its clear influence on signature sequences in both Michael Reeves's *Witchfinder General* (1968) and Stanley Kubrick's *The Shining* (1980), is a landmark in the British televisual grotesque. The complexity and density of ideas Kneale deploys throughout the film extend to the final seconds. While the production-pod crew celebrate the hysterical audience reactions, it dawns on Ugo Priest that Nat, in his murderously vengeful state, has attained a level of existence that's been denied to his fellows. The credits roll with that mental state of horrified consternation hanging in the balance.

Given the problematic nature of the production, with its hi-tech sets, screens within screens and all-terrain outdoor unit, as well as the industrial action by studio electricians that held up filming, it's a miracle *The Year of the Sex Olympics* ended up getting made at all. In addition, the script and its provocative title were catnip to the National Viewers' and Listeners' Association, with its founder, the clean-up TV campaigner Mary Whitehouse, trying to halt filming. If she had taken the trouble to read it, she might have realised that Kneale's position – as a critic of the effects of pornography and permissiveness, rather than a champion – was not so far from her own.

■

Susceptible youth versus the experience of age; expertise versus dumbing down; cult beliefs versus 'official' culture; state and mercenary control versus societal breakdown: the themes that saturated *The Year of the Sex Olympics* surfaced again in one of Kneale's final contributions to British televisual sci-fi, as well as his farewell to Professor Quatermass. The series titled simply *Quatermass*, sometimes referred to as *The Quatermass Conclusion*, filmed for ITV in 1978 but not broadcast until the following year, was a flawed but fascinating return to dystopian fiction from a writer in his advanced years. The four-part serial was directed by Piers Haggard and, like Haggard's earlier folk-horror classic *The Blood on Satan's Claw*, it featured a youth cult running blindly out of control. Its opening shots take us into the post-riot streets, hollowed-out cars and feral hinterland that junior audiences had already been shown, as we've seen, in *The Changes*. Both series show machinery reviled as an evil force, and in the final episode of *Quatermass* a group of youths smash up the last remaining technology capable of tracking alien activity. 'Bust it!' demands Kickalong, their Charles Manson-meets-Jim Morrison leader.

Professor Quatermass (John Mills) feels, more than ever, like a cipher for Kneale himself, conscious of his advancing years. Both achieved distinction for staying ahead of the curve and anticipating futures; both now find real-world events overtaking them. In this final series Quatermass is an old man caught in the crossfire of a factionalised, devastated Britain, rife with no-go areas and ripping itself apart. 'Someone remembered his name . . .,' Quatermass comments, while waiting to make an appearance on a TV chat show to discuss his 'comeback'. 'Glad of a few pence, the usual thing . . . Perhaps, you know, he was too soon – premature, I mean, he did strike trouble . . . Took appalling risks . . .' It might have been Kneale himself at a gloomy dinner party, talking about the launch of the first *Quatermass Experiment*. He even makes a slight return to the Shell processing plant of *Quatermass II*, during an exchange with rogue scientist Joe Kapp about the misuse of North Sea oil.

As stragglers cower and the dwindling authorities hurtle around this new world in armoured vehicles, the Planet People roam the ruins. Kneale has been criticised for the way he depicted this youth cult. Already outdated in the late-1970s era of punk, these ragamuffins are a tabloid caricature of late-1960s hippies – refugees from the earliest Glastonbury Festival. Given the script's slow gestation (Kneale began writing it in 1972), punk had not yet happened when the show was first conceived. But we should remember that those right-wing plotters of the Wilson era were trying to anoint a strong caretaker to put a stop to what they feared was coming: economic and civil meltdown, riots and industrial action. The Britain in *Quatermass* is Kneale's representation of the hard right's worst nightmares. Looked at from another angle, the cult is unconsciously prescient of a later generation of New Age travellers, greboes and the ring-road acid house devotees of the late 1980s and early '90s. What goes around comes around: Kneale's world view in a nutshell.

Here, what comes around again turns out to be an invisible alien presence that first tasted human meat five thousand years ago and is now returning for second helpings. Megalithic monuments and stone circles mark the locations of the sites where gullible humans, singing wyrd pagan songs, were zapped into the ether, leaving only a ring of white ash. Scientific rationalism and/or religion (Kapp reveals he's Jewish) insulate humans from indoctrination. It's the amoral, ignorant young, Kneale argues, who are most vulnerable to the mysterious pull towards the tempting lights.

Professor Quatermass begins the series as a fugitive, tracking his vanished granddaughter, who has been rescued from a mugging by Kapp in his ramshackle Ford Transit and whisked off to the countryside. Kapp's house is more like an Arts and Crafts wigwam; his wife Clare uses a weaving loom. Nearby stand a seventeenth-century space observatory and a Neolithic stone circle. A clay beaker excavated by Clare is the link between the ancestors of five thousand years ago and the present. She imagines a pair of lips drinking from the cup in the past – 'It was as if they were standing next to me.' They drive to Ringstone Round, a newly discovered stone circle that Clare believes could be linked to Stonehenge. There they find themselves in the middle of a stand-off between the children and the acting police force. Six years after broadcast, fighting between police and travellers would take place for real at the 'Battle of the Beanfield', when Wiltshire Police, acting on government orders, forcibly prevented peaceful festival-goers from making their way to a free festival at Stonehenge (where Kneale originally envisaged key scenes taking place).

Britain's approaching civil war is constantly evoked by small details. Quatermass talks with the district commissioner (a royal 'CR' (Charles Rex) coat of arms is stencilled on her Land Rover bonnet) and says her title reminds him of the old Empire, when Britain put down the natives. Now, she replies, 'putting down our own natives' is her role. Riot police, mounted knights in plastic vests, quell violent outbreaks.

Kneale remained disturbed by the hypnotic power of mass entertainment. 'These great gatherings,' observes Quatermass, 'they're another freak of our time. Huge assemblies, mindless, enormous – supposedly to listen to some leader or pop star, but really just to crowd together.' At the same time, when he falls in with an underground community of the elderly, some of them express anger at what the older generation (with a memory of growing up under wartime austerity) missed out on and envy that the young now have the chance to experience the rapture: 'Why should they? They got the lot off us, didn't they?' In these sequences emphasising the usefulness of the elderly, Kneale plants his feet firmly on the side of conservatism. The story becomes a rebooted Pied Piper fable: the extraterrestrials are luring young humans to open meadows in order to harvest them for some unknown purpose. Tracker beams detect living human protein. Kneale synthesises folk culture (the nursery rhymes and songs of innocence, such as 'Huffity Puffity Puff', sung by the celebrants), prehistoric archaeology and close encounters of the destructive kind. Quatermass theorises that Britain's megalithic landscape must be a system of markers left thousands of years ago by visitors from an advanced civilisation.

The final instalment finds Quatermass assembling a coalition from the local army, a Russian scientist colleague and a veteran workforce comprised of his pensioned-off friends to rig up a nuclear booby trap, luring the aliens by simulating a human crowd and sending them a nuclear 'sting' to encourage them to back off. This somewhat optimistic plan, relying on a large measure of British 'make do and mend', is executed in the final episode, under eerie chlorine-coloured skies, as more and more human remains are floating in the atmosphere. The melodramatic conclusion, on the 'sacred turf' of Wembley Stadium, ties together the lost granddaughter/Quatermass-as-hero narrative with a final appearance of the Planet People, who almost but not quite manage to screw up the plot. Despite the return to pastoral, childlike innocence in the shot of gambolling kids in the meadows under the closing credits, Kneale's valediction to Quatermass is not quite the happy ending you might expect. His vision for humanity and for the prospects of the young appears to be either a retrenchment to idealised innocence or a sticky end for those who aspire to personal change. Quatermass sacrifices himself for humankind, leaving the planet to an uncertain fate. Went the day well?

3

This Nation's Undermind

Went the Day Well?, Nineteen Eighty-Four, It Happened Here, The Other Man, The Guardians, An Englishman's Castle, 1990, Years and Years

The fading world maps on my classroom walls in the mid-1970s still showed countries coloured in the British Empire's shocking pink, even though I now know many had claimed independence before I was born. Britain, a fortress nation surrounded by a giant moat, held on to its global power after the Second World War, but total victory, not just self-defence, required the help of the US, the Soviet Union and forces from its various colonial territories. Adding to the feeling of instability, just a couple of years after VE Day several key jewels in the imperial crown began the process of decoupling. The Suez debacle of 1956 shook public confidence in the moral superiority of the British state. These factors plus post-war domestic austerity combined to make Britons exceptionally prone to fevered imaginings of their own national demise. Complementing the science fictions of the previous chapter, many films and TV programmes on this theme have taken the form of alternative histories, entertaining the possibility that the Axis powers won the war and invaded Britain, or imagining what a Britain run by an autocratic government might look like.

One of the most unusual wartime domestic movies convincingly crossed the line between civilisation and barbarity and, in doing so, set itself the task of imagining the unimaginable – an alien invasion of the sceptred isle. *Went the Day Well?* (1942) was Alberto Cavalcanti's adaptation of a story by Graham Greene, in which a tranquil English village is seized by a German advance party disguised as English troops, as a forerunner to a full-scale invasion

by the *Wehrmacht.* One of the few wartime films to temper any
sentimental patriotism with a stark portrayal of extreme measures
taken in adversity – such as the old postmistress Mrs Collins killing a German guard by stoving in his head with an axe – *Went the
Day Well?* prepared the population psychically for an invasion. (The
1976 film *The Eagle Has Landed,* directed by John Sturges and based
on Frederick Forsyth's jingoistic pulp novel, used a similar premise,
this time with the Germans, disguised as Polish troops, attempting
to kidnap Winston Churchill.)

During the Second World War, the island nation preserved its
thousand years of security by fighting off the Germans – a mere local
enemy. But in the 1950s alien matter was infiltrating from the other
side of the pond. Comics, pulp fiction and beat poetry, jazz and consumer durables were all increasingly visible, along with Hollywood
movies of all stripes. The American way of life, which had Britain in
its pocket, changed society through its special relationship at least as
much as a Nazi takeover could have done.

■

Nigel Kneale's other big project in 1954 – between *The Quatermass
Experiment* and *Quatermass II* – was his BBC adaptation of Orwell's
Nineteen Eighty-Four (1954), starring Peter Cushing as Winston
Smith. *Quatermass II* already contained Orwellian overtones. At
Winnerden Flats, Newspeak about overshots and synthetic food
effectively suppresses the locals' desire to find out what is really hap-
pening at the plant. In Kneale's adaptation of Orwell's dystopia, pro-
duced only five years after the novel was published, Winston Smith's
London is an atomic wasteland. The pyramidical headquarters of the
Ministry of Truth, decked with propaganda slogans, looms above
Big Ben. Britain has hardly appeared bleaker than in the fogged
frames of this *Nineteen Eighty-Four.* Its outdoor locations, shrouded
in a deathly mist, were largely filmed in White City, on the western

outskirts of London, at a site that would soon be demolished in order to build the new, gleaming, modernist 'ministry of television', aka BBC Television Centre.

Orwell's political insight channelled via Kneale's visionary tele-visual storytelling is a stark prospect. The opening sequence includes a heartless exchange between Syme (Donald Pleasence, in one of his most shiftily fanatical roles) and Winston on the conversion of the official language to Newspeak. Syme speaks witheringly of the proles, his attitude a continuing symptom of the divided kingdom: 'They're not human, they've no minds, they live by instinct.' The proles, he says, have no memory, no inkling of the past. Another Kneale preoccupation: the degradation of culture and erasure of his-torical memory.

Kneale invented a scene with two child 'spies', one reading a his-tory textbook that tells of the sorry fate of children in the squalid London of old, not the beautiful city they know today; the other blames a blocked sink on revolutionary infiltration. Indoctrinated, tyrannical kids who rule the roost at home, winkling out traitors with the promise of medals. All of this had been witnessed at first hand by Kneale's generation – not least by his own wife, Judith Kerr, as a Jewish child in Nazi Germany. Kneale exhibits a particular inter-est in Winston's research into what the past was really like, having him visit an antique dealer who delights him with the song 'Oranges and Lemons'. Folk memory conveyed by remembered nursery rhyme is the sole means of uncensored preservation now. Here, crucially, Winston learns that the antique trade is drying up; all metal objects and china goods have been destroyed or melted down. The destruc-tion of the past – in which Winston is also reluctantly complicit via his position in the Ministry of Truth, altering Big Brother's pro-nouncements so that they retrospectively chime with reality – is for Kneale the most salient factor in this future Britain.

In a premonition of Kneale's *Year of the Sex Olympics*, he goes beyond the scope of Orwell's novel to invent Julia Dixon's workplace:

PornoSec, where they are developing 'Pornorite', an automatic pulp
fiction device designed to satiate the masses. She is creating a 'situation kaleidoscope', randomising configurations of six basic plots.
Julia's first overture to Winston is a rushed instruction on their first
tryst, promising an escape from the inner city exactly like the old
London Transport posters used to, when they depicted green belt
suburbs and the countryside as a haven from the city – 'down the
lane and meet at the forked tree' . . .

Secrets emerge, not from a crack in the earth this time, but from
Winston's hidden alcove, a nook in his surveilled and compartmen-
talised bedsit, a freak of architecture in the old converted block he
lives in that allows him to write a diary and exist in a chink of freedom
that's a blind spot for his two-way television screen. Here Winston
is free to read illicit political writings and thus gain insight into how
Big Brother has become the illusory face of an autocratic Party, and
how it enforces ignorance to enslave its citizens.

Kneale no doubt especially relished the speech of Inner Party and
Thought Police member O'Brien (André Morell): 'We are the dead.
Our only true life is in the future. We shall take part in it as hand-
fuls of dust and splinters of bone. How far away that future is there
is no knowing – perhaps a thousand years of spreading our knowledge outwards from person to person, generation to generation.'
Morell – soon to be the suave and reassuring gentleman in a succession of Hammer films, including *The Hound of the Baskervilles*
(1959) and *The Plague of the Zombies* (1966) – is sinister by vir-
tue of his apparent culture and humaneness. As he brainwashes
Winston with electro-convulsive therapy, O'Brien affirms that the
Party has invaded the British system from within and has spread,
gaining 'power over the human mind; and power over all matter,
climate, disease, the laws of gravity'. When Cushing, who throughout strikes a perfect figure of reluctant resistance and whimpering
anxiety, regards his broken face and body in a full-length mirror,
the image is not only a bolt of Munch's *Scream*, but also a parallel

with Richard Wordsworth's Carroon. Even the scars on Cushing's face are almost identical to the marks transmitted by the exploding overshots of Winnerden Flats.

∎

The film *It Happened Here* and the TV series *The Other Man*, both released in 1964, speculated on alternative outcomes of the Second World War, if the alien Axis powers had managed to conquer Britain. Behind the protective insulation of its natural moat, Britain has proved redoubtably resistant to invasion and conquest, but it sure has harboured some disturbing speculations about what kind of country it would be if it was run by the far right.

It Happened Here began in 1956 as a hobby for teenage amateur film-maker Kevin Brownlow. It was a project that snowballed into an eight-year labour of love, involving countless volunteers, week-end shoots, borrowed uniforms, memorabilia and army vehicles, and substantial reshoots of botched scenes. Andrew Mollo, a seventeen-year-old collector of war memorabilia, was drafted in to advise on historical and period detail, and eventually joined Brownlow as co-director. Their fake archive footage, shot in black-and-white *vérité* documentary style and painstakingly constructed in the streets of central London and various English villages and countryside, accurately foreshadowed the sombre style of the epic 1970s TV documentary series *The World at War*, which featured real footage from all the world's battlefields.

Brownlow and Mollo, plus cinematographer Peter Suschitzky (a cine enthusiast who would eventually film *The Empire Strikes Back*), were prepared to think the unthinkable and recreate it on screen. Nazi forces have overrun Great Britain immediately after the retreat from Dunkirk in 1940, and the pattern of occupation in France and even the Channel Islands is repeated with greater intensity on the British mainland, with the Germans taking over major cities

and a resistance movement slowly organising in the south-west and
Wales. As the film opens, the Nazi forces are clearing out a village,
forcibly relocating rural citizens into cities and shooting anyone
who resists.

Details of this occupied Britain are skilfully imagined: in
Westminster a Jewish ghetto has been created behind barbed wire; the
wireless pours out German Schlager; posters advertise job opportunities in Germany; tin-hatted police officers work on the streets hand
in glove with *Wehrmacht* infantrymen, who sample English tea with
suspicion and hilarity. On a propaganda newsreel the new European
union between England and Germany is celebrated, reminding
viewers that the two nations had already fought shoulder to shoulder
against Napoleon at Waterloo. The invading Reich seduces rather
than crushes its victim; the bitter enmity is gone, replaced by a common cause against communism, and the hostilities in the Great War
were engineered by 'propagandists'.

Jackboots in Westminster: alternative history in *It Happened Here* (1964).

The lens homes in on the busts of German genius carved into the Albert Memorial opposite the Royal Albert Hall in Kensington: Goethe, Schiller, Bach, Gluck. These reminders that the British monarchy has strong German family ties, plus the bomb-damaged sites with piles of rubble and weeds, did not need to be invented or built from scratch. Neither were the real-life English fascists who were invited to appear as part of the largely amateur cast and recorded discussing a British final solution, both informally and at a demagogic rally. Jews are described as parasites, 'fleas on a dog'; solutions include 'sending them all to Madagascar' and extermination ('getting rid of useless tissue').

The euthanasia these extremists propose is relevant to the later part of the film, when a story takes shape around Pauline, a Northern Irish nurse who acts as the viewer's avatar within this alternative universe. She is of necessity co-opted into the fascist party, working as a medic in the Immediate Action Organisation. Behind the black serge uniform with lightning-strike armband she retains a conscience, and her blank expression veils her vigilant scepticism. She is loyal to no one: she does not agree with fascism, but also nearly loses her life during a raid by anti-German partisans.

Renting a room in a basement owned by Dr Richard Fletcher and his wife Helen, both covert anti-fascists, she takes part in a conversation in which Fletcher ends up declaring: 'When you get two sides fighting a battle, and you don't agree with either, life does get a bit complicated . . . The appalling thing about fascism is that you've got to use fascist methods to get rid of it. We've all got a bit of it in us. And it doesn't take much to bring it to the surface.'

The family are secretly harbouring a wounded partisan fighter, but they are eventually discovered and arrested. Pauline's experience as a nurse excuses her from suffering the same fate, but she is sent out to the country to work in a remote hospice. At first, with its cheery birdsong and almost empty wards, it seems like a cushy posting, until a party of East European workers with tuberculosis, including a small child, are brought in for inoculation. Pauline is asked to vaccinate them, but discovers, next morning, that the injections were lethal and she has unwittingly taken part in an official euthanasia programme. It's all part of what Dr Walton, the head of the centre, calls 'a great cleansing operation' of the sick and infirm.

For such a low-budget film, the attention to detail is staggering, particularly props such as the German-language newspapers and road signs and the nationalist party costumes, and the mass execution scenes familiar from European documentary photography transposed to English settings. It ends with Pauline being captured by the Anglo–American resistance force as she tends to a dying soldier. As she is seized, we hear the distant sound of a machine gun mowing down German troops who had surrendered peacefully. In stark contrast to the patriotic Second World War blockbusters of the time, such as *The Dam Busters* (Michael Anderson, 1955), *The Guns of Navarone* (J. Lee Thompson, 1961) and *633 Squadron* (Walter Grauman, 1964), *It Happened Here* is more closely linked to a film like *Went the Day Well?* in lingering on the moral choices presented to civilians when tyranny appears in their midst.

One wartime speculative fiction that failed to survive the tape-culls, transmitted once in September 1964, was *The Other Man*, part of Granada Television's 'Play of the Week' series. Like *It Happened Here*, this drama, written by Giles Cooper and directed by Gordon Flemyng, asks difficult questions. Although at the time it was the longest TV drama ever transmitted, now only eighty-one minutes of the original transmission survive, which were screened at the National Film Theatre in London as part of a series called 'Missing Believed Wiped' in 2007. The story starts out with an opening ceremony for a new military museum but takes flight in the mind of one man present, George Grant (Michael Caine), who imagines an alternative history as Britain capitulates to the Nazis to avoid aerial bombing in 1941, reconquers India and allows its home-grown culture to be infiltrated by the ideology and methods of the Third

Reich. His situation accelerates into a fever dream, as he is gradually but inexorably assimilated into Nazi conformity, betrays his wife and friends, orders executions and tries to kill himself after he is recorded confessing doubts to a prostitute. He is revived and transplanted with new limbs courtesy of hi-tech German surgical procedures – a symbolic capitulation to the new order. The real and imaginary worlds fuse at the end as Grant gives a nationalistic speech about 'why we are here' that could fit equally well in both outcomes. As one entertainment magazine reported at the time, 'The ending makes clear that the play as a whole reflects critically on England's present state and lack of self-awareness, rather than being the comfortable celebration of British survival that such a plot device might have elicited from a different writer. Cooper's eye and ear for minute verisimilitude, minimal exposition, and images that convey violence and degradation without mere sensationalism, make the parable convincing. A devastating portrait of Britain with its middle class "virtues" corrupted.'[1]

■

> You get to the top, and you realise it's only the middle.
>
> Tom Hawkins (Gabriel Byrne), *Secret State* (2012)

Paranoia and a right-wing takeover by stealth has become a running theme on British television, from the 1965 ABC series *Undermind* to Channel 4's political conspiracy thrillers *A Very British Coup* (Mick Jackson, 1988) and *Secret State* (Ed Fraiman, 2012). *Undermind* – which featured several future *Doctor Who* screenwriters – remained in the sci-fi realm. Key figures in the Establishment are becoming afflicted or undermined, destabilising the nation. Attacks occur without warning or discrimination; confidence in institutions is gradually eroded.

Such fictions have begun to feel alarmingly plausible in the early twenty-first century, featuring the manipulation of data, money and voting systems by powers subverted from the inside or by corporate political donors. Reflecting 'the belief that British decline had worsened into national crisis; the need for a strong, quite possibly authoritarian right-wing government to stop the slide',[2] the industrial actions and economic meltdowns of the 1970s provoked a surprising number of prophetic alternative-history scenarios in which England slides imperceptibly (or violently) to the right. The proliferation of conspiracy tales went hand in hand with genuine fears of a hard-right takeover. From 1964, Harold Wilson's term as Labour prime minister featured several plots, real or imagined, by the shadow opposition, who believed CIA suspicions that Wilson was a covert Soviet agent. In the spring of 1968 both Enoch Powell's notorious 'Rivers of Blood' speech and the failed attempt by the League of Empire Loyalists to depose Wilson and crown Lord Mountbatten as PM demonstrated British fascism on the rise. Britain's National Front organisation emerged during this exact time frame, and *The Guardians* (various directors, Granada, 1971) revisited the idea of Britain's government in fascist hands, this time from an invisible British dictator controlling a puppet prime minister. 'England Is Great Again' is visible on a placard in episode one – Trump-style populism ahead of its time. The story is told from the viewpoint of one of the fascist guards and revolves around loyalties, trust and how far people will go to bring down tyranny from within. *The Donati Conspiracy* (Vere Lorrimer, 1973) portrayed Britain ruled by a military dictatorship, and its follow-up *State of Emergency* (David Askey, 1975) added a home-grown terrorist group resembling the real-life Angry Brigade.

An Englishman's Castle (BBC, 1977) poignantly starred Kenneth More, homely hero of so many war movies, such as *Reach for the Sky*, *The Longest Day* and *The Battle of Britain*, as ageing scriptwriter Peter Ingram. (He was not the only grand English actor to be placed in dystopian jeopardy towards the end of a long career: see John Mills in *Quatermass* and Alec Guinness in *Tinker Tailor Soldier Spy*, both transmitted in 1979.) Ingram is writing a successful soap opera set during the Blitz, three decades earlier. But as he's living in an England that was conquered by Germany, the story starts to look different from the one we're familiar with. As the series starts, Ingram is an old man, too tired to care any more about the nation that existed prior to losing the war (in many respects, German soft power has allowed the British way of life to carry on with most of its features intact). He reminisces about being a member of the resistance after the surrender and of living for a time 'like ancient Britons' up in the hills. He's one of the many who have simply acquiesced and justified defeat to themselves by pointing to the peace and stability that now reigns, while Germany gently steers policy from a federal base in Berlin.

Ingram catches the authorities' attention when his scripts begin to include references to Jewish characters, despite the Holocaust having officially ended. His loyalties are tested to the limit when he discovers that Jill, the leading lady in his show (who's also his lover), is not only Jewish, but actively working for the underground resistance movement. Jill opens his eyes to his own complicity in rewriting British history for the next generation – 'You present the image of a calm and beaten people patting itself on the back' – and his controller Harmer (Anthony Bate, displaying all the cynical sangfroid of his role as Oliver Lacon in the BBC's *Tinker Tailor Soldier Spy*) expresses his anguish at being caught in a double bind. Strict codes forbidding any mention of the Jewish 'problem' must be adhered to, so that the BBC may be permitted to continue broadcasting at all. Thus, the series contains a mini-essay on the dilemma of broadcasters' responsibilities and argues the distinction between editing and censorship. In this world, for the Fourth Estate to hold on to its licence, the line must be toed.

Running over two series in 1977 and 1978, the political thriller *1990* remains the broadest panorama of an imaginary totalitarian Britain ever to appear on television. The press is moved centre stage as we follow hardened investigative journalist Jim Kyle (Edward Woodward, more laconic and cynical, and far more in control of his destiny, than his Sgt Howie in *The Wicker Man*). Projecting thirteen years into the future from the date of its recording, *1990* envisions a Britain run by the Public Control Department (PCD), an openly autocratic home office that has demoted the House of Lords to a 'Leaders' Club' and regularly 'disappears' dissidents. Partly guided by 'Faceless', a government deep-throat informer in a green Citroën 2CV, Kyle investigates the underground economies that have sprung up within this new Britain, such as a people-smuggling ring that enables the brain drain of high-skilled émigrés. Dissident voices critical of the regime are arrested and detained at various ancestral homes that have been converted into psychiatric hospitals (Adult Rehabilitation Centres) to treat social misfits.

The contracted state of the National Socialist Britain of *1990* – bankrupted in 1981, a new government voted in by only 20 per cent of the population, people living under rationing, business under state ownership – is unrelentingly dark, grey and wet. *The Star*'s newspaper offices are crammed into an untenably small space; the pub walls are plastered with government propaganda. Kyle juggles a number of tense relationships, from the gangster underworld to high-level PCD officials such as the alluring Delly Lomas. His quick-thinking actions, above and below the law, as he assists in the illegal emigration racket transform the Fourth Estate into a kind of rogue underground network. His eventual trial and relegation to non-citizen status, denied work, food and home ownership, involve all the coercive powers the government can muster. As Woodward commented in a promotional interview before the series was broadcast, he sometimes felt *1990*'s storylines were a little far-fetched. 'Then I would pick up a newspaper and read some ordinary item of day-to-day life – and there it all was already. Red tape, the VAT man, forms, identification. It's much more frightening than *1984* because it's closer to us than Orwell's book was to his own generation. It's really just around the corner. I mean, just think how difficult it is to find who's responsible for things nowadays.'[3] One month before Woodward's comment appeared in the *Radio Times*, the same magazine had trailed the documentary series *My Country: Right or Wrong* – which investigated the modern-day role of the secret service – with a strident Nazi swastika emblazoned on its cover. On the TV screen, fascism seemed to be closing in on all fronts in late 1977.

1990's screenwriter, Wilfred Greatorex, had already explored boardroom and union relationships in his two series for ITV, *The Plane Makers* (1963–5) and its spin-off *The Power Game* (1965–9). He was also one of the writers on *The Battle of Britain* (Guy Hamilton, 1969). When it came to *1990*, he moved from real-world politics to the speculative, in a series whose sophistication is only partly lost now, with its dour BBC production values. Woodward is splendid as the 1970s alpha-male cynic Kyle, who is called a 'doom-drip' by one crowing minister ('I bet you see the rainbow in various shades of black'). The politicos are cast from hammier cloth, but a number of throwaway lines revealing their casual sexism and racism display a consciousness rare for British television of the period.

As union leader Wainwright declaims before his brain is ECT'd into a Brussels sprout: 'I live in a sceptred isle surrounded by barbed wire.' 'Common or garden idealism,' murmurs the psychiatric doctor Vickers, 'quite easy to treat.' *1990* is a nuanced examination of what happens to idealism, the compromises it is forced to make, when governments over-extend their authority.

■

Alternative histories have continued to occupy screen time on British networks sporadically over the ensuing decades. *The Aerodrome* (Giles Foster, 1983), adapting Rex Warner's 1940s novel, featured the construction by a fascist government of a mysterious new airbase outside a tranquil Cotswolds village. *A Very British Coup* (1988), the adaptations *Fatherland* (Christopher Menaul, 1994) and *SS-GB* (Philipp Kadelbach, 2017), and Russell T. Davies's near-future mini-series *Years and Years* (Simon Cellan Jones/Lisa Mulcahy, 2019) would also tick the 'fascist Albion' box. *Years and Years* crammed a catalogue of conjectured future shocks into its six episodes. During a period spanning 2019–36, a Manchester-based extended family experiences huge political, demographic and technological changes: the rise of a populist female prime minister, compulsory voting, financial melt-down, a catastrophic loss of income, transhumanism, black-market cybernetic body modifications, sex robots, violent anti-immigration policies and extermination camps. Added to all of that, in Davies's version of history a re-elected and hawkish President Trump launches a nuclear missile at an artificial Chinese island in disputed territorial waters. A mushroom cloud such as this (which gives one of the family siblings radiation sickness) had rarely exploded onto the screen since the end of the Cold War, but for many who grew up in the shadow of bomb culture, some of the most unforgettable TV memo-ries stemmed from the many earlier examples of films about domes-tic nuclear apocalypse.

4

The Bomb Will Keep Us Together

The Road, Threads, The Bed Sitting Room, The War Game,
Day of the Triffids, The Old Men at the Zoo, 28 Days Later,
Z for Zachariah, Doomwatch, Stronger Than the Sun,
Edge of Darkness

I am fifteen years old, and I know how the world will end –
because I have seen it on TV. When the four-minute warning
sounds, there will be nowhere to hide, so I have designated
the parkland outside my house to be my final resting place
(or rather, the place where my skeleton will instantly light
up through my skin). There I will lie flat on my back, shut
my eyes and wait for the nuclear warheads to detonate over
Bristol. Although I can't deny that seeing your skeleton
lighting up through your skin would be spectacular, I really do
hope to God that this fiery death will be instantaneous.

But of this I am not entirely sure. In the BBC's *Panorama*
documentary 'If the Bomb Drops' (1980) and the QED film
A Guide to Armageddon (1982), the effects of thermonuclear
explosions on the human body are horrifically illustrated by
flash-roasting pig carcasses. Rapid cuts between footage of
shocked and surprised humans and the seared, melted meat
are, to say the least, disconcerting. As is the programme's
enactment of the government's 'Protect and Survive' strategy
for the actions Britons should take in the event of a nuclear
war. Those makeshift shelters made from salvaged timbers
and doors unscrewed from their hinges don't look too secure.
It isn't clear how whitewashed double glazing will hold off the
ravages of Soviet megatons. And the prospect of hibernating

out the nuclear winter with my family, lying in a shallow
trench in the garden covered by wooden planks, sustained by
a couple of buckets of tap water and some tins of baked beans,
appears bleak.

But I am a citizen of a nation that has managed to keep
its borders protected from invaders for almost a millennium.
I shouldn't be surprised if this well-preserved emerald isle
expends so much of its cultural imagination fretting over its
own downfall and destruction.

■

When, directly after the Cuban missile crisis, Nigel Kneale imagined
Britain's roads crammed with people fleeing the cities after a
nuclear attack, in his television play *The Road* (1963), he reverse-
engineered Armageddon as a premonition intimated by denizens
of Enlightenment England in 1770. Annually on Michaelmas Eve,
there are eerie aural hallucinations in a nearby forest – 'all screams
and screeching – as if all the dead people was risin' out o' hell an'
covering' the land!' This was a frightened reaction to the nuclear now,
reframed as a warning from the future to a historical country that, in
many respects, still existed in 1963.

Threads (Mick Jackson, 1984) and its US counterpart *The Day
After* (Nicholas Meyer, 1983), on terrestrial television, plus the
Raymond Briggs animation *When the Wind Blows*, in cinemas in
1986, were pretty much all the primers you needed on the inescap-
ability of the coming apocalypse. *Threads*, filmed in Sheffield and
involving members of the local community as extras, was exceptionally devastating in looping the local and domestic into global
politics. What was most frightening was its depiction of the frantic
minutes before and after the explosion – electricity and cars instantly
crippled, local infrastructure wiped out, familiar streets annihilated. *Threads* was not afraid to let its central characters perish in

the aftermath, agonisingly and grotesquely, and ended with a young mother's scream of disgust when confronted with the deformed baby she had just given birth to.

With its descent into utterly nihilistic obliteration, *Threads* left no room for comic relief – not even the lamp-black humour of Richard Lester's bitter, post-apocalyptic *The Bed Sitting Room* (1969, based on a play by Spike Milligan and John Antrobus). Britain has never looked so desolately razed as in Lester's nightmarish limbo of ash heaps, timber-clogged lagoons, smashed teacups, skeletal TV sets, rusting vehicle hulks and the dented dome of St Paul's Cathedral. The surviving handful of citizens are all going whimsically insane, keeping up appearances and bureaucratic formalities, and refusing to mention the 'nuclear misunderstanding' that has blasted their world to smithereens. A formidable comic cast – including Ralph Richardson (as the former cabinet minister who believes himself to be the bed sitting room of the title), Michael Hordern, Dudley Moore, Peter Cook, Rita Tushingham, Arthur Lowe, Mona Washbourne, a magnificently deranged Marty Feldman and Harry Secombe, and Milligan himself – scatter bathetic one-liners among the squalor ('This is Paddington – don't you know your London?' one lost soul is informed, adrift on a slate quarry). With Ken Thorne's mock-heroic soundtrack parping away throughout, this succession of absurdist vignettes is a genuine curio, offsetting Goonish comedy against ghoulish post-nuclear satire. Cinematographer David Watkin – fresh from the set of Tony Richardson's *Charge of the Light Brigade* – applies colour filters and misted lenses that cast a pall of damp greyness over the absurd theatre of subsistence-level survivors engaged in futile errands and routines.

The TV broadcasts of *Threads* and *The Day After* opened the way for Peter Watkins's film *The War Game* to finally appear on television in July 1985. It was considered too horrific for national viewing and banned from its original October 1965 transmission slot. Like Watkins's earlier *Culloden*, *The War Game* was a faux-documentary: it turned its lens on the experiences of ordinary people, but particularly on the various authority figures tasked with their protection. Public understanding of the realities of nuclear war was less than ideal in the mid-1960s, while the leaders and organisers appeared woefully inadequate, and in some cases blindly negligent. *The War Game* set out to penetrate the illusion of media-created reality around a global disaster and remains compulsive viewing.

In addition to the destruction they projected, these post-crisis dystopias often served as a negative version of the flight from city to countryside. If one important facet of the British dream was to leave the city behind and find a safe haven in a cottage in the country, the inverse of that was the idea that rural areas offered a refuge from societal collapse. The pattern was laid down in one of the first great English post-war science-fiction fables, *The Day of the Triffids* by John Wyndham (1951), which has been filmed (by Steve Sekely in 1962) and adapted for television twice, in 1981 and 2009. Combining Cold War paranoia with a very early ecological consciousness, Wyndham's story involves menacing, carnivorous plants bred in the Soviet Union and cultivated worldwide for their rich oil. These triffids run rampant after the human race is collectively blinded by either a meteor shower or a space weapons test gone wrong. In the novel and its adaptations, the protagonist, Bill Masen (John Duttine in the 1980s BBC miniseries), quits an increasingly perilous London and lights out for the countryside, passing through safe havens, including a country house, an enclosed commune of the sighted in Sussex, and finally the Isle of Wight. The survivors' precarious stability is, in the end, threatened as much by a newly installed autocratic government and its military law enforcers as by the rogue triffids themselves.

◼

For a good old English apocalypse narrative, the key ingredients are generally a catastrophe, an authoritarian regime, a flight from the city and an attempt to find shelter and preserve some of the former culture. The three seasons of *Survivors* (1975–7), written by Terry Nation, were an adult counterpart to the contemporaneous children's series *The Changes*. A deadly virus, originating in China, obliterates most of the world's population. The series focuses on a small assembly of British stragglers from the old world making sense of new realities – throwing together individuals from disparate walks of life. As in *The Changes*, the imperative is a back-to-the-land approach, in which the characters gathered at 'The Grange' must relearn the agricultural ways of yore. *Survivors* was filmed at multiple rural locations, from Monmouthshire and Herefordshire to Suffolk, Derbyshire, Wiltshire and the Scottish Highlands, with one episode featuring a return to the barren streets of London.

Another type of post-nuclear Britain emerged in the five-episode *The Old Men at the Zoo* (Stuart Burge, 1983), adapted by Troy Kennedy Martin from an Angus Wilson novel of the early 1960s. This version took its cue from the fascist takeover dramas of the 1970s, such as *The Guardians* and *1990*. The London Zoo in this story is a microcosm of the British state, and its leadership is co-opted into the authoritarian regime that takes charge after a nuclear strike. The zoo becomes a holding compound for political prisoners; they are eventually forced into a gladiatorial arena and fed to the lions for sport. The series came a year after the Falklands War, which shored up Tory power, and with the government on the attack against perceived left-wing bias in the media, there was a feeling that criticism and interrogation were harder to project via the news and current affairs department. 'I see fiction as a bulwark against the economic demands of television,' said *Old Men at the Zoo* producer Jonathan Powell,[1] who had previously worked on the classic John le Carré serials *Tinker Tailor Soldier Spy* and *Smiley's People*.

In any case, whenever the world threatens to turn upside down, the countryside is usually the only place to run to. In *Children of Men* (Alfonso Cuarón, 2005), Michael Caine looks after a massive library of books in his eccentric home concealed deep in the woods, safeguarding these precious, radical texts in case the book burnings begin. In *28 Days Later* (Danny Boyle, 2002) – which opens with the famous abandoned central London cityscapes that would eventually come to pass during the 2020–1 coronavirus lockdown – frantic townies scramble for the relative safety of the north of England. They take temporary refuge at a mansion now taken over by the military, enjoy a peaceful interlude at some ruins (the location was Waverley Abbey in Surrey), and the film ends with the young protagonists, having evaded the zombies and the virus, ensconced in a rural cottage in Cumbria.

These scenarios underscore a basic trust in the endurance of the land as a place of sanctuary. In the event of a thermonuclear war, the quirks and contours of Britain's more undulating regions might inadvertently offer some shelter from the firestorm. That is the premise behind *Z for Zachariah* (Anthony Garner, 1984), one of the last BBC 'Play for Today' dramas in a strand that had been running since 1970. An adaptation of a science-fiction novel by the American Robert C. O'Brien, it featured an extraordinary, unnerving performance from Anthony Andrews as scientist John Loomis, building on his performance a few years before as the diseased and alcoholic Sebastian Flyte in *Brideshead Revisited*.

Essentially a two-way between Andrews and Pippa Hinchley as teenager Ann Burden, the film is remarkable for its sparse script – the first half-hour unfolds almost entirely without words. It's a year into the aftermath of a nuclear war, although it takes time for that information to seep out. The Burden family and their dog Pharaoh are keeping a normal life going as much as possible, with communal meals and regular farm activities. Their green valley in the Welsh mountains, and the nearby village post office/grocery shop, have been shielded from the blasts and, apart from the sputtering radio bulletins and absence of other humans, life seems relatively unchanged, though lived in silent shock. Ann is left alone when her parents and

younger brother drive away to seek help, and her realisation that they
are never coming back is expressed when she silently disposes of their
toothbrushes. The electricity and water are cut off, and she finds dead
sheep in the pasture and lifeless fish in the stream. She learns which
of her farm's two rivers is contaminated with radiation and continues to birth calves and cultivate crops. Over the hill, a mysterious
tent, white and yellow like some giant egg, has been pitched, and
she watches from afar as its inhabitant, a young man named Loomis,
arrives at her farm towing a metal trailer full of equipment and a rifle
and bathes elatedly in her stream.

Given that it deals with a safe spot in the demise of civilisation,
Z for Zachariah is full of eerie passages, such as when Loomis, wearing his protective suit and helmet but clearly suffering from radiation sickness, enters the farmhouse and examines the parlour with
its piano and antique furniture. Familiar human habits and routines persist in the knowledge that everything just beyond the horizon must be a ravaged, hellish landscape. At the same time, human
morals and boundaries are rendered obsolete in this new year zero.
Although glad of human contact, Ann seems rightly wary of Loomis
after nursing him back to health. With good reason, as in the second
half, a male instinct to dominate and procreate kicks in, and the pair
are thrown into the role of mortal enemies.

All the while there lurks the awareness that the land and its waters
are being gradually but surely poisoned, and that this tiny preserved
paradise cannot hold out for ever. In this narrative it is not secrets or
unpleasant home truths buried under the earth, but radioactive con-
tamination with a long half-life. What could have been a reversion
to a Garden of Eden story, with an Adam and Eve for the new post-
nuclear age, is inverted into a dark and horrific tale of rape, pursuit
and revenge – a Fall with devastating consequences for the survival
of the race.

■

Pollution – a new invisible enemy from the 1970s onwards – does not have to come only from nuclear weapons. *Doomwatch*, a television series (now partly erased) and a 1972 film directed by Peter Sasdy (immediately before working on Nigel Kneale's *The Stone Tape*), dealt with a long-concealed outbreak of acromegaly among inhabitants of Balfe, an island off the coast of Cornwall. This disfiguring disease, which affects the frontal lobes and causes aggression and violence, is caused by an overdose of growth hormones. In *Doomwatch*, the source is illegally dumped canisters of the hormone chemicals, which are reacting with nearby radioactive waste sunk by the Ministry of Defence and 'bursting open like shelling peas', in the memorable words of protagonist Dr Del Shaw (Ian Bannen in the film version). Shaw is the medical scientist dispatched to the island by the eco-watchdog Doomwatch to investigate a reported recent oil tanker spillage. The parallels with the opening of *The Wicker Man*, filmed the following year, are striking here, from Shaw's arrival at the tiny harbour front to the raucous pub and defensive hostility of the locals. The cinema version of *Doomwatch* makes great use of its Cornish locations, both on land and at sea, as well as Doomwatch's scientific laboratory back in London. There is no superstition or witchcraft here, only the islanders' existentialist fear that their community will be torn apart if their secret is uncovered.

That secret is the deformation and mutations affecting those who have consumed seafood, who are now 'goin' ugly', contaminated with the pituitary hormone that is exploding into the seawater in a silent, submerged environmental catastrophe. 'Old Mother Nature has a way of dealing with these things,' laughs off Sir Henry Leyton, boss of the company responsible for ditching the chemicals. But *Doomwatch* warns of the effects of unintended consequences, when the private sector and the Ministry of Defence cumulatively unleash monstrous deformities and refuse to face accountability. The human cost is the dismantling of the village and its inhabitants' removal for treatment, the necessary step with which the film finishes.

As far back as 1977, nine years before Chernobyl blew its stack, *Stronger Than the Sun* (a BBC production written by Stephen Poliakoff) was picturing the effects of radiation sickness on a young worker, Kate, at Caversbridge, a nuclear reprocessing plant. Concerned by dangerous practices and cover-ups at the facility, she realises the only way to draw attention to the problems is to steal a lump of plutonium. Forsaken by both the media and anti-nuclear campaigners who suddenly get cold feet, she smuggles the plutonium back to a hotel, where she quietly disintegrates before being hauled off by hazmat-suited police.

There's also a chunk of half-inched plutonium in *Edge of Darkness* (Martin Campbell, 1985), this time in the hands of rogue CIA operative Darius Jedburgh. This six-part drama was a triumph for screenwriter Troy Kennedy Martin after *The Old Men at the Zoo*, combining nuclear threat, Cold War spycraft, US covert operations, UK deep state cover-ups and a burgeoning ecological consciousness. On top of all this it even managed to throw in a neo-Arthurian chivalric undertow, ghostly apparitions and the suggestion of Gaia-type Earth magic. In an age of overexposure to nuclear war movies, *Edge of Darkness* was prescient in anticipating later theories of the Anthropocene and presenting the nuclear threat as a harmful blight on the planet. As Jedburgh says: 'Honour went out the window when they invented that stuff . . .' As such, the series has remained more future-proof than other atom bomb films. In a UK that Jedburgh calls 'Third World', tech corporations keep governments on a leash. Detective Ronald Craven is searching for the truth behind the murder of his daughter Emma, an activist with a Greenpeace-type organisation called Gaia, who was shot in front of him on his doorstep. Her ghost appears next to him from time to time, giving him hints and advice and reminding him why he is undertaking this hellish quest.

Craven's enquiries take him to Northmoor, a nuclear waste plant which Emma and some fellow protesters previously infiltrated. He learns that she contracted a lethal dose of radiation from a secret cache of plutonium that had been illegally stashed underground. What the series does so brilliantly is to overlay the computer science, delicate spycraft and atomic power with an armature of mythology. Kennedy Martin was inspired by a book about the pagan origins of the legends of Camelot,[2] and Jedburgh became his avatar for one of the Knights of the Marches who defended the western lands from the barbarians of eastern Europe. (Jedburgh is also a village in Scotland famous for containing a two-thousand-year-old tree; Operation Jedburgh was the codename for certain Second World War guerrilla missions behind enemy lines.) His reason for piggy-backing on Craven's mission to find the truth about his daughter is that he's on a mission of his own to ensure the plutonium doesn't fall into the hands of Grogan, the American boss of the Fusion Corporation, which recently bought the ownership of Northmoor, and who is 'part of the dark forces that would rule this planet'.

Emma's ghost materialises by Craven's side in almost every episode, but after stealthily obtaining a 3D map of the subterranean tunnels from MI5's computer centre, Craven and Jedburgh enter the labyrinth underneath the power plant. It may have started as a political thriller, but from here on a larger overstory seeps through the cracks. Craven is a modern-day green man, associated with the primal forces of nature. A psychiatrist he consults tells him he has a 'bush soul' and refers to the ghosts that revisit him: 'In some societies, the dead are thought to be reluctant to proceed on their way because they fear what might happen to them in the next world.' When he arrives at his house in Yorkshire, he stops to look at the trees growing on his front steps, on the spot where Emma was shot, and discovers a bubbling well has sprung up. 'O Jeptha son of Israel, what a treasure hadst thou,' says Jedburgh. On another occasion Craven is described as being 'freeze-dried from some earlier epoch'.

Craven and Jedburgh's expedition in the radioactive tunnels under Northmoor is a supremely tense episode. They worm their way to a safe room, shut off since 1962 and provisioned with nostalgic objects, like a grim replica of an English drawing room: gramophone horn, model Second World War planes, stuffed animal heads, masks, ancient TV set, Union Jack, harp, dusty dressing table, pinned butterflies, vintage wines – 'the Doomsday equivalent of Harrods', as Jedburgh puts it. As they eat a candlelit dinner in the near darkness, Jedburgh observes there are no clocks: 'Time stands still.'

Someone has also installed a life-size statue of Jesus the Redeemer down in this infernal hellhole. One of the many undercurrents of *Edge of Darkness* is the rise of born-again Christianity; an overheard radio programme speaks of the new popularity of the Rapture. The eternal life of redeemed humanity is set against the long half-life of radioactive waste. The only constant is the planet itself. In one of her visits from the other side, Emma tells Craven how in past ages a certain species of black flower evolved that could absorb the sun's heat more quickly and warm up the planet. Already they have been discovered in the mountains of Afghanistan, returning to melt the ice caps and purge the planet of its deadly humans. As *Edge of Darkness* goes on, it gets harder to understand who are allies and who are enemies. Only in the final episode does it reveal its true hand: that the only meaningful battle left to be fought is the one pitting humans against planet Earth. After Jedburgh has created a nuclear singularity by bashing two bars of plutonium together at an industry conference in Scotland, and been hunted down and killed, Craven retreats to the hills, to fulfil his destiny and merge with the earth. He screams Emma's name from the side of a mountain, in a bestial release. Kennedy Martin's original script called for him to be seen mutating into a tree, but in the end the producer rejected the idea. Instead, we see a shot of the black flowers spreading across the Scottish Highlands: Gaia's self-healing process is gaining momentum.

Edge of Darkness's prophecy was more accurate than any of the nuclear war scenarios, more acutely aware of the concerns that would come to plague the Anthropocene. While its labyrinth of political connections, allegiances and double-crossings becomes almost unfathomable, its conclusion proposed a healing force, even a form of regenerative magic. Gaia is always ready to heal and restore itself when the Earth is wounded.

THE THREE FATES OF FOLK HORROR

5

Return to the Rural

'Home Counties Horror', Dead of Night, The Hound of the Baskervilles, The Droving

Between 2012 and 2020, I counted at least eight academic conferences in Britain on the subject of 'folk horror'. In the second decade of the twenty-first century, the term began to be used with increasing frequency in a multitude of newspapers, podcasts, blogs and magazine articles on film, television, music, fiction and art. Folk horror was discussed in relation to films like *Midsommar*, *The Hallow* and *Apostle*; TV series like *Requiem* and *The Third Day*; novels like Max Porter's *Lanny*, Fiona Mozley's *Elmet* and Ben Myers's *The Gallows Pole*; and musicians such as the Haxan Cloak, Bat for Lashes, Dylan Carlson, the Heartwood Institute and much of the roster of the Ghost Box label. Even a high-profile group like Radiohead got in on the act: the video for their nerve-jangling 'Burn the Witch' (2016) inserted pagan sacrifice into the lovingly recreated claymation toytowns of *Camberwick Green* and *Chigley*. The ongoing blog/label/publishing imprint A Year in the Country epitomised this confluence of interest and dark synergy between nature, myth, occultism and ghost traces of hauntological memory.

At the same time, 'folk horror' could easily be applied as a rather lazy critical shorthand. Even at the conclusion of a book entitled *Folk Horror: Hours Dreadful and Things Strange*, the writer Adam Scovell laid down his quill admitting that 'the genre resists such a direct question; it is not any one thing but in fact a multitude of creative ideas . . . It is not simply a few British films and television series from the 1970s, and it is not just a presentation of landscapes imbued with a sense of the eerie; it is all of these things and more. Essentially . . .

the term "Folk Horror" can be seen as a type of social map that tracks the unconscious ley lines between a huge range of different forms of media in the twentieth century and earlier.'[1]

Like so many discussions of folk horror, that's a stab-in-the-dark definition whose boundaries are so loose as to practically strip it of any claims to being a genre at all. In this section, in order to try to map out some of the key features of folk horror on screen, I have picked out the three British films glamorously referred to as folk horror's 'unholy trinity' – *Witchfinder General* (Michael Reeves, 1968), *The Blood on Satan's Claw* (Piers Haggard, 1971) and *The Wicker Man* (Robin Hardy, 1973) – and held them up to the light. Because they are each so different in the stories they tell and the vantage points they adopt, I'll spin them out into three distinct threads; three fates following their own lines of destiny, revealing markedly different meanings and perspectives, and each trailing their own separate lineages of films and programmes that came before and after.

These three films were the central topic of a documentary made by the actor, novelist and screenwriter Mark Gatiss for BBC Four, part of his three-part series *A History of Horror* (2010). The middle episode, 'Home Counties Horror', looked at the rise of British Gothic films after the war but ended with a consideration of these three as epitomising the tendency of 'folk horror'. This was the first time the term had reached such a wide audience, but it wasn't the first time the phrase was ever used. Appropriately enough, it seems to have been the director Piers Haggard himself who used it in the context of British cinema, discussing his film *The Blood on Satan's Claw* in the horror film magazine *Fangoria* in 2004. 'To me the countryside was terribly important,' Haggard told interviewer M. J. Simpson. 'I grew up on a farm and it's natural to me to use the countryside as symbols or as imagery. As this was a story about people subject to superstitions about living in the woods, the dark poetry of that appealed to me. I was trying to make a folk-horror film, I suppose. Not a campy one. I didn't really like the Hammer campy style, it wasn't for me.'[2]

If folklore can be defined as ritual remembering, a mutable process via the oral transmission of culture through generations, then rural horror frequently demonstrates the effects when forgotten things, long buried, are caused to erupt suddenly upon an isolated community or individual. Before we start unwinding the threads from the spindle of folk horror, it's helpful to consider this most nebulous of genres (perhaps 'tendencies' is more accurate) as a reaction to the earlier incarnation of British horror movies which Haggard found so camp, and which in turn was a cinematic outcrop of the fiendish legacy of English Gothic.

■

'Can you see the witch hiding in the bush?' I'm running my fingers through hot pebbles as my mum rubs suntan lotion on my three-year-old arms. We've spread our towels in a tiny sheltered cove in Majorca, where stones become fine sand as the coast trails into the ultramarine surf. It's my first time abroad, and after this package holiday my family dialled down the foreign vacations – summer holidays were typically spent self-catering in Devon, Wales or the Lake District.

But this particular afternoon, which I remember in the fuzzy haze of an infant dream, there is, as my dad excitedly points out, a hunched old crone in a black robe skulking in a knot of palm trees about twenty metres away who seems to be hiding from the small, single-masted wooden skiff that's even now approaching the shingle. Out jumps a robed man in a flat golden mask and a bearded, turbaned fellow carrying a raven-haired woman clad in red and gold. The company strides up the beach, looking about them in wonder and curiosity. Then they get back in the boat, row a few strokes and come back in to land. This happens several more times, and each time the witch peeps threateningly from the bush.

At last, this fairy-tale crew heads over to the catering tables under the cliff.

Back home I had a pop-up book of Sinbad the Sailor, so I know something about this legendary hero from the *Arabian Nights*. Here he was in the flesh, pitching up on my Mediterranean beach on this sultry afternoon in 1972, when I barely knew what a film even was. A year later, I'm a seasoned cinema-goer, and my dad takes me to see *The Golden Voyage of Sinbad* (Gordon Hessler, 1973) at the local Odeon, and there it is, the heroes' arrival on our holiday beach – the Grand Vizier in his shiny mask, the slave girl Margiana and Sinbad himself. Thankfully, the Ray Harryhausen animated monster they encountered shortly after this scene was having lunch with his agent on the day of the shoot.

■

As we'll see throughout this book, so many British films and television programmes hinge on some form of digging up or unearthing. The image is so prevalent as to be almost an alternative national mythology. In Italy, the remains of Pompeii and Herculaneum, which had been discovered under their layer of volcanic sediment in the mid-eighteenth century, began to be seriously excavated, along with the nearby city of Pompeii, under the French occupation of Naples between 1799 and 1815. The extraordinary, sometimes gruesome finds from the classical era that began to emerge out of the archaeological explorations – artefacts, buildings and human bodies preserved from the pre-Christian era – came to haunt northern European culture. The 'neopaganism' of artists like Henry Fuseli and William Blake, and the fascination with ancient history and classical Arcadias in poets such as Shelley and Keats, fed into the broader stream of Romanticism, an artistic movement that venerated nature, individual expression and inward reflection.

The presence of the root 'Roman' in the word 'Romantic' links it indelibly with the pagan world. In part a reaction against the Enlightenment and the early social effects of the Industrial Revolution, Romanticism predominantly looked beyond cities and headed to the country for its subject matter and setting. The *Lyrical Ballads* (1798) of Wordsworth and Coleridge delved into rural folklore. In the broad brushstrokes of this timeline we can discern the lineaments of folk horror, and appropriately enough, one of the first published uses of the phrase came in a review of an exhibition at London's Tate Gallery of paintings by Henry Fuseli, a painter whose images possess qualities of nightmare and phantasmagoria that would influence the design of horror films a century and a half later. (A print of Fuseli's painting *The Nightmare* hung on the wall of psychoanalyst Sigmund Freud's office.) 'Fuseli impressed from the start', wrote Caroline Tisdall in the *Guardian* newspaper in 1975, 'with his mingling of history painting, Shakespeare and dramatic folk horror of the changeling kind,' also noting that his work was 'sprinkled with imagined oddities and grotesque expression'.[3]

Right in the middle of all this, on a unique, fantastical night in 1816, the monster of English Gothic was birthed in a secluded villa by a Swiss lake. The legendary colloquium of Mary Shelley, Percy Bysshe Shelley, Lord Byron, Dr John Polidori and others at the Villa Diodati, by Lake Geneva, gave rise to Mary Shelley's *Frankenstein*, the prodigiously imaginative novel that generated the chief mythology of the machine age, and Polidori's *The Vampyre*, a direct antecedent of Bram Stoker's *Dracula* and its countless iterations in film, TV and popular culture. The notion of a human group forced into companionship to while away the dead of night telling each other their stories while the fire blazes in the hearth and the tempest rages outside has become the clichéd setting for the recitation of ghost stories.

In the first such film to appear in the wake of the Second World War, *Dead of Night* (Alberto Cavalcanti/Charles Crichton/Robert Hamer/Basil Dearden, 1945), architect Hugh Grainger is driving through rural by-roads towards a half-timbered Elizabethan dwelling. All around is sunshine and the trilling of garden birds. He has been summoned to discuss a proposed extension to the house. We can detect in this the green shoots of optimism and forward-thinking as the war drew to a close. The four directors involved in *Dead of Night* were among the generation of young left-wing documentary-makers of the interwar years, scions of the John Grierson school of realism. The same cadre included Humphrey Jennings, whose talents were turned towards a patriotic form of propaganda in works such as *Fires Were Started* (1943) and *A Diary for Timothy* (1945), films which drew on enduring images of England as a reminder to audiences of the national inheritance that was being defended.

The framing device for *Dead of Night*'s portmanteau of ghost stories and uncanny yarns is a meeting at a historic house, whose owners wish to improve it by adding a modern extension. Grainger has his self-confidence visibly ruffled the moment he steps inside the door; he claims to have met everybody gathered there before and has had a premonition of various specific events connected with the place and the group of people. The yarns spun by the guests turn on glitches in time, strange forgotten rooms in the attic of a mansion, a premonition of death that allows a character to evade a fatal bus crash, and a spooky ventriloquist's dummy with a cruel mind of its own. Most disturbing is the Robert Hamer-directed 'The Haunted Mirror'. An antique ornamental mirror is bought by Joan as a present for her fiancé Peter. He hangs its lavish frame on a wall amid the clean lines of his modernist apartment and begins to see the reflection of a wholly other room behind him – a Victorian parlour with blazing hearth, different furniture and decorations. Struggling with his own sanity, he almost succumbs to the pull of the room as it appears to become the real one. Even after moving into a new house the reflection comes back, and Joan's enquiries at the antique shop where she bought it reveal that it was salvaged from an apartment that had been shut up since 1830 and where a grisly murder had taken place. The husband witnesses the deed in his mirror and is just about to mimic the crime in his own home when the wife smashes it, destroying this insidious portal to the past for ever.

The power of traumatic events to imprint themselves upon an object, building or place is an idea explored many times over in ghost stories – it is the foundation of Nigel Kneale's BBC drama *The Stone Tape* (1972), which we will come to later. The past and its stranglehold on the present is an ever-present tic in Britain's psyche, especially at the end of the war, just as it almost takes over Peter's mind in *Dead of Night*. Smashing the antique mirror and its window on an earlier age is a revolutionary act of destruction that Cavalcanti and the documentary brigade would have sympathised with.

■

For all its eerie effects and unsettling atmospheres, *Dead of Night* still feels like a decidedly studio-bound effort. Wartime films such as *The Halfway House* (Basil Dearden, 1944) and *A Canterbury Tale* (Michael Powell, 1944) were early instances pointing the way to the use of real outdoor locations and natural light. After the war, as film-making increasingly moved outside the studio to encompass real country locations, this sense of the outdoors would be roughened and refined. Rural horror tends to have a distinctive look, with glimpses of countryside that range from textbook tourist board village pretti-ness to agrarian wildernesses whose remoteness strongly contributes to the sense that help is nowhere near at hand. As the film historian Peter Hutchings put it in his essay 'Uncanny Landscapes in British Film and Television', 'This is not a landscape where we find ourselves as modern national subjects; it is instead a landscape where that sense of identity is diminished or removed entirely.'[4]

The English countryside – the term already comes with an inbuilt cosiness – has been exploited in different ways by poets, writers and painters. For the Romantics it was a sympathetic resonator, a mirror for the internal lamp of feeling and sensibility. In Emily Brontë's novel from 1847, the few square miles around the bleak moors of Wuthering Heights doubled as a psychic wasteland for an exploration of subtexts including the status of society's inequalities and outcasts; domestic security and the force of untamed nature; male cruelty; passions that attain an almost cosmic scale; and life and death itself. Cathy and Heathcliff are a part of that grotesque nature, even when denied access to it; the sheer physicality and sensuality of the out-doors, with its louring skies, impassable downpours and blizzards, and tenebrous burial places, is a continuous music – a *ground* – that drones sonorously throughout the novel.

British film has naturally absorbed this deep sensibility for land-scape into its own syntax. But until the early 1960s there were sur-prisingly few instances where the camera actually roved out of the film or television studio to record the landscape in its own natu-ral colours. Even a picture like Hammer Films' Sherlock Holmes remake *The Hound of the Baskervilles* (Terence Fisher, 1959), which did use some outdoor locations (Chobham Common, Frensham Ponds and Dartmoor itself) to depict the blasted heathland of Dartmoor, retreated inside the studio confines of Bray, with earthen and tree-lined mock-ups of the moors, for its more dialogue-heavy set pieces. Here Hammer's lighting technicians could really get to grips with casting an English winter light upon the action, but the real menace comes from the shots of the actual landscape at night, with the solitary secret signal gleaming out of the uncertain dark. The books of Charles Dickens inspired two other examples of intensified terrain in this period, both in films directed by David Lean: the Kentish marshes in which Pip meets the desperate escaped convict Magwitch in *Great Expectations* (1946), and the rain-lashed wilderness in which the orphaned hero is delivered to a workhouse in *Oliver Twist* (1948).

Nineteen fifty-seven was an important year for the fortunes of Hammer Films. That was when the company shifted direction, from purveyors of monster movies to what we might call 'heritage horror'. Flagships here were the legendary *Curse of Frankenstein* (1957) and *Dracula* (1958), vehicles that iconised the acting careers of Peter Cushing and Christopher Lee, at the same time establishing a new film language – a serendipitous alchemy cooked up by production designer Bernard Robinson, scriptwriter Jimmy Sangster and producer Anthony Hinds – for the telling of dreadful tales that would pervade almost every area of popular culture for the remainder for the century. Here, for instance, was born the mad scientist's bubbling laboratory, the bloodstained fangs of the vampire and its crumbling to dust in the light of day. The fodder of the new horror: sadism, vaulting ambition, isolation, obsessions with ruins, innocence and its defilement, death or the Promethean quest for life, the Persecuted Woman or Belle Dame sans Merci, the vampire with origins in the 'Fatal Man' (aka Satan in Milton's *Paradise Lost*). The films' archetypes of English Gothic – derived from the writings of Mrs Radcliffe (*Udolpho*), Matthew Lewis (*The Monk*), Sheridan Le Fanu, and the

Charles Maturin of *Melmoth the Wanderer* – were played out on sets constructed at Hammer's Thameside Bray Studios, all airless mansions and dilapidated cottages, and on location in dusky Home Counties wildernesses. Hammer's cinematographers passed on Technicolor, opting instead for the slightly less saturated Eastmancolor film stock, lending the frames a patina of age and dried blood.

Storylines that moved to the outdoors inevitably involved shooting scenes in the English countryside. Production companies such as Hammer and the smaller Amicus simply stepped right outside their studio doors. Certain Hammer movies from the late 1950s and the '60s feature the same recognisable stretches of lake shore, woodland bridleway, battlegrounds in clearings and porticoes of manor houses, all of which were in the vicinity of Bray Studios in Berkshire. These places provided sets that were ready-made and dressed, with outdoor light and realistic weather effects to boot. English nature rarely boasted the solar flare of West Coast movies, but its misted atmosphere, its rural palette of terracottas, russets, dark greens and white overcast skies, marked it as forever England.

The changing seasons defined the mood of a great many films, and attempts to keep up led to uncanny effects (*The Wicker Man*, shot during the autumn months, is supposed to be taking place in spring). These are some of the visual qualities that often mark out the films labelled as 'folk horror', although 'rural horror' would be a more inclusive term, and more accurate. But as I have already argued, the words 'folk', 'rural' and 'horror' come with a lot of complexity stitched in. This ends up with a mass of diverse films and programmes being lumped together, causing a pile-up of agendas and ideologies that are wildly at variance.

Bookended by *The Witches* (1966) and *The Wicker Man* (1973), the main period of classic vintage folk/rural-horror films precisely coincided with the golden age of British folk rock and its countercultural revival. This was a period when the likes of Shirley Collins, the Incredible String Band, John Martyn, Pentangle, Fairport

Convention, Bert Jansch and Sandy Denny spearheaded a marriage of folk tradition with contemporary song and electric instruments. Folk became a touchstone for a decidedly British aesthetic in the sound and presentation of the music, with period instruments, acoustic and electric hybrids, and songs written in the vernacular of an idealised neo-medieval minstrelsy.

As with the folk-rock revivalists, folk-horror films draw on an idea(l) of the British landscape and tradition to subvert and cloak it with an evocative feel garnered from the experience of the retreat to the rural. By getting back to the country, artists, musicians, directors and cinematographers exploited the otherness produced by the city/country dichotomy. Beyond the merely picturesque, this was a neo-Romantic landscape that had the potential to conceal persistent folk memories, supernatural doings and secrets – even, in its most extreme cases, abject horrors.

There is an unsurprising correlation between, for example, the album sleeves of the late 1960s and early '70s and the folk-horror films of the same period (think the Watersons' *Frost and Fire*; the Incredible String Band's *Hangman's Beautiful Daughter*; Black Sabbath's first LP; Trees' *On the Shore*). Grain in the frame; green and brown hues in the palette; pale light under clouded skies. Alternative dimensions and time zones riffling through landscapes that don't feel quite right. How much 'folklore' is present is open to question, since much of that era's folk rock is just creative, post-Dylan songwriting. Folk is an aesthetic choice rather than a direct link with the canon of folk song collected in the late nineteenth century by the likes of Cecil Sharp, Ralph Vaughan Williams and others. When younger artists like Fairport Convention, Pentangle, Sandy Denny, Anne Briggs and others did go back to the source, it was the pastoral, magical folk tradition that attracted them more than the 'industrial' canon of workers' songs espoused by the likes of Ewan MacColl. Social justice gave way to mystery and the sense of tapping into a bedrock of song and poetry that emerged through the fog of time, bringing with it tales of fairies, earth magic, shape-shifters, vampiric beings. The films referred to as 'folk horror' do not always reference folk culture or tradition, and are not always concerned with the supernatural. They do, however, address the tensions between younger and older generations; you could say that if folk corresponds with seasonal cycles, and with birth and regeneration, then many of these films investigate the survival of older beliefs and entrenched ideas against the arrival of the new. Authority and order are challenged and assaulted by pagan or anarchic impulses. Which side is the audience supposed to take?

Each of the three core films – fate lines – in the folk/rural-horror canon is built on very different assumptions. In *The Blood on Satan's Claw*, a murderous youth cult, in league with the devil, forms a separate anarchic faction in a village and are hunted down as enemies of the people. This is about the potential for evil to emerge from within the heart of a society.

By contrast, the island-based pagan society of *The Wicker Man* emerges strangely triumphant over the doomed police officer from the mainland, Sgt Howie. The film enacts a clash between authority and the unfamiliar customs of a remote community, but offers little in the way of condemnation of the sacrificial logic of these cultists and their charismatic leader.

In *Witchfinder General*, the unspoilt fenlands of Suffolk are despoiled by the inquisitorial regime of Matthew Hopkins, witch-finder. There are no supernatural powers at work here, only the unchanging open spaces of the fens as an eternal canvas against which acts of pain and suffering are enacted in the name of law enforcement.

As I mentioned at the start of this chapter, to fully understand the scope of folk/rural horror, I have found it helpful to group various films and television productions around these three 'fates'. All three films examine questions of identity, morality and who represents the laws, but from very different moral positions. *Witchfinder General* overturns the stereotypes of prince/princess versus ogre. In fighting back against the abuse of power perpetrated by the witchfinder, the hero/heroine is forced towards a moral snapping point where they themselves must descend into savage violence. *The Blood on Satan's Claw* features a satanic cult violating the morality of a village – the viewer effectively wears the witchfinder's hat and is assumed to be on the side of 'good', which requires the cult to be destroyed. In *The Wicker Man*, the witchfinder is Sgt Howie, who has the law (and God) on his side, but we move from empathy – sharing his confusion – to pity and an ambiguous response to his sacrifice. Because on Summerisle, the pagans come out on top.

■

In *The Droving* (George Popov, 2020), a film produced in a period of more expanded consciousness about the genre of 'folk horror', all three fates converge. Popov's debut feature, *Hex* (2017), was a refreshing take on the witchfinder/superstition/battle of wills encounter of a Cavalier and a Roundhead in the English Civil War. In *The Droving*, Popov and writer Jonathan Russell returned to the present day in Penrith, in Cumbria, on the eve of an annual folk fair and fire festival called the Droving, with origins in medieval market days. Given its associations with Romantic literature, its wild expanses and dramatic tarns and fells, the Lake District remains surprisingly underused in English Gothic cinema. Here Popov takes his cameras out into the razor-edged valleys and heathery slopes and sets key scenes in several bleak and mysterious locations: mysterious free-standing brick portals in the forest, a hermit's cottage that looks almost naturally sculpted from the slate shingle on a mountainside, and a shimmering, mirror-calm lake. Because of the verticality of this landscape, a camera lens pointing straight ahead can be filled with land rather than sky, which, combined with an electronic drone soundtrack, enhances the menace and claustrophobia of the wilderness.

Landscape, myth and menace: *The Droving* (2020).

Martin is a modern-day crusader, returned from soldiering in the Middle East, with a belt-mounted whittling knife replacing a magic sword. He's searching for his sister, who disappeared the year before on the eve of the Droving. After waterboarding Brendan the hermit in his isolated stone bothy, Martin learns of a legend that every year, the Droving is attended by a Merchant who promises to resurrect a dead soul in exchange for a new one. Martin suspects his sister Megan was sacrificed by a local hiker, Simon, who wanted to bring his deceased wife back from the dead.

The film precariously holds the line between folk tale and realism, and as in *The Wicker Man*, plot and the background of various characters are revealed only teasingly. Martin is a Howie but also a Hopkins; he has right on his side but is a trained interrogator from the cells of Bahrain, where he extracted secrets from 'some of the sickest men in the world'. Like Richard in *Witchfinder General* and the Judge in *The Blood on Satan's Claw*, he must commit brutal acts in the pursuit of revenge. And as with Jay in *Kill List* (Ben Wheatley, 2011), a film *The Droving* resembles in many ways, Martin slowly comes to feel he is a pawn in a larger game that will eventually grant him unlooked-for powers. Some details read like a folk-horror playbook: silent, faceless figures watching from a distance; a hair-raising night-time encounter with attackers wearing creepy animal heads; a final showdown with the Merchant – or is it just some murderous sadist getting kicks out of persuading humans to kill each other? – in a prehistoric cavern. And when Martin makes the deceptively innocent comment, 'When you're new to an area, the sweet local stuff can seem quite alien at times . . . you're never too sure what to trust,' it's a prime rural-horror plot point in a nutshell.

Some of the script's lines also testify to that crucial instability around 'folk' in the British imagination: that it is forever feared to be disappearing or becoming papered over by materialist desires. When Martin first asks the hermit about the Droving ceremony, he complains it's being corrupted and mainly continues as a tourist attraction – 'most of the people end up watching it on their mobile phones'. That's what makes one of the final scenes of the film so compelling: when Simon attempts to contact the Merchant, ready to make his grisly soul trade, he's a man desperately yelling into an empty cave in the hope of animating something he wants to believe in. That's the question folk horror so often puts on the table: is there more to this than what I can see?

6

Fate the First: Evil Heritage

*Masque of the Red Death, The Black Torment, The Tomb of Ligeia, The Plague of the Zombies, The Reptile, **Witchfinder General**, Cry of the Banshee, The Bloody Judge, Twins of Evil, The Devils, The Shout, A Field in England*

The mid-afternoon is my time in the study, the post-school hours known as 'Watch with Mother', although Mother is usually elsewhere getting on with something important. Between around four o'clock and five forty-five, a string of children's programmes are unleashed. In the winter we flick on a bar of the electric fire, catching a whiff of scorched fibres as the coil turns orange. On sunny days we pull the curtains closed to stop the sun's rays falling across the screen. It's like a little cinema, and we habitually sit there with glasses of orange squash and a plate of custard creams. Softened up by comfort fodder such as *Play School*, *Jackanory* and *Vision On*, the young audience might sometimes find itself served with more disturbing fare: the persecution of a Romany orphan girl in *Kizzy*,[1] leading to an arson attack on her caravan – petrol is poured over straw and deliberately set alight, the flames eating into the floral paintwork; the weird, dissonant cacophony of *Children of the Stones*.

Once, in the late morning during the summer holidays, with a builder doing some paint-stripping in another room, my brother and I were watching TV. Maybe it was *Rainbow*, or *Jamie and His Magic Torch*, or *Why Don't You Just Switch Off Your Television Set and Go and Do Something Less Boring Instead?* but life was just about to get interesting.

Over the course of about twenty minutes, we slowly became aware that the screen seemed to be dimming. Thick dust was swirling upwards and around our armchairs. But the dust was accompanied by an acrid, smoky stench. When our eyes began to ooze and the screen became invisible, we opened the door and were hit by a blast of grey smoke, invading the hallway. At the same moment my mother's alarmed voice called from the garden, 'What's going on? Something's not right . . . Run next door and call the fire brigade.' We sprinted down the path, observing as we went the French windows of the living room ablaze. At least the TV wasn't in that room.

A stray spark from the builder's blowtorch – he having disappeared on a lunch break – had probably ignited some ancient cobwebs in the woodwork and set the room on fire, we speculated in our neighbour's kitchen, over the lemon barley water and Rancheros that were sympathetically furnished after the frantic 999 call. Gleaming fire engines quenched the blaze before it spread to the whole house, but the stink lingered for months and the television sat amid smoke-stained paintwork for a spell. The trauma lent extra force to any programme depicting fire, which was surprisingly often – for instance, the horrific finale of *Carrie's War*, when the heroine curses her school and teacher and a skull bursts into flame, granting her wish.

■

Folk horror mythologises the arguments Britain has been having with itself for generations about who it wants to be. Many of these arguments have swelled into battles that have left their mark on the land itself. Consequently, British history is written clearly on the landscape, from battlefields to burial mounds and megalithic monuments. You can travel from the City of London to King's Lynn, on the Norfolk coast, on a straight road laid down by the Romans. In some parts of the country, there are paths and hollow ways once trodden by prehistoric hunter-gatherers. County and parish borders lie on top of prehistoric boundary lines. The weirdness of the past remaining visible in the present is transposed to the stories that can be told about these places. It's hard to quell the imaginings of the people who once inhabited/haunted these places and the forces that allowed some to hold dominion and others to be subjugated. The macabre story inscribed across Britain's fields and furrows, its castles and churches, is one of mastery and servitude; violence and rebellion; power and its abuses.

Added to which we find that odd quirk in the British island mentality, which is so bafflingly conflicted about its own miscegenated heritage. No matter that, since the farmers of the Mesolithic era, the islands' population has been infused with waves of migration and invasion: Neolithic Anatolians and Iberians, Bronze Age peoples from the Steppes and Rhinelands, Roman occupiers, Anglo-Saxon migrants, Viking marauders, Norman conquerors, wandering Flemish and Romani people, Huguenot refugees and immigrants from the imperial dominions of India, Africa, the Caribbean and elsewhere. A fear of the outsider and the 'other', coupled with the urge of an elite few to rule over the scattered many, are constructions that make their way into the strand of folk horror explored in this chapter. As we approach the keystone of *Witchfinder General*, we'll see a shift from earlier English historical horror being played out in Gothic castles and aristocratic homes that conceal literal or metaphorical chambers of horror towards an aesthetic of the outdoors, (un)natural light and menacing country locations.

Although there were economic factors that largely drove American director Roger Corman to shoot his Edgar Allan Poe adaptation *Masque of the Red Death* (1964) in England, the British crew – including cinematographer Nicolas Roeg – made it something else. With its protagonists isolated in a castle to avoid the plague of the Red Death that is ravaging the land beyond its walls, the film has a sumptuously theatrical look, its castle-interior sets at Elstree having been left over after Peter Glenville's film *Becket* (1964) had wrapped production.

With its brilliant and vivid colour design, *Masque* might be wonderfully atmospheric, but its stylised interior and exterior settings belong to an age of film-making that was on the wane. Hard on its heels – and in the wake of *Tom Jones* and other historical films already discussed – came producers Tony Tenser and Michael Klinger, after spending the early 1960s producing exploitation and 'nudie' movies. Following his work on Roman Polanski's *Repulsion* and *Cul-de-sac* in the mid-1960s, Tenser graduated to producing English horror pics, such as Michael Reeves's *The Sorcerers* and *Witchfinder General*, Piers Haggard's *The Blood on Satan's Claw* and Peter Sasdy's *Doomwatch*. He kept an eye on what was coming out of Hammer's studios, impressed by its factory-floor churn of popular sci-fi and heritage-horror flicks. Under the wing of his production company Compton-Cameo, Tenser took a historically-set script by brothers Derek and Donald Ford, hired director Robert Hartford-Davis and made *The Black Torment* in 1964. This film's use of the woods and lakes around a castle is a foretaste of the muted palettes of later ghostly tales and films, its wintry natural light and misty dawns placing it nowhere else than southern England.

The action is focused on the Queen Anne mansion of Fordyke House, which appears in several establishing shots. The opening pre-credit sequence, notorious in its day, remains a powerful prologue (the most suspenseful moments of the entire film, in fact) – Lucy stalked through a forest to a lakeside by an unseen assailant in black leather thigh boots. The intrigue – an aristocrat with anger management issues who can apparently be in two places at once, and with rumours about his wife's and a local girl's murders swirling around him – eventually resolves into a *Scooby-Doo*-style unmasking, but the theatricality is beginning to be offset by a more naturalistic placement of this action in the now-familiar nexus of aristocratic mansion and the wildness of the surrounding estate. 'You're just a carriage ride away from terror,' squeaked the trade advert.

In the last of Corman's 'Poe cycle', *The Tomb of Ligeia* (1964), the wheels kept on rolling. Hammer's cinematographer Arthur Grant shrouded Swaffham village, in Norfolk, in mystic fog and concealed the Byronic figure of Verden Fell (Vincent Price) – an aristocrat surrounded by a sinister cloud of suspicion – behind eyeshades, adrift among spectacular Romantic ruins. In the story, death reaches out from beyond the grave to exert its hold on those still living. The spirit of Fell's dead wife Ligeia pursues his new spouse, Lady Rowena (Elizabeth Shepherd plays both roles), who is symbolically equated with a hunted fox in assorted scenes. Despite the occasionally leaden pace, the film excels at conjuring an atmosphere of subdued fear and oppression, the shattered church walls of Ligeia's burial place a Gothic metaphor for Fell's (and Rowena's) crumbling sanity. The image of the sacrificial woman as the fox was not new: Powell and Pressburger's *Gone to Earth* (1950) had used the same idea, as would Hammer, not long after *Ligeia*, in *The Plague of the Zombies* – a very English horror film.

Two heritage-horror films shot back-to-back on the same sets by Hammer in 1966 are perfect examples of the English landscape changing its emphasis from backdrop to player in the story. *The Plague of the Zombies* and *The Reptile* share more than just locations, props and director John Gilling. Both are informed by post-colonial anguish, where what should be a bucolic and uneventful country life – where everyone knows their place – is problematised by exotic imported rites and sacrificial impulses. 'This', we're told in *Plague of the Zombies*, which takes place in 1860, 'is a Cornish village inhabited by simple country people. Riddled with superstition and all dominated by a squire.' Yet in the film's opening scene, 'savage' Afro-Caribbean drummers in full warpaint are gathered in some stuffy cavern, thundering out infectious voodoo rhythms on congas and bongos. Where and how do these two worlds collide?

Sir James Forbes and his daughter Sylvia travel to Cornwall to pay a visit to the unnamed village, after Sir James has received a disturbing letter from his old friend Dr Tompson, the local physician. As they approach the outskirts, they spy spots of blood in the fields from the carriage window – the local red-jacketed hunt, in pursuit of a fleet fox. Later, Sylvia herself will turn out to be the quarry. The huntsmen, whom they encounter on their arrival in the village, show no consideration for a village funeral and carelessly knock the coffin into a stream. This not only allows the corpse to be seen (thus proving it has vanished later), but is a literal illustration of what the hunters are also up to – exhuming bodies to order for their master, the local squire. Not only have the graves been defiled, but so has the social stratification of mid-Victorian England. Servants refuse to attend Dr Tompson's scruffy house, so Sir James and the doc have to conduct a strategy meeting while wearing pinafores and cleaning the dishes. The local economy is as undernourished as its suspicious peasantry. There are echoes here, whether conscious or unconscious, of Britain's parlous economic situation in the mid-1960s. The highest level of national debt since the war had led to a slump in 1964 and a deflationary government package a year later, and when this film was made, Britain was undergoing a full-on sterling crisis, with a devalued pound and wage freezes across the land.

The tin mines on the squire's land have recently been shut down, as no one wanted to work down there after too many accidents: 'They said it was unlucky.' Most of what we see of the village itself is a cramped open-air cemetery surrounded by houses and narrow footbridges. Then there's the mine itself: a desolate pit head on top of a ragged structure of beams and pulleys.

The dark horse here is Squire Clive Hamilton, who was away for years – overseas, say the villagers – and came back with an entourage of younger people – the huntsmen – spending money like water. Hints at his motives can be seen from the interior decor of his mansion (in real life, Oakley Hall, on the estate of Bray Studios). Where the doc's terraced house is hung with paintings and engravings of picturesque country views, Hamilton's mansion is an Aladdin's cave of exotic souvenirs, antlers, a stuffed bear, muskets and assegais, a grinning 'golliwog' statuette, trophies and paintings of the hunt. He kills to collect, but his most precious collection lies in the underground chambers beneath the estate. There, he has secretly reopened the mine shafts and populated them with 'zombies' – the animated husks of deceased villagers. This undead labour force is enslaved and lashed into working the mine, to a soundtrack of Haitian trance rhythms from the aforementioned drumming troupe.

In this film occurs one of the first instances of zombies rising from the grave, a cinematic trope that would become familiar from works as diverse as George Romero's *Night of the Living Dead*, David Gladwell's film *Requiem for a Village* (which is discussed later in this book) and Michael Jackson's 'Thriller' video. The earth piled over recently dug graves begins to stir and hands, limbs and heads push up out of their coffins, clawing at the air. The image of workers being coerced from their last resting place and forced into back-breaking labour is a potent one, especially as those benefitting from it are the landed aristocracy, who remain free to indulge their whims, from fox-hunting, grave-robbing and sorcery to the attempted rape and murder of young women.

The scenes featuring the zombies are well executed for this type of film, ghoulish make-up combining with pallid day-for-night photography when the body of the doctor's wife, Alice, is dug up. In fact, all the outdoor scenes have a slightly sickly grey humour, the misting quality of a fading photograph, rising to squalls of ground fog every time a grave is ruptured. In a race against time to discover whether Alice's body is still in her tomb, Hamilton's henchmen stalk the streets in grey cowls and sinister voodoo folk masks, in scenes eerily prescient of the carnival procession in *The Wicker Man*, seven years later.

The Reptile, Gilling's third movie of that year, also nominally takes place in Cornwall; this time, pub sea shanties, the yelps of seagulls and the croaking of frogs are higher up in the soundtrack mix. The Spaldings, Harry and Valerie, have arrived in Clagmoor to take up residence in Larkrise Cottage, which formerly belonged to Harry's deceased brother. It's the classic country-retreat model: Harry says he's sick of working in London and has always desired rural bliss – 'It's what I've always dreamed of. Roses round the door.' By contrast, the rooms of nearby Well House – yet another role for Oakley Hall – are filled with bushy arrangements of exotic, rainbow-coloured flora, spiky and fecund, arranged by Anna Franklyn, who lives there with her father. Dr Franklyn is awkward and standoffish, cruel to his daughter and attended by a silent Malay servant.

A disfiguring 'black death' has been causing fatalities around the village, but the locals Harry meets in the pub don't want to answer questions. Innkeeper Tom Bailey is the only one prepared to talk, and he affirms that he just wants his own comfort and security, not to rock the boat by enquiring into what's going on. Perhaps realising his custom is about to decrease unless he does something about it, Tom becomes Harry and Valerie's only ally. He is the film's rational, moral centre – a role traditionally given to members of the professional or aristocratic classes in horror films of this period.

As in *The Plague of the Zombies*, subterranean activity is revealed, in the same underground tunnel set that was used in the previous film. (Outside its entrance stands the grinning black boy statuette too.) Here the Reptile – the cold-blooded Anna, now with a lizard attached to her face – keeps her lair, protected from the outside world at her father's instigation.

If the plot again doesn't entirely hang together, it remains a film of multiple unforgettable moments and visual impressions. The entwined stone dolphins supporting Oakley Hall's fountain act as macabre guardians in the twilight. The impossibly vivid hues of Anna's flower arrangements leap off the screen. Elsewhere, images of archetypal Englishness are juxtaposed with the foreign and strange. When the Spaldings are invited over for a toe-curlingly uneasy dinner

at Well House, they are served unfamiliar oriental dishes, are told
about the doctor's research work in Borneo, India and Sumatra, and
are invited to listen to a music recital by Anna, who is dressed in a
lurid pink sari. She plays an Indian raga on a sitar, becoming more
and more agitated (under the mental influence of 'the Malay'), until
her father, anticipating Pete Townshend's guitar abuse, seizes the
buzzing instrument and smashes it against the fireplace. The film's
final scenes are a suspenseful attempt to exit a burning building while
the study doors are locked. *The Plague of the Zombies* ends with the
mineworks in flames; the final scene of *The Reptile* shows Oakley
Hall itself ablaze.

Released in the year of Indo-jazz fusions, the rise of the sitar and
tabla in pop music, Jimi Hendrix's arrival in the UK and the dawn
of English psychedelia, both these Gilling movies play on fears about
potentially malignant external influences as they take root and subvert
English culture from within. Both use evocative settings and outdoor
location work to situate them in the English countryside, far from
urban influence; both ultimately fall down in their plotting, as the
motivation for attacking and transforming the women involved (Sylvia
in *The Plague of the Zombies*, Anna in *The Reptile*) is never satisfactorily
explained. Ultimately, these films are simply about the menace of the
Other, effecting its transformative powers in the very heart of all that
is most familiar and comforting in the homeland. To that, *Plague* adds
the idea of ruling-class power and its abuses – the zombies as a cipher
for the exploited individuals of a crushing labour system. And power
– and the desperate measures that must be taken to combat it – is the
central theme in the decade's climactic rural-horror film.

■

Witchfinder General contains nothing of the occult, no monsters or
undead, no witchcraft or black magic of any kind. From the savage screams that open and close the film to the duckings, burnings,

pokings with a giant pin, brawls, vicious beatings and rapes, director Michael Reeves hammered home an anti-violence message. The
catalogue of brutality was also framed by hypocrisy, corruption, violation, innocence, greed, vengeance, partisan politics, dictatorship,
collusion and tyranny. Fab!

It was made in the months immediately following the Summer
of Love, in 1967, and finished off in the early months of 1968 –
a historical moment marked by Vietnam, the Six Day War, race
riots, student protests, civil unrest and political assassinations. On
17 March, Reeves made his final touches on the edit of *Witchfinder
General*, then went out to join eight thousand protesters outside the
American Embassy in London's Grosvenor Square in a siege that
ended with a mounted police charge and two hundred arrests – the
day that English flower power woke up and realised it had to take
direct action or be forever impotent. Such a moral dilemma comes to
the fore at the film's climax, when a conventional dashing hero must
transform himself into an axe-wielding butcher.

Following his performance in Reeves's *The Sorcerers* (1967), Ian
Ogilvy was again cast as the male lead, Richard Marshall, a Roundhead
whose sweetheart Sara lives with her uncle, the local priest, in the
nearby village of Brandeston. When we first meet Richard, he is about
to go on leave, his boyish smile eagerly anticipating a reunion with
Sara, his lover and intended wife. As the daughter of the local Catholic
priest, Sara promises to fulfil Richard's dream of a secure and happy
family life, which we see triangulated as he gallops into Brandeston:
house, church and forest. All of these, during *Witchfinder General*,
will be penetrated and violated by amoral force.

The unease begins with the priest's troubled look outwards as he
ushers Richard inside and closes the door. Sara immediately informs
him they are being pilloried, bullied as Papists, made to feel like outcasts in their own village. Suspicion and division are already latent
in this community. When he arrives, the witchfinder merely exploits
this bubbling hatred.

The film's opening minutes establish a remote agrarian scenario, where the silence of the fields smothers the anguish in the community. In scenes that unashamedly ape the leading of Christ to the crucifixion, an accused witch, screaming in terror, is led by impassive villagers to the gibbet being constructed on a hill on the edge of the woods. On the soundtrack, once the stool has been kicked away and she falls silent, the creak of the rope is magnified. Behind all the human folly and fallibility, the East Anglian landscape maintains its regular breathing, playing its eternal, traditional part, sure-rooted and softly rustling. Many of the film's most sadistic scenes take place in the cold light of day; there is little dirty work conducted in secret chambers here. The roving inquisition conducted by Matthew Hopkins (played, famously, by Vincent Price) and his sidekick John Stearne necessarily takes place in the open, under the docile gaze of the local populace. When accused witches are dunked into a moat to see if they float or lowered into flames on a giant toasting fork, such acts are arranged in public spaces, effecting a normalisation, even a banalisation of such barbarism (Betjeman-like church bells peal out over the burning). The inaction of the spectators at these grotesque entertainments is clearly intended to reflect back upon Reeves's audience, and the effect is chillingly similar to the passive consumers of *The Year of the Sex Olympics*, which appeared on TV screens in the same year.

The interiors were filmed in a converted aircraft hangar near Bury St Edmunds or within the stone keep of Orford Castle in Suffolk, but much of the film's action takes place outdoors, in natural light. There is nothing of the twilight Gothic about *Witchfinder General*; it is a cloudy late September, with the sun only occasionally breaking through. Cinematographer John Coquillon, a Dutchman who would film several more rural-horror films for AIP (American International Pictures, the company associated with Roger Corman) in the coming years, cut his teeth in the 1950s as a wildlife photographer in the Belgian Congo and East Africa, where he learned how to capture fleeting natural light.

Power corrupts: *Witchfinder General* (1968).

The first establishing shot is a long pan around an oak tree, while a voiceover sets the scene in the age of the English Civil War. The tree plays the role of the hypnotist's swinging watch. Our viewpoint glides around its gnarled bole, and a troop of red-tunicked Roundhead soldiers trot into distant view. The spell is cast, and we are back in 1645. Here under a swishing layer of ferns, danger is concealed. One of the resting Roundheads is shot by a rogue Cavalier. The ensuing revenge raid, as the soldiers sweep through the woods, takes place under a cacophony of birdsong. Later, a flock of sheep scatters around Richard's urgent pursuit of the witchfinder. England's inner peace is troubled. In *Witchfinder General*, Reeves found a way to film the particularity of English nature, while not making it play any kind of psychological or symbolic role. Nothing takes place according to natural laws; rather, human laws and ethics are sidestepped or transgressed ('There'll be no magistrates involved,' insists

Richard). Nature is, instead, a picturesque frame around an outbreak of entirely man-made barbarism.

Shortly after the English Civil War, Diggers and members of other revolutionary movements quit their armies and went in search of a new Eden, and a new deal with God. When Hopkins is asked what he is looking for in the village that is his destination, he replies, 'A man who may not be what he seems to be.' It's a motif that applies to the whole film, one full of men – and women, for that matter – whose role and moral position shift according to circumstance, or who wilfully conceal their underlying motivations. Hopkins the witchfinder, for instance, is himself a sadist masquerading as a lawyer. His purging methods are stated to come from God but trespass outside Christian ethics. Marshall is a fairy-tale prince who's capable of bloody murder. Stearne's only business is 'extermination', and he will do whatever it takes to keep one step ahead of the law. Even the apparently virtuous and faithful Sara immediately offers her body to Hopkins in an attempt to purchase back the life of her father, who has been condemned to death.

In *Witchfinder General* the chambers are psychological and internal: the voyeuristic sadism of Hopkins and Stearne; the blood vengeance wreaked by Marshall. More than a bloodthirsty horror film, it's a treatise on power and the repression of liberalism that ends with a scream and a discord on Paul Ferris's soundtrack. Hopkins has invaded the body politic just as the aliens in *Quatermass II* subverted the British government from within. Although widely misunderstood by contemporary critics, Reeves defended his film as a humane statement against violence. This was no morbid obsession with esoteric and creepy material purely for exploitative purposes; he wanted his audience to come away with a sense of self-loathing. 'Violence is horrible, degrading and sordid,' Reeves wrote in a riposte to a savaging in *The Listener* by reviewer Alan Bennett. 'Insofar as one is going to show it on the screen at all, it should be presented as such – and the more people it shocks into sickened recognition of these facts the better.'[2]

■

'Degrading and sordid' – words often used to describe what went wrong in British cinema in the early 1970s, as style turned to smut. Reeves was making his film at a point in time when the British film industry was beginning to take a nosedive. Horror movies from Hammer and other studios, which had been among the national cinema's biggest successes, increasingly shoehorned sex, nudity and sensational violence into the frame (helped in no small measure by *Witchfinder*'s producer Tony Tenser). Meanwhile, the innuendos and double entendres of the long-running *Carry On* film franchise had seen better days. From *Carry On Camping* – the biggest box-office earner of 1969 – onwards the much-loved series declined into the full-blown sauciness and tawdriness of the 1970s. But it was only being dragged out by the tide. Nineteen sixty-nine saw the *Sun* news-paper, which had been founded as a 'radical newspaper . . . championing progressive ideas', being purchased by the Australian media tycoon Rupert Murdoch, who transformed it into the familiar populist tabloid of page-three girls, scandal and sensational headlines. The new-look paper caught the national mood: circulation rose from 1.5 million in 1970 to four million in 1975.

With its strong moral position, *Witchfinder General* shines crystal clear out of the churned muck of the horror movies of its period. Its combination of historical setting and inhumanity spawned a sub-genre which, itself, appears to misread or ignore Reeves's motivations, and witch-hunting, female persecution and sadistic masters became popular on-screen sport in the ensuing few years after his film slipped out.

Right off the bat (and recasting Vincent Price and Hilary Dwyer, who had also just appeared together in *The Oblong Box*, as well as hiring cinematographer John Coquillon) was *Cry of the Banshee* (Gordon Hessler, 1970). This was a tale akin to a murder ballad, with gypsies inveigling their way into the castle, sleeping with Lord

Edward Whitman's daughter and bringing doom on the estate
by means of unaccountable magic. This world – the date is never
clear – is a hotchpotch of historical styles: Tudor clothing for the
lord and his court; eighteenth-century firearms and blunderbusses;
Reformation-era torture chamber; a sleek Victorian hansom cab;
and location filming at Grim's Dyke House, the former home of
eminent nineteenth-century librettist W. S. Gilbert. A witch hunt
is afoot in the village, instigated by Whitman's heirs (the eldest son,
Sean, looks like the young folk singer John Martyn, a reminder that
this movie was made during the Indian summer of British folk rock)
and their henchmen, but there is no doubt that a coven actually
exists, a swooning, harmony-singing, white-robed sect led by the
ageing high priestess Oona. They hold nocturnal rites in the local
cemetery, which is dotted with stone pagan effigies. Although this
group seems happy enough to conduct its affairs in secret, with
no ill motives, the lord and his sadistic sons (Roderick has already
referred to the local Romani as 'Gypsy vermin') are determined to
stamp it out.

In the well-stocked dungeons of the Whitman residence, torture,
rape and forced confessions are depicted in crimson detail, but unlike
Witchfinder General, in which no black magic is practised, there
seems genuine reason to be afraid of the black arts in this scenario.
Aside from the asymmetrical violence perpetrated against them, *Cry
of the Banshee* cannot drum up a reason to generate sympathy for
the witches, and by painting them in hippie-ish hues, it suggests an
ambivalence as to their social status.

Jesús Franco's *The Bloody Judge* (1970), set in Restoration England
in 1685 but shot in Portugal, took the exploitative dimension even
further. Christopher Lee plays the real-life inquisitor Judge Jeffreys,
and he and his executioner Satchel are the counterparts of Hopkins
and Stearne, this time acting on the supposed authority of King
James II. Jeffreys runs the courtroom as his own personal fiefdom,
and Lee's intense gaze transmits meaningfully across the chambers

to the eyes of the young women on trial for witchcraft. The film is an excuse for Franco to recreate the racking and bleeding of girls; its gratuitous violence crosses boundaries Reeves never intended to, but the themes of prejudice and a figure representing the law exploiting his authority for personal gratification run on parallel lines.

As well as authority clamping down on occult practices, there is a counter-strain of film that turns the tables, in which it is the aristocracy – a warped and depraved version thereof – that is courting Satan in the hope of achieving absolute mastery. *The Devil Rides Out* (Terence Fisher, 1968) is the most famous example, but a film like *Twins of Evil* (John Hough, 1971) is a more direct inverse of *Witchfinder General*, in that the figure on the side of Christian righteousness – Uncle Gustav Weil (Peter Cushing) – is pure and unstained, while the local baron, Count Karnstein, is busy pursuing his desire to commune with the prince of darkness. In this macabre tale, loosely based on Sheridan Le Fanu's 1872 novella *Carmilla*, Karnstein's disdainful and sadistic attitude to the peasantry culminates in his unmasking as a vampiric parasite sucking on the blood of his subjects.

Cushing's character is a forerunner of *The Wicker Man*'s Sgt Howie: almost virginally pure, uncorrupted by local customs and pedantically righteous, especially when confronted with his twin nieces Frieda and Maria, denigrating their flamboyant attire when they are supposed to be mourning their dead father. As in *The Wicker Man*, when facing black mischief, the law's claim to purity and uncorruptedness is an object of ridicule. 'The young must be chastised,' says Weil, displaying a blooded and gory corpse to an assembled schoolroom. 'Let them all see.' Unwittingly, this idea could be taken as the premise behind a number of these late-1960s and early-'70s films, in which youthful cult worship was held up as evil, requiring persecution and punishment and leading only to destruction. Let them all see.

After all, this was the Season of the Witch. In parallel with the rise of the Beats, flower power and psychedelia, cults and covens represented the darker side of the counter-culture's love affair with magic. The secret history of the black arts in pop culture is partly ushered in by the films of Kenneth Anger and the weird rites of Donald Cammell's *Performance*. Black Sabbath's self-titled first album (1970), the *Four Symbols* album of Led Zeppelin (1971) and Donovan's 1966 hit 'Season of the Witch' (covered in an electrified version by Julie Driscoll and used on the soundtrack to the 2016 series *Britannia*) all contained a shadow side. Zeppelin's Jimmy Page purchased a Scottish property that formerly belonged to legendary occultist Aleister Crowley. Alex and Maxine Sanders, the self-anointed royal family of British pagan witchcraft, recorded an LP of satanic induction rituals, *A Witch Is Born* (1970), while in the same year the couple collaborated with heavy-rock outfit Black Widow, resulting in the band's one hit, 'Come to the Sabbat'. Graham Bond, a former jazz keyboardist turned Crowley disciple, bellowed invocations to Lucifer on albums like *Holy Magick* (1970) and *We Put Our Magick on You* (1971).

TV series like the BBC's Gloucestershire-set *Witch Hunt* (1967) and cheap movies like *Virgin Witch* and *Black Death* (both 1971) rejoiced in the on-screen presence of witch covens. Children's television got in on the act with drama serials like *The Witch's Daughter* (1971), *Lizzie Dripping* (1973) and *The Witches and the Grinnygog* (1983). (In the 1980s cartoon *Willo the Wisp*, the witch morphed into a television set.) A corollary form of exploitation documentary sprang up too, at exactly the same moment. *Legend of the Witches* (1970), the BBC documentary *Power of the Witch* and *Secret Rites* (both 1971, the latter directed by Derek Ford and with an extraordinary experimental Wurlitzer organ soundtrack by the mysterious band the Spindle) all featured appearances by the attention-loving

Sanders couple and their sky-clad followers. These films were directed unashamedly at voyeurs of the prurient, and now stand as luridly fascinating period pieces.

■

'I guess I've been a voyeur all my life,' admitted Ken Russell in his 1989 autobiography,[3] and he always assumed his audiences were the same – that voyeurism, in fact, defined cinema's appeal. By the time he came to make *The Devils* – in which he found a subject matter that fully justified the hysterical pitch of his movie-making – it was 1971, and he had just come off *The Music Lovers*, his pyrotechnic ode to Tchaikovsky, in which the composer's obsessions with both work and his male lover cause his wife to seek male attention elsewhere. *The Devils* would put Russell in similar straits: while he was consumed with work, his wife Shirley, the film's costume designer, began an extramarital affair that ended in divorce from her husband.

The Devils, Russell also conceded, was 'the last nail in the coffin of my Catholic faith'. The story it tells is of a political conspiracy in the name of Christ, and as in *Witchfinder General*, powerful men claiming to represent the tenets of their religion take advantage of others' faith and gullibility for their own perverse gratification. Sister Jeanne (Vanessa Redgrave), head of an enclosed Ursuline convent in the walled town of Loudun, begins having blasphemous fantasies about the popular local priest, Father Urbain Grandier (Oliver Reed), who already has a reputation as something of a ladies' man. Jeanne's possession eventually spreads to the rest of the order, and before long the whole convent is seething with lewdness. Cardinal Richelieu, puppet-master over the weak king Louis XIII, scents an opportunity to break down one of France's last independent walled strongholds, part of an ongoing campaign to reduce the power of the feudal aristocracy. So he engineers an Inquisition, directing the nuns' possession against Grandier. Russell plays up the tragedy by focusing on Grandier as a happy, romantic newlywed, wrenched from marital bliss, shaved, tortured and delivered up to a kangaroo court. The conclusion is an epic immersion in the sensation of pain, as the camera tracks the bloodied, broken Grandier on his final, agonised journey towards the stake.

The film was an adaptation of John Whiting's play, itself a staging of Aldous Huxley's *The Devils of Loudun*, which novelised real events that took place in the 1630s. The film was butchered by the censors, especially in America ('circumcised', Russell called it): the first cut had included a dream sequence of Christ being raped while hanging on the cross, and two quack exorcists (one played by a leering Brian Murphy, later of *George and Mildred* fame) analysing Jeanne's syringed stomach contents for a blasphemous admixture of sperm and communion wafer. Hideous it might have been, but these were facts drawn (by Russell's brother-in-law, a Medieval French lecturer at the Sorbonne) from the historical record.

Plot aside, Russell contrived to make *The Devils* an orgy for the eyes and ears. Derek Jarman's production design is exceptional by any standard: Loudun is a colossal walled city/amphitheatre in tiled white brick, more like a public convenience than a fortress (the sanitised interior is contrasted with the filth and plague-ridden bodies piling up outside). The sets provide an arena for the film's many arresting images: Redgrave's incredible study of wracked, twitching, frustrated lust; plague pits bursting with swaddled corpses; Richelieu's monstrous, Borges-like scriptorium; Grandier's residence ransacked before his eyes; Louis XIII sportingly picking off peasants with a blunderbuss.

During shooting, Russell installed a quadraphonic sound system around the set, getting his cast in the mood with blasts of Prokofiev's *The Fiery Angel*. But even that demonic opera was trumped by Peter Maxwell Davies's original soundtrack, a discordant orchestral nightmare that exudes total religious dementia. It's a marvellous use of dissonant music in cinema and churns in the mind long after the closing credits.

This is the film that runs closest to the legacy of *Witchfinder General*: despite hysterical scenes of female possession that prefigure parts of *The Exorcist*, there is no actual sorcery here, only manipulation of suggestible psyches in order to tip the balance of power. Like Michael Reeves, Russell needed to put violence explicitly on the screen in order to deter it. 'Corruption and mass brainwashing by Church and State and commerce is still with us, as is the insatiable craving for sex and violence by the general public,'[4] was Russell's later justification for the film's existence.

In medieval and modern times, the village is especially vulnerable to the potent influence of outsiders. In *The Shout* (Jerzy Skolimowski, 1978), Crossley (Alan Bates) arrives in a Devonshire village and promptly cuckolds Anthony Fielding (John Hurt), the husband of Rachel (Susannah York). While Anthony, an avant-garde composer, beavers away in his electronic music studio, Crossley seduces Rachel using domineering powers that he claims he obtained from Australian Aboriginal shamans. In contrast to Anthony's rarefied noises, Crossley's terrifying shout is a sonic weapon capable of killing a human at twenty paces.[5] A seemingly magical influence holds Rachel completely in his power, while deflecting Anthony. Crossley's lethal scream disrupts the sleepy enervation of an English village. Like the witchfinders we have already seen, he is abusive and self-gratifying, with the addition of actual eldritch powers to control people and satisfy his whims.

The archetype of the rogue witchfinder has endured through innumerable films and television programmes, including the *Inside No. 9* episode 'The Trial of Elizabeth Gadge' (Dan Zeff, 2015), which featured dialogue culled from transcripts of actual Elizabethan witch trials, and even an episode of *Doctor Who* ('The Witchfinders', Sallie Aprahamian, 2018). Forty-five years after Vincent Price galloped the bridleways of Suffolk, his image was reborn in a field in England. The costume and physical outline of Michael Smiley, who plays the character of O'Neil in *A Field in England* (Ben Wheatley, 2013), is unmistakably a tribute to Price's Matthew Hopkins, down to the white collars, cloak and hat. Shot over twelve days in the autumn of 2012 at the Hampton Estate near Farnham, Surrey, Wheatley's film is a black hole that sucks *Witchfinder General* and *Winstanley* (Kevin Brownlow and Andrew Mollo, 1975) into its vortex, and while visceral, scatological and hallucinatory, this film, which takes a group of characters spat out of the English Civil War as its starting point, ends up as pure metaphysics.

'There are no sides here, friend.' Most, if not all, of this enigmatic film plunges its five characters into a disorientating limbo state. Its frantic opening shots are out of focus, a camera crawling through ferns and undergrowth, while martial drums tattoo in the distance. We hear the desperate panting of the hunted. When we finally see the quarry, and the film locks focus, it is Whitehead (Reece Shearsmith of *The League of Gentlemen* and *Inside No. 9*), pleading, 'Please, God, don't let him find me.' The finger of his pursuer, Commander Trower, wearing a castle-shaped ring, points Whitehead towards an empty field. As we are pulled in, there are no edges, no loyalties, no sense of logical time, no north, south, east or west. It's never even quite made clear whether the characters are Roundheads or Cavaliers. But it's not, in the end, important. Wide-angle cameras, loosely hand-held, rove into the faces of the actors, almost as if the viewer is one extra presence in the field.

The field itself is a temporary autonomous zone, a collective mushroom trip, maybe even an afterlife where, as Sartre put it, 'Hell is other people.' A plangent folk song with its roots in Scotland, 'Baloo My Boy' (aka 'Lady Anne Bothwell's Lament', written at any time between 1558 and 1791), lingers over the entire film like a curse, a suggestion perpetually hanging in the air that all these boys are already dead, butchered in a war that defines England's eternally divided kingdom. While on the run, Whitehead breathlessly speculates he might write a book called *A Field in England, or, The Myriad Particulars of the Commonweal*. So this field stands as a symbolic landscape, a microcosm of the land.

And what kind of land is it? This field lies fallow; ferns and nettles grow in abundant drifts; it has clearly not been ploughed or cultivated for some time. It is one of those fields peculiar to England that appears able to be left ignored, which feels, if you are in it, like some kind of end of the world; artificially bounded by man-made hedgerows, but somehow of a piece with the wild. *A Field in England* is the product of what the then Tory prime minister David Cameron named 'broken Britain': a casualty of austere times, with few green shoots of recovery in sight.

Wheatley's film – written by his partner Amy Jump – encapsulates at least some of the myriad particulars: from the ruthless greed of O'Neil, who has been studying under the same alchemist master as Whitehead and stolen the sorcerer's notebooks, to the innocent coarseness of Friend, to the wry cynicism of Jacob. O'Neil, an Irishman and apparently a Royalist (although none of the characters' allegiances are ever stated outright), asks his prisoners, 'This is your country, is it not?' He has 'claimed a small corner which I intend on raping a little'. In one sense the film can be interpreted as portraying the deep split in British culture between idealism and self-interest: the idealism of nationhood and the appropriation of resources for the venal few. O'Neil is essentially using the chaos of war to make a land grab, enriching himself while coercing the others into slaving for him. 'All the world is turned upside down,' he spits, 'and so is its pockets.'

In the process, Wheatley returns to the now-familiar image of unearthing, of digging into the soil. The original Diggers of the post-Civil War period intended to cultivate the land as a gift from God

The world turned upside down: *A Field in England* (2013).

and a return to the innocence of the Garden of Eden. Here Jacob and
the hapless Friend are put to work excavating the assumed treasure
site, under the threat of violence from O'Neil's bodyguard. When
they eventually strike the prize, it is a gold skull leering from the
loam: an alchemical conjunction that recalls the discovery of skeletons at the start of *Quatermass and the Pit*.

While digging in the pit, which has been located by the hypnotised and tortured Whitehead, Jacob repeatedly intones, 'I am my
own man.' The conflict of self-interest and collective effort is one
of the film's principal dynamics, and O'Neil brutalises and enslaves
these men just as Squire Hamilton did in the tin mines of *Plague of
the Zombies*. Like Richard and Sara in *Witchfinder General*, the pac-
ifist Whitehead must eventually resort to the measures he abhors in
order to remain his own man. Blowing O'Neil's brains out after the
violence escalates appears to alchemically transform Whitehead too.
Dressed in O'Neil's 'witchfinder' outfit, he stalks alone through the
field with the confidence of power (although one long shot makes
him ghost-like, as if he is the walking dead) and intuitively senses
how to finally exit the confines of the field. Plunging through the
perimeter, we are back in the panic of the opening shots, until the

film's climax, in sharp focus: Whitehead, Jacob and Friend, death-
lessly facing the camera. This enigmatic conclusion will never be
fully explicable. Whitehead, the underdog, assuming the mantle of
authority by wearing O'Neil's costume, hints at a belief in the possibility of wresting control from bullies who mistreat it for their own
ends. On the other hand, the psychedelic trippery leaves the door
open to the idea that the whole interlude is nothing but shroom-dust
puffed in the face, a psilocybin dream. But through its hazy clouds of
unknowing, you can dimly make out the roots of England's utopian
urge, as well as its susceptibility to the abuse of power.

7

Fate the Second: The Ghouls Are Among Us

Night of the Demon, *Night of the Eagle*, *The Skull*,
The Blood on Satan's Claw, *Psychomania*, 'Baby'

Occult powers, weird cults and transgressive youth movements hostile to the established order manifested themselves in popular culture from the late 1950s through to the 1970s. Combined with the mind-altering effects of drugs, the psychedelicisation and radicalisation of rock and pop music, and the darkening of the hippie dream at the very end of the 1960s (with the infamous acts of the Manson family and others), such ideas and images penetrated the mainstream as never before. (In the cinema, it was the kind of horror and science fiction already discussed in these pages where such imagery secured its back channel.) Michael Reeves and his generation were the ones teetering over the fissures opened up by the post-war youthquake, and the plethora of witch-hunt narratives in the previous section reflected a general unease in society at large about the covert presence of dark and subversive impulses. For Reeves, this was a misguided belief wrongly tackled by the cinematic slide even further into extreme violence.

The Blood on Satan's Claw (Piers Haggard, 1971) and a number of other films looked at the problem from an entirely different angle. Here cults and counter-cults spring up, meet in secret and are quietly tolerated, until they begin to disrupt the status quo in their surrounding communities. What's interesting is the differing degrees to which each film sympathises with the cults, or ultimately sides against them and pushes back towards a 'normalised' state in which the elders (the forces of order and repression) retain control.

■

In 1969, two years before Haggard's film was released, the ornamental gardens of a mansion in Lymington, Hampshire, were ploughed up by workmen who had come to demolish the grand former country home of the author Dennis Wheatley. Wheatley was one of the most successful writers of the twentieth century, whose dozens of adventure, historical and spy novels have been largely overshadowed by the handful of books he published on the occult. Along with Agatha Christie, Barbara Cartland and Hammond Innes, few bookshelves of the 1960s and '70s did not contain yellowing copies of Wheatley's *To the Devil – A Daughter* and *The Devil Rides Out* (Terence Fisher's adaptation of the latter from 1968 remains one of Hammer's last great productions from that decade).

What those builders dug up from Wheatley's garden was a time capsule: a letter he had buried inside an urn in November 1947 as a message to the future. Wheatley's 'Letter to Posterity' rambled over many typed pages and detailed the upheavals that had already shaken up society, politics and technology during his lifetime, and would continue to do so, he feared, for generations to come. He wasn't happy. The overriding impression one gains of this well-travelled, broad-minded war hero's perspective is of a deep conservatism, a fear of Marxist encroachment and a sense of British exceptionalism that is still very recognisable in right-wing rhetoric more than seventy years later. Lamenting how post-war employers 'have become the bond slaves of socialist state planning', and railing against the power of trade unions, Wheatley opined that 'All men are not equal. Some have imagination and abilities far above others. It is their province and their right to take upon themselves the responsibility of leading and protecting the less gifted.' The document is riddled with hard-right attitudes: low regulation; a minimal welfare state that would not breed lazy scroungers; the free market offering 'the rewards of ability and industry' in a Darwinian 'rise to the top'. But what's striking is Wheatley's proposal to future generations. Fearing that state intervention – 'protection from all the hazards of life' – would produce a cowed and emasculated population, he urges, of all things, revolution. 'If when this document is discovered, the people of Britain are bound to a state machine, my message to posterity is to REBEL,' he writes, proposing the formation of small, secret groups of friends, leading to ever greater acts of rebellion. 'Then numbers of people can begin systematically to break small regulations, and so to larger ones . . . and eventually the boycotting, or ambushing and killing of unjust tyrannous officials.' Overall it's a strange tract, hijacking methods used by the Tolpuddle Martyrs, Luddite machine-breakers and union activists as a strategy to reassert the rights of the sovereign individual over liberal values. But to those inured to the way terms like 'control', 'freedom' and 'sovereignty' are still bandied about in the arguments over Britain exiting the European Union, Wheatley's language will sound uncomfortably familiar.

The point here is the complexity of rebellion and revolution in British history, and this is relevant to the films discussed in this chapter. Revolution isn't always about reaching for a shinier future. Many English rebels – for example, the Puritans and Levellers after the Civil War – had in mind an earlier unsullied age, even the Garden of Eden, as their societal model. In our own time, modern conservatism has increasingly co-opted the language of radicalism and liberty as a sleight of hand while removing freedoms from its supporters. In folk horror, the 'enemy within' often takes the form of a sect, a coven or a rogue magus. In all cases, these elements are trying to exercise their liberty. *The Blood on Satan's Claw* and the other films and programmes in this thread tend to view the breakaway movement as an evil entity to be quashed, so that normality can be resumed.

■

Night of the Demon, directed by Jacques Tourneur in 1957 (an adaptation of M. R. James's 1911 short story 'Casting the Runes'), is one of the first examples of the rebellious arch-mage brought to heel. In this film we begin to see the portrayal of magic not as something hidden away in subterranean chambers, but as a power being exercised out in the world in a variety of threatening and non-threatening guises. The black-and-white movie works hard to achieve its dramatic conflicts between rationalism and superstition, science and magic – a key line is: 'I know the value of the cold light of reason, but I also know the deep shadows that light can cast.' At the same time, it offered a vision of how the English landscape could assist in framing a sense of the uncanny.

The opening shot of Stonehenge comes across as the sinister inverse of a British Transport Films documentary-style portrait of the countryside. The prehistoric site, which will later play a determining role in the plot thanks to secret inscriptions found on its megaliths, helps to introduce a pagan otherworldliness, a reminder of mysteries of past ages. (In his 1981 film *Excalibur*, John Boorman would cast Stonehenge as a megalithic radio through which King Arthur makes contact with Merlin.) Headlights emerge, beaming like will-o'-the-wisps through trees and thick fog. These spears of light are echoed, a little later, on a transatlantic plane carrying Dr John Holden: he requests an eye mask from a stewardess, as sunbeams are shining in his eyes. Dr Holden is the film's representative of enlightened thinking, science and rationality, but this first view of him presents him as being blinded by the light.

The frantic car journey was the film's first casualty, Professor Harrington, racing through the night to the mansion of Dr Julian Karswell, the leader of a satanic cult. Karswell has taken professional rivalry a little too far by casting a curse on Harrington, but promises to cancel it if the latter stops his ongoing investigation of Karswell's practices. Harrington refuses, drives off and is confronted by a monstrous, furry and visibly artificial demon that makes him crash fatally into power lines.

Landing in Britain for a conference, Holden soon encounters Karswell, and once he hears of Harrington's death, determines to get to the bottom of it. Karswell gives Holden three days to live and serves him with a cursed scrap of parchment, which the psychologist dismisses (but keeps in his jacket). When he visits Lufford Hall, the mansion where Karswell lives with his mother, he finds the magus, togged up as a conjurer, hosting a children's magic show, while a seance is taking place inside. The dark arts are being gently embedded in apparently harmless social situations. Each situation slides from innocent charlatanry into something more sinister. The curses bestowed during this tale are real, in the sense that deaths foretold do come to pass. And the cult has its human collateral damage. Former acolyte Rand Hobart, arrested on suspicion of murder, has produced drawings of demonic figures that resemble the imps of medieval woodcuts, in particular the fire demon invoked by witches to destroy an enemy. Driven insane by his visions, he commits suicide while under hypnosis, when he believes Holden is trying to pass the deadly parchment back to him.

Karswell's pact with the dark side brings a parade of magical summonings and eerie sensations into the film. From the cyclone whipping through the children's fete to a mystic fog, a spontaneous forest fire and a cat that shape-shifts into a panther, he bends nature to his will and summons supernatural beings to eliminate his enemies. Elsewhere reference is made to the magical properties of music – an Irish folk melody to summon up the devil and an Indian tune used for enchantments. Meanwhile, Holden's journey from the searchlight of reason to a foggier condition of unknowing – deriving from M. R. James, this film does not dismiss the 'truth' of these supernatural elements – forms the narrative mainframe. It's appropriate that the evil genius is eventually killed, the victim of his own curse (Holden's quick wits diverted the hexed parchment back to its issuer), by a demon riding a train. Is he mauled to death by a monster, squashed on the tracks by the product of industrial engineering, or a combination of the two? The cult is destroyed, but it is not a question of rationalism triumphing over superstition, more a case of evil neutralised for now. The last line is: 'Maybe it's better not to know . . .'

In the similarly titled *Night of the Eagle* (Sidney Hayers, 1962), witchcraft was brought even more intimately into the public sphere – this time the suburban household of public-school teacher Norman Taylor (Peter Wyngarde, fresh from appearing as the ghastly Quint in Jack Clayton's *The Innocents*, which will be discussed in more detail in the next section). Norman is the innocent here; it's his wife Tansy he needs to keep a close eye on. The film very subtly introduces her superstitious 'protections' and charms (medicinal herbs, but also toxic ones, like her namesake flower). Rationalist Norman's first appearance in the film is in front of a blackboard chalked with the words 'I do not believe', but as he slowly discovers, he is sharing their wood-panelled home with a practitioner of Anglicised voodoo. He'll end up backed up against the wall, accidentally erasing the word 'not'.

When Norman's career and private life slip out of control (accused of rape by a female student; physically attacked by her boyfriend), it's clear Tansy is not the only necromancer in the village. The rest of the story unfolds as a case of professional revenge via occult spells. The melodrama of the final scenes in the Gothic school buildings is less appealing than the sequences in which Tansy's magical practices and talismans emerge into the light and the peculiar details of the set dressing take on a heightened significance.

Night of the Eagle and *Night of the Demon*, two films made five years apart, are evidence of the dawning realisation that Britain's landscapes could provide a more spooky presence than when they were recreated in the film studio. In the former movie, fine use is made of the deserted Cornish coastline and the gargoyled pinnacles of the school building, with its carved stone eagle menacingly overlooking events from the rooftop. There are some brilliantly taut performances – Janet Blair as Tansy, panicking at the loss of her protections, gives an acting masterclass – and the (professionally and sexually) jealous teacher Flora Carr ruthlessly racks up the torments that disrupt the couple's formerly tranquil domestic life. The destructive aspects of witchcraft are employed here not for their own sake, but arise out of very precise psychological conditions. It is a practice not available to the elite, the leisured landowner or the initiated wizard, but to the denizens of middle-class homes and the professional class. The illusion of magic spilling into recognisable everyday life was perpetuated at the US premiere (where it was retitled *Burn, Witch, Burn*): audience members were reportedly handed a packet of salt and the text of a protection spell to ward off any evil the film might conjure.

In this chapter, heading towards *The Blood on Satan's Claw*, we are looking at situations where the innocent surface of things conceals secret outbreaks of black magic and anarchic cults. This dormant mischief and violence often emanate from an antique artefact, just waiting to be dug up and unleashed. A good example is the 1965 Amicus production *The Skull*, directed by Freddie Francis on a Shepperton set that recreates the claustrophobic interiors of obsessive collectors of grisly artefacts. A head purporting to have once belonged to the Marquis de Sade finds its way into a London auction room. The invocation of de Sade here represents the innate cruelty and sadism of the human heart, and the skull exerts a compulsive magic upon those it encounters, forcing them to do unspeakable things to each other. The film ends up enacting a battle of wills between Christianity and pagan witchcraft, eventually suggesting that occult magic should not be dismissed in the modern world. Peter Cushing reprises the impotent terror of his Winston Smith in *Nineteen Eighty-Four*, hounded this time not by rampant state power, but by the hollow mind of an impassive skull. A similar accursed relic kick-starts *The Blood on Satan's Claw*, a film that combines a satanic unearthing with its effects on the breakdown of society.

■

Are you bent on reviving forgotten horrors?
The Judge, *The Blood on Satan's Claw*

There is a profound sense of instability around the second film in
the folk-horror triptych, *The Blood on Satan's Claw* (Piers Haggard,
1971). The more you watch it, the more you notice the shifting
equilibrium of power and control, as characters appear and disappear from the narrative, throwing its power balance into wobbling
disarray like bricks removed from a Jenga tower. The action takes
place in the early years of the eighteenth century – at one point a
leading character, the Judge, drinks to the health of the pretender
to the throne, James III in exile. The Catholic James never took his
place as the monarch, and was replaced instead by the German-
speaking George I of the Hanover family. A Jacobite such as the
Judge would have considered George an unwelcome invader, usurp-
ing the righful claim of the House of Stuart. Thus, the film is set
at a moment in history when England's royal bloodline is being
transplanted by an alien strain, creating dissent and destabilisation
throughout the land.

The schlocky title of *The Blood on Satan's Claw* was slapped on
the film just before release by the legendary producer Tony Tenser
himself (the US release was titled *Satan's Skin*). Although it sounds
like a camp Hammer or Amicus effort, this movie has made its mark
thanks to having a very different look and character from anything
those studios were producing at the time. In its use of outdoor locations and natural southern English spring light, as well as the significant role for Patrick Wymark as the Judge and a scene featuring the
drowning of a suspected witch, there are certainly similarities with
Witchfinder General, although its writer and director later claimed
not to have seen that movie while they were in the preparatory stages

in early 1970. The film ended up substantially different from its original conception, which was as a three-way portmanteau film set in different historical periods, including the Victorian age of steam.

Around Christmas 1969 the young writer Robert Wynne-Simmons, recently graduated from Cambridge after making a film based on the writings of William Blake, wrote about a hundred letters to British film production companies, requesting work as a scriptwriter. His one reply came from the small Chilton Film Enterprises, which at the time was contracted to produce a film with Tony Tenser's Tigon studio. Wynne-Simmons had written macabre stories while still at school, as a way of escaping from some of the traumatic experiences he had there. One image from these formed the basis of *The Blood on Satan's Claw*: a man, made to feel uncomfortable while visiting the house of his future in-laws, ends up cutting his own arm off in his bedroom. Wynne-Simmons also wanted the film to include a battle between a judge and a pagan cult, and to contain a version of the real-life Mary Bell, the eleven-year-old convicted of child murder in a case that shocked Britain in 1968. In its final form, *The Blood on Satan's Claw* compacted these elements into ninety minutes, united them all into a common time period and location, and succeeded in transcending an English horror-film style that was fast descending into pantomime.

'It's rural mythology with the smell of the country earth and without any modish, urban confidence tricks. We're treating it as realistically as possible,' said director Piers Haggard of his second feature, in an interview during the filming.[1] *Satan's Claw* was played and shot as a straight historical drama, outside the theatrical artificiality of the studio. Its exteriors abound in leafy greens, terracottas and overcast skies. Inside, the frame often flickers with fire-glow and candlelight, and in some of the most terrifyingly tense scenes the rooms are almost pitch black. Cinematographer Dick Bush had been behind the camera on the film *Culloden*, as well as television productions such as Jonathan Miller's *Alice in Wonderland* (1966),

Ken Russell's *Song of Summer* (1968, based on the life of composer Frederick Delius) and the inaugural BBC Christmas ghost story *Whistle and I'll Come to You* (Jonathan Miller, 1968). All of these combined naturalistic landscapes and light in the service of creating believable locations and period atmospheres. Now working in colour, with occasional hand-held sequences, Bush distilled the essentially Ruritanian qualities from the fields, woodlands, half-timbered farmhouses and ruined old church at Bix Bottom in Oxfordshire.

The third element in the film's magic triangle is the music of Marc Wilkinson. For the main theme and incidental music, Wilkinson pulled off the feat of layering Vaughan Williams-style country rhapsodies and a folkish zither with a descending thirteen-note motif of tritones, otherwise known as the devil's interval. Moments of tension and suspense were punctuated by tuned kettle drums and the unearthly swoops and glides of the electronic ondes martenot.

Evidence of this alchemy of scene-setting, camerawork and music comes in the very opening sequence: a still life of a ploughman's lunch – bread, apples and a flagon of drink – placed in the mud, while a silhouetted ploughman toils with his horse in the background. A young girl, Cathy Vespers (Wendy Padbury, fresh from appearing as Patrick Troughton's sidekick in the late-1960s *Doctor Who* TV series), who we'll later learn has designs on marriage, calls to Ralph the ploughman across the valley. With the early-morning mist, the cawing of crows and the wide rolling slopes of English farmland, it's a wonderfully evocative introduction to the film's topography. Some of these shots are made with the camera dug down in the earth, an ultra-low viewpoint that recurs throughout the film. It's right that the lens should peep out of the ground, for the action in *The Blood on Satan's Claw* is triggered during this furrowing of the soil, as the crow sounds grow more intense and the plough blade churns up a hideous skull with one decomposing eye. As a result of this unearthing, the peace of the village is upset: the malefic influence causes mysterious

fur patches to appear on people's limbs; fevers and hysteria spread
through the population as it becomes clear that the devil is attempting to incarnate on Earth.

Evil in *Witchfinder General* was embodied in a human, Matthew
Hopkins. In *Satan's Claw*, no corrupt dark magus directs proceedings
by persecuting innocents or conducting grim rites in subterranean
cellars. Instead, evil is a force released from the earth that appears at
first only as shadows and in fleeting attacks, materialising as hairy
human deformities, an incorporeal Satan ruthlessly assembling the
constituents of a body, limb by limb. The pressure of evil presses in
on all sides, and by the end has almost forensically dismantled the
settled order of this rural community, threatening morals, causing
elders to disappear and corrupting innocents.

The central figure here is 'the Judge', Patrick Wymark's larger-than-
life character, whose status as pillar of the community is rendered
unstable in subtle ways. When first sighted, he is visiting the house
of Isobel Banham, aunt of the local landowner Peter Edmonton.
Peter brings his fiancée Rosalind home to meet her, and following
an awkward dinner-table scene where Isobel makes it clear she does
not approve of Rosalind's lowly status, both she and the Judge highlight the impropriety of Rosalind staying under the same roof as her
intended. Later, it transpires the Judge and Isobel have some kind of
romantic history. It's the Judge who is given the lion's share of significant lines. 'So, young people, your elders triumph,' he gloats on
winning at cards. By the end of the film, it will indeed be the elders,
spearheaded by the Judge himself, who will 'run this devil of yours
to earth' and defeat the dark forces taking over the village's youth –
at least for now. Yet there is also something of the night about the
Judge: his black attire and flamboyant black ostrich plume suggest an
affinity with the crows that appear whenever Satan is released from
the earth. Both he and the devil are referred to during the film as
'the Master'. At one point he tells the blustering Squire Middleton (a
wonderful supporting role for veteran James Hayter), 'Unfortunate

you could not sup with me' – a line that recalls the old proverb about using a long spoon to sup with the devil. He also abandons the village just as its crisis is mounting, telling the squire to 'let it [the evil] grow'. Has this judge gone over to the dark side, or is he taking a calculated risk?

Just as the local doctor bleeds his patients ('Open a vein and the humour will perhaps pass out'), the Judge allows the boil in the community to swell up until it is big enough to be lanced. The collateral damage from this strategy includes Cathy, who is violently raped in a scene so brutal that Haggard later declared he would have shot it differently had he had a second opportunity; the priest, falsely accused of lechery by the manipulative Angel Blake; and the unfortunate Margaret, Angel's passionate disciple who, after having a patch of fur scalpelled off her thigh with no anaesthetic and being caught in a bear trap, ends up drowned in a woodland pond, accused of being a witch.

Nature underscores the events. The ploughed field is where Angel and her schoolfriends become 'infected' by the satanic hysteria, even as they hurl clods of earth at each other. In the same field, the Reverend Fallowfield catches a grass snake, allowing the symbolically charged serpent to writhe around his fingers as he chats with the Judge. '*Ubique opera domini*' (God's work is everywhere), he states – but the folly of such complacency is soon to be revealed in the village. Later, he is seen to keep a live hare tethered by a ribbon to his writing desk. Piety tames and controls nature's bestial instincts.

The film's enduring appeal is also down to the details of its design. Peter's anxious statement, 'There is evil in this house,' is affirmed thanks to a masterful martialling of effects, from the creaks under the attic floorboards to the wind whistling through the walls. Following that first night, the weather ramps up as the film progresses, but the ensuing rainstorm and thunderclaps feel like the natural rhythm of the season rather than the clichéd lightning strikes of vampiric horror. The rape scene's viciousness is compounded by the sunlit forest and May blossoms, and the way the camera stalks between the tree trunks. Likewise, Bush's camera-handling is brilliant in a scene where the boy Mark is forced to play blind man's buff in the ruined, roofless chapel before being murdered by Angel. As our viewpoint swings around, we catch sight of Angel at the altar, then the camera, which has been moving randomly, seems to lock on to the victim and drag him into the sacrificial chamber. These rites feel convincing, very different from the conventional dungeons, sacrificial slabs and pentagrams of earlier horror films. The cult's chanting – 'Rise now from the forests, from the furrows, from the fields, and live' – is a convincingly pagan invocation of a satanic presence that has lain dormant in the land.

Class differences and power relations are rendered unstable in this unholy interregnum. Peter's romance with a lowly peasant girl has already been mentioned; there is also the increasing subversiveness of the children in Reverend Fallowfield's schoolroom, defying his authority as they defect to Angel's cult. Angel herself explicitly tempts the pastor by making a sexual advance to him in the church, which requires all his powers of restraint. Until the absent Judge returns from London at the eleventh hour to direct his 'undreamed-of measures' against the foe, and after Peter has chopped off his own right hand, it's farmer Ralph who has taken charge in the village. The return of the Judge, with his pitchfork and cross-shaped Sword of Justice (weapons of the devil and the avenging angel), is a kind of Restoration. The three-pronged fork slays Angel, the sword heals Ralph's furred leg and awakens the villagers from their nightmare. Although, in one last destabilising image, the final shot of the film freezes on his eye, echoing the wormy sockets we saw in the original skull and perpetuating the film's running ambiguity about where evil resides.

Ultimately, then, the elders representing the established church and state – and the burgeoning Enlightenment – restore peace and

Worm's-eye view: a soil-level camera angle in *The Blood on Satan's Claw* (1971).

harmony and vanquish the rebellious forces of youth. This is the enduring plot of *The Blood on Satan's Claw* – the anarchy let loose from the earth flares up in a brief spate of decadence and amorality, and is then violently quelled. The parallels with the generation gap, the permissive society and the increasingly negative portrayals of hippie licentiousness in the media at the dawn of the 1970s cannot be ignored. Angel's mob retreat deep into the woodland to conduct what are repeatedly referred to as 'their games' – involving coercive sexual violence and human sacrifice. Her attempted seduction of the priest displays the potency of Britain's latent paganism in graphic terms. The fascinating problem in this film is that while the forces of conservatism win the day, the figure who represents those forces is himself no angel. Before the final confrontation, the Judge asserts, 'Only the most strict discipline will save us in our hour of trial.' Permitting subversion to breed will in turn justify the imposition of authoritarian force.

In 1988 Haggard would direct *A Summer Story*, a post-Merchant–Ivory rural idyll based on John Galsworthy's short story 'The Apple Tree' (1916). Although it's not a horror film, as in *The Blood on Satan's Claw* it's about memories unlocked from the earth threatening the

social order, before leaving it essentially untouched. It's a tale of forbidden love across class divides, between privileged student Frank
and fascinating peasant girl Megan. The sunlit Exmoor villages and
farmlands, and the nostalgic revisiting of events, place this squarely
in *Go-Between* territory (see Chapter 14), but viewed through the
right prism it can offer an interesting parallel with *The Blood on
Satan's Claw*. Most of the film is a flashback, with Frank's memories
triggered by a symbolic pile of earth – Megan's grave. She's buried
outside the churchyard, at the spot she intended to meet her lover,
although for various prosaic logistical reasons (local train timetables,
slow communications between banks) he never returned to sweep
her off her feet.

Their union – transgressive by the social standards of the day, and
involving Megan breaking her troth to another of her own class – has
been thwarted, and despite Frank's sadness, the film offers little sense
that Megan's death was unjust and fails to cast judgement on Frank's
negligence. He does not even step out of the car when passing his
eighteen-year-old son, whom he's never set eyes on before. Decades
later, revisiting the area, the memories haunt his eventual fate in life
(themes of destiny versus free will are raised explicitly in the dialogue), but however unhappy the outcome, by the end the social
hierarchy has been preserved.

■

A youth cult of amoral mischief-makers, retreating to a historically
charged spot in the countryside, recurs in the 1973 romp *Psychomania*
(Don Sharp). Here, though, it's set in the present day and the cult is
an English motorbike gang calling themselves the Living Dead. With
helmets retooled to look like skulls, speeding around the suburban
backroads and assembling at an Avebury-like stone circle next to a
river, this relatively well-spoken wild bunch is led by square-jawed
longhair Tom Latham. The son of a local lady (played improbably

by Beryl Reid) who lives in a mansion, Tom is obsessed with death and immortality, and cheerfully encourages his girlfriend Abby, who seems much too nice a girl to be a member of a necrophilic Hell's Angels gang, to join him in a suicide pact.

There are subtle continuities with previous British horror movies (Nicky Henson, who plays Tom, has a small part as a cavalier in *Witchfinder General*; Denis Gilmore, who plays gang member Hatchet, is familiar as the red-headed youth in *The Blood on Satan's Claw*), but rather than being in thrall to some devilish supernatural being, the Living Dead's motivation for cheating death is simply to live for ever and be able to make mischief with no consequences. Tom gleefully imagines escalating his disruptions to eliminating the Establishment, police, judges – the whole apparatus of law and order. That their quaint havoc extends to hassling pedestrians at a newly built shopping centre in Walton-on-Thames is merely a measure of this film's budgetary limitations.

Home Counties death cult: *Psychomania* (1973).

Behind the death wish, and seemingly holding the key to the undead resurrections, lie the mystical machinations of Mrs Latham's butler, the shady Mr Shadwell (George Sanders, the voice of Shere Khan in Disney's *Jungle Book*). The film never makes clear why he would want to facilitate the breakdown of society using an undead biker gang as a proxy revolutionary army, but while this is not a film with much purchase on ulterior motive, its edgeland aesthetic makes it an important addition to the legacy of British movies dealing with the fallout from 1960s liberalism through a prism of folkloric horror.[2]

■

Every time Jo Gilkes ventures outside her new country cottage, she's assailed by shrieking crows. You never see them, but the birds of ill omen are a constant rasping presence on the soundtrack of 'Baby' (1976), one of six episodes in an ITV series, written by Nigel Kneale, called *Beasts*.

In the tradition of macabre/uncanny short stories by the likes of John Wyndham and M. R. James, *Beasts* includes plenty of creature-based horror, but the 'Baby' episode is the most gruesome and disturbing. The situation of urbanites moving to try out a new, simpler life in the country is by now a familiar dynamic in British narratives, as is the buried artefact that causes havoc once excavated. In 'Baby', you get both.

Jo and her husband Peter seem divided from the beginning by their different attitudes: she grew up in the country and therefore doesn't think much about it, while he, a city lad, romanticises the move as a life-changing event. Peter, a veterinary surgeon, is invigorated by his new surroundings and treats the move as a utopian and psychologically enriching new start in life. But his new-found enthusiasm for his job, which takes him racing from the cottage in his Land Rover and finds him forging a raucous and boozy friendship with his new boss/colleague, Dick Pummery, paradoxically distances him even more from his heavily pregnant wife's concerns. Meanwhile, Jo is left to keep house while two builders, who appear to know more than they are prepared to let on, chip away at the fabric of the building with sledgehammers.

This being a Nigel Kneale story, it's only a matter of time before the old brick walls deliver up a sinister secret. A clay urn, roughly the size of a womb, is lifted out of a smashed brick wall in the kitchen. From it, Peter extracts the hideous, desiccated corpse of some unidentifiable creature. No one who examines this shrivelled homunculus – recalling the rotted remains of the devil's body parts in *The Blood on Satan's Claw* – can identify it, although there are plenty of speculations. A cat? A monkey? The farmyard monster brings down a curse on the house: Jo's cat goes missing; a spell of contagious abortion takes hold of the beasts in the fields; and while searching for the cat in the woods, Jo appears to be threatened by unseen, anarchic forces of nature – convincingly yet simply conveyed through a roaring noise on the soundtrack and a brief chaotic flocking of birds. The crows squawk their dark menace from the treetops.

Once again, Kneale explores ideas around power and coercion from several angles. It is not only about the power of the buried familiar, whose pagan purpose is explained by the builder Arthur Grace (a name with faint overtones of 'Angel Blake'). 'Wise men' had familiars, he says, and buried them in walls in order to exert power over each other. It's also about masculine power, the way the natural authority assumed by patriarchal males effectively silences female viewpoints. As a screenwriter Kneale had already included this theme in his earlier BBC play *The Stone Tape*, which will be discussed later. In 'Baby', it is illustrated by Peter's relationship with Dick. After the two vets fall out after a quarrel, Jo is delighted when Peter agrees to leave the cottage and move back to the city. But after one patch-up visit from Dick and his wife, to Jo's dismay the pair are man-hugging and chortling together again. While Peter and the Pummerys are carousing over whiskies in the sitting room, Jo slips into the deserted kitchen, and with the sounds of partying still audible from the next room, she is visited by menacing growls and a briefly spied black shape on the stairs.

This split second of murky television can now be replayed and freeze-framed, but it was designed for one-off 'live' broadcast. In its very indistinctness – you don't quite know what you see, and then it's gone – resides the fear and the horror. There is no final confrontation with a definable creature, only more murk, a lingering question mark in the mind, and a presence apparently released back into the wild. Whatever this thing is or was, it escapes, to be revived another day as one of the uncountable 'forgotten horrors' of the British psyche. This thing lay dormant for so long, right in the home's hearth, but like Dennis Wheatley's letter to posterity, or the skull in *The Blood on Satan's Claw*, once it's dug up and exposed to the air, it threatens to push domesticity and the stability of the local community off a precipice. In the next chapter, we'll see examples of this in mirror image, when the local community itself has already gone over to the other side.

8

Fate the Third: Pagans Rule OK!

The Witches, Eye of the Devil, The Owl Service, Robin Redbreast, Tam Lin, Doctor Who and the Daemons, **The Wicker Man**, *Children of the Stones,* 'The Breakthrough', 'Murrain', *Kill List*

Our appointment with *The Wicker Man* draws near.

This chapter explores the enduring attraction of imagining how ancient belief systems – paganism in particular – survive and hide in plain sight in the modern age, even after Judaeo-Christian religions, the Enlightenment and urbanisation have elbowed them out of the way. *The Wicker Man* is the Stonehenge of British film archaeology. It's the one movie of its type that most people have heard of; it's a high-water mark that feels like the summation of a genre; and it has undergone several controversial restorations.

The films and television programmes that cleared the ground for *The Wicker Man* contain mythologies buried in the landscape and its people, legends ready to be reawakened, reactivated, often by an innocent. Like an Arthurian king under the hill, these powers lie dormant, awaiting rediscovery and reanimation through ritual and sacrifice. Underlying such actions is the idea of a horrific self-sacrifice in the service of a greater good or a higher power. Sacrifice forms a kind of gaping bear trap stretched across the film, into which the protagonist – innocent in certain respects – is coerced, through magical or other means, into becoming the victim, while their previously held certainties crumble in the face of an entirely other system of belief. These films also delight in the revelation of both hidden and imaginary pagan presences beneath the surface of modern Britain.

Rural horror thrives on the mutual suspicion between city and village, between rational sophistication and earthy essentialism. The country is the site of secret doings; urban aliens will only disturb things that are better left untouched. It lives by its own rules, rules that have evolved at widdershins to civic priorities. *The Wicker Man* and its precursor films often include a sense of bewilderment on the part of the protagonist, as they try to uphold the behaviours and values they have imported with them from the world we know. Those values break down as they become living participants in a myth retold.

When paganism and rural horror combine, legends are the driving, fateful force, and the notion of predestination – the retracing of the footsteps of folklore, the impossibility of dodging destiny – is stronger than ever. The subtitle of productions like *The Owl Service*, *Tam Lin* and *The Wicker Man* itself could have been, 'I fought the lore, but the lore won'.

For an early glimpse of the dark energies that eventually produced *The Wicker Man*, try *The Witches* (Cyril Frankel, 1966). This film began as a story by Peter Curtis (a pseudonym of historical novelist Norah Lofts), *The Devil's Own* (1960); Nigel Kneale adapted it for Hammer Films, and in his hands the surface prettiness of a village is a smokescreen concealing a coven whose activities are subtly camouflaged by everyday life.

Before we get there, we're shown the heroine's backstory: teacher Gwen Mayfield (Joan Fontaine, in her final screen role) in her African mission school, frantically packing her suitcase to leave in the middle of a tribal rebellion. Warlike witch doctors bearing a gigantic tribal mask burst through the wall, leaving Gwen traumatised and causing her to be sent back to England to recuperate.[1] Back on her feet, she nervously attends a job interview with Alan Bax, who co-owns a private school in the village of Heddaby with his sister Stephanie. Alan, dressed in his vicar's collar, offers Gwen the job straight away. After Gwen arrives in Heddaby and is shown into her sunny cottage, she discovers Alan at home in plain clothes, his 'church' a private museum of religious and architectural fragments and taped organ music from Salisbury Cathedral. Later, she meets him in the roofless ruins of the original church, a ruined shell that can no longer be anyone's spiritual home.

Kneale sets up the conditions for a pagan revival in a village whose Christian heart has been torn out. With her effortless smile and permanent goodwill, Gwen brings her trusting spirit into the community but begins to perceive an inexplicable undercurrent: mysterious trysts between two of her adolescent pupils, Ronnie Dowsett and Linda Rigg (Ingrid Boulting, step-daughter of English film-maker Roy Boulting), involving the exchange of, and obsessive play with, plastic dolls. Ronnie warns Gwen in a note that Linda is being cruelly treated by her grandmother, and when she goes to visit their cottage, the boggle-eyed 'Granny' reveals some classic witch-tells: home-brewed wine and a preference for medicinal herbs. Mouldy bread on Linda's injured hand: what's the difference between that and penicillin? Granny asks. Modernity is often tradition in confusing new garb.

Secret rites in the village: *The Witches* (1966).

Arthur Grant's camera emphasises spring brightness; much of the action occurs in sunlight, amid the family grocer shops and cottages of the village or in the nearby meadows and riverbanks. But isn't Bob Curd, the butcher (Duncan Lamont, who was cast as Victor Carroon in the TV version of *The Quatermass Experiment*), just slightly too jolly, as he cheerfully guts and peels the skin off a rabbit before Gwen's eyes? Is that a warning or a mark of her own fate? At one point she drinks tea from a ridged green mug that also appears, containing a sleeping draught, in *The Reptile*. Alan Bax constantly falls silent and drifts off into a trance whenever Gwen asks too many questions, and gradually we discover it's his sister Stephanie who really rules the roost, having secretly embroiled most of the locals in a black magic coven and plotting to secure for herself 'a skin for dancing in', in a spell intended to keep her youthful and extend her life – with Linda as the intended sacrifice. Gwen discovers a headless doll stuck with pins in a tree; she upsets Ronnie's parents with her probing questions, and his father turns up drunk at her house before being found dead in the river.

The black magic is then directed at Gwen's efforts to uncover the truth. A startled herd of cows stampedes towards her while she is investigating multiple footprints at the spot where the body was found. The animals leave the crime scene a blank expanse of churned mud, erasing all the evidence. Gwen then becomes feverish while staying at Stephanie's house, and she is admitted to a care home for several months, while Dr Wallis (Leonard Rossiter), the Baxes' creepy family physician, tramples her own memory into mush. It's only a chance sighting of a toy doll that triggers her recovered memories, and Gwen escapes in a lorry. She uncovers the full truth about Stephanie's plans and attends the sacrificial Lammas-time ritual – along with many of the other villagers – where Linda is about to get skinned, but slices into her own arm to shed blood at the crucial moment, foiling the spell. She survives, and the film ends with Alan installing his music system into her classroom, with romance clearly blossoming.

The Witches is folklore viewed through the prism of the atomic age. At one point Stephanie speaks of 'a power, a force that we're going to release' – magic acting like the detonator of elements within a nuclear bomb. Kneale reported he was not happy with the way his script was eventually edited, cutting passages that clarified his more mocking take on witchcraft, but what remains is the way he places full responsibility for the horror on individual human choice, not on possession by forces beyond anyone's control. 'What we admit we believe could destroy us,' says Alan Bax early on. The folk of Heddaby keep their dark secret veiled behind an illusion of country innocence – breaking that circle of trust is equivalent to dynamiting the entire project. Kneale's most memorable scripts over the next ten years would similarly explore notions of complicity, pagan belief and persecution in rural environments.

■

Films like *The Witches*, picturing secret cults and covens in the nation's hinterlands, reflected a growing awareness in the 1960s about the rise of British pagan witchcraft. A genuine grass-roots movement with its own hierarchies and 'monarchies', pagan witch-craft was a patchwork religion advanced in the 1940s by Gerald Gardner, a former civil servant in the British colonies. Stepping into the void left by the decline in Christian worship since the begin-ning of the twentieth century, Gardner stirred up a cauldron of texts and rituals from Freemasonry, the writings of Aleister Crowley and esoteric Christianity to construct the framework of British pagan witchcraft. By the time he published his book *Witchcraft Today* in 1954, Gardner was at the centre of a disparate yet growing com-munity of British occultists, including druids, Rosicrucians, the-osophists and Wiccans.

Gardner died in 1964, but the network of covens expanded after his death, their imagined rites and rituals inspiring numerous prurient articles in the sensationalist press. But the occultists themselves rarely sought publicity, and the practice was generally conducted quietly by private citizens. It was hard to shake the impression that this was a very English form of witchery. Far from being a subversive spearhead of the radical New Atlantis, Gardner – himself a *Daily Telegraph* reader and a member of his local Conservative Party – was more likely to refresh himself after a nudist ritual with tea and biscuits rather than a goblet of virgin's blood.

But the underground spread of pagan witchcraft satisfied a need for something beyond what the secular civic state could provide. An attraction to paganism and pre-Christian beliefs and ceremonies often went hand in hand with the revivals of folklore that started in the late nineteenth century. Therefore, one of the common threads in *The Wicker Man* and its attendant films is the remote community that has chosen to isolate itself, suspicious of outsiders, so that it can practise its own brand of pagan living.

Released, like *The Witches*, in that sultry year of 1966, *Eye of the Devil* (J. Lee Thompson) included many of the elements later deployed in *The Wicker Man*. The vineyards are failing on an old estate in rural France, and the marquis, Philippe de Montfaucon (David Niven), and his wife Catherine (Deborah Kerr) travel to the castle, with its medieval chill factor and diabolical history. We'll soon discover the ancient halls are a 'fortress of heresy'. The estate is full of suspicious, anonymous local agricultural types ('The people of Bellignac have always been steeped in strange rituals'), deceptively jolly folk music and the hypnotic strains of a harp (a quintessential pagan instrument). All aspects of civic life, we'll discover, are involved in the pagan conspiracy. Police chief, priest and doctor: all these pillars of morality, rationality and law and order have been effortlessly co-opted by the persistence of the ritual.

The priest wields a locket that suggests the evil eye, which, when placed on the de Montfaucon family Bible, holds a talismanic power over designated targets. Young couple Christian de Caray (David Hemmings) and Odile (Sharon Tate) are already under its spell. She is an enchantress who lures the lovers to their near deaths on the ramparts and sows suspicion between man and wife; he the bowman who, in a trance, conducts the sacrifice. When Odile sedates Catherine with a belladonna infusion – a drug that, as the doctor (John Le Mesurier) explains, prepares the user for 'some glorious pilgrimage of the soul' – she begins hallucinating and wakes to find herself imprisoned in her bedroom. The scene prefigures *The Wicker Man*'s Sgt Howie in the bedroom at the Green Man pub, listening to the siren song of the landlord's daughter.

There's a recurring image – enshrined in a painting hanging on the wall – of a ring of twelve dark, hooded figures, with a thirteenth, clad in white, at the centre of the circle. Philippe's line 'Am I seeking, or am I being sought?' twitches upon the entire *Wicker Man* thread. Even the marquis is not fully in charge; it is the priest, eventually outed as a pagan, who ensures the perpetuation of the cycle by initiating his son Philippe, inducing him to kiss the devil's eye. The sacrificial act is a command that must be obeyed, with everybody complicit. That is why there is so little passion displayed by the participants. Emotions are reserved for the one(s) outside the circle, like Catherine, who perceives the horror. From inside the ritual, all the actions and events (including the slaughter) are logical, consequential, propitiatory acts. 'It's our belief in something', says Philippe, 'that makes that thing, for a moment or for ever, divine.'

Also foreshadowing *The Wicker Man*, the film ends with a series of ritual processions – first, the outwardly Christian festival of the Treize Jours (Thirteen Days), where a saint is paraded around the streets. Even here the villagers dance to the strangely hypnotic bell music as if under hypnosis, and as Catherine learns, the name 'Treize Jours' can also be interpreted as 'Treize Joueurs' (Thirteen Dancers)

– the twelve plus one seen in the painting. The image simultaneously refers to the twelve disciples and Jesus Christ – another sacrificial figure – and older rituals. 'There are people who see in the midst of the twelve, a thirteenth . . . These people are not Christians, and never have been . . .' explains Philippe's father, whom Catherine discovers locked away in a room in a high tower.

The propitiation appears to work. The closing scenes are drenched in rainfall: the crop will flourish once more.

■

The novelist Alan Garner characterised his early books for young audiences, such as *The Weirdstone of Brisingamen* (1960) and *Elidor* (1965), as 'expressions of myth'. In these strange, earthbound elaborations of the fantasy genre, Garner had no need to invent a pseudo-Nordic mythology and language (see J. R. R. Tolkien) or a mystical Christian symbolic landscape (see C. S. Lewis), since he had all of ancient Britain's Celtic legacy to draw on. Referring to the collection of Welsh stories that are the earliest of their kind in Britain, he wrote, 'The *Mabinogion* is less a text than a state of mind or being,'[2] and in his fiction, myth-action is transposed to modern-day settings, where it replays like a tape loop. Characters lose their agency to these preset narratives, which are linked in turn to place and landscape. In *Elidor*, it was the northern ballad of Childe Rowland and Burd Ellen. In *Red Shift* (1973, filmed as a BBC series in 1978), it was Tam Lin, Burd Janet and the Queen of Elfland. 'The difference', Garner explained, 'between [my present-day activity within myth] and what are usually called "retellings" is that the retellings are stuffed trophies on the wall, whereas I have to bring them back alive. It is a process not without risk.'[3]

When characters find themselves caught up in the retelling of a myth, their destinies are hijacked by a power beyond their control. That is what makes Garner's novel *The Owl Service* – and its 1969 TV adaptation – another precursor to the fatal trajectory of Sgt Howie in

The Wicker Man. Broadcast over eight twenty-five-minute episodes, *The Owl Service* was Granada Television's second-ever colour production.[4] Garner himself stated, 'The feeling is less that I choose a myth than that the myth chooses me; less that I write than that I am written.'[5] In *The Owl Service*, an old legend ordains certain people to relive its roles, defying them to alter the course of destiny.

The filming location of this retelling, Poulton Hall in the Wirral, contained real trophies hanging on the wall: the stuffed heads of a boar, a stag and a badger. They are creatures of both the natural world and fairy tales. The house was owned at the time by Garner's friend and fellow author Roger Lancelyn Green – familiar in school libraries as a reteller of world mythologies for the Puffin imprint. To reduce the external signs of modernity even further, the set dressers stuck white tape over the light switches and electrical sockets. The house they originally wanted – Bryn Hall in Wales – was where Garner had first dreamed up and begun writing the tale in 1963. Tucked away in the valleys of North Wales, with its ghostly legend of a child once killed by its mother, and guarded by an old man who had served there since 1898 and seemed to know more than he would let on, it was 'a house with more electricity than most people found comfortable',[6] according to the series's producer and director, Peter Plummer, a friend and fan of Garner who visited at the time the novel was being written. Although the owner of Bryn Hall did not allow permission to film on the premises, a few outdoor scenes were shot next to the entrance gates and on the hills overlooking it.

Watching the series with eyes accustomed to twenty-first-century narrative techniques is an odd, sometimes queasy experience. The television shares a degree of obliqueness with the book, although of course on a screen it is harder to read between the lines. The book's heavy dependence on impressionistic dialogue is replicated by the use of modernist filmic and editing techniques, subliminal cutting and disconcerting effects, including discordant sounds and the non-appearance of one of the principal characters. The production

– between May and July 1969 – also took place under mostly overcast Welsh weather, but at the end, during what is supposed to be a torrential rainstorm, actually in a rare Celtic heatwave.

The three teenage protagonists – middle-class Alison, her stepbrother Roger and Gwyn, the Welsh housekeeper's son – each have one missing parent and are all going through some kind of personal transformation or silent crisis. Thrown together, they will exert difficult and dangerous effects on one another. The holiday home is a jumble of competing friendships, sibling relations and desires, but also of simmering class differences and resentments. All three protagonists are in that uncomfortable stage of life between adult and child, school and work, innocence and experience, town and country, myth and reality. They are aliens – to the valley, to the dimension of myth and to the future of jobs and responsibility that awaits them out there. The stylised dialogue is matched by striking and unusual camerawork: scenes filmed from high or low vantage points; wide-angle lenses in the huts, sheds, telephone boxes, darkroom, kitchen, bedroom and attic that box the characters in. The three main characters are frequently arranged in a triangle within the frame or conduct conversations via mirrors. Further, their clothing is colour-coded – red for Alison, green for Roger, black for Gwyn (red, green and black were, at the time, the standard colours of the three wires in a British mains plug). The stylisation contributes to a sense of predestination. Like the endpapers of a book, the first shot of every new episode, and the return after the ad break, is a static shot of trees, branches or leaves waving. The image locks the viewer into this natural world and casts its spell, like Kipling's Puck of Pook's Hill waving his enchanting sprigs of oak, ash and thorn.

The 'service' of the title refers to a set of dinner plates with magical properties that is discovered in the opening minutes in a sealed and dusty attic. The plates act like batteries, storing a huge charge of mythic power. (Garner referred to myths held in the human subconscious as 'engrams'.) The energy is discharged when Alison becomes obsessed with their floral, owlish patterns, which she traces from the plates onto paper and folds into origami owls. The plates turn blank.

The story behind the story comes out of the *Math fab Mathonwy*, one of the books of the medieval Welsh *Mabinogion*, which Gwyn and Alison are seen reading in the series. Essentially a brutal love/revenge triangle, it recounts how the hero warrior/magician Lleu Llaw Gyffes is cursed by an enraged queen never to marry a human. His adoptive father, the wizard Gwydion, conjures up a magical wife for him from a cocktail of 'flowers of the oak, flowers of the broom, flowers of the meadowsweet': Blodeuwedd.

Garner's strength here is to not draw precise equivalences between the three modern kids and the myth protagonists; it would have been too easy to simply update the myth by reclothing the characters and action points in the present time. For example, the Welsh name Lleu means 'the fair-haired one', but Gwyn, his equivalent, has dark hair. It's as if the psychogeographic weight of the legend is exerting a pressure on current events in the locality, and the trio are drawn into its electromagnetic space–time eddies while time is suspended in the valley and its exits sealed off. The characters turn out to have the power to divert the course of events, if only they can summon it.

The estate is managed by the eccentric handyman Huw Halfbacon (Ray Llewellyn); and a local woman, Nancy, has been engaged as housekeeper. Both Huw and Nancy seem to know more than they let on about the property and its secrets. 'Story and setting all came together as if waiting to be married,' said Llewellyn many years later. 'They were willing us to make the film.'[7] He recalled the weird coincidences around the production: Garner had seen one of the only extant copies of the Victorian plate (only about five examples have ever been discovered, and one of them happened to belong to Garner's mother-in-law); they kept finding owl-shaped decorations and trinkets around the house; and just when the crew needed to film close-ups of a real owl, they found one trapped in a hedge.

The production had a kind of magic spell cast over it. Dafydd Rhys, the real-life individual Huw was based on, had worked at Bryn House since 1898, and during the shoot was found scratching letters on a stone that turned out to read 'Blodeuwedd'. He told them a story about a man having been killed there with a bow and arrow. Gillian Hills recalled Garner himself ushering the young cast into his world as he had lived it, in a claustrophobic room at Poulton Hall with 'a fisheye feel'. He had eyes that 'seemed to see right through walls', and his initiation of the actors left them 'jangling and ready when we began filming'.[8]

Whether coincidence or magic, the production is shot through with editing sleights of hand – a kind of *cinéma enchanté* – that suggest the explosive release of magical power. When Gwyn knocks the *Mabinogion* out of Alison's hands, a subliminal image flashes up of her face tattooed with the owl/flower pattern, marking the moment she has synchronised with Blodeuwedd. Later, during a game of snooker the red, black and green balls collide, apparently triggering the cracking of the room's panelled walls to reveal a flowery fresco of Blodeuwedd (reproduced from Botticelli's *Primavera*, a masterpiece of pagan Renaissance iconography). In a scene Garner wrote especially for the television version, Huw distracts Clive by inviting him to admire his 'bonny-fire'. When Clive asks what kind of wood he is using, Huw replies, 'Burning alder' – a tree with the same colour combination of green leaves, red sap and dark-brown bark, and which for the Celtic druids symbolised the harmony of male and female, as well as death and resurrection.

The TV version's conclusion is even more enigmatic than the book's last chapter. Roger finally breaks into a locked outhouse and finds evidence that the youngsters' parents also once enacted their own iteration of the myth. The three-pointed engram of love and vengeance turns out to have been lived and handed down by the previous generation. Nancy's slow-motion smashing of the site foreshadows the ecstasy of Whitehead emerging, bound, from a tent in *A Field in England*. And in scenes eerily prescient of *The Wicker Man*,

Nancy and Gwyn are thwarted in their attempts to leave the village: gurning locals (one of them a cameo by Alan Garner) crowd around her telephone box as she tries to order a taxi; children cheerfully chop down a telegraph pole to block the exit road.

In the end the cure is simple. Roger seizes the moment to soothe Alison with a mantra about flowers (the loving aspect), not owls (the violent and vengeful spirit). This generation stumbles on a strategy to short-circuit the hard-wired myth by clipping its wires. If they had stuck to the story in the *Mabinogion*, Gwyn would have been allowed a revenge throw of the spear against Roger. Instead, he backs off, and Roger saves the day. But just because the myth-cycle has been interrupted this time, it does not guarantee the course of events in the future. In a final scene, three Welsh-speaking village children – the future offspring of Roger, Alison or Gwyn? – play in the fields and drape an ominous daisy chain over the Stone of Gronw. The story is never laid to rest; the engram batteries are set to trickle-charge.

■

To be cut off in a remote island, valley or village, and at the same time trapped in a narrative beyond your control, are two key elements of this fate of folk horror. Britain's pagan past survived, by the late twentieth century, as a mishmash of half-remembered eccentric rituals, lightly mocked by the sophisticated metropolitan middle class. Sherds – fragmented prehistoric relics – remain to be found in the garden, although it takes a trained eye to spot them. In the BBC 'Play for Today' episode *Robin Redbreast* (transmitted 10 December 1970), Norah Palmer refuses be rattled by the appearance in her newly acquired cottage garden of Fisher (Bernard Hepton), an oddly out-of-time, self-educated peasant in a deerstalker with a penchant for Frazer's *Golden Bough*. Fisher pointedly enquires whether he might have permission to trawl her backyard for such 'sherds': 'One often finds them, you know, in freshly turned earth.'

The writer of *Robin Redbreast*, John Bowen, would later adapt the first and penultimate of the BBC's 1970s Christmas ghost stories (*The Treasure of Abbot Thomas*, 1971, and *The Ice House*, 1977). Elsewhere in Bowen's work, both as screenwriter and novelist, he has referred to the short span of humanity in the vastness of history, and there is something allegorically archetypal in *Robin Redbreast*'s dramatic collision between the sophisticated urbanite Norah and the rural propitiators of the harvest gods who swarm around her cottage like busy, unstoppable ants.

Robin Redbreast encapsulates the often-recurring narrative line of the city arriviste confounded, and eventually imprisoned by, the old ways of the countryside. 'Everything seems to be slowed down,' Norah complains to her effete, world-weary London friends about the new life she has sought at Flaneathan Farm after the collapse of a love-less long-term relationship. 'Flaneathan', she discovers, is an Anglo-Saxon term meaning 'the place of birds', and on first making Fisher's acquaintance she learns that birds often get trapped in her chimney breast 'until they die'. The play brilliantly and remorselessly accumu-lates its wyrd details around Norah's urbane insouciance. Half of a glass marble, found outside, is taken into the house and remains with her as a charm. The young man, Rob/Edgar, is first glimpsed by Norah on a walk through a wood appropriately filled with the cawing of rooks – a sound-library effect heard in almost every example of rural drama on television during the 1970s. Half-naked and built like a Greek god, he's practising an energetic form of martial arts. Strong-bodied but intellec-tually empty, he tells her he was brought up in an orphanage and was given his name by the locals ('There's always one young man answers to the name of Robin round these parts'). Norah is half attracted to him on a purely physical level, half irritated with herself for thinking of it, but nonetheless before Rob arrives for an intimate dinner date, she reaches into her drawer for her contraceptive cap. BBC prudes objected to the implication of a woman in control of her sexuality, but director John McTaggart fought for the detail to stay put. Anyway, the disappearance of the cap is crucial to the story, being the removal of the last barrier to Norah becoming impregnated, as the locals intend. The cabal of villagers – Fisher in cahoots with housekeeper Mrs Vigo, Peter and the butcher Wellbeloved – are almost zombie-like in their determination to seed Norah's womb with a newborn at harvest time. The secrets are all in the doing, not in the explaining: Mrs Vigo wants to bring her to church, even though Norah turns off the radio at the first hint of a panel debate featuring a bishop; her car is sabotaged; the phone is monitored and then cut off at the local post-office exchange. 'This is 1970 – if she really wants to get away, she will,' drawls Norah's complacent London friend Madge. The utter isolation of Norah in this country setting is unimaginable in twenty-first-century terms, but without a mobile phone, with the post office able to steam open her correspondence, a conspiracy among local ladies to move the local bus stop without warning, and with no access to railways or a taxi service, Norah can be comprehensively locked down in her cottage prison. She is merely playing an anonymous part in a secret ritual engineered behind her back.

The penny takes an awfully long time to drop, but finally she realises and drops the bomb on the hapless Rob: 'We had *arranged* sex – the bull was brought to the cow.' Still-life shots of the church altar prepared for the harvest festival show a Church of England site peppered with pagan sherds: corn dollies, dead hares and bird corpses. Earlier, Fisher had mentioned his disdain for the local vicar, who's only a temporary 'Brummie' visitor from Birmingham: 'In rural areas, the church puts up with what it can afford.' This was a trenchant detail added by Bowen: Birmingham is the city most symbolic of the agricultural labouring class shifting to the factory drudgery of the Industrial Revolution, and of an urban sprawl that spread across the country heartland of England, even as the aristocracy indulged in the mammoth land-grab of enclosure in the mid-eighteenth century. If anything was designed to rub out any last vestiges of paganism languishing in the backwoods, it was this. In dramas such as *Robin*

Redbreast, small pockets can be imagined where wanderers might discover not so much the collapse of modern values as a landlocked zone into which those values have so far failed to penetrate.

As Bowen himself pointed out in subsequent interviews, neither was this entirely fantasy. The house used as the location for the shoot was his own, in Banbury, Oxfordshire. Many details, including the marble, the birds stuck in the chimney and the passer-by looking for sherds, were real. So was the case, reported in the paper, of a local 'cunning man' found dead in the woods near the village of Little Quinton, in what appeared to be a ritual murder (the corpse had been dragged around so that the blood could fertilise the soil). At the conclusion, Norah flees in her Triumph Spitfire and casts a last look back. The four locals who have silently terrorised her for nine months stand ranged outside the cottage; suddenly – in one of those fleeting yet unforgettable shots that are so essential to this genre of televisual haunting – they metamorphose into a band of medieval sorcerers, witches, executioners. In this apocryphal battle between rationality and instinct, the superstitious impulse appears to have won.

■

> Michaela: 'I'm immensely old. I shall love you and leave
> you for dead.'
> *Tam Lin* (1970)

Here's another privileged commune, hidden from prying eyes and ruled over by the immortal embodiment of a fairy queen. In the baronial environs of a Scottish mansion, Michaela 'Micky' Cazaret (Ava Gardner) resides, holding court to a crowd of effete hippies and thrill-seekers, modern-day flappers, indolent, spoilt and privileged sprites of metropolitan bohemia. Around the castle this 'slippery bunch of breast-feeders' lounge and flop, building houses of cards, trudging around the Monopoly board. Tom Lynn (Ian McShane) is their nominal leader and currently shares Micky's bed.

Tam Lin (titled *The Devil's Widow* in the US) was the only film directed by Roddy McDowall, a Hollywood actor, photographer and socialite with English roots and a distinctively British-weighted trans-atlantic accent. In the late 1960s, the ballad 'Tam Lin', an old Scottish folk song included in the *Child Ballads* collection, was one of the central pillars of the ongoing folk revival. It dates back at least as far as 1549 and had been a staple of the folk club movement that sprang up in the mid-1950s. At exactly the time the film was made, the song was being re-spun by the Watersons, Dave and Toni Arthur, and Anne Briggs, and electrified by the likes of Fairport Convention. But in this movie version from 1970, it's another of the era's pioneering folk-rock groups, Pentangle, who supply the mystic music, their acoustic trac-eries perfect for the summer skies over idyllic Scottish countryside, laced with mossy stone walls.

Like *The Owl Service*, *Tam Lin* is a series of tableaux set in a Celtic landscape. The opening credits play over scenes from the 'Tam Lin' ballad etched on a large sheet of glass. The camera tracks over the various vignettes from the story: the court of the fairy queen at Carter Hall; the encounter of Tom Lynn (the queen's lover) and local girl Janet in the wilderness; Tom, as he escapes with the pregnant Janet, being turned into a series of magical animals, while she holds him to protect him from the fairies trying to claim him back. Through this decorative frieze, we first view Tom and Micky, post-coital in bed, their respective fates etched out in front of them just as this story is forever engraved on the pane.

The glass merges with a chandelier above the bed that holds the mortal man hypnotised. Entrancement is a running fugue in *Tam Lin*, but a more appropriate term would be 'glamouring', used both for the mesmerism of vampires but also literally here, as Tom is part of a chic, superficial, cosmopolitan set who form Micky's retinue. Tom is the latest in a long line of male lovers whom Micky 'glamours' by making them wear a pair of acid-yellow-tinted sunglasses. 'I live in a bloody daze,' he tells an outsider. For now, he is the favourite, but his likely fate is there for all to see in the pathetic hanger-on Alan (Bruce Robinson), a lank-haired sub-Jagger type who is Micky's former conquest, now wrung-out and bawling. Here he is, in precisely the milieu Robinson would lovingly, hilariously satirise twenty years later in *Withnail & I*, whose sequences up the motorway to the remoteness of Cumbria are foreshadowed by the driving scene at the start of *Tam Lin* – a convoy of luxury cars zooming up an M1 that's newly opened and squeaky clean, like the scrubbed arteries of a new utopian city. Micky's heartless disdain for Alan's misery represents, in essence, the relentlessness of myth. Its mortal victims must submit to its immutability, while she bestrides time, impervious to it. 'What very forgettable ruins this town will make,' she drawls, as they speed out of London.

On the outdoor terraces of Carter Hall in Scotland, the hipsters (including a young Joanna Lumley) while away the hours in an enervated stupor, drinking and smoking, making rubbish jokes and playing games – gaudy captives, just like the caged parrots who also hang there. This is essentially the backstory to Lumley's character in the BBC comedy series *Absolutely Fabulous*: the dilettante deb with a glamorously louche past. McDowall's vision of the Scottish landscape, realised by director of photography Billy Williams (who learned his trade on the British Transport Films of the 1950s and '60s), is expansive, locating the castle and the pastoral security of the nearby village where Janet (Stephanie Beacham) lives with her father in the midst of the imposing grassy glens. Tom and Janet's significant encounter next to a waterfall is rendered stiffly dreamlike by the use of stills. The principal outdoor locations – stream, bridge, church, cottage, forest and castle – add up to a magical landscape, navigated and occasionally trespassed upon by the various characters.

It's not clear to what extent director Roddy McDowall was a fan of Pentangle, but the group's filigree of acoustic guitars, lightly dusted

rhythm section and the angelic vocals of Jacqui McShee are the perfect choice, casting an elvish musical spell over the glowing Scottish
hills and glens. It was happening for real, not too far away: on Lord
Glenconner's estate in the Scottish Highlands, the Incredible String
Band and their lunatic courtiers rented labourers' cottages and acted
the jester–minstrel role for aristos, including Princess Margaret.

As the daughter of the local vicar, Janet comes from the kind of
upstanding Scottish Christian community that might have spawned
The Wicker Man's Sgt Howie, but which also contains its white witch
in the shape of Miss Gibson, who gives Janet counsel. Reversing the
standard trope of the time, the city is the escape route from the country. For Janet, it's the abortion clinic in Edinburgh, and for the run-
away lovers, it's Tom's dockside caravan hideaway in the shadow of
the Forth Bridge.

Tom is given a foretaste of his fate by Micky's shady fixer, Elroy
('the king'?), who subtly warns him by reading out newspaper reports
of the accidental deaths of two of her former lovers in 1955 and 1962
– it's 1969 now, so do the math. Elroy's intervention introduces the
tale's moral dimension. 'Don't Think was made to think; Don't Care
was made to care,' he snaps. This is the 'Tam Lin' ballad in a nutshell:
Tom and Janet's love will only survive when he overcomes the spell
he is under, with her invaluable help, and regains his mortality. As
her father attests in his sermon, 'We must love one another and die.'

Tam Lin's slow pace and ravishing camerawork seem appropriately
dreamlike, a kind of cinematic weirding. The last fifteen minutes
or so are an unsuccessful attempt to update the hunt sequence to
the psychedelic age. After Tom is forced to drink a drugged cocktail
during his final appearance at Micky's court, he is ordered to flee in a
white sports car (replacing the white horse of the ballad). He crashes
in thick fog, loses the yellow shades and dashes through the forest, in
the changing guise of a bear (furry suit) and a serpent (rubber python
strapped to arm). Finally, he catches fire, Janet holds him close, and
the spell is broken. Micky, meanwhile, is jetting back to the US with

Tom's replacement, who willingly dons the tinted eyewear. The cycle of fate is restored, but Tom has escaped the preordained doom.

■

This mingling of the folkloric with the modern world was a potent scenario at the dawn of the 1970s. It percolated into the long-running *Doctor Who* franchise, in the shape of *Doctor Who and the Daemons* (1971). Of all the *Doctor Who* series, *The Daemons* is one of the most overt homages to the work of Nigel Kneale, and it fits here because it depicts a demonic cult that's sprung up autonomously in a postcard-perfect English village. As in *Quatermass and the Pit*, the premise is of dormant alien presences disturbed by an archaeological dig. As in *Quatermass 2*, the village of Devil's End is sealed off, this time by a hemispherical firewall. A running theme is the conflict of superstition versus science. Merging Jon Pertwee's suave Doctor with a rural English location (Aldbourne in Wiltshire), this is one of the best vintage *Who*s, and episode one plunges into the action with a live outside broadcast relay of the opening of a prehistoric burial chamber (covered by the then non-existent 'BBC3', complete with the obligatory effeminate director) at the Devil's Hump, near Devil's End. (The local manor is Satanshall. How could those names possibly arouse suspicions?) 'Very exciting,' says the dashing Captain Yates, heading off to watch the proceedings with the Doctor's assistant, Jo Grant. 'Forecasts of doom and disaster if anyone disturbs the burial chamber.' The place has long been associated with pagan rites and witch covens: there's a name-check for 'witch-hunter extraordinary' Matthew Hopkins. A white witch, Miss Olive Hawthorne, still practises there, offering tea, sympathy and piles of occult reference books on request.

Meanwhile, the Reverend Magister, the newly appointed vicar of the parish, turns out to be none other than the Doctor's long-standing foe, the Master. The saturnine, Aleister Crowley-quoting vicar has designs on harnessing the supreme power of these sleeping giants. When the horned beast Azal – a daemon from the planet Daemos who arrived on Earth 100,000 years ago to 'help *Homo sapiens* kick out Neanderthal man' – is eventually summoned, the Doctor's response to this folkloric apparition is to try to banish it from the planet, while the Master appropriates it for tyrannical ends. ('What this country needs is strength, power and decision,' he intones to an assembly of village elders. The squire, ironically named Winstanley, replies, 'If that's your brave new world, you can keep it!')

> Brigadier Lethbridge Stewart: 'So the Doctor was frozen stiff in the barrow, and was then revived by a freak heatwave. [Sergeant] Benton was beaten up by invisible forces, and the local white witch claims to have seen the devil.'
> Yates: 'I know it sounds a bit wild.'

The brigadier's stiff-lipped evaluation of events provides one of the many comic moments; among these are the appearance of the Headington Quarry morris dancers in the final episode, beating the Doctor with a pig's bladder and (anticipating a similar scene in *The Wicker Man*) capturing his neck in a headlock with their sticks. At this moment in history, *The Daemons* appears to argue against the retention of national folklore – a dangerous force – but nevertheless ends, after the destruction of the aliens and the arrest of the Master, with a maypole dance on the village green. Miss Hawthorne smells the flowers again, and birds chirrup on the soundtrack. Like a fairy tale, *The Daemons* enacts the transition from darkness to light, from death to rebirth.

■

But now it is time for our appointment with the one film that has survived its initial botched release in 1973 to become perhaps the most celebrated and revered of cult British movies: *The Wicker Man*.

In this chapter we have uncovered a lineage of films dramatising one or more of the following themes: the 'innocent' party arriving in a new and unfamiliar rural location; the remote community hostile to incomers; characters forced to relive myths or preordained narratives; the propitiation of nature via sacrifice; and the revival and prolongation of pagan rituals and customs. What makes *The Wicker Man* such a monumental movie in the canon of folk horror is that it contains all of these at once.

A central tenet of paganism is not so much that the journey from life to death described above is linear, but that it is cyclical. The yearly rounds of the seasons, the orbits of sun and moon, the reproductive cycle of humans, animals and plants, and the equilibrium of the four elements were believed by early societies to be governed and propelled by their respective divinities. *The Wicker Man* – whose plot spirals in intensity like a vortex as menacing forces circle around the lead character – posits the existence of a fully functioning pagan community in 1970s Britain. Its masterstroke is to paint this cult in a favourable light when set against its haughty and self-righteous protagonist, Police Sergeant Neil Howie (Edward Woodward). Arriving on the island at the request of an anonymous inhabitant of Summerisle, a private island in the Hebrides, to investigate the disappearance of a young girl, Rowan Morrison, Howie gradually uncovers the topsy-turvy yet relentlessly plausible logic of the pagan mindset. In the process, he becomes less likeable and more like a fool. As a viewer it's easy to find yourself admiring and complicit with the pagan tribe and its charismatic leader, Lord Summerisle (Christopher Lee) – right up until the closing minutes, when the lengths the cult is prepared to go to preserve its way of life are revealed in all their barbarity.

Although often cited as the quintessential folk-horror film, *The Wicker Man* is not so much a horror movie, more of a musical, a mystery, a police procedural, a pageant, a moral homily, and the ballad of a murder committed in plain sight. It falls into the lineage of strange, self-sufficient and remote societies that began with the *Utopia* of Thomas More, the *New Atlantis* of Francis Bacon, the imaginary lands of Jonathan Swift and the *Erewhon* of Samuel Butler. So many of the themes and tropes of the films discussed earlier are drawn together: the lone individual pitching up in a distant rural locale; the tight-lipped community guarding its secrets; the clash of values and beliefs; the unfolding suspicion that the interloper is unwittingly fulfilling a destiny proscribed long in advance, by forces he does not understand. Howie, representing the law, arrives as a king; he ends up a mere pawn in someone else's game.

Scripted by Anthony Shaffer as an adaptation of David Pinner's 1967 novel *Ritual*, and directed by Robin Hardy, *The Wicker Man* was loathed by its studio, British Lion, under the helm of Michael Deeley, who simply never understood it. An eighty-seven-minute version, heavily cut, premiered right at the start of 1974 in the UK, and after interventions from Roger Corman and Warner Brothers, a seventy-two-minute cut was released to US theatres as the accompanying B-movie to Nicolas Roeg's *Don't Look Now*. Hardy attempted to piece together his own preferred version over the years, during which time swathes of original footage disappeared (some have hinted it may have become landfill under various British motorways). The *Director's Cut* (2001) and *Final Cut* (2013) seem as close to his artistic intention as we are likely to get.

One of the most significant elements of the restorations is the revealing glimpses they give of Howie's life on mainland Scotland. The policeman's puritanical streak and austere propriety are introduced much sooner than in the first theatrical cut. His colleagues in the force mock him behind his back and tease him to his face: when he asks the younger Constable McTaggart what has been happening in his absence, he is told there has been the usual 'rape, sodomy and sacrilege'. Howie not only fails to see the funny side of this police banter, but he'll soon be witnessing such depravities at first hand. Meanwhile, he's reading a prophetic lesson in church about the first

Holy Communion of bread and wine, in which the Jesus Christ he'll soon be howling for offers up his own body as a sacrifice for mankind.

He begins and ends the film encased in different types of capsule. The first is the solo seaplane in which he rules the skies, with godlike views over his allocated domain. In stunning aerial shots en route to the island, his plane soars over jag-toothed black mountains, like the exaggerated backdrop to some medieval wilderness painting. Summerisle from above is verdant and cultivated, with orchards, vineyards and palm trees neatly laid out. Howie will observe, too late, that growing apples in Scotland is 'against nature'. Once moored near the village quay, the aircraft's communication systems are easily disabled by the islanders, so that he is cut off from help. At the finale, of course, he is bound into the blazing cockpit of the islanders' sacrificial effigy.

Behind the scenes, the whole of *The Wicker Man* location shoot went against nature. The film's uncanny visual character is a result of being seasonally off-kilter. Filmed entirely in western Scottish locations between 9 October and 25 November 1972 (Woodward called it 'seven frantic weeks of sleepless nights, heavy socialising, fantastically hard work and a kind of wartime Blitz camaraderie'[9]), it is set over a few days around May Day, the apex of spring. Woodward recalled rain, snow, the ground awash with sleet and mud. Whatever sunshine penetrates the clouds – see, for instance, the maypole dance or the naked fire leap scenes – is intense and autumnal, throwing long shadows. Actors tucked ice cubes into their cheeks to prevent their breath condensing. Fake fruit trees with plastic blossom were transported to the set and shifted around during extended takes to create the illusion of large orchards. This was improvisational cinematic magic in action, which contributes materially to *The Wicker Man*'s uncanny enchantment.

David Pinner's *Ritual* was at one time pronounced 'unfilmable'. The book is set in rural Cornwall, but a Scottish island is so much more convincingly faraway and alien, and the late 1960s and early

'70s were notable for the creation of a plethora of privately owned offshore fiefdoms in the region, bought up by rapacious aristos or newly enriched pop stars for the pursuance of libertarian ideals. In an interview, Hardy mentioned that the main image he carried away from the book was the dead hare that had been substituted for human remains, which in the film is discovered inside Rowan's coffin instead of the child's body. From the bones of the tale, Shaffer wove a tapestry that added up to a panoply of pre-Christian magic, ritual and superstition. Entire cycles of life and death are fed into it: fertility rites, sexual initiation, ancient healing arts, propitiation hymns, dances of death, ritual sacrifice. The maypole song sung by the village schoolchildren is a classic Russian doll encapsulation of nature's pattern of growth, death and resurrection.

Myths in *The Wicker Man* aren't recreated. These pagans are not nostalgic for a vanished age, but dwell in a contemporary world where paganism is a living, breathing reality. It is not a reconstructed fantasy or hypnotised cult. It is a functioning society, and all are willing participants. The silent conspiracy of the locals is particularly well achieved. Impassive, gently smirking fishermen and bluff, aloof shopkeepers who all clearly know more than they are telling keep Howie trapped on the island, and the longer he stays, the more fervent becomes his moral outrage and, linked to that, his sense of being on a mission. But for the islanders, the longer he wants to stay, the more easily he falls into their trap.

Throughout, there are equal measures of the eerie and the weird. If eeriness can be defined as discomfiture caused by an absence, then the first half of the film is all about that, with Rowan inexplicably vanished from the island, no one apparently mourning her, a total lack of the expected sorrow over a disappeared child. For all of its production headaches, *The Wicker Man* is remarkable for the wealth of visual detail that elevates it from the run-of-the-mill low-budget flick. Throughout Howie's traumatic spell on the island, eerie details are picked out by an unrhetorical camera: the evil eye painted on the prow of a rowing boat; the sinister confectionery on the post-office counter (chocolate hares, skulls and animal heads, cakes shaped like naked pregnant women); the magic spells written on the school blackboard; the beetle tied to a nail in Rowan's abandoned desk; the 'navel-string' (dried umbilical cord) hung on a sapling on Rowan's 'grave'; the copulating dolls Howie finds when searching a house; and the suspiciously empty space on the pub wall from which the previous year's harvest queen photo has obviously been removed.

When Howie tries to fly back to the mainland but finds his plane has been sabotaged, the weirdness kicks in. *The Wicker Man*'s famous animal heads pop up from the parapet. From here on, the film is a parade of outlandish costume and behaviour – truly midsummer madness – with the walls closing in fast. The gathering pace of the action as Howie is sucked into the masked procession, dressed in fool's clothing stolen from the unconscious pub landlord, is a deft piece of direction and editing. Just when he thinks he has completed his quest – rescuing Rowan – the game is well and truly up.

The charred stumps of the wicker man's wooden legs – from the second of two effigies constructed on set – stand to this day in a caravan park on the cliff edge at Burrowhead. This is the version that was set alight and whose conflagration was timed so perfectly with the clouds rolling away, revealing the setting sun, which could only happen at this autumnal time of year. Howie's shocked response to his first sighting of the wicker man itself was genuine: it was the first time Woodward had clapped eyes on it. Towering, impassive, grotesque in its grisly purpose – a killing machine – and its squawking cargo of animals and poultry, which are also destined to be crisped up in aid of Summerisle's apple crop, its final form was a compromise that worked more brilliantly than the original design. The plan was for it to have a face, as in several eighteenth-century engravings showing an artist's impression of the wicker men described in Julius Caesar's annals. By reducing the head to a featureless node, it became more sinister and better represented the cult's manifest intractability.

A compilation of pagan beliefs, superstitions and folkloric symbols: *The Wicker Man* (1973).

In one of the restored early scenes, Howie is seen with his bride-to-be in church, reading a lesson about the Last Supper, when Christ offered himself as a human sacrifice and instigated Holy Communion. In the moment before he is brought before the wicker man, Howie calls for divine aid, then confronts the fact that he is slated to be the sacrificial lamb. The final moments are a pagan–Christian sound clash – Howie attempting to drown out the islanders' atonal 'Sumer Is Icumen In' with a hysterical Psalm 23. There's no salvation, Howie's God forsakes him to the end, and the pagans are victorious. The blazing head collapses to reveal the eternal sun, which governs all this human activity. 'I look forward to the day when we *are* all pagans again,' said Anthony Shaffer. 'I think . . . we'd have a lot more fun . . . I think we'd have a lot more immediacy with the things unseen.'[10]

But is their triumph everlasting? That's the question hanging in the air, drifting with the ash particles as the wicker man burns down to its straw toes. If you could fly back to Summerisle on the first May Day after the disappearance of Sgt Howie, or after the drought of 1976 a few years later, what might you have found? Barren trees, and the Laird himself being served up to the gods in a basket, with a side order of roast goose, duck and lamb? Or perhaps just the emptied-out cottages and ghostly, silent pub, after the mainland police have arrived looking for their vanished colleague, shut down the community and dispersed all to the four winds? Or perhaps, as Lord Summerisle confidently declared, the crop flourishing once more and a healthy bunch of bonny babies, conceived last May Day eve in the Green Man's garden?

■

The notion of a secret pagan society hiding within British public life remained almost as strong a theme as the idea of the political enemy within. A version of the *Wicker Man* story – one, at least, featuring an isolated village ('Milbury') acting as a 'pagan storehouse of energy' – was aimed at junior viewers in *Children of the Stones*, the HTV West series that has become one of the most celebrated and notorious examples of the wyrdness of children's programming.

'You'll never leave' was the strapline for the fictional village of Royston Vasey in the late-1990s series *The League of Gentlemen*. In the double-edged slogan lay the small-mindedness of village life and a veiled yet undefinable threat. The lines that inspired this comic catchphrase were once spoken by actor Freddie Jones, playing the Welsh idiot savant Dai in *Children of the Stones*, a character who knows all too well how real that threat can be.

Transmitted at the start of 1977, *Children of the Stones* overflows with scientific terminology, political philosophy and esoteric astro-archaeology. Shared with *The Owl Service* are a relationship between

an adolescent boy, Matthew Brake, and his father Adam, the suggestion of awakening teenage sexuality, a landscape humming with
ghost presences and mystery, and a misanthropic Welshman who
seems to know more than he lets on.

The script by Jeremy Burnham and Trevor Ray portrays Matt as
a studious, multitalented boy, with a working knowledge of Latin
and astronomy, who can jerry-build his own theodolite, analyse a
painting and practise psychometry. As in *The Wicker Man*, there's a
local squire/pagan despot, Rafael Hendrick, who is controlling his
hermetically sealed domain with a system of black magic rituals.
Thankfully, Lord Summerisle never had access to portable oscillo-
scopes, megalithic dining rooms or a vast IBM computer installed in
a parish church.

Like Summerisle, Milbury is a hermetic village-state held in a
mystic time bubble, hemmed and henged in by the visible survivals of its prehistory. Nobody can leave; the population is happily in
thrall to the aristocratic magus striving to fulfil a cosmic destiny. It is
a warning from history of the powerful intoxicants of racial memory,
exclusivity, landed power and control. By becoming one of the con-
forming tribe of 'happy people', each villager is complicit in 'deny-
ing the existence of that which exists' – in other words, oppression
and tyranny. But it is all the more disturbing for being tyranny of
a distinctly English kind, one in which eavesdropping, covert surveillance and snitching are one step away from village gossip and
nosey-neighbourism.

The shooting schedule fell across the famous drought of summer
1976, when the grass in southern England turned a pale shade of
yellow. The desiccated community is amplified by the backdrop, and
the aerial shots of Avebury in the title sequences show a green circular settlement sequestered amid a sea of brown and withered fields.
Close-up camera sweeps superbly intensify the visual presence of the
stones themselves, revealing eerie facial features weathered into their
craggy surfaces. There's an organic grain to the film, offset by the

peculiar but common practice of intercutting 16 mm outdoor footage with video-based interiors. Sidney Sager's dissonant choral music
adds an eerie and disturbing undertow.

The series deftly interweaves technology, folklore, prehistory and
astrophysics. The incorporation of ley-line theory into the mix feels
timely too. Adam calls Milbury 'a primitive Jodrell Bank, immovably
aligned with . . . something up there'. It all smacks of the writings of
John Michell, whose 1969 book *The View Over Atlantis* posited hidden connections between ley lines, Earth energies, magnetism and
the flight paths of alien spacecraft, and was required reading for the
early-1970s Aquarian generation and formed one of the founding
principles of the nascent Glastonbury Festival in 1971. Michell saw
England as a site of spiritual redemption in the New Age. *Children of
the Stones'* neo-Celtic font adds to the atmosphere and helps the title
sequences to look a little like the sleeve of a progressive folk-rock LP
from the same period.

It didn't look all that different from the Public Information Films
and Children's Film Foundation material circulating at the time, some
of which have gone on to become classics in their own right: *Lonely
Water*, for instance, made in 1973, with its macabre voiceover by
Donald Pleasence and lugubrious air of doom. *Apaches* (1977), which
Children of the Stones most closely resembles, has a bunch of rumbustious schoolchildren literally running amuck around a farm, with
fatal results in the form of a series of unlikely but gruesome deaths.
But *Children of the Stones'* turbulent argument between rationality
and belief, and between critique and acceptance, remains potent, surrounded as it is by the interface of superstition (Dai's casting of a toad
bone), ritual landscape (Milbury was an augmented Avebury, with
extra polystyrene monuments) and technological rationalism.

The *BBC2 Playhouse* production 'The Breakthrough' (1975, a
Clive Exton dramatisation of a story by Daphne du Maurier) also
wrote its characters into a narrative landscape of mythology. Steve
(Simon Ward) comes to Saxmere research establishment on the

remote Suffolk coast to mend a faulty computer system. The small skeleton crew are researching high-end technologies and ultrasonic sound waves. There is a similar power dynamic to *The Wicker Man* – chief Maclean is the magus (is it a coincidence that his towel and cardigan are the same solar yellow as Lord Summerisle's polo neck?). Steve is the 'innocent', rational man, trying to maintain his stability in a sealed-off environment where a different set of rules and norms prevails. Among the crew is Ken, a boy-man with leukaemia who has just a couple of months to live. With a dog named Cerberus, a caretaker/cook called Janus and a computer installation nicknamed Charon (Steve previously worked on Hermes), there's no attempt to conceal the myth–science connections. Away from prying eyes, the team attempt to pinpoint what happens to consciousness in the moments immediately after dying – 'an answer at last to the intolerable futility of death'.

This rarely seen work has some fine character acting: Ward is brilliantly buttoned-down; the two scientists have a seen-it-all, hands-on professionalism even as they coldly gamble with people's lives and possible deaths. When Ken eventually dies, local girl Nicky, who seems to have some kind of sixth sense, is sent to follow him down the dark tunnel, compelled by Maclean to dangle at the tip of the metaphorical lifeline. This electronic seance (which recalls key moments in *Quatermass and the Pit* and *The Stone Tape*) scares her half to death, but Maclean twice forces her into this near-sacrificial role, believing this breakthrough has allowed him to detect what he calls 'Force 6' – the essence of life. He craves this human sacrifice in the pursuit of science, but is stopped at the last minute.

■

And here's yet another village – this time unnamed and in the Midlands – where the locals have their own superstitious way of doing things. To get there, veterinary surgeon Alan Crich has to drive his Mini estate under the railway bridge, past the factory and out into the country lanes. A symbolic threshold is crossed. He runs the gauntlet of menacing road sweepers, reluctant to get out of his way, at the entrance to Beeley's Farm.

'Murrain' (John Cooper, 1975) was a contribution by Nigel Kneale to a short-lived ATV drama series, *Against the Crowd*, devoted to exploring the condition of outsiders in society. Not surprisingly, Kneale's effort diverged from the realist prerogative, yet its haunting power comes from being grounded in a damp, miserable and austere hamlet (in real life Wildboarclough in Cheshire, with some scenes shot in Hollinsclough, Staffordshire). Its title referenced a word of very ancient origin, a medieval conception of a plague affecting livestock, but often with the overtone of a divine curse.

Kneale's script followed *Robin Redbreast* and *The Wicker Man* in portraying a city dweller entering a detached area where decidedly other values hold sway. Crich, who's been dispatched to the farm to treat farmer Beeley's sick pigs, is quietly steered into the bedroom of a boy who's been sick for a month with a mysterious debilitating disease, just like the animals. Neither Crich's rationalism nor his medical training have equipped him to explain why the village's livestock and people have been afflicted. The superstitious locals therefore suspect the lone inhabitant of the neighbouring cottage – old Mrs Clemson. Beeley explains he's been waging a silent war of attrition against this woman, whom he believes to be a witch. He has already murdered her pet cat, and now she has been banned from the village shop (which his wife runs). Accused of casting 'a thing called a murrain' across the village, Mrs Clemson is effectively being starved into submission in her own home. Crich naturally views her as the unfortunate victim of cruel intimidation and rounds on the farmers: 'Kill her cat in the name of magic and then go home and watch your colour telly!' Following this memorable line comes an irresistible Kneale-ism, as Beeley compares the television set to the ancient magical art of 'scrying' into a reflective black mirror.

Determined to get to the bottom of things, Crich realises he's being gently coerced into collaborating in an unspoken ritual practice, as the local farmworkers mutter among themselves, 'He's a stranger . . .' His medical bag has been stuffed with swept-up grit from the village crossroads, and as he makes his way up the lane to her hovel, the farmers beg him to pour the stones over her, which 'breaks the power'. Instead, he empties the bag of its dust and knocks on the old woman's door.

'They want to get rid of me,' attests Mrs Clemson, once she allows him inside. She's presented as a survival from a fairy tale – the type of mostly harmless old lady who provides refuge to lost wanderers with her gruel and wormy cabbages. Odd talismans in the house – including a voodoo-like doll that triggers her traumatised memories of wanting to be a mother – could be interpreted as magical objects, but equally could be just prosaic household objects.

'Murrain' was shot on video, and of all the televisual rural-horror tales, this one paints the grimmest, most anaemic vision of the English countryside. With its overcast skies and rain-dampened lanes, this is the rough underbelly of the pastoral dream, a quarantined parish where the rule of law is handed over to the superstitious lynch mob. The village shop, where Crich cunningly disguises his purchases of staple foods for Mrs Clemson by adding requests for middle-class Continental salami and stuffed olives, is a study in paltry austerity, all tinned foods and dried-up perishables. This combination of entropic environs, gruff blankness and passive aggression towards outsiders, in a landscape not noted for its luxury, would again be be satirised by *The League of Gentlemen*.

Kneale himself never professed to have any active belief in the supernatural. But he allowed his dramas to remain on the fence. 'Murrain' is no exception: as in other works, he implies mystical powers held in suspension in the land itself, 'Just waitin' there, see . . . till someone has the trick to come along and use them.' Patched into this belief is a timely nod to the great utopian hope for the

British economy at the time the play was written: 'It's like finding oil and gas in the North Sea: they said there was none – then there it was.'

Against the odds, more and more uncanny events begin to stack up. Mrs Clemson's cash, handed to the shopkeeper (the mother of the sick boy) via Crich, appears to transfer the murrain, with its swollen hands, to the adult woman too. Crich makes Mrs Clemson his special case and returns the next day to find an assault in progress. Beeley collapses dead of a heart attack during the melee; Mrs Clemson's squealed 'Yes!' is forever open to interpretation.

■

'Murrain' is so effective because it keeps its secret close to its chest and holds back the killer blow until the final seconds. Leaping forward several decades, we find another film that recasts the pagan supremacy in an innovative and shocking form. *Kill List* (Ben Wheatley, 2011) confounded many viewers when released for the way it 'begins in one generic mode and jumps, or modulates, into another'.[11]

For most of its duration, it seems to be a relatively straightforward, if sometimes uncanny, crime/buddy movie tracking the engagements of a pair of hired assassins who are also former military comrades. The marvel of the film lies in the way its scattered enigmatic details at first swirl delicately around the main action, only to clump together in the final minutes, revealing an entirely different outcome to the one expected.

Repeat viewings are helpful in revealing the details that writer Amy Jump sprinkles throughout the script, stitching a mythic (specifically Arthurian) lining into the cinematic fabric of documentary realism. The names of the two male leads, Jay and Gal, evoke the Camelot knights Kay (often associated with hot-headedness and boorish behaviour) and Galahad – appropriately, as they are both warriors, or ex-servicemen. Jay's wife Shel is Swedish, of Viking stock. Jay and his son Sam are seen duelling with toy swords, he reads bedtime stories about the Knights of the Round Table, and at one point suggests naming a puppy 'Arthur or Gwinnie'. Behind his and Gal's comradeship lies an incident in Kiev, which is referred to several times, in which it seems Jay committed some unnamed atrocity as a mercenary. 'We're doing a fucking job, man,' says Gal. 'It's not a crusade.' But a crusade – not, admittedly, of their own making – is exactly what they turn out to be involved in.

When the pair are hired by an unnamed client to commit a series of killings – a pact brutally signed in blood when the client slices Jay's palm with a knife – they embark on a gritty journey around anonymous motels, seedy storage facilities and suburban homes to carry out their gruesome task. Gal leaves Jay to deliver the death blows, first to a priest, then to a librarian, and suspicions grow that they have been hired to take out an underground paedophile/pornography ring. But there's the nagging fact that each victim appears to welcome their fate, prefacing the final blow by recognising Jay and saying 'Thank you' for the fate he is about to mete out. The uneasy feeling develops that the job is in fact a quest whose endpoint the men have no idea about. The client knows more about their past than they expect: they find a file on the Kiev incident that includes images of medieval knights and tombs.

Wheatley himself has talked of 'the idea that the whole of this film has been this big bear trap'.[12] An accumulation of small details attests that Jay is being drawn into a magical circle, a secret pagan society run by anonymous powerful figures. Early in the film, Gal's girlfriend Fiona (Emma Fryer, evidently cast for her raven-haired witchy looks) is seen carving an occult symbol on the back of a mirror in Jay and Shel's bathroom. Later, Shel tells Jay that Fiona has begun visiting the house regularly while he is away. Fiona apparently bewitched Gal in order to gain access to Jay. Unconsciously confirming her magical attributes, Jay jokingly describes her as a 'glary-eyed phantom', while Gal calls her 'a demon in bed'. She later appears in a vision, waving from a field and apparently clad in a wedding dress, as Jay stares out of his hotel window.

Why this recruitment of two washed-up warriors? Fiona's job, she says, is in human resources, where she helps organisations to downsize and terminates underachievers. Is the bear trap in fact an opportunity for Jay to be headhunted as the new leader of a failing pagan cult? When Jay and Gal revisit their hirer to try to extricate themselves from the job, they end up asking, 'How long have we been working for you?' Jay has been groomed as a cult saviour for some time, and the Kiev incident was the testing ground for his ability to carry out a sacrificial act. 'At least we're not killing a toddler,' Gal tells him at one point, giving him a meaningful look.

The client explains that their mission is part of a 'reconstruction', picking up a thread running through the film about sectarian divides. This cult has fallen on hard times and is desperate for a new leader to perform the necessary sacrifices and unite its divided factions. There has already been discussion at Jay's dinner table about the sectarian divides in Ireland, during which Fiona stated that, to her, Protestant and Catholic is 'all the same religion'. What sounds at first like naive ignorance turns out to be pagan logic – after all, a committed pagan occultist is unlikely to draw much distinction between Christianity's various divided houses. Jay later angrily confronts an evangelist self-help group in a hotel who are singing 'Onward, Christian Soldiers' to an acoustic guitar. The choice of hymn is telling: it was written by the Victorian folklorist and song collector Sabine Baring-Gould, and its crusading theme asserts the confidence of a unified church ('We are not divided / All one body we'). The cult that has appropriated Jay and Gal as its cogs could use some of that confidence itself, and its undercover HR department is carrying out its own structural adjustments.

The last assassination, of a 'politician', takes place in the wooded grounds of a country mansion. In these nocturnal outdoor scenes, and in the relentlessness of ritual behaviour, comes the most obvious homage to *The Wicker Man*. Humans, white-robed or naked and bearing

Twisted chivalry: *Kill List* (2011).

flaming torches, converge on a clearing, their faces hidden behind straw masks. Among them can be recognised the client, Fiona and a doctor who earlier replaced Jay's usual GP when examining his septic hand.

Jay – captured after a chase through an underground labyrinth in which Gal is killed, and after briefly reuniting with Shel and Sam – is forced into gladiatorial combat with a hooded hunchback. When he eventually stabs it with a sword, it turns out to be Shel carrying little Sam on her back. She lets out a sarcastic laugh, the meaning of which has been much speculated over; but the final shot lingers on Jay as he appears to come to terms with the consequences of his actions and prepares to assume the mantle of cult leader.

Would there be order or more chaos with someone like Jay in charge? Jump and Wheatley leave the question unanswered. In fact, *Kill List* is a case study in stripping away backstory and context and leaving the bare bones, which has led to multiple readings and inter-pretations. Watching the film in the wake of the pagan high-water mark of *The Wicker Man*, it might be instructive to consider the cult as a microcosm of British society – racked by factionalism, oppositional politics and deep economic and ideological divisions. Seen through this lens, *Kill List* becomes almost revolutionary in scope, advocating the replacement of the aristocratic leadership class with a wholly other type of chieftain. As in the legend of King Arthur, an unsuspecting 'commoner' finds himself at the centre of a coronation after an unprecedented show of strength. What legendary deeds Jay will go on to perform are left to the unfilmed future.

Kill List, then, is the culmination of a small genre in which mythology prowls around the edges of society or even totally dictates it. At the centre of it all, the shamanic leaders and their followers are driven by a higher calling, a belief system that goes deeper and further into Britain's past spiritual life than Christianity, but which somewhere along the line has become mixed up with the game of power for its own sake. It is as if the ghosts of ancient Britain are seeping out through the medium of these films and stories. But there are many more ghosts than this swarming inside the magic box.

CATHODE WRAITHS

9

Spooks and Stones

The Innocents, The Haunting, Symptoms, 'The Exorcism', The Stone Tape, Tarry-Dan Tarry-Dan Scarey Old Spooky Man

> Television . . . has become the new influencing machine
> on all our minds. It also sets the scene for a new afterlife,
> where the past meets the future and turns into an ever
> repeating, eternal present: 'Television archives store
> millions of images of the dead, which wait to be broadcast
> . . . to the living . . . at this point, the dead come back to
> life to have an influence . . . on the living . . . Television is,
> then, truly the spirit world of our age. It preserves images
> of the dead which then can continue to haunt us.'[1]
>
> Marina Warner

> The annual M. R. James adaptation is a television
> tradition, now: a more than satisfactory replacement for
> tales whispered round the hearth.[2]
>
> Angela Carter

Since it was first constructed, the magic box has displayed a peculiar affinity for the paranormal. Electricity in the form of street lighting has chased nocturnal horrors from once-dark city streets. Once it began coursing through the loops and wires of a television set, however, it became a lightning rod for phantoms and ghostly apparitions.

The word 'television', coined in 1900 by the Russian scientist Konstantin D. Perskyi at the first International Electricity Congress in Paris, is an amalgam of the Greek '*tele*' (far) and the Latin '*videre*' (to see). Distant events made visible somewhere else in space and time? There's sorcery afoot, for sure. The screen acts as a strange attractor of ghostliness. In the era of the cathode ray, the static-ridden void between the channels tuned in to a paranormal dimension. The internet abounds with weird urban myths and anecdotes: spectral hands materialising on a TV in Minnesota; faces of the recently deceased popping up on screens everywhere; disembodied voices howling from speakers; a supposedly haunted television set banished to the Himalayan village of Tsento; the apparition of Swedish 'electronic voice phenomena' researcher Friedrich Jürgenson on a screen during his own funeral. The rumour mill churns ever on.

If you were to shrink yourself down and take a fantastic voyage inside a cathode-ray tube, your observation port would reveal electron streams moving around in vacuum tubes under low pressure. The reason the television could earn the nickname of 'the box' is because a three-dimensional container was needed to house the cathode-ray tube, which converts the signal received via the antenna into the images on the screen. The technology to steer electrons to their correct location, forming an image on the inside of the phosphor-coated glass, has existed since around the middle of the nineteenth century. The cathode-ray tube was utilised in experiments by Sir William Crookes, a distinguished English scientist and electrical researcher who harboured a vivid interest in spiritualism. Crookes, who died in 1919, aged eighty-seven, developed a T-shaped tube in which charged particles could be emitted from a cathode and picked up by an anode inside a near vacuum. The process would make the remnants of air inside the tube glow, and when all air was forcibly removed, the glow would 'attach' itself to the phosphorescent side of the glass. Crookes apparently attended late-Victorian seances with his bulky apparatus, partly to test spirit mediums for the electrical energy they emitted during their ceremonies.

Given these early associations with attempts to contact the 'other side', it should be no surprise that television culture has been drawn to the spirit world. There was, after all, something ghoulish and dissonant about the output of the earliest TV receivers – or, as inventor John Logie Baird called them in the 1920s, 'televisors'. Shapes and objects emitted ether waves that registered as sounds on early sets. A contemporary survey of television technology observed how 'A hand with fingers extended, if passed in front of the transmitter, sounds like the grating of a very coarse file, and an inanimate object, such as a box, gives a single, steady note.' As for moving subjects such as a human face, 'the slightest movement of the features is turned into sound waves by the transmitter'. The primitive apparatus of the 1920s was highly susceptible to distortion and interference, whose 'effects are almost as distressing as distortion in a loud speaker . . . The image of a face may appear flattened out as in a concave mirror, or a twisted effect may be produced, so that the face seen on the screen may have a flattened nose and a chin higher on one side than the other.'[3]

As early as January 1937 – barely three months after the BBC began transmission – the sound stage at Alexandra Palace hosted a televised performance of *The Soul of Nicholas Snyders*, a supernatural short story by Jerome K. Jerome. At the end of that year, a carriage-load of abandoned travellers experienced hauntings on the platform of a lonely railway station in *The Ghost Train*, an adaptation of a 1923 stage play by Arnold Ridley. Nineteen thirty-eight, the last year before television was brought to a temporary halt by the Second World War, featured at least three plays with a ghostly theme.

After the war, ghost stories cropped up sporadically, notably a Christmas Day 1950 broadcast of Dickens's *A Christmas Carol*. A youthful Tony Richardson adapted, directed and produced two M. R. James stories for the BBC in 1954: *Canon Alberic's Scrapbook* and *The Mezzotint*. In the 1960s Marshall McLuhan conceived of the new electronic telecommunications media as nothing less than extensions of the human nervous system. Later still, films such as David Cronenberg's *Videodrome* (1983) and Hideo Nakata's *Ring* (1998) make explicit connections between TV sets and the spirit world.

In the early 1970s a certain strain of British horror on television and on film recognised that the age of latex mummies and ersatz monsters was over. The buckets of blood and the threshing melodrama of vintage Hammer were drying up. As were the Victorian and Edwardian characters who routinely participated in the shenanigans, and who were too easily dismissed as historical caricatures. The BBC's 'Ghost Story for Christmas' strand, plus a significant clutch of films and other programmes, acted as psychological studies of fear, unease and harried states of mind and relied more on atmospheric scene-setting and the imaginative use of locale. Added to this was a bracing jigger of eccentricity, sadism and antiquarian oddity that the English imagination has always been strangely well equipped to provide.

The ghost story's affinity with the small screen derives in part from the TV's physical position in the home itself: it becomes a transmitter of fearful events and unexplained hauntings, right there in the domestic living room. A woman screaming in terror on a cinema screen, punctuated by dramatic orchestral music, is theatrical. On the television screen, the woman screaming in an otherwise silent house is a frightening invasion of domestic privacy. When a character leaves the light and companionship of a living room filled with friends, and in the next scene finds herself suddenly alone in the dark faced with unknown terrors (with the sounds of the party still faintly audible in the background), she's only going through what the viewer is experiencing: the irruption of the uncanny into a supposedly secure and familiar environment. Television haunts us in our own home.

The Victorian and Edwardian eras gave us the classic English ghost story. What gave rise to this cacophony of supernatural horror? There's a phantom thread that connects the 'spectre . . . haunting Europe: the spectre of Communism' in the opening sentence of Karl Marx and Friedrich Engels's 1848 *Communist Manifesto* with the unease at the pace of change expressed by preservationists like

William Morris, who worried that the ugliness and barbarity of industrial London would kill off the arts and the entire 'invention and ingenuity of man'.[4] Early communism drew on Marx's first-hand observations of capitalism's ghosts on the streets of England's capital, where imperial wealth had steadfastly refused to trickle down to the poor and destitute. Such impressions were reinforced in the popular novels of Charles Dickens, where London's abject underbelly found vivid expression. His critique of greed and the inhumanity of wealth, *A Christmas Carol*, might well be the most famous ghost story in world literature. Marx sought liberation through the removal of religion and superstition from the minds of the proletariat, but the backlash led to a revival of interest in spiritualism, seances and esoteric traditions from the near and far east. The old gods and departed ancestors proved mightily resistant to socialist materialism.

Beyond the many screen adaptations of period ghost stories, TV spookery has gravitated to the modern era, undercutting twentieth-century rationalism with the persistence of the supernatural in works like *The Stone Tape* (1972) and *Symptoms* (1974). Transplanting horror scenarios into the present day necessitated a re-engagement with the British landscape and a reinsertion of horror tropes into it. Chilling effects, the best directors discovered, could be created using very little in the way of costume or trickery. Director Jack Clayton discovered this as far back as *The Innocents*, his 1961 adaptation of Henry James's *Turn of the Screw*, whose aura of unease and ratcheting psychological intensity was taken up by directors such as Jonathan Miller (*Alice in Wonderland*, 1966; *Whistle and I'll Come to You*, 1968) and Lawrence Gordon Clark, who updated and extended the tradition of the Yuletide ghost story.

Sometimes one can't help imagining things.

Miss Giddens, *The Innocents* (1961)

Haunted houses have become the kitsch stock-in-trade of horror movies, making the transition to fairground ghost trains, Addams Family comedies and Scooby-Doo cartoons in which pesky kids unmask costumed crooks. But the notion of a house or mansion as a staging post for unquiet spirits is still a powerful one. *Room to Let* (Godfrey Grayson, 1950) made early use of Down Place and Oakley Court at Bray (the latter would become familiar as a location in so many Hammer pictures). The Gothic aura of menace, as a spooky doctor inexorably possesses a house and its inhabitants, was not lost on Jack Clayton.

The Turn of the Screw, a short novel published in 1898, was an odd divergence in the fiction of Henry James. With its precocious and flirtatious children; hauntings by the deceased former governess and her lover, servant Peter Quint, who may have abused the children while he was alive; and the perplexity and possible complicity of the visiting governess Miss Giddens, it reaches levels of disturbance rarely matched by James's society novels. In his 1954 opera version, composer Benjamin Britten latched on to the same sensation of malignant enchantment in one of his most spectrally haunting scores. (One of Britten's protégés at that time, James Bernard, went on to become a prolific soundtrack composer for Hammer.) Following a Broadway version of the story in 1960, Truman Capote and John Mortimer together wrote a screen adaptation, which became the follow-up to *Room at the Top* for director Jack Clayton and cinematographer Freddie Francis. Filmed at Sheffield House near Brighton, *The Innocents* (which also had its roots in a 1950 Broadway stage adaptation by William Archibald) almost single-handedly injected British film with an ectoplasmic shudder that would later become standard procedure.

Retitling James's story *The Innocents* raises the question of who, really, are the innocent ones. It's certainly not the children, Flora and Miles, who have clearly witnessed sexual shenanigans around the house between the former servants and take visible delight in watching a spider dismembering a butterfly. Incidentally, the boy who played Miles – Martin Stephens – arrived fresh from appearing as the goggle-eyed child genius David Zellaby in *Village of the Damned*, which prepared him well for his performance here. (His final film role was in *The Witches* in 1966, before he went on to train as an architect.)

Deborah Kerr, in one of the finest roles of her career as Miss Giddens, can't regain control over her charges' childlike qualities and allows Miles in particular to get the upper hand over her, even to the point of provocative flirtatiousness. In her first scene, in London for a job interview with the children's uncle, she is asked whether she has 'an imagination'. It's her imagination that gradually takes over the whole film.

Bly Manor may be 'a heaven for children', as their uncle puts it, but it rapidly becomes a hell for Miss Giddens. The grounds, as her first morning dawns, are a landscape worthy of Arthur Machen's uncanny fictions, with the statue of a Greek soldier looming near the shrubbery. Whiteness, of a piercingly bone-bright kind, is the signature (non-)colour of *The Innocents* – Clayton even introduced innovative fades to white instead of black between key scenes. Using over-lit scenes and cameras that sometimes ranged only inches from the principals' faces, he engendered an intensity that dazzles the viewer, offering a similar disorientation to that which afflicts Miss Giddens as she discovers that the children's innocence has been corrupted by the deviant public sexual acts of the now-departed nanny and manservant. There's an extraordinary moment while she's taking a tour of the estate. As she approaches a garden gate (which resembles a wrought-iron spider's web), a white butterfly flits momentarily into view, and a trail of white petals scatters in its wake. A white dove flaps past. These details flash onto the screen only for microseconds, like interferences at the edge of the eye, but they mark out the main

There's a ghost in my house: *The Innocents* (1961).

character as enchanted. White – the traditional symbolic colour of innocence – is more ambiguous here.

There are several more instances of white petals falling around the house; at the same time, Giddens learns of 'something secret, and whispery, and indecent' that has previously taken place in full view and with the knowledge of the brother and sister. The house is suddenly no protection against the harsher forces of nature: 'Rooms', the housekeeper tells her, were 'used by daylight as if they were dark woods'. Then you start to notice the tapestries hung on the walls, depicting hunting fables. Finally, Giddens herself is stalked by terrifying apparitions. First, there is the wraith-like Miss Jessel, half glimpsed hovering over an ornamental lake in the middle of a downpour. Later, as Giddens stands in front of a large bay window, with no musical warning cues Quint's face lurches into view behind the glass. It is a genuinely shocking moment, all the more so for its lack of the traditional horror trappings, and it triggers the first suspicions that all of these spooks might, after all, be Giddens's own hallucinations. What strikes me on subsequent viewings of this film is how much the glass window itself resembles a television set. Quint's materialisation activates the screen's potential to haunt and disconcert us. (In Chapter 11 I'll go into more detail about the self-reflexive relationship between the spirit world and the medium of television.)

These effects are truly ghostly, in that they seem to vanish before you've had time to register them, and you're left not quite knowing what you have seen. There are no elaborate special effects involved; instead, the focus is on creating a shiver of presence where by rights there should be none.

■

The Haunting (Robert Wise, 1963), another supernatural movie set almost entirely in a remote country mansion, contains the playbook for all the elements that would later make up the most creepy, memorable and insidious televised ghost stories. Although set in New England and adapted from 1959's *The Haunting of Hill House* by American writer Shirley Jackson, the ambience is far more British than American (reinforced by the casting of Claire Bloom as the lesbian inmate Theodora), and indeed it was filmed at the MGM-British studio at Borehamwood. The exteriors for Hill House itself were shot at Ettington Park in Warwickshire, using infra-red cameras to intensify the grain of the stonework and its leering gargoyles.

A paranormal researcher, Dr Markway, invites two women with mediumistic abilities to take part in a research project at a house that is notoriously haunted by its past, where many inhabitants have met untimely or murderous ends. Psychologically frail and adrift after the mysterious death of her mother, Eleanor Lance appears on Markway's list of likely candidates because she reported seeing poltergeist activity when she was a child.

Wise remained influenced by the late Val Lewton, the Russian-American film producer behind *Cat People*, *The Leopard Man* and others. Throughout his career, Lewton found it necessary to fall back on budget-saving measures, which led to the art of evoking terror through a few simple effects – shadows, reflections in mirrors, sound and music. 'The stories [Lewton] produced', wrote DeWitt Bodeen in a 1963 magazine article on the producer, 'are dramatizations of the psychology of fear. Man fears the unknown – the dark, that which may lurk in the shadows . . . That which he cannot see fills him with basic and understandable terror.'[5] *The Haunting* is an essay in achieving maximum effect with minimum spectacle. Examples include the lingering shot that Eleanor sees in the night of the scary face in some carved oak panels; the infernal pounding noise heard by the two women on their first night in the house; the steamy breath the actors exhale as they enter localised 'cold spots' in the passageways; and a wooden door bending inwards, pushed by some unknown force (the door was made of thin laminated wood and pressed from behind by a stagehand with a timber joist).

Nelson Gidding's script even embeds lines that appear to endorse the Lewton/Wise philosophy. 'Ghosts are a visible thing,' says Dr Markway in his welcoming speech to the two women. Ghosts instil an unseen, shivering terror, but they have visible manifestations – which is what suits them ideally to the medium of film and television. The rooms and corridors for this waking nightmare, constructed by Elliot Scott, are famously disorientating. 'Add up all the angles, and you get one big distortion,' Markway observes. A mishmash of moving camera viewpoints, 'incorrect' reverse angles, widescreen shots and the deliberate use of a defective anamorphic 30 mm prototype lens combine to give the building's interiors a disjointed and claustrophobic perspective. The rooms seethe with too much furniture, tangly William Morris textiles and oxidised mirrors. These reflective surfaces constantly distract your vision throughout the movie, building up the dread expectation that something awful is going to appear in them, as well as suggesting the way in which Eleanor's fraying mind holds reality at one remove. 'Nothing in the house appears to move until you see it from the corner of your eye,' comments Theodora – a sentence that would go on to instruct many genuinely eerie supernatural films and television programmes that came after.

As we've already seen in folk-horror examples such as *Robin Redbreast* and 'Murrain', here also was the required character of the disconcerting local guardian, suspicious of the urban visitors ('You city people think you know everything') and who knows more than they let on – in this case, the husband-and-wife caretaker team of Mr and Mrs Dudley. In these respects, *The Haunting* cemented many of the elements that would feed into British big- and small-screen ghost stories in the future.

■

The opening sequence of *Symptoms* (José Ramón Larráz, 1974) sets the tone for a movie that, like *The Innocents*, is all about ambience. We're looking through the windscreen, driving through a long, over-grown driveway, as if discovering some overgrown Mayan temple complex. It's autumn – that time in southern England when the trees are still heavy with the last leaves of summer, but the ground is also covered with the leaf-fall. The morning air is frosty, the sunlight is harsh. Morning sunbeams through trees and mist. Dawn chorus salted with crow squawks. Pan across a gloomy ornamental lake – the kind of pond that looks like it would suck the unwary to their doom, like the fated children in *Lonely Water*, the notoriously malignant Central Office of Information film from 1973 narrated by Donald Pleasence. The English riverbank idyll, turned stagnant and chilly. It is a place of death, of frozen stasis, where there's no wind to lift the fallen leaves from the riverbanks. A dour, Charon-like groundsman rows up and down the black mottled lake.

Fourteen years after *The Innocents*, *Symptoms* wallowed in this pure atmosphere. As we'll see in Chapter 14, the English country house is often portrayed as an island detached from the outside world. These buildings become architectural time capsules, repositories of countless heirlooms, memories and secrets – an atmosphere, in other words, in which ghostliness can flourish in rural England. In *Symptoms*, a pair of female friends, possibly on the verge of starting an affair, arrive at a closed-up mansion. It's a deathly place where time stands still: they open up a Victorian sitting room with caged stuffed birds and an inevitably stopped clock. 'Life, again,' says the morbid Helen (Angela Pleasence, daughter of Donald), as she winds the grandfather clock. She has just returned from a boring work trip to Switzerland – Geneva, to be precise – which might put us immediately in mind of the Mary Shelley/Villa Diodati provenance of English Gothic horror. Helen experiences heightened sensations: she can hear things nobody else can (an owl in the woods) and fills the house with the aroma of a mysterious herb growing in the grounds. Anne contents herself with nosing round the house's opulent yet faded glories. Brady, the shifty groundsman seen earlier in the rowing boat, adds an extra disconcerting presence.

The house's interiors are lit with a sickly, wan gleam. It creates faint, gauzy halos around the electric lamps, as if the air is full of dust motes. The friends warm their evenings with a real fire and candles. Out in the real world of 1974, as Larraz was shooting his movie, ordinary British households were being forced to do the same during the energy strikes and power cuts of the Heath era.

In the heyday of Hammer horrors, the camera rarely got close enough to a human face for it to occupy the screen completely. In *The Mummy* (1959), the entire film is a tease in which Christopher Lee's bandaged and muddied visage, with its expressive eyes peeping or scowling through holes in the gauze, is progressively shown in more and more intimate detail. The year before, Lee's classic Dracula had also flapped onto the big screen, fangs bared, dripping crimson with stage blood. The full-screen facial close-up was reserved for the ultimate revelation of horror and deformity, while most action was kept at a convenient viewing distance, under an invisible proscenium arch. *Symptoms* is composed of many head shots, especially of the two female protagonists, playing a delicate cat-and-mouse game with each other, friends in some unspecified way, without fully reaching an understanding. There's even a nod to the 'Peter Quint moment' in *The Innocents*, when Brady's leering face appears at the window of the house.

Symptoms derives its title partly from the headaches Helen keeps suffering. As well as the pain, uncomfortable memories hover at the fringes of her consciousness: flickerings, unseen yet latent in the crackling fire, of the empty rowing boat, the leaf-covered water, the ladder leading to the sealed attic, the dried flower posy attached to the bicycle. Add to this her possessive and jealous behaviour around Anne, especially when the latter's ex-husband turns up, and her erotic lesbian fantasies, and the pressure cooker is set to explode. The house turns out to be a psychic crime scene, but the real reason for returning to *Symptoms* is to be immersed in its ever-present edginess, and to appreciate the superlative rendering of the moist, chill English climate (credit here to cinematographer Trevor Wrenn) and the fleeting presences half seen in mirrors.

Symptoms was set in the present day, but in a rarefied and out-of-time setting that alluded to the Gothic, Romantic origins of the traditional ghost story. At the same time, though, ghosts were also piggybacking on the social demographic by relocating from castles and manor houses to the blander regions of the suburbs. Britain's suburban drift had been gathering pace since the 1960s and was in full spate by the early '70s, as aspirational nuclear families fled the city centres or abandoned them to largely poor and immigrant communities. Suburban housing, meanwhile, was a less edgy substitute for tower-block living. Typically featuring architecture harking back to Tudor or Georgian heritage, suburban towns and housing estates occupied a transition zone between city and country, and were frequently built on old farmland, burial grounds or former aristocratic property. A few decades after the Second World War, suburbia was fully mapped into Britain's cultural geography. As one social historian of the period has noted, 'The fact that so many sitcoms [in the 1970s] were set in greater Metro-land, from *Bless This House* and *Happy Ever After* to *Butterflies* and *George and Mildred*, was a testament to its newfound place at the centre of Britain's physical and imaginative landscape.'[6] Add to that list *The Good Life*, a comedy of manners juxtaposing two couples, lower- and upper-middle-class neighbours in a semi-rural street that they have each chosen for very different reasons: Tom and Barbara are rat-race dropouts living a bohemian dream of eco-self-sufficiency, while Margo and Jerry are commuter-belt social climbers. The fact that they have ended up having to get along merely illustrates the all-pervasiveness of the British dream of retreating from the city.

The drain of urbanites from metropolises like London, Manchester and Birmingham between the 1960s and the '80s led to streets upon streets of newbuild housing distinctive only in its lack of architectural inspiration. Suburban sprawl was an in-between non-place badly in need of re-enchantment – above and beyond the gnomes and other faery-land effigies that dotted the gardens. Perhaps this in part explains the gravitation of ghosts to blank suburbia. 'The Exorcism' (Don Taylor) – an episode of the BBC's *Dead of Night* series from November 1972 – is a classic of this mode. Bored married couple, husband away at work, housewife confined to the house . . . and an impish spirit that infiltrates her sleep. The house may be a 1970s travesty of spangly wallpaper and brown and orange paint-work, but a traumatic memory is burned into the fabric of this historic building which even a vicar's exorcism can't dislodge. Later in the decade, TV spirit-hunter Maurice Grosse would produce real-life documentary reports on ghost sightings in similar dwellings. 'The Exorcism' happened to bring the supernatural into a tale of malaise in the stockbroker belt that would supply the subject matter of scores of realist dramas from this decade. But even as this episode was being broadcast, another BBC crew was in the process of filming a one-off production that took the premise of a building replaying the imprint of tragedy, amplified it via the imagery of science fiction, and made for one of the all-time greats of uncanny television.

■

The Stone Tape was the BBC's 'festive' 'Play for Today' offering on 25 December 1972, fixing a Christmas ghost-story tradition that continued for much of the rest of the decade and beyond. It sits awkwardly among the costumed Victorian and Edwardian horrors, but effectively gave permission for future episodes to take place in the present day, or some semblance of it.

When narratives engage with paganism and ritual, actions get stuck in a loop. This continues indefinitely, or at least until disrupted by conscious will – or by carefully deployed modern technology. The clash of ghosts with electricity is played out to devastating effect in *The Stone Tape*, which focused on the archetypal conflict of rationality versus human sacrifice with the forensic precision of a magnifying glass held to the sun.

The Stone Tape was another triumph for screenwriter Nigel Kneale. Like episodes of *Doctor Who* from the same period, its nearly windowless Television Centre interiors feel claustrophobic and constricted. The action occurs in both the minimalist-chic apartment of Peter Brock (Michael Bryant), head of research at Ryan Electrics, and the grisly chambers of the country house the company has leased in order to develop a new audio recording technology that will give it an economic edge over its Japanese competitors.

Let's just consider that aspect for a moment. Nineteen seventy-two was a watershed year in Britain. It was the year after decimalisation and the disappearance of a currency of shillings, farthings and half-crowns that dated back to the Georgian era, and the year before the referendum on joining the (proto-EU) Common Market, a decision supported by the incumbent Conservative government. Unemployment figures jumped, and there were the first in a series of power cuts and strikes that characterised the following couple of years, as the oil crisis in the Middle East kicked in. This was a time of national instability, when, with immigration rising, institutions and old ways of life were tangibly altering and even disappearing.

At such times of change, a culture will often reach back in time for reassuring certainties. Towards the end of the Victorian era, when industrialisation had comprehensively changed the face of the English countryside and its cities, a counter-movement began to reconnect with folk culture and the old ways of life. Radicals such as William Morris and the collectives that sowed the seeds of institutions like the National Trust, the Society for the Protection of Ancient Buildings, and English Heritage were appalled by the shrinking of green space and the demolition of historical architecture to make way for railways, factories, canals and slum housing. Preservation was linked to radical politics.

Preservation is always self-contradictory. Revolutionaries and utopians often wish to return to a lost age of perfection rather than imagine an unknowable future. From Blake's dark satanic mills to the fiery forges of Sauron and Saruman in Tolkien's *Lord of the Rings*, British culture frequently depicts industry and technology as enemies, destroying and encroaching upon the last remaining patches of natural beauty. Old places and buildings thus become repositories of history: they literally trap time. In *The Stone Tape*, an instant in time is trapped in the foundations, and humans develop a method of extracting this recorded information. But this Promethean discovery comes at a price.

An old country house, Taskerlands, built or renovated in the Victorian era and requisitioned by American forces, has stood derelict since the war. (The house's exterior was filmed at Horsley Towers in Surrey, once owned by Ada Lovelace – daughter of Lord Byron,

and a pioneer of Regency computer engineering alongside Charles
Babbage.) More recently, builders have refused to work there, believing it to be haunted. Brock and his experimental research team of
Open University-styled colleagues arrogantly believe in technology,
and in their own rampant masculinity. Like mortal Time Lords,
they banter phrases like 'Randomised . . . with an accelerated uncertainty principle', 'Direct injection of sound and vision', 'No need
for the TV set – no box, not even a visor – the thirteen-channel
earring!' When the team sets up in Taskerlands, they find that the
dark stone chamber in the basement is a remnant of the house's
ancient foundations dating back to the Saxon period. The research
team hears unexplained noises in this stone room – the sound of
running footsteps, followed by a piercing scream. Enquiries in the
local village reveal that a maid died in the room in the last century
and that a priest had once performed an exorcism upon it. Clearly,
it hasn't worked. The 'duppys in the stone' – a phrase the pub landlady remembers being used by an African American soldier – have
clung on.

The team members develop their own theories about the mystery, tailored to their own advantage. The stone blocks have acted
as a 'tape', a form of psychic recording technology. Can they crack
its code and incorporate it into a music reproduction system that
will revolutionise the recording industry? Ghosts, says Brock, are 'a
mass of data waiting for the correct interpretation'. Jill Greeley (Jane
Asher), the nervous, superstitious member of the team, who has previously been involved in a subservient relationship with Brock, suggests that the recorded sensations are some kind of interface with the
brain's electrical nerve endings, triggering a psychic response. Brock
tries to overload the system, but the plan backfires, leaving some of
his team with concussion. His superiors order the research to pivot
towards designing a new prototype washing machine.

Jill, meanwhile, proves to be a scientist with a sixth sense, or an
above-average sensitivity to the spirit world. She realises that there

are deeper layers underneath the haunting they have experienced; the stones have recorded older deaths, with a subliminal flash of ancient stones suggesting that this loop stretches back into prehistory. 'It's about something very deep – a core . . .' she tells Brock, who angrily dismisses her from the project. Ignoring his stern banishment, she plunges into the heart of the older recordings and dies in their grip, becoming the latest high-fidelity presence imprinted on the stone tape.

'Something very deep – a core': Kneale was surely telling us something with this phrase. Something secretly buried underneath the visible surface of things, something with the power to speak about the past, revealing a truth about the myth of origins. Folk traditions, which often rely on repetition and refrain, deliver a polished version of tunes sung and sung again over time immemorial. *The Stone Tape* imagines a direct connection with a historical event through the reiteration of its essentials, mediated by the geographical place where it is experienced.

∎

Those pagan spirits and their birthrights. Peter McDougall, a Scottish screenwriter, grew up in Glasgow and worked as a docker. His earliest effort at writing, *Just Another Saturday*, drew on his experiences as a drum major in Orange marches and explored sectarian divides. Although admired in the BBC's 'Play for Today' office, its sensitive subject matter meant that it was not made initially, although director John Mackenzie finally filmed an acclaimed version for 'Play for Today' in 1975. The Orange march is a prime example of a traumatic historic event in the British Isles continuing to have a searing and controversial effect in the present day. McDougall applied a similar notion, but threw the historical net much wider, in *Tarry-Dan Tarry-Dan Scarey Old Spooky Man*, made in 1976 and broadcast only once, in May 1978. Directed by John Reardon, this forty-seven-minute drama again played with the notion of Britannic pagan spirits haunting one particular charged geographical spot and waiting to reclaim it and perpetuate its cycle of regeneration.

To tarry is to linger, loiter; those who tarry are waiting for something. In this insular village (unnamed, but filmed in Port Isaac on Cornwall's northern coast), Tarry-Dan is a taciturn, white-bearded tramp who has become the butt of taunts from local youths. Among the group of teenage boys constantly testing out each other's masculinity, sixteen-year-old Jonah Grattan seems strangely drawn to the old man, transfixed and unsettled by his sentinel-like presence. Jonah's dreams have been consumed by nocturnal visions of the medieval stained-glass figures in the local church, by warlike violence and fire. His schoolteacher, Mr Johnson, has taught him the local legend: that the village was once a prosperous medieval maritime city, before it was attacked by sea raiders, who were aided in breaching the walls by some mysterious force. He also learns that the etymology of his own name derives from '*gratneit*', a Celtic word meaning 'night guard'. On all sides, the snare of history seems to be pulled tighter.

When Jonah and his mates end up in a cave, speculating about the cavemen that might once have lived there and the rituals that prehistoric teenagers had to undertake in the dark in order to reach adulthood, Jonah becomes increasingly nervous and aggressive. Running through the dark on a stormy January night, he confronts Tarry-Dan in the church, where the old man breaks his silence to reveal he is a spirit '*gratneit*', part of a centuries-old line of guardians of the local people. Realising that Tarry-Dan is his direct ancestor, Jonah bludgeons him to death, but is unwittingly committing a ritual sacrifice that allows the older guard to pass on and Jonah to take his preordained place as the next 'scarey old spooky man'. It's time for a new guard to tarry a while. That's the thing about myths and the humans that come into contact with them: they are forever doomed to repeat themselves.

10

Ghosts of Christmas Past

Whistle and I'll Come to You, The Stalls of Barchester, The Tractate Middoth, A Warning to the Curious, Lost Hearts, The Ice House, The Treasure of Abbot Thomas, The Ash Tree, The Signalman, Stigma, The Woman in Black, 'The Devil of Christmas'

> The modern rebirth of the Christmas ghost story tradition: no longer told around the fire, but emanating from the eerie glow of the television screen beside the Christmas tree.[1]

Winter 1972 was the high-water mark for ghostly tele-fantasy. Between late November and the new year the BBC transmitted their *Dead of Night* series of modern-day hauntings, the M. R. James adaptation *A Warning to the Curious*, and *The Stone Tape* on Christmas Day. By this time, television was becoming good at the macabre. Learning from *The Innocents*, and rejecting the screaming bloodbaths of the Hammer and Amicus stables, the small screen refined the kind of pure atmosphere and haunting-by-suggestion that we've already examined in certain feature films.

Montague Rhodes (M. R.) James (1862–1936) is revered as a master purveyor of supernatural tales. His books remain in print, and even today there are entire podcast series devoted to analysing his short fictions. Actor, broadcaster and screenwriter Mark Gatiss, who made a BBC documentary about James in 2013 that was broadcast on Christmas Day, immediately following the version of *The Tractate Middoth* that Gatiss adapted and directed, calls his writings 'the finest and most frightening ghost stories in the English language'.[2]

An old Etonian who began writing his short stories while still a schoolboy, James lived the kind of life he reproduced in many of his stories – an antiquarian academic, at home in the dark, wood-panelled confines of a dingy library or church sacristy. While cataloguing the book collection at the Fitzwilliam Museum in Cambridge (a Herculean task he undertook largely while still an undergraduate at the university), James was exposed to manuscripts and illustrations depicting demons, bloodthirsty martyrdoms and enigmatic alchemical iconography. As Gatiss discovered when he inspected the Fitzwilliam's documents, there are certain examples of devils seizing the souls of sinners and gleefully transporting them away for an eternity of torment that seem directly to have fed James's visceral descriptions of fierce yellow eyes, horned bodies and savage teeth. James's arachnophobia also played into several of the stories, particularly the terrorising insectoids of 'The Ash Tree' and the spiders accompanying the deceased man in 'The Tractate Middoth'.

James's short stories formed the backbone of the BBC's legendary 'Ghost Story for Christmas' strand, which was produced in an unbroken sequence between 1971 and 1978 (although the 'canon' extends back to 1968 and has been revived sporadically since 2005). These films were never intended for more than a single transmission, which makes their attention to detail all the more remarkable. They are chilling screen-mares, designed to pelt the psyche with half-seen, subliminally macabre horrors. James knew about the intellectual fantasies that can plague the overworked minds of bachelor academics and reclusive autodidacts all too well. Mostly adaptations of his *Ghost Stories of an Antiquary* (first published in 1904), but with one very special exception from the oeuvre of Charles Dickens, the BBC versions are full of eccentric, foolish antiquaries, secrets unlocked from ancient grimoires and ghostly guardians of accursed spaces. Bastions of science, enlightenment and rationalism become swamped with night sweats and fever dreams, isolated sounds and unsettling silences, malevolent survivals from pagan times. James himself, who hated arithmetic and science at school and held strong Christian convictions all his life, was an inheritor of the world that late-Victorian capitalism and science had left behind – one whose soul and inner life were on the wane. The lamps of innovation were eating up the shadows where the unexplained still lurked. A haunted world, on the other hand, was one that still retained the possibility of mystery. Perhaps that was even more important to an academic and lifelong bachelor who rarely strayed outside his regular haunts of Eton College, Cambridge University and the Fitzwilliam Museum.

Frequently making use of eerie outdoor locations and dimly lit heritage interiors, the BBC's retellings of James's tales form a series of tableaux captured on grainy film stock that retains the foxed, cracked quality of a dusty oil painting. Remote country houses and libraries are shrouded in a stillness that is broken only by ticking clocks, a sense that time is standing still and sprouting mould. Landscapes lidded by low cloud; interiors shadowed and half lit. There is a feel of the dog days between summer and autumn, or between autumn and winter. In *A Warning to the Curious* (1972), England is in the midst of an economic slump (announced on a newspaper's front page), and the sense of enervation in the remote Norfolk village of Seaburgh is palpable.

James once wrote that in concocting a ghost story, the principal characters should be 'introduced in a placid way, undisturbed by forebodings, pleased with their surroundings; and in this calm environment let the ominous thing put out its head'.[3] His stories gain their effectiveness because their atmospheres of horror and suspense are achieved with impressively minimal means – a combination that has uniquely transplanted itself to television. As in *The Innocents*, with its single tear on a blotting pad, the tiniest objects or traces of activity can activate the chill factor – special effects with a low impact on the licence-payer's tariff, such as two flowers slowly stiffening (*The Ice House*), rumpled sheets on an unused bed (*Whistle and I'll Come to You*), or even an open railway carriage door, through which, in *A*

Warning to the Curious, a porter tries to usher an invisible passenger. In 'The Exorcism', part of the BBC's *Dead of Night* series, it's the lights going out, a haunting baroque melody on a clavichord, a stopped clock, doors and windows that refuse to budge.

Through the 1970s and into the '80s, the televisual spooky tale became refined and rarefied, via the eight episodes of the BBC series *Supernatural* (1977), to its essence as adult *Jackanory* fireside yarn. Over the years, such seasoned actors as Michael Bryant (1980), Robert Powell (1986) and Christopher Lee (2000) have been installed in classic panelled-library settings to retell James's short stories, relying solely on intense readings, well-placed props and the occasional impressionistic sighting of an actor or two in the background. Bryant (one of the leads in *The Stone Tape*) particularly excelled as a narrator who seems faintly rattled by his own recitations.

Eventually, the BBC even solicited ghost stories from its own viewers, leading to the early-1980s series *West Country Tales* (1982–3). 'Based on an experience sent in by . . .', these half-hour episodes dipped into the postbag and dramatised weird, unexplained events and apparent hauntings or visitations described by members of the public. By commissioning these tales, the BBC (and ITV, in their series *Worlds Beyond* (1986–8), consisting of adaptations of accounts from the Society for Psychical Research archives) returned the ghost story to the realm of confidences shared among strangers, via the medium of the screen.

■

Whistle and I'll Come to You (Jonathan Miller, 1968) was the first, unofficial BBC 'Ghost Story for Christmas' and featured an unforgettable lead role for Michael Hordern. As Miller's first effort since his masterful *Alice in Wonderland* (1966), whose stuffy Victorianisms cut to the dark heart of Lewis Carroll's whimsically surreal classic (and arguably sparked off the burgeoning British psychedelic movement⁴), it came full of promise, sharing some characteristics (not least its stark black and white) while confining itself to more minimal elements.

Hordern turns in an impeccably eccentric performance as Professor Parkin, an introverted and intellectually conceited don on vacation from Cambridge University. As in many of these ghost stories, his purpose in coming out to the coast is never adequately explained; he requires rest and relaxation, brisk walks and fireside reading, but doesn't want company (the few conversations he has with his fellow guests are largely soliloquies, delivered while avoiding eye contact). With its relatively long focal lengths, the camera does not offer much wide angle around any of the action, resulting in a sense of blinkered vision. In this way the film brings the viewer inside the carapace of oddness surrounding this man, who constantly accompanies his actions with a mumbling commentary, laughing and raising his eyebrows at his own words as if performing to himself. It sets up a possible interpretation: that he is mildly insane, and that the hallucinations he experiences are evidence of that.

'Burnstow' is a fictionalised version of Felixstowe. This stretch of the Suffolk coastline is famously rich in lore and decay. Dunwich, which had been one of the largest and most prosperous ports in medieval England until a storm in the late thirteenth century tore it to shreds, was eventually swallowed up by waves and land erosion and is now just a memory on the pebbly shingle. The opening shot, of a bloated sun that might equally be the moon, casts a weird pall over the scene. The next thing we see is a white sheet being stretched taut over one of the beds in the guest house where Parkin will stay. The camera lingers on this blank sheet – is this an assertion from Miller that this is a *tabula rasa*, a new deal for the British horror film? It also reflects the peculiar blankness of the landscape where Parkin (and others in future episodes) will roam. Parkin's entry into the room is viewed in a lingering shot of the dressing-table mirror, in a clear homage to *Dead of Night*'s 'The Haunted Mirror'.

Parkin strides out, full of the joys of spring, kitted out with knickerbockers and walking stick. In a cemetery on the edge of a crumbling cliff he wanders among pagan Celtic crosses and gravestones of more recent provenance. 'Finders keepers,' he mutters, tugging a bone fragment out of the loam. Once more, a long-buried artefact is disturbed from the sleep of ages. Here the transgressive moment is specifically keyed to a sound: the rasping whistle as he blows into the bone, which is inscribed with the Latin words *Qui es iste, qui venit?* (Who is this who is coming?). As he strides back to the hotel, a hooded figure silently watches. That night, the terrors descend. It's only sleeplessness, nightmares; next morning, he is right as rain, joshing with a fellow in the breakfast parlour on the meaning of death. 'There's no broad consensus about what a ghost is, is there?' he argues. It's the argument made by all the BBC's ghost programmes. Ghosts are suggested, imagined, often signified by the most mundane of objects, sound effects or weather conditions. In *Whistle*, there is no music, and for some stretches it's to all intents and purposes a silent film. In his later nightmare, accompanied by the noise of a squishy heartbeat, Parkin is chased along a beach – but we never see his pursuer. What haunts this intellectual is precisely that invisible, inchoate presence: the persistence of the irrational.

■

'The BBC gave you the space to fail,' said Lawrence Gordon Clark, who was handed the job of directing the next in what would become the institution of the BBC's 'Ghost Story for Christmas'. Miller's *Whistle and I'll Come to You* had been a one-off, but it set the tone and pace. Gordon Clark, with colour now at his disposal, took on the eerie Victorian ghost story tradition with gusto and updated it to present-day settings. Unlike much BBC drama at the time, these were shot on film rather than video.

Gordon Clark's entry into the Jamesian world came in 1971 with
The Stalls of Barchester. M. R. James's stories frequently involved the
'masterly use or misuse of history', as Gordon Clark himself put it.
The director spent some weeks driving around England in search of
locations, eventually settling on Norwich, with its medieval cathedral and rectory. While Gordon Clark held that the only point of a
ghost story is to scare people, he recalled that in tandem with film
editor Roger Wall, he learned to apply different rules to the ghost
story from accepted film-making practice. 'You cut unexpectedly,
make people jump, rather than smoothing everything out. The great
moment, if you can achieve it, is what I call the "*Marnie* moment"
. . . when the whole audience stands up and screams.'[5] In fact, the
climactic moments were often fleetingly glimpsed, often indistinct
and silent, so that the effect was achieved far more insidiously. It was
the *absence* of melodrama that made them so powerful.

In *The Stalls of Barchester*, and in the following year's *A Warning
to the Curious*, Gordon Clark introduced an invented character, Dr
Black, to frame the narrative. Black is a somewhat smug and complacent historian, but with slightly more clubbable social skills than
Michael Hordern's professor in *Whistle and I'll Come to You*. In *The
Stalls of Barchester*, Black is listlessly cataloguing the contents of the
library at Barchester Cathedral, when he is shown a locked chest that
turns out to contain the papers of a former archdeacon, Haynes.
Black's research takes us from his own present in 1932 back to 1872,
when the supercilious Haynes arrived in town and had to endure
years of waiting to succeed Archdeacon Pulteney. Strange presences
reveal themselves to Haynes in the church, with a mind-bending
force that is accentuated by the psychedelic echo effects applied to the
choral singing. The carvings on the ends of the wooden stalls appear
to come to life; one mutates into a furry mammal under Haynes's
hand. Pulteney seems to have some kind of charmed immortality
that leaves the newcomer impatient, after several years, to take up
the position. So impatient that nothing short of murder will suffice

to clear the way for the furtherance of his career. Alone in the vicarage, with nothing but his guilt for company, he begins an 'incipient decay of the mind'. As Dr Black relives Haynes's breakdown through studying the diaries, we accompany Haynes around his increasingly menacing rectory, wandering in and out of a sepulchral darkness.

Gordon Clark adds a further refinement to James's original tale. In the course of a ramble in the local forest, we learn that the timber for the cathedral interior came from the 'hanging oak', located in a clearing associated with covert pagan ceremonies. On closer inspection, the wooden figurines resemble heathen artefacts that have infiltrated the supposedly enlightened Anglican church. Haynes's inevitable demise – foreshadowed by the mutation of another carving into a death's head skull – is a visceral disfigurement and fall, but could equally be explained away as a cat scratch and a misstep on the landing. Once again, the irrational does away with the rational, represented by a lonely, introverted, arrogantly pious (unmarried) man.

The dusty library was the most disturbing feature of a much later James adaptation, *The Tractate Middoth* (2013), directed by Mark Gatiss. From his documentaries on folk horror, occult artists and James to his work screenwriting for *Doctor Who* and various other supernatural shows, Gatiss's fascination with this genre of television has reawakened it in the twenty-first century. It is impossible to shake off the feeling of homage in this version of 'The Tractate Middoth', but as with the 1970s James adaptations, it achieves an extraordinary eeriness through simple expedients, such as dust motes floating in a deserted corner of a library (a trick that would be later copied in the US Netflix series *Stranger Things* to denote the impending presence of horror). Gatiss's scene-setting relishes the Edwardian time period and its antiquarian fustiness.

Like *Whistle and I'll Come to You*, *A Warning to the Curious* (1972) takes place on the East Anglian coast and makes similar use of its expansive blankness. A character even comments on the vista at one point, announcing that it is impossible to distinguish land from sky

– the horizon melts the two together, as in a painting by the surrealist Yves Tanguy. In his second adaptation, Lawrence Gordon Clark adeptly painted the dusty corners of English institutional life, and the strange timelessness of its neglected rural spots, onto the television screen. Much of the action of *A Warning* takes place in day-for-night conditions or at the golden hour before sunset, giving its rich, saturated colours an unearthly intensity. The matter of Britain is at stake. Like the legend of the ravens at the Tower of London – when they desert their perches, England shall fall – here James invented a myth of three crowns buried along the Norfolk shore as talismans to ward off Viking attacks.

'No digging here!' the last remaining descendant of the Ager family, which safeguards the burial place of the last remaining crown, hisses to an earlier excavator, as he starts poking about in the sand dunes with his spade. Paxton's visit, 'twelve years later', slowly penetrates to the heart of a community where pagan survivals rule the roost. Even the local vicar declares his Christian mission is almost impossible out here. As in *The Wicker Man*, which was being filmed at almost exactly the same time in Scotland, we find ourselves in an isolated domain where paganism has closed its ranks (the shot where the ghost hunches over Paxton's butchered body, facing into a streaming sunset, is very similar to *The Wicker Man*'s final shot too). Paxton's murder at the end is filmed from a distant viewpoint. In the centuries-old battle to protect England's sea defences, he is just one more piece of collateral damage, a mere speck on the broad event horizon of coastal history.

■

A horse-drawn carriage rumbles out of the mist, on country lanes bounded by muddy, ploughed-up fields, waiting to be sown anew. A lonely flute starts up the motif heard throughout *Lost Hearts* (1973), breathy echoes of a pagan voice through the mists of time.

Eleven-year-old young gentleman Stephen is arriving at the remote country seat of Mr Abney, his middle-aged cousin, who welcomes the lad with uncommon enthusiasm. Introducing himself as an enthusiastic amateur scholar with interests in alchemy and history, Abney is particularly interested in Stephen's age. He repeatedly asks for confirmation that he will soon be twelve and calls on his house-keeper to feed him well, so it's clear Stephen is being fattened up for some secret purpose.

From the gardens to the wilderness, nature out here bristles with vague threat. Right up against the camera lens, Abney's secateurs snip off a sprig of borage, the herb traditionally added for centuries to claret or port to bring courage and happiness. Later, when Stephen is out in the fields flying a kite, with Ralph Vaughan Williams's *English Folk Song Suite* on the soundtrack, the trees and bushes appear to whisper to him, undead voices rustling through the foliage. Stephen catches sight of a girl's washed-out face around the estate.

Apart from a split-second glimpse of a bleeding chest ravaged to the ribs, the horrors in *Lost Hearts* are all cloaked in smiles. Abney chuckles at his coming misdeeds; then there's the demented grin of the ghost of Giovanni, a Gypsy boy taken in by Abney more than ten years before. He finally makes his gruesome appearance to the haunt-ing strains of his hurdy-gurdy. The dead children, victims of Abney's attempts to achieve immortality, are returning zombies, conscious enough of their own fate to warn the new boy and to exact revenge on their cheerful murderer. The undead Giovanni is surely one of the most ghoulish, gruesome visions in the entire history of British horror television: the deceptive tinkling drone of his hurdy-gurdy, the over-grown fingernails and startling zombie eyes, the wheyish grey–green face with its impassive, threatening grin. Tracing its origins in the ghastly materialisations of Quint in *The Innocents*, the undead visage, confronting the lens and filling the TV screen, produces nightmares.

Jumping ahead five years to *The Ice House* (1978), we find a similar cold-hearted bid for immortality. In the hands of writer John Bowen (also responsible for *Robin Redbreast*) and director Derek Lister, the story takes place in a nominal present day, although its setting in a secluded country-house spa gives it a flavour of yesteryear. Clovis and Jessica, the unnerving brother–sister duo who run the spa, conduct their business with the aim of helping people get through life, but like so much of what they convey to visitor Paul, their manner is more graveside than bedside. 'Our guests come in search of peace,' says Clovis, in one of many sentences tinged with menace.

The frozen theme also applies to the country-house ambience, upsetting the common portrayal of an English dream of easeful leisure away from the urban sprawl. Tea is taken on the lawn in a chill summer light. At the spa, the passive, indolent lifestyles lead to stasis and paralysis. 'One pays for it,' says one character of the experience, in another deathly double entendre. Out in the real world, since November 1978 Britain had been suffering an unusually cold snap, and when *The Ice House* was broadcast at Christmas that year, it was effectively a prologue to the coldest winter for sixteen years, a national infrastructure cryogenically frozen by strike action and the politically disastrous Winter of Discontent.

■

In 1974's M. R. James 'Ghost Story for Christmas', *The Treasure of Abbot Thomas*, the camera woozily follows a path underground, through a sinister portal in a cathedral churchyard. Seeking buried treasure deep in a subterranean passageway, the Reverend Justin Somerton (Michael Bryant, looking considerably older than when he appeared in *The Stone Tape* two years earlier) hacks into the stonework and unleashes 'a thing of slime . . . darkness and slime, it's an unholy thing', that recalls the creeping sludge of *X the Unknown*. Wells Cathedral and other sacred buildings in Somerset and Wiltshire are used to great effect in this chiller, which abounds with wintry sunbeams and menacing, hooded forms. One of those finally approaches the gibbering, deranged Somerton in the final scene, as the helpless vicar is left alone in his bath chair to confront his vengeful demons. Somerton's greed and hypocrisy have goaded him into excavating something that should have remained covered up for all eternity.

The stirred-up past is the basis of the episode that led off the twenty-first-century revival of M. R. James on television. *A View from a Hill* (Luke Watson, 2005), a tale in which a pair of old binoculars, discovered in a guest room of an inn, unveil hidden histories of a particular rural location. Director Watson and screenwriter Peter Harness play the story fairly straight in its depiction of the consequences of 'ransacking and rummaging all the history of the place'. Its dream sequence – brackish water, shapes in the dark and skull masks – harks back to the hallucinatory passages in the earliest entries in the 'Ghost Story' series.

■

The M. R. James adaptation of Christmas 1975 was put in the hands of playwright David Rudkin, in the year after the broadcast of his classic BBC 'Play for Today', *Penda's Fen* (discussed in Chapter 21). Here it's not the selfish actions of an individual man that bring him to his doom, but the revenge of a condemned and executed witch, Mrs Mothersole, wreaked on the descendant of a sinful landowner who apparently abused his authority in an affair with a local woman. Haughty, pious and serious by turns, Edward Petherbridge plays both Sir Richard Fell (inheriting Castringham Hall in the eighteenth century) and his father Sir Matthew (in flashbacks to 1690).

Much of the action takes place out in rural East Anglia. Pursuing themes he had explored in *Penda's Fen*, Rudkin adapted *The Ash Tree* as a fable about the Manichean struggle between the pagan/dispossessed and the Christian/powerful. The nominal inheritor of the estate, Sir Richard, is a Regency progressive and self-styled 'pestilent innovator' who wishes to rebuild the house as an Italianate country retreat. He might read racy literature like *Tom Jones*, and his fiancée Augusta might gaily hang paintings of nudes on the walls, but like Haynes in *The Stalls of Barchester*, the present Sir Richard drifts into confusion and discomfort when left alone in his house, plagued by demons dispatched by the spirit of Mrs Mothersole (whose grave is now discovered to be empty). At first her hauntings are achieved through the intense use of sound effects: the beating drums of the execution party; her ghostly scratching at the base of the tree trunk outside Sir Richard's bedroom; and the strangulated squawks and gurgles of the creepy-crawlies that inhabit the tree branches and invade Fell's bedroom at night.

As one of the magical folkloric trio of 'oak, ash and thorn', the ash tree was traditionally held to possess healing properties, as well as being cast as the pillar of the Earth in the Yggdrasil of Norse mythology. Here the tree (which actually stood in director Lawrence Gordon Clark's own garden) is weaponised by Mrs Mothersole, who sends the spiders clambering up its boughs and into Sir Richard's waking nightmares. When the tree is eventually burned to the ground by his household staff after a particularly difficult night, her corpse is revealed at its base, splayed out as a life-sized Sheela-na-gig effigy. Her unjust fate has taken the ultimate toll on the aristocratic family by snuffing out its own line. The pagans have inherited this patch of earth, at least.

■

Brimming with malevolent energy, one of the most powerful of the 1970s line of BBC period-drama ghost stories was *The Signalman* (1976). This was a version – one of the first projects by Andrew Davies, who would go on to become synonymous with adapting English costume drama on television – of Charles Dickens's short story, which had been published in the run-up to Christmas 1866 (five years after Dickens had been involved in the Clayton Tunnel

train crash, in which he witnessed the deaths of twenty-three travellers due to a signal failure). The resurgence of the supernatural in
late-Victorian fiction points to an unease with the pace of change
in the engineering revolution. In the repetitive work of a Signalman
in his solitary box, Dickens glimpsed the alienation of mechanised
labour. The Signalman's minimal physical gestures have huge effects
down the line, on the rail system and on passenger safety. Like other
Victorian campaigners against industrial spread, such as William
Morris, Dickens was profoundly concerned about the human flot-
sam and altered moral universe churned up in the wake of material progress. Railways sliced through previously unspoilt spots in
the landscape, sending the middle and upper classes speeding into
forgotten rural haunts – or at least chuffing past them for a few
seconds. In *The Signalman*, a bride, falling from a railway carriage,
appears to be the victim of spectres awakened by the train's chilling
whistle shrieks.

Most of *The Signalman* occurs in the crepuscular shadows of a railway cutting in an undisclosed but apparently remote part of England.
Dickens's narrator calls the place an 'unnatural valley', and here (it
was filmed on a stretch of the Severn Valley Railway at Birchen
Coppice, near Kidderminster, in October 1976) the long, straight,
deep vale of shadow, with the vibrations of the wind causing the
overhead telegraph wires to act as a 'wild harp', seems too uncanny to
be real. A brumal autumn light, blue–black, and the sinister red lamp
attached to the outer face of the tunnel's mouth suffuse the screen.

In what is essentially a two-hander played off between 'the
Traveller' and 'the Signalman', both characters are equally mysterious
to the viewer. The Signalman – a fascinating, nervy performance by
Denholm Elliott – appears stiff and wary at first, gradually warming
to the Traveller's repeat visits for tea and a chat by his glowing coal
fire. As they talk, the Signalman carries out his mechanical duties –
throwing a few levers and switches, responding to the electrical warning bells that ding and hum in his tiny signal-box home. His dark

domain – with the tunnel mouth like some looming portal to a nebulous underworld – is lit by the discomfiting glows of the red lamp
and brazier. The fateful figure that appears at the tunnel's opening is
hardly there at all – a barely discernible shadow within the shadows.
These two men, both in their own ways confined, end up changing
places. The Traveller is the harbinger of the Signalman's death, but *he*
may end up in the cramped signal box, until he too is released by the
onrushing locomotive.

The 'score' fizzes and crackles with the raw electricity that transmits messages down the telegraph wires; the buzzing silver bell that
jolts the Signalman's nerves is beautifully rendered, and Stephen
Deutsch's electronic music drapes a membrane of menace across the
vale, connecting technology with the world beyond as profoundly as
in Dickens's original conception.

■

Folklore is a mess of survivals, half-remembered tales, traumatic
events whittled down over time and tarrying in children's songs and
nursery rhymes. But these ditties' very triteness is a function of the
cyclical process of folklore and tradition (its social manifestation) –
the way it seems to compel repetitive actions. Memories linger too in
the soil, awaiting their uncovering.

The BBC's 'Ghost Story for Christmas' 1977 told a tale of subur-
banite country dwellers – Peter, Katharine and their teenage daughter
Verity – impaled on the ley lines of destiny. *Stigma* – the last in the
sequence directed by Lawrence Gordon Clark – is set around a cottage on the edge of a megalithic stone circle. (Avebury in Wiltshire
must have been teeming with film crews around that time, as it
was also the location for HTV's *Children of the Stones*.) The fateful
unearthing gets under way in the very first scene, as a menhir is excavated from the garden by a mechanical digger. It's the tracking camera that makes the connection from the garden find to the broader

stone circle on the village green, accompanied by a clanging discord on the soundtrack.

Clive Exton, the writer of this episode, made his name working on the BBC's apocalyptic dramas, such as *Doomwatch* and *Survivors*. A similar dread hangs over the events of *Stigma*. The stone is shifted only slightly after strenuous efforts by the two men working for Katharine, but its disturbance is clearly a violation. The house shudders under an earthquake; Katharine and Verity suddenly start bleeding from previously non-existent sores. These are not the stigmata of religious martyrdom, but – judging by the damaged skeleton and knife blades that eventually emerge from the pit – a revisitation of the scars and burns of a persecuted witch. *Stigma* ventures much further into explicit body horror than any previous BBC ghost story, influenced by the more violent horror films that were being made in the US by the mid-1970s. But the idea of a lingering curse from some pagan spirit, released from its long slumber, seems indelibly British. 'We don't even know what's coming out from the earth yet,' announces the radio in Peter's cramped Citroën, ostensibly discussing the launch of the Voyager spacecraft towards unknown galaxies. As *Stigma* and other familiar dramas such as *Quatermass and the Pit* imply, there may be uncharted galaxies still lurking under our noses in undiscovered chambers. This was the age of no-punches-pulled in television drama, and *Stigma* ends as hopelessly as a post-holocaust story, with a nuclear-style wind whipping around Peter's ears as he mourns Katharine's death.

■

The ghost story reached its screen apotheosis in two adaptations of *The Woman in Black*, the 1983 novel by Susan Hill. ITV's Herbert Wise-directed version, broadcast on Christmas Eve 1989, featured the last great contribution to British screenwriting from the venerable Nigel Kneale. In its conjunction of eerie landscape, haunted house and buried secrets, it represented a pinnacle in mystery period drama. Invoking the aesthetics of the BBC's early-1970s Christmas ghost stories, and filmed on classic Eastmancolor stock, cinematographer Michael Davis brought out the white-sky bleakness of the fictional Crythin Gifford, on the north-east coast of England, and the fog-shrouded remoteness of Eel Marsh House, an empty dwelling cut off from the mainland at high tide. Wide, threatening shorelines and suspicious locals were a key ingredient, and Bernard Hepton practically reprised his role from *Robin Redbreast* as Sam Toovey, a local businessman of questionable loyalty.

In Hill's original novel, itself a pastiche/homage to Victorian/ Edwardian Gothic fiction, young solicitor Arthur Kipps (the name a direct lift from H. G. Wells's *Half a Sixpence*) is dispatched by his head office to oversee the funeral and estate of the late Alice Drablow, a reclusive widow. For his TV adaptation, Kneale swept in and changed the hero's name from Kipps to Kidd and set it in 1925 (signalled by a legal clerk who has just seen 'the new Charlie Chaplin – *The Gold Rush*'), but more significantly, as he had with *The Stone Tape* seventeen years earlier, Kneale emphasised the role of the house. The disturbing sounds and disembodied voices locked into its stonework perpetuate an older, nameless horror, but Kidd uses a combination of psychic and technological antennae to detect them. His mission to Crythin Gifford is framed as being crucial to his advancement in the law firm, but his first inkling that something is not right comes during his long train journey, where he shares a carriage with Toovey. Toovey's reply when Kidd mentions he expects to spend a few days going in and out of the house – '*Do* you now?' – is uttered by Hepton in a masterfully weighed tone of ominousness. Under Toovey's clubbability lie feelings of futility: Kidd discovers that Toovey buys and sells land as a 'hobby', with no other purpose, and that he lost his only daughter at the age of four.

The woman in black makes herself visible to Kidd at Alice Drablow's funeral (attended by no one), at the back of the church and in the cemetery as the coffin is laid to rest. Her appearance is believed to foreshadow the death of a child, and local solicitor Mr Pepperell becomes flustered when a gaggle of schoolchildren are clustered at the churchyard wall, with the dead woman's silhouette materialising on the horizon. She appears again, in a brilliant act of directorial sleight of hand, in the grounds of Eel Marsh House, when Kidd surveys the gravestones there. In a single take, we watch Kidd from a low angle as he stops for a moment and clutches his neck, as if the hairs have begun to prickle. He then whirls round, revealing the revenant's thin form materialised behind him. It's at this moment, as we see her blanched, bloodshot face in close-up, that he begins to realise that she is no solitary mourner, but a ghost. This is surely the most sinister spectre to haunt British TV since the murdered children of *Lost Hearts*.

Electric light offers a reassuring bulwark against the blackness, and Kidd gratefully cranks the handle of the outhouse dynamo to generate enough power for a day's work. Among the paperwork he discovers a primitive recording device and wax cylinders that have preserved the voices of previous inhabitants; meanwhile, out on the regularly flooded Nine Lives Causeway, he hears the commotion of stampeding horses and a carriage crashing into the sea. The notion of a ghost road plagued with alarming sounds takes Kneale on a winding course back to his lost television masterpiece, *The Road*, from 1963, in which eighteenth-century characters hear the screams of the victims of a future nuclear holocaust. Here, as Kidd deduces from his own perusal of the family papers, a trawl of Alice's wax cylinders, and the landscape, the screams are the dying cries of Nathaniel, the illegitimate son of Alice Drablow's sister Jennet. Her family adopted the child to avoid shame. Denied the chance to live as his mother, she could only watch helplessly from an upper window as he perished in the carriage accident. Jennet is the woman in black; Nathaniel is the unquiet spirit of the house. 'She', speaks the voice on the wax cylinder, 'has found ways to make me hear their calamity in the marshes . . .'

The rest of the film is entirely infected by this calamity. A poltergeist sequence is remarkable for its depiction of an active presence in
the house using nothing but static objects, sound effects and lighting. Hearing a repetitive thudding from the only locked room in
the house, there are echoes of *The Shining* as Kidd runs manically to
fetch an axe, only to find the previously firmly locked door standing
ajar. An old leather ball seems to be the culprit behind the noise,
but there is also a child's voice and a tin soldier that makes its way
into Kidd's hand. As the power goes down, the acoustic hallucination
from the accident begins again.

Kidd is rescued from this nightmare by Toovey, but he is marked
psychologically by his spell in the house. Eel Marsh House has now
burned to the ground, but the toy soldier continues to act as an
antenna, summoning the dead child. 'It's for you,' says a voice in the
middle of the night, as Kidd wakes in a cold sweat with the soldier in
his hand. The camera pans around him as he sits bolt upright in bed;

She's behind you: *The Woman in Black* (1989).

in the murky painting on the wall behind him a shadowy figure scuttles. Even though the soundtrack has previously included shrieking violins during moments of tension, this is eerie through being perfectly silent. You might even wonder if the fleeting animation within the frame was nothing but an aberration of your own vision. It's a moment far scarier than the next, when the grimacing woman in black herself almost suffocates him with his own bedsheets.

Even back in London, Kidd cannot shake free from the curse. This is a ghost that denies life to the children of any individual who comes into contact with it. Kidd sets light to the papers, burning most of his wood-panelled office in the process, but he and his family still pay the ultimate price.

The Woman in Black was adapted again in 2012, this time for the cinema by the newly relaunched Hammer Films. In Jane Goldman's adaptation, directed by James Watkins, Kipps's original name is restored and the role handed to former *Harry Potter* star Daniel Radcliffe. With its cawing crows, suspicious locals, ghostly presences, cursed dwelling, possessed and deceased children, discomfitingly silent rooms, clashing sounds of horrific historical events, macabre ornaments and automata, 'madwoman' (Elizabeth, wife of the local doctor, who has lost her son) and spiritualism, this take on *The Woman in Black* is a bingo card of ghost-film traits since the late 1960s. What's emphasised in this chiaroscuro version is the raking up of the past and the trouble it causes, with Kipps literally embedding himself in the muddy flats – the concealing murk of history – around Eel Marsh House in search of the vanished coach.

Early on in the film, he is warned against the whole thing ('Don't go chasing shadows, Arthur'), but the shadows – this is a black-clad ghost, after all – can't fail to lure him in. Despite the dark, this is the age of electric light, as well as machinery with enough horsepower to raise the dead. One of the film's most impressive moments is the dredging up of the carriage with its corpses. Watkins also extracts maximal creepiness from the scenes where Kipps is exploring the old

house and finds objects moving by themselves in the locked nursery. When Kipps is alone in the building out in the dead marshes,
there are long, silent passages where he doesn't speak, and we are with
him, uncovering the mystery at the same pace, subjected to the same
unaccountable hauntings. Where the TV version ended in tragedy,
this film manages to extract some kind of triumph, even as Kipps and
his son are killed: as he is reunited with his wife on the 'other side',
there is the sense that the curse has now been vanquished.

■

And yet the unquiet spirits of Yule have still not been exorcised.
Towards the end of the 1970s, depictions of horror and the macabre increasingly devolved into anthology series such as *Tales of the
Unexpected*, based on Roald Dahl's adult short stories, and ITV's
long-running 'Armchair Thrillers'. These episodes, mostly taking
place in contemporary settings, are clearly much loved by the *League
of Gentlemen*'s Steve Pemberton and Reece Shearsmith, whose series
of half-hour comic horror films, *Inside No. 9*, finely balance awkward
British humour with a dark seam of sick malevolence. Their 2016
Christmas special, 'The Devil of Christmas', which opened the third
season, brilliantly recreated and lampooned one such TV drama from
1977, with its studio-bound cameras, exaggerated lighting, wooden
acting and stilted script. Into this was woven a meta-narrative that
drew attention to the medium itself, with a behind-the-scenes element whose deconstructive function ended up providing the episode's unexpected, nasty twist.

A white middle-class family arrives at an Austrian chalet to celebrate Christmas, and are shown to their accommodation by the hir-
sute local landlord, Klaus (Shearsmith). The episode was filmed on
an old set at the BBC's Elstree Studios, using genuine vintage 1970s
television cameras, and we're instantly plunged into an environment of flaring candlelight, brown furnishings and half-rehearsed

hamminess. Minutes in, the picture freezes. The voice of Dennis Fulcher (Derek Jacobi), the director of the fictitious original, is discussing the production in the present day, in the manner of a DVD commentary track. At first, he points out a continuity error: the painting of a Krampus, the demon of Tyrolean folklore who visits homes and punishes bad children at Christmas time, has shifted from one wall to another between shots. The sinister threat of the Krampus slides in among the family's comic caricatures: father Julian's mansplaining; his wife Kathy's awkward relationship with her mother-in-law Celia; and their son Toby's unquestioning obedience. Kathy is unnerved to find evidence of the Krampus's nocturnal visits – boots filled with clumps of twigs; scratches on Toby's and Kathy's backs – but as in, for example, the Nigel Kneale *Beasts* episode 'Baby', the husband is insouciant and dismissive of any superstition, while the wife descends into a private paranoia, unheeded by anyone around her.

The time-slip spell woven by the finely observed period costumes, mannered camera zooms and the repeated breaking-in of the director's commentary, as he remarks on the vanity of a lead actor or the artificiality of various props, appears to be leading towards a more farcical denouement. There's a conventional, Roald Dahl-style plot twist (Kathy and Klaus, real name Simon, are having an affair and murder Julian). But then comes 'The Devil of Christmas''s final turn of the screw. The filming is over, but before the actress playing Kathy can get up from the bed, there's an extra, unscripted scene. 'Klaus/Simon' ties her to the bedposts, placing her on a plastic sheet. 'I'm Krampus!' he bellows, words that place us right inside the fear 'Kathy' must be feeling as, now a terrified actress in a vulnerable and compromised position on a closed set, she faces a psychopath in a gargoyle mask. From her stiff delivery of lines to screams of the doomed, this is a masterful and genuinely disturbing transition, one that extended and revivified the Christmas horror story with a brutality even the originals never stretched to.

Like the BBC's *Life on Mars* a decade earlier, 'The Devil of Christmas' was a kind of televisual time machine that brought us back into the world of the 1970s. In the wake of the Jimmy Savile and Rolf Harris child abuse scandals, it fed into contemporary revulsion at the darker secrets of the entertainment industry that came to light in the twenty-first century. And, as we'll discover in the next chapter, it joined a darkling tradition of haunted television in which the medium itself seemed possessed by the demons of electricity.

11

Imps in the Valves

'A Woman Sobbing', *A Child's Voice*, 'The Keeper',
Ghostwatch, 'Dead Line'

I am half in, half out the door when the battle-weary Bush
television, many years old, has an ectoplasmic seizure and
blows up. On the news at five forty-five, Alastair Burnet has
been updating the nation on the progress of the Falklands
War. It occurs in a nanosecond, like a smack of fear at the
back of the cerebral cortex – a shooting vertical triangle of
pale blue flame, smeared like film against the wallpaper
behind the television, its apex touching the ceiling. No sound
except a faint pop from the expiring valves. The picture cuts
out, and with it the pallid light it shed over the armchairs.
This is how a television gives up its ghost: a fleeting projection
of its electrostatic soul.

■

Wherever electricity has been connected, phantoms have found a
conduit. Given these early associations with attempts to contact the
'other side', it should be no surprise that the television set has been
such a strong attractor for hauntings. These may be as much aural as
they are visual. For television productions on a shoestring, the acoustic hallucination comes with a budgetary advantage. In 'A Woman
Sobbing', written by John Bowen for the BBC's *Dead of Night* series
in 1972, middle-aged housewife Jane lies awake in her new house
in rural Sussex night after night, plagued by the noise from the attic
of a weeping woman. With the assent of her husband Frank, she is

given medication, then psychiatry and finally ECT therapy to try to remedy her terrors, which draw her up to the loft in search of the origin of the noise. The expected reveal might be that a former housemaid died by jumping out of the upper window, but that never comes. Instead, the house – filmed here amid dreary autumn dampness – becomes a symbol of menopausal, loveless matrimony. It's also a good example of the way this type of drama could really turn the dry acoustics of the TV studio to its advantage. With no incidental music, the silence of the suburbs or the country retreat becomes almost a tangible presence, part of the lonely listlessness of the (usually female) protagonist. The sobbing sounds that never leave her at night grate and chafe against this silent backcloth, taking the viewer into the wife's psychosis.

The voice in the head is a classic ambiguous signal for the potentially insane, bridging the point where haunting and insanity become indistinguishable. Nineteen seventy-eight's *A Child's Voice* – another one-off late-night ghost story – features T. P. McKenna as 'the disturbing gentleman of the wireless', a nightly narrator of creepy tales. When he broadcasts a story about a magician who uses a small child as part of a disappearing act, he receives a mysterious phone call in the middle of a stormy night. 'I would prefer you to go no further with it. It troubles me a great deal,' says the shrill voice on the end of the line, before hanging up in a buzz of static. When the presenter persists in continuing his spooky yarn on air, his studio blacks out, the microphone feeds back, and he is palsied by a stroke and never finishes the story. BBC productions were now adept at evoking this kind of atmospheric, looming sense of unease, enhanced here once again by a particular emphasis on acoustic hallucinations.

The paranormal-investigating couple in 'The Keeper' (an episode of ITV's 'Spooky' *Dramarama* strand of children's programmes from 1983, written by Alan Garner) unwittingly discover ways to channel the latent voices of a run-down keeper's cottage where they plan to stay the night. Empty for several years, Beacon Lodge has a history of tragedies over the previous centuries, including shooting accidents and suicides. After positioning thermometers and tape recorders and settling down to wait with their sandwiches and thermos flasks, these amateur ghostbusters speculate that 'we convert the energy – we're transistors', and begin to feel as if it's they – an extension of their technological scanning devices – who are being hunted, not the ghosts.

■

With the radical, Halloween water-cooler special *Ghostwatch* (1992), things seemed to move beyond the mere telling of a tale to making the medium of television into . . . a spirit medium.

There have been moments in the history of all art forms, and not least television, when the medium takes an unexpected evolutionary leap. One such occurred in 1992, with a programme created by the BBC that ended up being so disturbing and disorientating that cases were reported of post-traumatic stress in children who stayed up beyond the nine o'clock watershed to watch it, and even the suicide of a teenager who had become obsessed with it.

Ghostwatch (Lesley Manning, 1992) arrived ahead of the era of reality TV in Britain (*Big Brother* on Channel 4 was still another eight years away), but the programme assumed the shape of established BBC actuality shows such as *Crimewatch* or *Comic Relief*, with a high-profile anchor (Michael Parkinson), an outside broadcast unit fronted by Sarah Greene and Craig Charles, and with Greene's real-life husband Mike Smith manning the telephone switchboard. The programme switches between studio formality, hand-held documentary and footage from CCTV cameras, combining three genres in one. Although presented as if it were a live broadcast, all the material had been pre-recorded during the previous weeks, using a script written by Stephen Volk, who has claimed to have been profoundly influenced by such unsettling films as *The Stone Tape* and *Don't Look Now*.

At times, *Ghostwatch* feels like a direct descendant of the former, with its recording and detection technologies installed in a house whose foundations appear to have malevolent memories entombed within them.

The outside broadcast unit draws up at a council house in Foxhill Drive in Northolt, in the north London suburbs, where a mother and her two daughters have been experiencing poltergeist activity. 'Dr Lin Pascoe' sits in the studio with Parky, playing the evangelical researcher to his cynical unbeliever, in a double act that is surprisingly convincing. The early sequences build up a sense of Halloween jollity: the house is decked out with the typical pumpkins and skeletons, and Greene and Charles play frivolously genial hosts. Pascoe, however, has brought along surveillance videos that she has previously recorded, in which the children endure a midnight poltergeist attack in their bedroom. Parkinson is mildly dismissive; part of the show's success is that it contains far more scepticism than horror.

The brilliantly cast, household-name TV presenters gave the whole enterprise a polished credibility and authority. Add to that the breaking of the fourth wall – the outside broadcast crew are frequently in shot, racing up and down the staircase and being addressed directly by Greene – and you have a masterful exercise in postmodern, metadimensional television. When we see footage of the camera crew loading up their van with equipment, flashing their spotlights, there is a sense that television's glare is bright enough to exorcise whatever spooks haunt the house. By the end, we'll be in darkness, groping after Greene with a thermal-imaging camera, while Parky stumbles around the remains of his smashed studio during a power cut.

Volk's original conception of *Ghostwatch* was as a six-part series. In the end, he condensed the multiple strands of his backstory down to the single programme's ninety minutes, which makes for a constant barrage of new information, gleaned either from 'members of the public' calling the BBC landlines or, in one case, a passer-by outside the house. The children veer from calm to moments of panic, and in one case teenager Suzanne is discovered by the cameras to be making some of the mysterious knocking noises herself in a cupboard. This deception appears to confirm one studio pundit's accusation that the family are 'disturbed attention-seekers'. But phenomena start to occur that cannot be explained away so easily. Suzanne is discovered with a scratched and bloodied face, and the switchboard starts to chatter – one caller tells Smith her glass coffee table suddenly smashed for no obvious reason. This fictional feedback anticipates the deluge of genuine complaints the BBC was to receive after transmission.

At several moments in the programme, the lineaments of a human figure can be discerned, behind curtains or even in the small crowd gathered outside the house, although some are so subliminal that they are only revealed through analysis of the VHS tapes afterwards. This chimes with the children's description of 'Mr Pipes', a shrouded, indistinct figure with a damaged, bloody face whom they have noticed in the house during the hauntings, and who has now been isolated in the 'glory hole' – a boarded-up cupboard under the stairs. He got his name because of the knocking sounds in the central heating pipework that have been plaguing the household.

From the on-air callers' contributions, it becomes clear that a feared child murderer, Mother Seddons, and her nephew/lodger, Raymond Tunstall, who was convicted of child assault, used to live where the house now stands. In a direct reference to *The Stone Tape*, Dr Pascoe speculates that things may have been happening on the same site 'way into prehistory'. In the climactic sequence, visual contact with the inside of the house is severed. The studio feed of the Foxhill Drive living room, where the kids are calmly playing a board game with Greene, is discovered to be decoy footage taken earlier in the evening – a ghost has got into the machine, as Greene puts it. Suddenly, the formality of the live broadcast is ruptured, the house is overwhelmed with the sound of yowling cats, there is loud knocking in the basement and the electricity surges. Back in the TV studio, a gale whips up, light bulbs pop, a rostrum camera drifts unmanned across the floor. The final shot – of Parkinson as a kind of blinded Lear in his darkened televisual kingdom, in a disarranged composition fed from an unmanned camera, with the chilling whisper of Mr Pipes over the soundtrack – is peculiarly disconcerting, as a jumble of elements such as this is so rare in a professional broadcast. There is genuine mischief at work in this scrambling of televisual reality.

Ghostwatch works so well as a piece of television because the presenters possessed exactly the type of blithe spirit, jokey tendency to dismiss the superstitious and familiarity with viewers that could suspend disbelief over a long duration. In addition, the effect was enhanced by the actuality-style filming techniques, which played with the notion of broadcast space. The TV set took on a mediumistic role, lacking only an ectoplasmic emission to convince its audience that it is displaying supernatural events. If only the BBC engineers had found a way to make viewers' sets flicker or even explode at the same time, the impact would have been incalculable.

Swinging to the opposite end of the credibility spectrum, a TV illusionist such as Derren Brown could harness the rationality of the television to debunk the notion of ghosts as a collective hallucination, as he did in his 2004 special, *Séance*. Collecting a group of young students and persuading them in barely half an hour that they are contacting the spirit of a long-dead woman who died in a suicide pact, Brown used similar technological installations – closed-circuit cameras, archive footage and explanatory asides to camera – as well as psychological persuasion tactics, to overcome the participants' natural scepticism.

Despite the long-running and increasingly slick reality-TV series *Most Haunted* (2002–19), it was not until 2018 that anyone rose to the challenge posed by such mediumistic television productions. One of the striking details about the original *Ghostwatch* was the presence of Mike Smith and Sarah Greene, a successful celebrity couple whose Thatcher-era lustre had barely been tarnished by a helicopter crash in 1988. Though injured, Smith (the pilot) and Greene survived the catastrophic drop out of the sky near Cheltenham while on their way to visit friends. At their wedding a few weeks afterwards, they radiated an almost unearthly glow. Television brought them together and seemed to throw a charmed circle around them, until Smith's death at fifty-nine in 2014.

The *Inside No. 9* episode 'Dead Line', transmitted on 28 October 2018, was performed live on the night of broadcast, and siphoned its malevolent energy from several other real-life examples of past televisual tragedies. The programme was not only a hair-raising experience, but also extended *Ghostwatch*'s fiendish manipulation of the broadcast medium itself. What starts as a studio TV drama – man finds mobile phone in cemetery, tries to contact owner – is interrupted by technical glitches, a power cut and a continuity announcer's apology. A previous episode of the series starts up instead, but its action is subverted after about a minute by the protagonists appearing in ghoulish guise. Cut to CCTV feeds from the dressing rooms, in which the creators of the series, Reece Shearsmith and Steve Pemberton, are overheard grumbling about the technical faults and sending a live tweet, which followers could see popping up on Twitter. These two strands coalesce into a third, as the studio's backstage area itself becomes a zone of suspense and horror, and scenes are intercut with archive footage of earlier accidents at the 'cursed' Granada Studios in Manchester. The studios, home to ITV's *Coronation Street*, among other shows, are rumoured to be haunted by former stars of the soap, and other ghosts have also been spotted during public tours of the premises. These – a young girl and her mother – are briefly glimpsed as phantoms during certain scenes in 'Dead Line'. Comedian Bobby Davro is seen in a clip from a live 1992 episode of the game show *Public Enemy Number One*, in which he keels over while locked in a pillory and smashes his face on the studio floor. There's also an extract from a news report on the fire in a Granada warehouse that destroyed costumes and props from the series *Jewel in the Crown*. The episode's mangling of television's dramatic conventions was clearly inspired by the anarchy of *Ghostwatch*, but went a step further in suggesting imps lurking in the crevices of the medium. It was the perfect analogue response to the age of digital TV, in which a new retelling of Shirley Jackson's *The Haunting of Hill House* (Mike Flanagan) – streamed via Netflix in 2018 – was filmed with the same cookie-cutter lushness as a costume drama like *The Crown*. 'Dead Line' flayed the artifice of television itself and allowed its malevolent, ethereal spirits – lurking in its glowing coils since the first cathode rays were warmed up – to be unleashed.

THE VINTAGE LENS

12

Brush Off the Dust

Fingerbobs, Bagpuss, Dreamchild, Finding Neverland,
Goodbye Christopher Robin, Mary Poppins Returns

'These hands were made for making, and making they must do.' At around five or six years old, my kids suddenly became obsessed with my DVDs of *Fingerbobs* and *Bagpuss*. It gave me another chance to become immersed in these folksy children's television creations from that interesting moment in the early 1970s when the image of folk started to go all dusty and parochial.

Fingerbobs (1972) was a cornucopia of whimsical storytelling led by the slightly intimidating 'Yoffy' (Rick Jones), whose piratical black beard had already been sighted in episodes of *Play School*. In the Blitz spirit of wartime mend and make do, he whipped up a fantastical finger-puppet menagerie from coloured paper, string, glue and kid gloves: Fingerbobs the mouse, Flash the tortoise, Scampi, Gulliver and a hedgehog named Prickly Friend. These DIY fables were filmed in a grainy BBC Schools and Colleges ambience that served the folk arrangements of the accompanying songs very well.

The series creators were Michael and Joanna Cole, visionaries of the utopian age of children's television, who also stitched together *Ragtime* (a white-elephant stall of sketches and skits, with woollen sock puppets and presenters in chunky-knit sweaters, that ran from 1973–5 and is now wiped) and the legendary minimalist cartoon *Bod* (1975). Michael Cole was one of *Fingerbobs'* songwriters and devised the music along with Michael Jessett, a guitarist who had been involved with previous BBC initiatives in children's programming, including the album *Time and Tune* (BBC Records, 1971). This was music that was intended to be sung and acted along to in primary schools. In the universe of today's output for kids, it sounds extraordinarily avant-garde folky, composed in the altruistic hope of unlocking children's imagination and stimulating their sense of wonder. The album sleeve notes spoke of 'the magic and mystery of the unknown . . . pure nostalgia, the best kind of longing, the poetry that lingers in us all . . . explore the world the story sings about, the world of geography, of folk-lore, even of magic'. The lasting appeal of programmes like *Fingerbobs* and *Bagpuss* is that they used cheap and cheerful methods to introduce children to the adventure of living.

Bagpuss – the invention of Oliver Postgate's and Peter Firmin's legendary cottage industry Smallfilms – is deeply saturated with ghostly echoes of the previous decades of collecting and reviving traditional folk music, full of songs, nursery rhymes and lyrics set to ballads and rustic old tunes. Each episode turns on an old item or fragmentary relic that has been brought into Emily's antique shop. At first unidentified, it is then gradually unravelled or mended by singing its history and identity into being – almost a metaphor for the whole process of folk revival itself.

Professor Yaffle, the 'wise' old woodpecker, purports to be the authority on all the antiques, but like many professional folk historians of yore, he often makes wrong assumptions about their provenance based on conjecture and his own self-importance. *Bagpuss*'s resident singer-storytellers, Madeleine the rag doll and Gabriel the toad, are the ones who breathe life into all the broken fragments. They were voiced by Sandra Kerr and John Faulkner, real-life folkies who had been associated with Ewan MacColl and Peggy Seeger's hard-line Critics Group in the 1960s.

What I marvelled at, rewatching the series with a critical eye, is how subtly subversive it is; how it adheres to the spirit of folk as an alternative people's history and benignly anarchic force, upsetting the normal order of power and reversing stereotypical tales. At the end of an episode entitled 'The Frog Princess', the fairy-tale princess kisses her frog, but he doesn't change into a prince; instead, she is transformed into a frog herself, renouncing her royal status to live happily ever after as a lowly beast. In 'The Owls of Athens', the titular birds are great singers but become greedy to be rewarded for their talents, and their singing voices are confiscated by the moon – a cautionary tale, perhaps, for anyone seeking to make excessive cash out of the people's music (Steeleye Span, for instance, were enjoying their glam-rock-inspired commercial high-water mark with 'All Around My Hat' at exactly the same time as *Bagpuss* was transmitted). 'The Fiddle' draws on the common folk tale of a violin that drives its player and audience into uncontrollable fits of dancing – a legend also invoked by Kate Bush in 'Violin', from her 1980 album *Never for Ever*.

Being a Smallfilms production, *Bagpuss* had an endearingly home-made, crafts-y feel; the hand-drawn illustrations for the songs, for instance, are pretty shoddy, washed-out watercolours and scribbles. But what a world away from the junior entertainments on offer today, with their garish colour schemes and sense of having to compete for their audience's fickle attention span. The thought of anything with similarly encoded mild subversion being aimed at today's children is but a distant dream.

Bagpuss's sepia-toned title and credits sequences are bang in tune with the mood of the power-cut years in the immediate pre-punk era. Emily's chant to wake the sleeping cat – the wise, sleepy demiurge of the old curiosity shop – recalls the enchantments of other children's fables, such as 'Oak, and Ash, and Thorn' from Kipling's *Puck of Pook's Hill* – a song arranged by that folky fan of all things Rudyard, Peter Bellamy. *Bagpuss*'s hermetic world of lost and orphaned objects speaks directly to that profoundly British nostalgia for the antique and how to reconstruct it.

■

In a thesis written in 1688, discussing the homesickness of Swiss mercenary soldiers, a student combined the Greek words *nóstos* (homecoming) and *álgos* (ache, pain), coining the word 'nostalgia'. When the physician on Captain Cook's voyages inscribed the term in his journal a century later, he considered it a disease. Nostalgia is a bringer of mixed blessings: a sliver of pain freezing the glow of warm remembrance. Because of its origins the condition used to be known as the *mal du Suisse*, but filtered through the prism of Romanticism, it has become more of an English disease.

Nostalgia is usually defined as a yearning for past experiences, places and people, a mourning for the time that has passed and the changes it has exacted. Photography and film have played their part in stimulating a nostalgic industry, recording and visualising the ageing process, reminding us and our friends of how we once looked and how time has altered us. Social media even promotes and encourages nostalgia, with its algorithmic selections of experiences and Facebook posts popping up from bygone years. In the five chapters comprising 'The Vintage Lens', we'll look at how British film and television have represented the past, especially how period pieces, costume dramas and literary adaptations for the large and small screen have fused with depictions of landscape and the relationship between the country and the city. We'll scroll through some of the less Laura Ashley-fied adaptations of English literature and embark on a grand tour of country houses on screen, which reflect the concentration and abuse of power, while illustrating various degrees of social (im)mobility. There follows a gazetteer of the charismatic spirit guides of the British landscape, filmic psychogeographers, and hermits who have chosen to isolate themselves in natural surroundings. I then turn to films and programmes that strive to show the tensions between modern development and the 'old ways' of the countryside. But first we'll look at some films in which nostalgia – that sweet, seductive sickness – forms the main theme.

Nostalgic emotions are often most potent during times of war; memories are, after all, what nations fight to preserve. But memories may also become distorted, cannibalised and selectively perpetuated, creating an idealised version of a past that never quite existed. In a country like Britain, whose culture and landscape are so heavily freighted with events and achievements in history, nostalgia remains an inescapable yet potentially treacherous force in the national imagination. Regrets, and longings for a vanished age, are hardly the healthiest base on which to build a nation for the future.

In the mid-Victorian era, in the fearsome heat of industrial progress and imperial dominance, nostalgia was a luxury reserved for a few artists, poets and anti-industrialists (such as William Morris and the Pre-Raphaelites). For later generations, one of the most potent reservoirs of nostalgia is preserved in the rich body of children's literature from the Victorian and Edwardian ages. The adventures of Alice, Peter Pan, the fluffy protagonists of *The Wind in the Willows*, Beatrix Potter's mischievous mammals and the Winnie the Pooh stories are loved for their depiction of innocence, whimsical exploration and fantasy. Lewis Carroll's *Alice's Adventures in Wonderland*, published in 1865, has been filmed (or animated) around three dozen times since the first silent version in 1903. Walt Disney's 1951 animation has, for better or worse, ended up as the best known and most iconic version. Jonathan Miller's 1966 black-and-white *Alice in Wonderland* managed to evoke the stuffy cruelty of Victorian England, while arguably dovetailing with the emerging fantastical spirit of English psychedelia.

Carroll himself – or, to give him his proper name, the Reverend Charles Dodgson – was in many ways the opposite of a nostalgist. His chief interest was the emerging science of photography, and he actually made the acquaintance of the Liddell family – whose fourth child, Alice, would become the inspiration for his famous books – while he was photographing Christ Church Cathedral in Oxford in 1856. Many of his images of Alice, from the age of eight onwards, still survive; sepia-toned memorabilia now, but cutting-edge imaging technology in the 1860s. Is it far-fetched to think of Carroll as a premature film director, whose imagination would have been far better suited to the manufactured illusions of cinema than prose and poetry? After all, the originator of so much fantastical English literature was happiest while composing portraits and tableaux through a lens.

Carroll's Alice stories were conjured up during improvised storytelling on languid rowing boat trips along the River Isis. Although controversy still rages over what kind of relationship he shared with Alice, he celebrated her provocative humour, while these trips and his proximity to a family of ten children provoked deep feelings of summery bliss and the melancholy of her impending adolescence and loss of innocence.

> In a Wonderland they lie,
> Dreaming as the days go by,
> Dreaming as the summers die:
>
> Ever drifting down the stream –
> Lingering in the golden gleam –
> Life, what is it but a dream?
>
> Lewis Carroll, 'A Boat Beneath a Sunny Sky',
> in *Through the Looking Glass* (1871)

If Dodgson/Carroll came close to committing some kind of transgression with Alice, his robust and florid imagination was also at odds with the buttoned-up moralism and conduct of High Victorian society. This triangulation of the romantic and the repressed lies at the heart of Gavin Millar's *Dreamchild*, a film released in 1985, with a screenplay by the British writer Dennis Potter. Rarely remembered today, and for some reason never released in a home-viewing format, it intercuts the elderly Alice Hargreaves (née Liddell), during her 1932 voyage to New York to hand over a manuscript of the original *Alice's Adventures in Wonderland* to Columbia University, with flashbacks that reconstruct vignettes from her childhood encounters

with 'Mr Dodgson'. Fantasy and reverence for the innocent but play-
ful imagination of youth clash with venality and experience, encapsulated in the response to her arrival in the US by a frenzied yet
jaded press pack. The instant her feet touch American soil, the question is raised about how best to monetise Alice's legacy, and it's not
long before the respectable eighty-year-old is losing her dignity in
a radio studio by reading out the text of a soap advertisement. The
trip sparks involuntary memory-flashes from her own childhood, as
well as nightmares in which she re-enters a grotesque incarnation of
Wonderland: the outsize mannequins, created by the Jim Henson
Puppet Workshop, are threatening, accusatory, bullying. 'Dodgson's
coming back to haunt me . . .' she whimpers.

The stammering Dodgson (a masterful performance by Ian Holm)
is an object of pity in this telling, on the cusp of innocence and
sin, naivety and defilement. He is, however, a welcome guest in the
Liddells' English summer idyll of croquet on a long-shadowed lawn,
plashing wooden oars on a river of lily pads, overhanging willow
boughs and the late-afternoon call of songbirds. Perhaps a little too

Drowning in nostalgia: *Dreamchild* (1985).

welcome, as the mother (an ice-cold Jane Asher) treats him with
polite disdain, while frostily tolerating his role as a mentor to her
daughters.

Dodgson is largely confined to his rooms overlooking the girls'
garden, from which they literally beckon him towards affection and
temptation. Here he lives with the creatures and absurd logical games
he weaves into his storytelling, as well as developing pictures in his
darkroom. It's here, under the red light, that he comes achingly close
to confessing his love for Alice, who is shown as enjoying his stories,
but also as flirty and betraying his innocent trust when she is in the
company of her sisters and their male friends.

One of the elderly Alice's last reminiscences, as she sits on stage
waiting to deliver her address to Columbia University, is of the
humiliation of Dodgson on the riverbank. In the film's most devastating sequence, the family sits indolently for hours, fully dressed
under the blazing sun, doing absolutely nothing ('Girls are expected
to sit still'). Awkward silences hang like thunderheads. Alice taunts
Dodgson to sing one of his nonsense songs, but this time she does
not take his side, and the young people, including her youthful
future husband Reginald Hargreaves, fail to stifle their snickering
as he tremulously sings 'Won't You Join the Dance?'. Compounding
the agony, Dodgson's stammer kicks in. His brand of whimsy and
wonder requires a degree of faith from its audience, but the situation
is complicated by the suspicion that he harbours what Potter called
'sexual longing' for the girl.

■

Dreamchild remains the best of several revisitations of beloved children's stories and their authors that examine how these writers' fictional
creations bumped up against their everyday lives. *Finding Neverland*
(Marc Forster, 2004) revolved around J. M. Barrie's relationship with
the Llewelyn Davies family and the stage production of *Peter Pan*.

Goodbye Christopher Robin (Simon Curtis, 2017) contrasts the twee, sylvan world of the Winnie the Pooh books with the human sadness – and the cost to one particular childhood – behind them. *Tolkien* (Dome Karukoski, 2019) attempted to examine the early academic and romantic hardships of the creator of *The Hobbit* and *The Lord of the Rings*, as well as to show how the epic battlefields of Middle-earth were inspired by Tolkien's experiences in the Great War.

Many of these films deal with the commercialisation of their authors' creations but strive to reassure audiences that the magic survives commodification. The toll exerted on the real-life children who inspired the stories is also in focus. As an adult, the prim Alice Hargreaves has imbibed the Victorian values of moral rectitude and austerity; only at the very end of her life can she accept and acknowledge the love Charles Dodgson felt for her. The creator of *Peter Pan* – a story about growing up, and those who refuse to let it happen to them – falls in and out of favour with the children of the family, who rip up his books but finally restore them. In *Goodbye Christopher Robin*, the real 'Christopher Robin', who is known in everyday life as Billy Moon, has to endure a fantasy version of his young life being turned into an international bestseller by his father, A. A. Milne, in the Winnie the Pooh books. With this success comes parental neglect, mountains of unanswerable fan mail, awkward teas with strange prize-winning children, being singled out for bullying at school, and many other painful intrusions into his private life. On top of all that, his nanny Olive/Nou, the one constant in his life, eventually tenders her resignation in order to start a family of her own – which for Billy is the ultimate betrayal. Milne is portrayed in this film as a distant, awkward metropolitan socialite (alongside his brittle wife Daphne), but also as an ex-serviceman repressing the mental scars of the First World War. A scene in which he and illustrator E. H. Shepard are beginning to visualise the original concept to fit the Pooh books has them walking through a sunlit Ashdown wood, shot with a golden, paradisiac glow. As they survey the Sussex

Downs from a clearing, the English idyll rolls away beneath them, but their exchanged glances silently speak volumes about the horrors they lived through in the trenches a few years before. A shared adult knowledge even in the presence of childlike innocence.

Goodbye Christopher Robin is a film about manufactured innocence, about what it's actually like to lead a life inside the creation of an illusion. Winnie the Pooh and the Hundred Acre Wood have come to stand as symbols of eternal England, of the idyll of childhood, but even in this film's elegiac moments, they're a reminder that an idyll often appears desirable only from far away.

A running theme of gravity and weightlessness ran through the original Disney *Mary Poppins* (Robert Stevenson, 1964), a film that also concerns itself with how to shed the burdens placed on children in the Edwardian age, in a hangover from Victorian times. Not only does the heroine descend under an umbrella parachute, but there is a lightness of being in everything Mary Poppins touches, from the vertiginous dance scenes to her lesson that the more you laugh, the higher you'll float. Self-discipline and tidiness free up the child for uninhibited play – the sugar that helps the medicine go down – in the supercalifragilisticexpialidocious cartoon worlds she leads them through. The simple act of flying a kite marks the suspension of adult concerns about time, money and duty, and introduces a warmer, more empathetic family life, as the magic nanny floats off in search of another dysfunctional Edwardian family to make over.

When it came to the long-awaited sequel, *Mary Poppins Returns* (Rob Marshall, 2018), the period had shifted to the late-1920s Depression. The Banks children from the original, Michael and Jane, are now adults facing bankruptcy following a reckless loan, and are awaiting eviction from 17 Cherry Tree Lane.

Ben Whishaw plays Michael as a downcast widower who is not, apparently, much good at anything. Antiques and bric-a-brac from his childhood drive the action, rather than any resolve on his part. When he ventures into the locked attic, props familiar from the original film, having lain undisturbed for decades, are visible among the set dressing. The kite which is flown at the end of the first movie is dusted down and launched by his three children in the park. This has the effect of summoning Poppins, the enchanted nanny, once more to apply a firm hand to his failing household. It's never clear why of all families this one should be singled out for her particular form of magical intervention. A sense of entitlement prevails around the family – that despite their own error, they are somehow exceptional and must be saved by any means. After a new set of fantastical japes in parallel dimensions opened up by Mary Poppins and her friends, the last option to save the family fortunes is to literally, physically turn back time – in the shape of the hands of Big Ben. Only by holding the march of time back a while can the household, and the inheritance, be saved. The metaphor, in a nation that was already struggling with the unsolvable conundrum of Brexit and an overpowering nostalgia for an illusory golden age, was difficult to ignore.

13

Flickers in the Grate

Lancelot and Guinevere, The Mouse on the Moon, Culloden,
Alfred the Great, Gone to Earth, Far from the Madding
Crowd, Wessex Tales, Little Dorrit, The French Lieutenant's
Woman, Another Time, Another Place, Rainy Day Women,
A Month in the Country

> To know that everything around and underneath had
> been from prehistoric times as unaltered as the stars
> overhead, gave ballast to the mind adrift on change, and
> harassed by the irrepressible New.
>
> Thomas Hardy, *The Return of the Native* (1878)

In late 2020 the Conservative culture secretary Oliver Dowden complained about the depictions of the British royal family in the fourth
series of the lavish costume drama *The Crown*. 'It's a beautifully produced work of fiction,' he said of the series scripted by Peter Morgan,
'so as with other TV productions, Netflix should be very clear at the
beginning it is just that. Without this, I fear a generation of viewers
who did not live through these events may mistake fiction for fact.'[1]

Coming at the end of a year in which fact and fiction had become
highly malleable concepts in politics, it was no surprise that a culture secretary could be disturbed by truth-twisters being allowed
prominent platforms. But at the same time, his concern did appear
to be something of a patriotic knee-jerk – he wouldn't, presumably,
require the same warning to be added to a production of *Henry V*, or
Ivanhoe, or the film *Who Dares Wins*. Then there was the somewhat
overprotective worry that *The Crown*'s presentation might do 'lasting
damage' to the monarchy – as if there was much left to defile after

Edward, the Duke of Windsor's Nazi sympathising; the palace's failure to protect the physical and mental well-being of Diana, Princess
of Wales, and Meghan Markle; the 'Squidgygate' tapes of Prince
Charles and Camilla Parker Bowles; revelations about the pitifully
low salaries paid to courtiers and palace staff; and Prince Andrew's
reputationally destructive TV interview defending his association
with a convicted sex trafficker.

Britain's landscape is saturated in history, and the nation sells
itself as a tourist destination on the back of its past. Nature is rarely
unmarked; instead, the terrain is written-upon and enhanced by
its associations (and commemorative plaques) – Elgar country, the
Pilgrims' Way, Wordsworth's Lake District. There's little genuine
wilderness left, and it's hard to ramble far before you stumble upon
an ancient battlefield, a country church, a local museum or a drystone wall piled up by unknown ancestral hands. You can read the
landscape like a book and drop in to the visitor centre and tea room
when you're done. This chapter will examine the texture of a range
of British films and TV productions set in various historical eras,
almost all of them adaptations from literature, and mostly taking
place beyond the city outskirts. Taken together they exemplify how
the look and feel of history has become so bound up with fiction
and its representation on screen. Meanwhile, films set in country
houses are so numerous that they have been bundled together in the
next chapter.

In the early 1960s, with the jewels of its former empire taking
back control of their destiny, Britain reached a peak of parochialism,
even as it grew more desperate to keep its end up on the world stage,
while the US and the Soviet Union squared off. Even its own culture
was coming under new ownership. Ever wondered why there were
so few adaptations of classic English literature in that period? Hardly
any Dickens since David Lean's late-1940s *Great Expectations* and
Oliver Twist, and Brian Desmond Hurst's *Scrooge* (1951)? No George
Eliot or Thackeray, precious little Walter Scott? That's because of new

gentleman's agreement-type regulations, copied from the American MCAA, whereby once a production company had registered its list of desired out-of-copyright classics on the official record, they retained exclusive rights. That explains why it was Disney that secured the monopoly over some of the classic fairy tales and historical stories, such as *Treasure Island, Kidnapped* and *Alice in Wonderland*.

American producers favoured idealised, fairy-tale versions of the age of chivalry and legends of the Round Table (Disney's King Arthur-as-a-boy cartoon *The Sword in the Stone* came out in that significant year, 1963). Ever since Tony Curtis imported a Bronx twang to fifteenth-century Derbyshire in *The Black Shield of Falworth* (Rudolph Maté, 1954), the English Middle Ages had been retro-colonised by the New World. *The Adventures of Robin Hood*, a series produced for television by Sapphire Films between 1955–9 that ran to 143 episodes, racked up an incredible thirty-two million viewers per week in the UK and US. Its style was emulated in countless other productions. *Siege of the Saxons* (Nathan H. Juran, 1963), with its bugle fanfares and school-play jousts, portrayed a Hollywood mogul's image of medieval Britain: the pageant and the pomposity. In the half-century that followed, period films and costume dramas grew to become some of Britain's biggest cultural exports. Just as, in the 1960s, British folk music sought out a native voice that differentiated it from the American stylings of Pete Seeger and Bob Dylan, so British film-makers sought inspiration in their own enormous reservoirs of history and literature, and began to enjoy capturing the specifics of the land's natural light, colours and textures.

'Camelot!' In the light of Monty Python's 1975 take on the Holy Grail legend, you can't hear that gasped ejaculation without supplying the punchline: 'It's only a model.' But the Pythons were sending up earlier US-backed movies, such as *Lancelot and Guinevere* (Cornel

Wilde, 1963). Wilde, a Hungarian-American, co-produced, co-wrote, directed and starred in this Arthurian caper, and cast his own wife as Guinevere. *Lancelot and Guinevere* (also known as *Sword of Lancelot*) encapsulated the pantomime of British historical drama: stilted dialogue, painted theatrical sets and an uninformed notion of a time that might have been anywhere from the pre-Conquest Dark Ages to the early Tudor era. The historical dramas of the early 1960s were, as they had been since Laurence Olivier's memorably gaudy and patriotic *Henry V*, staged and stagey, scripted in cod-Elizabethan, dressed in costumes that were often reused for any film set in medieval times that needed them. In *Lancelot and Guinevere*, with its fixed cameras and hand-tinted colours, the jousting tournament to win Guinevere on behalf of the king looks like illustrations from a Ladybird Book of King Arthur and his knights. The castle of Camelot itself, nailed together at Pinewood Studios, was as flimsy as one of Terry Gilliam's animated cut-outs. This version felt as though the once and future king was being laid to rest again in his eternal slumber.

■

Nineteen sixty-three. The sun streams down on Cape Canaveral, Florida, as Margaret Rutherford, aged seventy-one, splashes in a hotel pool. She's there to launch *The Mouse on the Moon* (Richard Lester, 1963), and NASA is hosting an unlikely British delegation of comic actors, including Ron Moody, Terry-Thomas, David Kossoff, Bernard Cribbins and Frankie Howerd. She even receives a signed photograph from Scott Carpenter, the fourth man in space, and Gordon Cooper and Walter Schirra, his Earth-orbiting colleagues.

The Mouse on the Moon was shot on sets left over from *Lancelot and Guinevere*. Paradoxically, they looked much more convincing when recycled. Beginning with the earlier *Mouse That Roared* (Jack Arnold, 1959), the 'Mouse' franchise – based on the comic novels of

Leonard Wibberley – occupied a peculiar anachronistic position, a High Victorian fantasia on the post-war military–industrial complex. These films gently mocked a tiny nation with inflated ideas about its own status. Grand Fenwick – no resemblance to Great Britain, of course – is petty and parochial, yet ambitious and resourceful, scraping to success in its hare-brained schemes by the skin of its yellowing teeth. In the first movie, in which Fenwickian envoys wearing chain mail are mistaken for Martians and get hold of a nuclear bomb, Peter Sellers played three roles. Several years later Sellers would insert his madcap vignettes into Stanley Kubrick's mutually assured destruction lampoon, *Dr Strangelove*, but the British take on Armageddon was best served at this stage by pantomime. In *The Mouse on the Moon*, the creaking state joins the space race. The rocket cabin is a miniature drawing room: chintz drapes, pot plants, a steam kettle on a gas hob, a lute, a wooden barometer, bottles of wine on a tasselled shelf, framed oil paintings of romantic landscapes. Live chickens are brought in as sustenance: 'Fresh eggs on the way out, roast chicken on the way home.'

Grand Fenwick is prone to self-handicapping in defence of its national sovereignty. At one point, a political delegation from the superpowers visits the country, and protesters walk in front of the camera with placards saying, 'Keep Grand Fenwick off the Moon!' Another adds: 'And out of the Common Market!' A BBC Home Service newscaster, announcing the launch of the rocket, digresses about how a wristwatch worn by the astronaut is British-made. This is offered as evidence that the Grand Duchy is at the forefront of world events. 'Let no one say we British are lagging behind,' a worker at the watch factory is quoted as saying. Nineteen sixty-three was the year Britons were promised a rebirth in the 'white heat of technology', but it was also the year of *Tom Jones*, which as I argued near the beginning of this book, marked a new, more naturalistic and atmospheric cinematic language in which to imagine British history.

■

A year after *Tom Jones*, another gritty contender came along to joust the older film methods away for ever. *Culloden* (Peter Watkins), broadcast on BBC television on 15 December 1964, addressed the 1746 battle of the same name, the last to be fought on British soil. Watkins shot in antique black and white, like a newsreel preserved from the eighteenth century, and cast this battle as dirty in every sense, one that brought out all the brutality of the English monarchy's foot soldiers in their haste to repress the rebellious clans of Catholic Scotland.

In Watkins's treatment, the past is made eerily present. His direction had a dynamic physicality rarely seen on TV at the time: Dick Bush's hand-held camera crept close, the lens merely a bayonet-length away from faces that were visibly pockmarked, sleepless eyes hardened by famine and fear. *Culloden* was current-affairs reportage direct from the field of battle. All the flaws of the Scottish leadership are spelled out: the insistence on age-old hierarchies even in desperate times; a rigorously enforced caste system even within the clans; and their own internal rivalries. In the space of just over an hour the forces have been lined up, the Scots routed, innocent women and starved boys brutalised and executed, and the English Redcoats have run amok, their bayonets dripping blood.

Watkins's decision to present this conflict as newsreel brings the past alive in a radical new form. The untrained actors, mostly from Inverness, are convincing in their deadpan responses direct to camera; they are both archetypes and real individuals. Their smouldering anger at the English oppressor is perhaps rooted in the fact that many of the actors could trace their ancestry back to those who fought on the moor. Serfs, foot soldiers and forced conscripts are given an equal amount of screen time as the aristocratic Royal Army officers and the groomed Prince Charles Edward Stuart (aka Bonnie

Prince Charlie). Watkins did his research here: the narrator bombards the viewer with facts about the action, giving a nuanced and objective social history. The prince speaks with a cod French accent, and several of the oppressed Scots talk in unsubtitled Gaelic. Only at the end of the film does this become significant: the process of Jacobite suppression was a willed political decision to cleanse an entire people from the face of the British Isles. John Prebble, historian of Scotland's woeful treatment at the hands of the English, and whose own revisionist history of the battle had been published in 1962, acted as historical adviser. No one comes out looking good, least of all the Bonnie Prince, last seen skulking off through a sun-drenched glen with nary a backward glance at the people he hoped to rule with such glory.

In placing a traumatic event from Britain's past on national TV, *Culloden* was a major act of historical retrieval (the *Doctor Who* series *The Highlanders* (Hugh David, 1966) returned to the scenario). By then, more and more grim *vérité* footage was emerging from the modern-day battlefields of Vietnam. As Watkins pointed out, the US was engaging in its own clearances in the Vietnamese highlands, and just as in Scotland it was the poor peasantry who would bear the brunt of the fallout from this ideological war. As the film's final line of dialogue puts it: 'They have created a desert and called it peace.'

■

The decade and a half from roughly 1966 to 1982 produced an array of costume dramas that stepped further away from the theatrical presentations of the 1950s and early '60s. An enormous spectrum of British history was represented. From the realms of Albion's mythology, you could watch *Arthur of the Britons* (1972) on HTV, while cinemas offered Sherwood Forest's hero in *A Challenge for Robin Hood* (C. M. Pennington-Richards, 1967) and *Robin and Marian* (Richard Lester, 1976), and more medieval greensward in

Gawain and the Green Knight (Stephen Weeks, 1973, adapted by David Rudkin and starring singer Murray Head). From the pages of English literature, meanwhile, came a range of visions of the past: the Crusader-era heraldry of *Ivanhoe* (1982); Julie Christie and Alan Bates swinging around Hardy's Dorset in *Far from the Madding Crowd* (John Schlesinger, 1967); Ken Russell's decadent D. H. Lawrence adaptation *Women in Love* (1969); Joseph Losey's elegiac version of L. P. Hartley's Norfolk-set *The Go-Between* (1971); Stanley Kubrick's dusky iteration of Thackeray's *Barry Lyndon* (1975); the rugged Cornish coastlines of *Poldark* (1975–7 and 2015–19); the intricate intrigues of Trollope's *The Pallisers* (1974). The Tudor era proved exceptionally evergreen on screen: *A Man for All Seasons* (Fred Zinnemann, 1966, about Sir Thomas More), *Anne of the Thousand Days* (Charles Jarrott, 1969, about Anne Boleyn), *Mary, Queen of Scots* (Jarrott, 1971) and *Henry VIII and His Six Wives* (1972, itself a big-screen adaptation of the BBC's *The Six Wives of Henry VIII*), as well as Glenda Jackson's immortal star turn in *Elizabeth R* (1971). (Hilary Mantel's *Wolf Hall* and its 2015 BBC adaptation offered proof that this era of English history endures in the imagination.) The music for those series on Henry VIII and Elizabeth I was contributed by David Munrow, a pioneer of the 'period instrument' movement in the performance of early music. Munrow, an enthusiastic adopter of the shawm and crumhorn, also played on *Anthems in Eden*, the folk album released in 1969 by Shirley and Dolly Collins, at the high-water mark of the folk-rock movement. In that year artists such as Fairport Convention, Shirley and Dolly Collins and Pentangle were ransacking century-old folk archives for inspiration (a year later, Pentangle were commissioned to make the folky soundtrack to Roddy McDowall's *Tam Lin*). Nick Drake's *Five Leaves Left* invoked the pastoral chamber arrangements of English composers who had been inspired by the golden era of Tudor music, such as Vaughan Williams, Finzi and Warlock. In its own way, *Anthems in Eden* was an anti-war album, as it harked back to the First World War and the enormous losses to the rural populations as young men left, never returning to take their place around the maypole.

In addition to the various movies celebrating or reliving Britain's various efforts in the Second World War, the 1960s threw up a raft of pictures dramatising historical successes or failures from around the Empire. David Lean's majestic *Lawrence of Arabia* (1962) set an epically high bar, but following through were *Zulu* (Cy Endfield, 1964), *The Brigand of Kandahar* (John Gilling, 1965) and *Khartoum* (Basil Dearden, 1966). *Carry On . . . Up the Khyber* (Gerald Thomas, 1968), the sixteenth in the long-running double-entendre-laden franchise, laid into Britain's Empire fantasy with an uncharacteristically searing satire of colonial rule in Asia, ending with a preposterous black-tie dinner party in the midst of a rebel bombardment.

In this great age of period drama, 'history' and 'literary adaptation' often merge in the imagination. Beyond the ready-made theatres of castles, stately homes and palaces, there is a very British outdoor aesthetic of muted verdigris and umber, mud, filth, grey skies and rain, where landscape is more than simply picturesque backcloth. Then the full panoply of the British engagement with its own heritage is given free rein.

Early in *Alfred the Great* (Clive Donner, 1969), the young King Alfred (David Hemmings), clad in red and gold battle dress, is spattered with blood during a ferocious ambush on the marauding Danes. As the orgy of impalings, stabbings, spearings and dismemberments reaches fever pitch in a welter of clangs and war cries, the camera begins to rise up in a helicopter, affording a hawk's-eye view of the combat. This battleground is the white chalk of the South Downs, but as the vantage point becomes still more vertiginous, the whiteness underfoot is revealed as a giant horse etched in chalk upon the hillside, modelled on the Uffington White Horse in Oxfordshire. The king, who has earlier been shown renouncing the priesthood in order to lead his people, is fighting a battle for the nation's spiritual soul, warding off the pagan menace on land that's visibly scarred with indigenous pre-Christian art.²

There aren't many uncanny elements in your average Jane Austen movie, but there are plenty of other literary adaptations in which the landscape features as a mysterious presence. There is a natural affinity for those rural novels in which the land appears to be a harbinger of the tragedy that will overwhelm its protagonists. One of the first in which this is a central plank of the production design is Michael Powell and Emeric Pressburger's *Gone to Earth* (1950), a film that is often overlooked in the duo known as the Archers' exceptional canon and one which Powell barely mentions in his autobiography. The 1917 novel by Mary Webb is set in Shropshire at the end of the nineteenth century, when cottage cupboards could still contain handwritten books of spells and Gypsy charms. The film frequently cuts to composed shots of eerie outdoor locations around the village of Much Wenlock and is filled with spooky silhouettes of spiky trees, hulking rocks (carved by prehistoric humans?), deep valleys and long shots over the rolling countryside. This is a landscape of warning, primed to release its latent retributive force at any time. The use of Technicolor makes the muted colours of the English countryside strangely, unfamiliarly garish – trees drunkenly pushing back against the wind, mystic fogs enveloping a remote house.

The young heroine, Hazel Woodus, whose organic-sounding name might have belonged to one of *The Wicker Man*'s villagers, is marked for death almost from her first scene. She is consciously framed inside the half-finished carcass of a coffin built by her father, a folk harpist and undertaker. 'Foxy', the tame animal she cradles everywhere she goes, is her familiar and talisman, but also the decoy that will end up causing her to fall to her death down a bottomless shaft on the hillside.

The squire, Jack Reddin, who wants to drag Hazel away to his castle, is as lecherous as any blood-sacrificing grandee in a vintage horror movie. The ingredients of a Hammer picture such as *Plague of the Zombies* are all here: the hidden mineshaft, the dogs, the lusty landowner, the dependable, if meek (and impotent), male love interest (vicar Edward Marston). At the same time, the home movies Powell shot around the sets while filming *Gone to Earth* are a short step away from the rural/pastoral panoramas of documentarists such as Humphrey Jennings and the GPO Film Unit.

■

Period drama is a showcase for Britain's heritage industry. *Little Dorrit* (Christine Edzard, 1987), a slow-burning Dickens adaptation lasting six hours stretched across two films, was praised for its meticulous attention to detail in recreating a vanished age. Sands Films, the company Edzard runs with her husband Richard Goodwin, is a supplier of costumes and props for many historical films and TV productions, and its warehouse workspace at Rotherhithe on the Thames (not far from the site of Dickens's real-life Marshalsea Prison) contains a vast picture library from the Victorian era.[3] For *Little Dorrit*, bonnets, waistcoats and collars were hand-sewn, embroidered and plaited by a team of twenty-four staff, while others hand-painted china cups to resemble original Sèvres tea services. The resulting film is at times immersive and dreamlike, at others effective in representing the cold-hearted efficiency of respectable Victorian authority. A rapturous shot in the town garden of Arthur Clennam (Derek Jacobi) rivals the rhododendron bower in Powell and Pressburger's *A Matter of Life and Death* for Technicolor fantasy.

Thomas Hardy's Dorset lends itself well to film treatments. When cameras rove out into Hardy's fields and furrows, the requisite buildings, barns and moors are already there, the panoramas almost unchanged since the 1870s. The costumes are rustic torn flannels and muddy kerchiefs. By contrast, the average Dickens adaptation is an urban affair and requires the reconstruction of mid-Victorian interiors and costumes in all their flamboyant and finicky detail.

Hardy's stories frequently deal with inescapable fate, or how one poor moral choice can tragically affect the remainder of a life. His 1874 novel *Far from the Madding Crowd* has received several treatments, including John Schlesinger's celebrated 1967 version. Often cited as an example of 'swinging London transposed to Dorset', thanks to the presence of its leads Julie Christie (Bathsheba Everdene) and Terence Stamp (Sergeant Troy), its widescreen immersion in the rolling clifftop pastures, stone farmhouses and cornfields of the county shaped the look of many rural dramas to come, on both the big and the small screen. The red, white and blue flashes on the uniforms of the hussars who appear on the scene are like a gobbet of Mod graffiti spat on a Constable canvas. Schlesinger makes a good fist of rendering Hardy's vast empty landscapes and the folk music of Wessex. The film features a celebratory outdoor supper where Bathsheba's farmhands creak through 'The Seeds of Love'. It was this song, heard by chance in a Somerset garden in 1903 by the folk-music collector Cecil Sharp, that effectively launched the revival of folk music in Britain. Bathsheba sings a lyrical 'Bushes and Briars', accompanied by the stalwart Gabriel Oak on a wood flute, an instrument redolent of pagan Arcadias. Isla Cameron, a veteran of the authenticist English folk-music revival from the 1950s, was hired as music consultant, and fiddler Dave Swarbrick, soon to join the electrified Fairport Convention, can be spotted among the jig-players at Bathsheba's wedding knees-up.

Troy's irruption into the lives of these small farmers, with the consequent moral degeneration of the community, is a symbol of the wider tensions between country and city. He brings Bathsheba a lavish but frivolous trinket, a glass-cased automata depicting a miniature Victorian cityscape, complete with castle, steam engine crossing a viaduct and tall buildings thrusting up towards the skyline. The camera seeks out this clockwork miniature in the final shot before the credits roll. There are no madding crowds in Bathsheba's drawing room, but this small souvenir of the distant city remains, tinkling away on the mantelpiece.

The country infiltrated by city ways: *Far from the Madding Crowd* (1967).
The model town lurks in the background.

The BBC's series of Hardy's short stories, *Wessex Tales* (1973),
landed on an almost perfect form for the televised rural drama. These
six hour-long episodes were shot in external locations and are saturated in the daylight of south-west England and a Dorset palette of
yellow lichen and Portland stone. In yet another example of how
closely the British sense of the past cleaves to its stranger imaginings,
this series was masterminded by producer Irene Shubik, who was also
responsible for science-fiction series like *Out of This World* and *The
Mind Beyond*, for which Nigel Kneale was a contributor.

'The Withered Arm' and 'Barbara of the House of Grebe' would
make worthy additions to the BBC's canon of ghost stories. Shubik
commissioned high-quality scripts, and the marriage of brilliant acting and real-life Dorset backdrops ensures that almost every frame
is composed with a landscape painter's eye, in muted russets and
ash greens.[4] Interiors of farmhouses and country homes are shot
with little artificial light, matching the rustic simplicity of Hardy's

world, and much of the soundtrack consists of choruses of birds, distantly lowing cattle and chanting crows. Each episode begins with an establishing shot that – like a typical opening paragraph in Hardy – frames the humans within nature, with a shot of a landscape or organism such as a tree, and is bookended at the finale with a reverse pullback.

Two of the six standalone episodes contain supernatural or macabre elements. Wintry and wild, 'The Withered Arm' introduces witchcraft (or 'the old ways') to Hardy's Wessex. Spurned and impoverished, Rhoda puts a curse on Gertrude, the new feckless wife of the man who previously fathered her illegitimate child. Was Hardy's tale an inspiration for the deformed skin patches in *The Blood on Satan's Claw*? Gertrude's arm begins to wither away and she is recommended to visit 'a clever man on Egdon Heath' who will perform some white magic on the deformity. 'Medicine cannot cure that!' he exclaims. ''Tis the work of an enemy!'

And there is the plum weirdness of 'Barbara of the House of Grebe', the final episode of the series, in which unhappily married Barbara, who believes her former lover to be dead, is confronted with him returning, his face in a strange ghoulish mask to disguise his disfigurement in a fire. Her husband Lord Uplandtowers constructs a life-size waxwork with a hideously melted face to try to cure his wife of her love for his rival, and reveals it by whisking off its covering with a string while they are lying in their four-poster bed. This tale of jealousy, insanity and misplaced passions ends on an ambiguous note, implying with scattered jump cuts that Lord Uplandtowers has eventually, after forcing her to love him, caused Barbara to fall to her death.

The six *Wessex Tales* feel like the perfect marriage of period setting and televisual form, and the productions involved some iconic and well-known figures in British film and television culture. Screenplays were contributed by, among others, Dennis Potter (who would go on to adapt Hardy's *The Mayor of Casterbridge* for the BBC in 1978),

William Trevor and David Mercer, and the actors involved ranged
from Billie Whitelaw and Jane Asher to John Hurt, Ben Kingsley
and even Claire Bloom. Other televisations of Hardy would follow
in the 1970s and '80s, and it was left to Roman Polanski's film *Tess*
(1979) to sublimate the form. *Tess* includes some memorably painterly depictions of the golden hour of late harvest and the inexorable
coming of the machine into agricultural labour, finishing up with
evocative shots of the dazed Tess Durbeyfield (Nastassja Kinski) wandering in the pre-dawn fog around Stonehenge.

■

The high stakes around Victorian propriety and its rigid class structure are the drivers of Karel Reisz's celebrated 1981 film of the John
Fowles novel *The French Lieutenant's Woman* (1969). Harold Pinter's
screenplay, famed for its 'postmodern' alternative endings, constructed its own parallel storylines, nesting the historical narrative
inside a meta-narrative around the film crew and actors 'Anna' (Meryl
Streep) and 'Mike' (Jeremy Irons). Its first long, uninterrupted take,
on the Cobb in Lyme Regis, Dorset, starts with the clapperboard
and a film crew hastily retreating from the shot. Streep, reflected in a
hand mirror, receives a last dusting of make-up for her role as Sarah
Woodruff. Then we hear the director's shouted instructions, runners
scurrying for cover, and the snap of the clapper. The shot continues unbroken; modernity has been expelled from the frame, and we
flip into the reconstructed past, Streep/Anna/Sarah walking onto the
quay. The disconcerting spell of registering her simultaneously as a
twentieth-century actress and a Victorian waif has never been replicated in any film since. The location, the Cobb, is a geographic
feature that provides one of the settings in Jane Austen's *Persuasion*
and was where Austen's feet actually walked; John Fowles himself, a
resident of Lyme, would also have trodden it many times, as well as
his fictional protagonists.

The Undercliff, on the coast at Lyme, where Darwin enthusiast Charles Smithson goes foraging for fossils, and Sarah traipses moodily dreaming of her lost lover (who also turns out to be a fiction), is dark and dense as a prehistoric forest, binding the characters in a dream-like enclosure. Here, under the knotted roots and leggy branches, taboos are probed and gently breached. But all the while, the buttoned-up reticence of the Victorian characters is undermined by switching back and forth to the present-day infidelities of the actors. If anything, the lasting effect of this was to transfer greater jeopardy to the plight of Charles and Sarah, back in the imagined history. As a poor, dispossessed, 'fallen' woman, Sarah has little more to lose, and Charles's standing in society is entirely destroyed after breaking off a respectable engagement. The 1980s characters have relationships and marriages, metropolitan lifestyles and booming careers; the roles they play professionally are just another day's work. This self-consciousness about the artifice of period reconstruction was rarely repeated until *A Cock and Bull Story* (2005), Michael Winterbottom's freewheeling attempt to film Laurence Sterne's experimental eighteenth-century novel *The Life and Opinions of Tristram Shandy, Gentleman*.

■

These types of meta-critical methods of retelling the past are unusual. Still, several 1980s period dramas, set earlier in the twentieth century, played their stories deceptively straight, while managing to reshuffle the pack of tropes that are often in play around British representations of history – buried secrets, repressed emotions, ghosts and witchcraft. Director Michael Radford's finest achievement of the 1980s was his Orwell adaptation *1984*, starring John Hurt, but the previous year he directed *Another Time, Another Place* (1983), adapted from a novel by Jessie Kesson and featuring cinematography by Roger Deakins. In 1944 the fortunes of war are on the turn for the Allies. On the Black Isle in north-eastern Scotland, bleakly positioned at one edge of the world, time has practically stopped for the farmers on the periphery of a wilderness. Somewhere far, far away, in another place, Britain is waging its military campaigns. Three Italian prisoners of war have been transported back to this isolated Scottish community to work as farmhands, but as Italy has now surrendered, their status is complicated. Allegiances shift; in many respects, their position and that of the labouring crofters are not so far apart. All are united, despite their different backgrounds, in working the land and in the bare facts of survival.

The film's perspective is largely that of Janie (Phyllis Logan, later the housekeeper of *Downton Abbey*), whose fate appears to be chained to the locale. Her husband Dougal is fifteen years older than her and has few ambitions other than to keep on farming until he has worked himself into the ground. Frequently in these rural stories, newcomers are confused by local manners and customs, but here the Italians – billeted in a ramshackle, spartan croft on Janie's farm (earning her and her husband much-needed extra cash) – exhibit self-confidence, and the freedom and new worlds they represent break down Janie's own notion of normality. Dreaming of alternative futures and the world she has never visited, she is gradually seduced by Luigi, one of the POWs. The Italians' folk music and erotic dancing is effective here, as Janie is entranced by their hypnotic rhythms and hip-rotating dance moves.

This landscape is good for nothing but hard-won cultivation. The settlement lies almost next to the sea; the fields and skies are wide open. There is plenty of physical reaping, hoeing of potatoes and exhausting corn-threshing. The weather is heavy; the haymaking and harvesting takes place under a lid of dark, grey, saturated sky. Janie is stuck here for no other reason than that here is where here is.

The Scots treat the Italians humanely, and a fragile solidarity is even imagined – after all, the local farm labourers do the same work and have almost the same status as the Italians. United by work, wartime enmities break down. There is also some bonding along gender lines, as the Italians get drunk with the men of the village. Everyone knows this war is approaching its end, and the POWs will shortly be sent back home. In some ways, Janie speculates, these men whose clothing is branded with solar-yellow circles enjoy greater freedom than she does: they have access to bikes and can roam reasonably freely in the area. The croft has a wireless set, but news of the declaration of peace, when it arrives, is carried by POWs from neighbouring farms whooping it up on bicycles. *Another Time, Another Place* shows a location that exists somewhat out of time – in many respects it could be a medieval smallholding – being thrust up close to world-shattering historical events elsewhere.

The sexuality of this influx of foreign men is a threat and a challenge to the male farmers, and Radford's film ends with one of the Italians being falsely accused of the rape of a local woman. Another home-front film made a year later – the BBC television production *Rainy Day Women* (Ben Bolt, 1984) – also deals with a village, this time in England in 1940, that has 'lost its sexual centre of gravity'. That's the diagnosis of Dr Karen Miller, the resident physician in Darton, where German spies are suspected to be hiding out. Captain Truman (Charles Dance) is an investigator arriving to find that the land girls who have been assigned to help with local agriculture are the catalysts for even more division and intrigue than the spies. David Pirie, one of the foremost historians of British Gothic cinema, wrote this 'ghost story without the ghosts' (as the voiceover puts it), incorporating subtle elements of folk horror. There may be a war on, but there are entirely other conflicts being contested deep in the countryside. Despite the village's outwardly macho culture, the local males are secretly impotent. Alice Durkow, the landlady of the house where the land girls are billeted, has been arrested for suspected lesbian tendencies, and her husband Tom has already been interned. Alice invokes Yeats's poem 'Leda and the Swan' – 'a very potent myth' that includes an appropriate line about the 'brute blood of the air'. The mob have deemed her residence a 'witches' house' and are also after a family of

German refugees. A strange device they suspect to be a secret radio transmitter turns out to be an electrical hair remover. As the mob go on a violent rampage, Truman finds himself in a similar situation to the characters in *The Owl Service* and *Robin Redbreast*: he is thwarted in every attempt to reach the outside world, with punctured tyres and the only public telephone box held under armed guard.

Like *Rainy Day Women*, *A Month in the Country* (Pat O'Connor, 1987), an adaptation of the book by J. L. Carr, also repurposes several familiar ingredients of the English ghost story. The shell-shocked war veteran Tom Birkin arrives by train in a remote Yorkshire village in 1920, where he is faced with hostility and awkwardness, or is simply ignored. A foreigner in his own country, on arrival he immediately discovers division in the community (between 'church' and 'chapel'). His welcome from the local reverend is chilly, to say the least, in his barren vicarage with spartan rooms and cold blue light.

Birkin has come to this country backwater to uncover and restore a long-lost fresco that's been plastered over in the local church. At the same time, another recuperating soldier, James Moon (Kenneth Branagh), is toiling in the neighbouring field on a lone archaeological dig in search of an Anglo-Saxon basilica. Here we have the two efforts at revealing the hidden (chipping away at the whitewash, recalling the flaking fresco of *The Owl Service*) and digging up the past taking place simultaneously.

The film develops at a slow rural pace, as does the vicar's wife Alice's unspoken romantic interest in Tom. From the wartime trenches to this romantic front, and to Moon's suppressed homosexuality, everyone is involved in a form of self-sacrifice, to little avail. The action spans a melancholic interlude in these characters' lives; even a brief Garden of Eden-like woodland walk for Tom and Alice is ruined by a blazing gunshot that triggers his shell shock. This moment aside, there are no fireworks in a film composed of stillness and intimacy, with communication through unspoken silences, and shot through with physical sickness (Tom's stammer, a village girl's consumption), atheism and the voids of death and the open grave. With its resemblance to the string serenades of Peter Warlock and John Ireland, Howard Blake's orchestral soundtrack gives appropriate acknowledgement to the English music of the period. The contrasting cadences of secular music and a solemn hymn beat discordantly against each other during a trip to an instrument shop, when Tom helps a Nonconformist minister to purchase an organ for his religious services.

When Moon finally digs up ancient bones in the grave adjacent to the church and reveals the fresco's long-dead artist to have been a Moslem returnee from the Crusades, there are again all the hallmarks of a classic M. R. James tale of terror. But here the excavation brings not horror but healing, restoration and a sense of closure for the war-damaged protagonists, even if they will continue their lives somewhere other than this remote hamlet. In a nod to the spirit of the ghost story, Tom passes by his older self, a ghost from the future, as he departs the church for the last time.

■

The coronation chicken has been scoffed, the parades have dispersed, the flags taken down and the plastic Union Jack bowler hats stuffed in the bin. The Silver Jubilee summer is over. After this patriotic surge of royalist festivity, the centre cannot hope to hold. On the screen, things are changing. In the late autumn of 1977 something appears on the children's magazine programme *Blue Peter* that moves fast and breaks things: a trailer for a space-opera movie due to come out next year and a couch interview with its boyish leading man. Heroes clambering down ladders into laser-gun emplacements in a hyperspace-leaping spacecraft. Humming electric sabres that glow like the porridge-warmed kids in the Ready Brek advert. A walking carpet and a moist-lipped space princess. Evil imperial warriors in white plastic body armour.

Star Wars changed everything. I saw the film at least five times in the cinema over the course of 1978: with my father, as the birthday treat of various friends, and once with my mum just because I insisted she should see it too. It brought a new speed, a massive sense of cosmic scale, completely new sound worlds – from Chewbacca's glottal rasps to the raygun bolts (created by tapping long telegraph wires) – and a high-tech update on the idea of impending fascist domination. This last theme (in what I still think of as 'the first *Star Wars* movie', but my own children know as *Episode Four: A New Hope*) would perhaps not have been so evident to my ten-year-old self. Back then, it felt like a wholly other energy that made the efforts of the Children's Film Foundation and the BBC's teatime offerings of *Rentaghost* and *Grange Hill* feel small and all too quiet.

I storyboarded and cast my own private *Star Wars* remake, planning to use my mum's Super 8 camera and to reconstruct the cockpit of the *Millennium Falcon* in my wardrobe. The project never got further than production notes on a few lined pages at the back of my English exercise book. Just developing the three-minute reels of Super 8 – sending them away to the Kodak lab and waiting for the nail-biting results – would no doubt have bankrupted the family. But at least I had managed to grow my hair like Luke Skywalker.

Star Wars is often discussed as a fairy tale set in outer space. What I now notice most about that first (now fourth) movie in the franchise is that despite its American provenance and debt to Japanese samurai pictures, it also sucked the blood out of an earlier age of English macabre. There's Alec Guinness as Obi-Wan Kenobi, the builder–destroyer of the bridge over the River Kwai, the manic shape-shifter of *Kind Hearts and Coronets*, and soon to be the ultimate le Carré antihero, George Smiley of *Tinker Tailor Soldier Spy*. There's

Peter Cushing as the Grand Moff Tarkin, veteran of scores
of Hammer and Amicus chillers. There's big Bristolian Dave
Prowse in the asthmatic Darth Vader helmet, a bit-part actor
in a couple of Frankenstein movies and *A Clockwork Orange*,
and the beefed-up Green Cross Code man of public service
advertising. X-wing ace Wedge Antilles was Denis Lawson, the
urbane hotelier of Bill Forsyth's *Local Hero*. Chewie, C-3PO,
even the undersized Kenny Baker inside the R2-D2 tin can
(soon to show his face as one of the dwarves of the post-
Python weird-out *Time Bandits*): British actors all. In later
episodes Andy Serkis and Christopher Lee himself would join
the game. A couple of the sequels featured cinematographer
Peter Suschitzky, whose first experience had been with Kevin
Brownlow and Andrew Mollo on *It Happened Here*. Director
George Lucas admitted it was the finale of the Sunday-
afternoon Brit war classic *633 Squadron* that inspired the
climactic X-wing chase down the Death Star's missile trench.
Many scenes were shot on the sound stages of Pinewood and
Elstree, not Burbank. And the story arc – unlikely youngster
is handed a wondrous sword, discovers his true destiny and
embarks on a cosmic quest, slaying warriors and monsters
along the way – comes straight out of the King Arthur
playbook. Verily, in the ribcage of *Star Wars* beats the gnarled
oaken heart of wyrd old England.

14

Bleak Houses

*The Go-Between, Brideshead Revisited, The Shooting Party,
The Remains of the Day, The Draughtsman's Contract,
Downton Abbey, Mansfield Park, Wuthering Heights,
Jane Eyre, Sir Henry at Rawlinson End, Archipelago,
The Garden*

In 2019 it was estimated that Britain's television export market
amounted to £1.34 billion. This factored in all kinds of programmes,
but the majority was drama, much of it set in the past. In 2013
Downton Abbey clocked up a staggering 120 million viewers worldwide and reportedly sparked off a trend in China for hiring butlers.[1]
The grand house, the Englishman's castle, remains a potent national
symbol. This is due in large part to what author Adrian Tinniswood
calls 'the English country house's most powerful attraction, its ability to evoke stability, continuity, sanctuary, a still point at the centre
of a maelstrom of cultural and social change'.[2]

The country-house costume drama is one of Britain's most enduring cinematic and televisual exports. Many significant examples even
feature non-British directors. Within the gardens, parkland, woodlands, dining rooms, multiple bedrooms, kitchens and sculleries
of the estates that cover so much of Britain's land mass – as well
as beyond the ha-has – spaces open up for adventure, intrigue and
deceit, away from the hurly-burly of urban life and labour. Plentiful,
tactfully silent staff are on hand to take care of life's drab necessi-
ties, freeing up hours and hours of indolence and intrigue for their
employers and guests. The houses themselves are historical artefacts,
architectural islands preserving ancient family lineages and inheritances for generations, over centuries. Their inner proportions are

generous enough that many productions use their interiors as locations, rather than rebuilding them in studios.

In these narratives, non-aristocratic visitors from other walks of life, unfamiliar with these houses' quirks and traditions, may find themselves dazzled, yet permanently affected, even damaged, once they are invited within their walls. As viewers, we too may be seduced and abandoned by these filmic attractions. Even when they involve tacit or overt critique of a rigorously enforced class hierarchy, of injustice and inequality, or of the latent burgeoning of English fascism, the desirability and styling of heritage properties, filmed with loving attention to detail, may ultimately serve to hold their status in place, undermining any republican notion of sweeping it all away.

From *Mansfield Park* to *Downton Abbey*, the country-house estate is one of the backbones of English literature and drama on both stage and screen. It's a microcosm of class distinction and privilege; a vacuum-packed fortress of urbanity ensconced within the landscape; a self-sustaining time capsule where power dynamics can be explored and played out. If they are not actually haunted like *The Innocents'* Bly Manor, they certainly swarm with tales and memorials of their former inhabitants – who insist on being remembered by what they leave in their historical wake.

Jane Austen's novels are nearly all set in country houses and have been perennial favourites with the viewing public over many decades of television and film adaptation. In these sparkling comedies of manners, the grandeur and National Trustworthiness of the setting tends to be emphasised. But other auteur directors have wafted sickly airs into the rural mansion. Joseph Losey was always keenly attuned to the unease and entropy that can develop in confined domestic spaces, whether in the London pad of *The Servant* (1963), the suburban manor of *Accident* (1967) or his early country-house movie, *The Gypsy and the Gentleman* (1958). Losey's most enduring and poignant contribution to the genre was made twelve years later, in *The Go-Between*. Harold Pinter's adaptation of the famous novel by L. P. Hartley is the epitome of the 'middle-class outsider chewed up and spat out by upper-class host' narrative that will recur in this chapter.

■

The screen is raindrops on a misted window. Memory tries to shine a light through its opaque glass, a searchlight on another country, where they do things differently. This window, in its bluish-grey light, is in the fictive present (the early 1950s), but as the opening credits run their course in Joseph Losey's *The Go-Between* (1971), we're transported out and beyond it, into this vanished land of the past, a long hot summer in 1913, when the sun never seems to set. It may be the early twentieth century, but most of the landscapes on the estate of Brandeston in Norfolk look like Gainsborough or Constable canvases wrenched from their frames. The narrator, Leo Colston, arrives as a guest at the country house of his antagonistically joshing private-school classmate Marcus Maudsley, and the first minutes of the film follow his breathless exploration of its corridors, rooms, gardens and clandestine viewpoints. While Leo scampers around the halls and duffs up the spoilt Marcus, the camera laps up the furniture and lavish art treasures displayed on the walls and mantelpieces. As the wealthy house opens up around him, Leo finds patches of deadly nightshade ringing the garden's perimeter.

The first half of the film is marked by its reconnaissance and spying tactics. The camera constantly peeks through banister rails, glances through windows; the adults of the house are at first matchstick people whose social interactions and relationships, glimpsed from afar, can hardly be guessed at. Before Leo's first meeting with the whole family in the parlour, he listens at the door to check he's not being bad-mouthed. Only when he hears himself guardedly described as a 'very nice boy' does he allow himself in. But he's also already positioned as a go-between, one who does not respect the strata of class and function that drive the rest of the house: we see him nonchalantly entering the kitchens and being given a bowl to lick. Out of his depth and implicitly of lower status than his hosts, he must take what comforts he can from wherever he finds sympathy.

Solace is tentatively provided by the squire's eldest daughter, who's first seen as a shapeless lump dozing in a string hammock. Marian (Julie Christie) takes him under her wing, rescuing him from a clothing faux pas by gifting him a new suit of summer clothes. Their 'Lincoln green' colour fully confers outlaw status upon him in the heart of the English aristocracy.

He is not entirely without agency, though: the film contains its own magical undercurrent with Leo's handwritten book of curses, his gathering of belladonna from the garden, and the three-way pact sealed when local farm tenant Ted Burgess (Alan Bates) sends Marian a letter spotted with blood from Leo's injured knee. As well as Robin Hood, Leo is also cast as Mercury, the messenger (and as Mercury's Greek incarnation Hermes, the holder of secret knowledge).[3]

Life in this strange paradise goes on at a stultifying pace. Losey is marvellous at evoking the sluggardly passage of time in this hermetic atmosphere, in one of England's remote rural corners, where indolence among the wealthy breeds restlessness and muted disquiet, as well as rigid enforcement of manners and rituals. Conversations around the breakfast table are excruciatingly awkward, and no one ever seems to have any idea what to do today. Wealth has reached the point of stagnation. Servants and subjects are portrayed as dignified mechanicals: the church bells so beloved for their abstract evocations of eternal England are shown being rung through the physical effort of the working-class bell-ringers.

Marian's mother clearly suspects certain misdemeanours that she cannot bring herself to state outright. Leo has already discovered them, at first via his long-sighted spying tactics on a shopping trip to Norwich – Marian sneaking off for secret trysts with Ted. As the scorching summer blazes on, interspersed with subliminal shots of the adult Leo revisiting the village under the rainy skies of the

1950s, social divisions are gently reinforced through the understated means of the local labourers versus toffs cricket match. More subtly, Losey and screenwriter Harold Pinter insert subliminal hints of the approaching war to end all wars: Marian's officer-class suitor Hugh faces off against Ted on the cricket square; an elderly father, cautious at the crease, gets his young son run out (surely a reference to the cannon fodder being sent to their deaths by reluctant generals).

Around Ted's farm, the rooks are gathering; he threatens to give them a 'peppering' with his shotgun. He hardly knows that he is the rook being set up for a checkmate by Hugh, who is trying to persuade him to join the army. The build-up to the final shattering denouement, as a thunderhead finally breaks over the house in the middle of Leo's thirteenth birthday party, is beautifully handled. The mother rages at her betrayal by Marian, but Pinter and Losey leave us in no doubt that the betrayals in the other direction – of Leo and of the worker tenants who keep this charade going, and who will soon die en masse in the trenches – are on a wholly other scale.

Nevertheless, it is the bleakest of endings. Leo in late middle age is loveless, scarred by his traumatic loss of innocence at Brandeston, and he is still 'owned' by Marian, who wants him to recount his story to her grandson – also the grandson of the late Ted. In an ideal world, their transgressive union should have broken the deadlock between the ossified British classes. Instead, she has gone to seed as the estate has been sold off around her. Leo craved the knowledge from Ted that would lift him out of his innocent state, but it has simply left him scourged, outcast and unfriended, almost without the power even to communicate. He has been treated as an empty vessel to be filled with the whims of his masters and mistress. Condescension and contempt concealed under a hospitable lacquer: the trap that awaits the unwary visitor to the aristocratic house. No film better illustrates how far the English ruling class will go, how little it cares for human collateral damage, in preserving its reputation.

■

Charles Ryder, the middle-class narrator of Evelyn Waugh's *Brideshead Revisited*, is, like Leo, an outsider given privileged access to observe the preoccupations of the upper classes during his visits to Sebastian Flyte's ancestral home. Granada Television's epic eleven-part adaptation of the novel (Charles Sturridge and Michael Lindsay-Hogg, 1981), starring Jeremy Irons, Diana Quick and Anthony Andrews, with masterful cameos from Laurence Olivier, John Gielgud and Claire Bloom, provided a foretaste of the lavish literary adaptations of Merchant–Ivory and the preposterous upstairs–downstairs malarkey of *Downton Abbey*.

At the dawn of the 1980s, with a revitalised Tory government under Margaret Thatcher and the royal family riding high after the Silver Jubilee, popular respect for the ruling class was relatively healthy. Despite its initial production schedule being held up, in 1979, by an ITV technicians' strike (the same one that spannered the final *Quatermass* series), *Brideshead Revisited* succeeded in burying its cameras deep in the remote lives of the elite Marchmain family, one whose roots, in Waugh's story, trail back to the Middle Ages. The absolute, unquestioned notion of exceptionalism and supremacy was represented in the series by the perpetual presence of the house and estate itself, in a style that practically diffused the whiff of cricket leather, pomade and marble polish out of the screen. Transmitted in the same year as the multi-award-winning *Chariots of Fire*, its first episodes, set in early-1920s Oxford – where the student generation had been touched by the Great War, even though they were too young to fight in it – were as freshly laundered as a pair of cricket whites, giving little foretaste of the darker episodes to come. The series married a nostalgia for the interwar good life with a persistent thread of regret and melancholy, in no small part due to Jeremy Irons's lugubrious voiceover (a feature decided on only late in the production), which served to set the mood, even as it often advanced the action and revealed the inner life of his character, Charles.

Behind that, though, was the sense that there was something festering rankly at the heart of Britain's Catholic aristocracy, and as the doomed, alcoholic Sebastian gradually drank himself out of the story, a shade gathered over the later episodes, carrying with it a strong sense that all of this homoerotic puppy love, pampered aestheticism, class snobbery and parental indulgence had long since been whisked away.

For much of the series, the stately home and its environs – played both in this series and in the 2008 cinema adaptation by Castle Howard in North Yorkshire – have a starring role, with human actors dwarfed by its ornamental fountains, giant columns, paintings, sprawling rooms and hallways, and sumptuous furnishings. Such action as there is – and the series leans heavily on long, expository monologues, filmed while

'There doesn't seem room for the present at all':
Brideshead Revisited (1981).

the characters promenade around various properties, doggedly tracked by a telephoto lens – is framed by the dimensions of the house and estate, all endeavours encompassed and to an extent proscribed by its traditions and its history. The palatial house and its ochre, limestone building blocks are often formally and symmetrically framed by the lens, as if mocking the chaotic peregrinations of the protagonists. It holds firm, an unshakeable Palladian theatre, while human actors flit from innocence to experience. As the camera pans from the treetops over Castle Howard, Charles's voiceover speaks of 'Distant Arcadian days . . . Every stone of the house had a memory of [Sebastian] . . .' As much as the rooftop scenes of Charles and Sebastian sunbathing with newspapers and teddy bears, the scenes that linger are the later, autumnal, drizzling encounters between Charles and the younger Cordelia Flyte, after she has returned home from serving as a nurse in the Spanish Civil War. In episode eight, 'Brideshead Deserted', Charles is commissioned to record the rooms of Marchmain House (the London residence) in a series of oil paintings, before it is sold off to be converted into a block of flats. Lord Brideshead, aka 'Bridey', is indifferent to the architecture, but the camera lingers on Charles as the extent of the loss sinks in. 'What a terribly sad thing . . .'

The first shot of the episode that follows – 'A Twitch Upon the Thread' – is inconceivable without Losey's *The Go-Between*: a sweeping panorama of the baroque grounds of Brideshead, just after Charles and Julia have become lovers, with the couple minuscule in the shot as they perch on the rim of the fountain. War is looming, and Julia wants to get married so that she can enjoy a year or two of real peace. 'Sometimes', she says, 'I feel the past and future pressing so hard on either side, there doesn't seem room for the present at all.' 'We possess nothing certainly except the past,' purrs Charles in voiceover, and in the later episodes the weight of ancestry and family traditions pursued without rational thought comes crashing down. Afterwards, a lugubrious and downbeat mood takes over, rendering even Waugh's catty character assassinations muted in their comic effect.

By the end, the dream life Charles witnessed and embraced at Brideshead, underpinned by doting, liveried servants, has become a fading light. And this whole series is palely illuminated by the dimming of England's aristocracy, as it collapses under all the vice, decadence and a more general burden of sin. In the tortuous conclusion, the ailing Lord Marchmain (Sir Laurence Olivier) comes home from Italy to die, but lingers for months propped up in the gigantic Queen's bed in the frivolously decorated Chinese drawing room. He reveals that the entail ceased with him and the family inheritance is up for grabs. '*Quis?*' he cackles, offering this exquisite poisoned chalice to the first taker, in the classic public-school style.

This extended conclusion is steeped in the entropy of manorial life. The pulse of the house decelerates along with the elder's faltering strength as he wheezes towards his last hour. Outside, the world, which feels further removed than ever amid the claustrophobic ennui of the drawing room, is stumbling towards another war. Charles begins the episode looking every inch the future proprietor of the estate, but by the end Julia has broken up with him, a victim of her Catholic guilt. The break-up scene is, like so many other set pieces in this series, aspic-preserved: they sit on the stone steps of the entrance hall, their speeches reverberating in the chapel-like acoustic. Charles, devastated, barely raises his voice; he just gazes balefully into space, defeated by Julia's unquenchable sense that she has mortally sinned by being with him. To be in the grip of such a place, such a life, such obligation, is to lose all capacity for demonstrative emotion.

It ends as it began – in wartime, with Charles, now a commissioned officer, billeted at Brideshead, which his soldiers have been dismantling. His old frescoes, painted in the 1920s at the family's request, have been rudely defaced. The series avoids the temptation to run through a sequence of flashbacks at the end – Sebastian has vanished entirely by now – and despite the solace Charles takes in finding the old nanny still alive in her upper chamber and the burning red light of the ages aflame in the chapel, the last shots show him driving off into the future, in a military jeep, with the house almost vanishing behind him in a haze of dampness and mist. As the credits roll, it is little more than a grey ghost – an image that will gradually fizzle out, too, in Charles's memory.

As Brideshead shifts over time from glory to decay, it is as organic as the lives within and around it. Among those are the domestics and servants, who are seen and occasionally named, but in this story their lives are not examined at all. They are, however, included in other tales, featuring other houses.

■

Servants hover around and occasionally feed off the intrigues of the house guests in *The Shooting Party* (Alan Bridges, 1985). Adapted from the 1980 novel by Isabel Colegate, the film uses a game-hunting weekend at the estate of Sir Randolph Nettleby (James Mason) to create a microcosm of English social strata in the uneasy lull prior to the Great War. There's no Indian summer in this autumn of 1913, just the grey, monochrome, damp air of the woodlands and a mist lingering over the park (the film was shot in the house and grounds at Knebworth). Even though he was shipped in as a replacement for Paul Scofield, who badly injured his leg when a carriage overturned on the first day of shooting, Mason is brilliant casting. Sir Randolph can see the approaching disaster but is too invested in his lifestyle, and too ready to satirise himself, to effect any change. Mason plays up his charm – most effectively employed against eccentric animal rights campaigner Cornelius Cardew (John Gielgud), whose protest against the shooting is totally disarmed by a mutual interest in pamphleteering and a discussion of printers' prices.

In one classic set piece around the dinner table – the type of candle-lit luxury immortalised in a slew of TV adverts for After Eight mints in the 1960s and '70s – Sir Randolph surveys each of his guests with sad eyes – the Hungarian and the German Jew (or 'the Israelite', as he is referred to), the ladies and daughters having affairs or flirting with them – meditating on this soon-to-be-extinct image of the old society and of liberal interrelations between British and European grandees. War, he speculates in the film's opening voiceover, might have its benefits in defining and strengthening the national character. 'Should we not be fitter afterwards to make a better world? For that must, after all, be what we are here for.' He is not the only character here dreaming of better worlds, but he has very little agency when it comes to bringing one into being. Surrounding him are competitive males, latent anti-Semitism, unfaithful wives, spoilt and whimsical children, and the blithe spirits of the English upper crust. The two tragic lovers of the piece, Lionel Stephens and Lady Olivia Lilburn, share an altruistic love of the arts and the civilising aesthetics of John Ruskin, but their starry-eyed ideals are not strong enough to conquer all; not enough to change the way things are or 'change the illusion of England', as Sir Randolph puts it. 'It would work against the whole current of history.'

What the film does well is to illustrate how the prejudices and hierarchies of the landowners have trickled down to the rural labourers and servants. Out on the grouse shoot, where the sounds of repetitive shotgun blasts are sonically boosted to anticipate the howitzers of the Western Front, the rifle-loaders get first place in the queue for refreshments, before the beaters and estate labourers. They also harbour their own prejudices: 'Never trust a Welshman, or Gypsies, or Jews,' mutters the gamekeeper's son, apropos of nothing. He's also the one who shushes his colleagues at the approach of the squire, reminding them to look sharp and pay their respects; and it's also he who has been promised to be 'put through grammar school' by said squire, only for his father to refuse ('He might get ideas above his station'). Butler John retrieves Lionel's torn-up love letters from the wastebasket and plagiarises them to woo housemaid Violet. Upstairs and downstairs are mutually dependent, but the social barriers are almost impenetrable. That is at least something the coming war will begin to loosen up.

The insufferably haughty Lord Gilbert Hartlip (Edward Fox) illustrates the less desirable side of the English sangfroid. Goaded into stiff competition against Lionel both at the pool table and at the shooting range, and distracted by headaches and the infidelity of his wife Aline, he accidentally blows a hole in the head of the new chief beater, Tom Harker, who's literally a poacher turned gamekeeper. It's a powerful set piece: the blinded Harker's life ebbing away; Sir Randolph keeping him company but unable to summon the emotion behind the poacher's requests for prayers and songs; and Hartlip barely able to look at the man at all, grudgingly offering only financial compensation. Hartlip's wife, meanwhile, who is already in debt from a secret gambling habit, is alarmed at the thought of the medical liability. Hungarian Count Tibor, who was succeeding so well with the young Cicely Nettleby, repulses her with a callous 'He was only a peasant.'

As Tom expires – and even this rebel sits bolt upright and, after reciting the Lord's Prayer, adds a passionate 'God save the British Empire' before breathing his last – Mason conveys Nettleby's helplessness, the sense that this death cannot be prevented any more than the social order can be upturned. He makes the right compassionate noises – says the things he's expected to say – but never apologises on behalf of Hartlip, and ultimately there's a moral and emotional vacuum at the core of this man. It's as if he has been compelled to leave the safety and peace of his study to deal with a sheep that's been run over, and he just needs the mess cleared away.

The final shot is a bookend with the opener: a line of shooters and beaters, mingled now, trudging across a field in England, a slow march towards a future in which killing will no longer be a sport and many of them will not outlive the war. Lionel's letter to Olivia from the wastelands of Flanders is read out as the scene fades: 'If you have illusions, perhaps I have them too . . . While we can, for as long as we can . . . oh, let us believe . . .' But with the names of so many casualties scrolling up the screen during this voiceover, there is not a great deal left to believe in.

■

It is painful to see a historical monument broken up and dismantled, even if we know that its destruction must be necessary. Brideshead, higgledy-piggledy and shrouded in white dust sheets, is a mournful sight at the end of that series, but somehow liberating for its revisiting hero, allowing him finally to shake off the albatross of past entanglements. Another literary adaptation, this time Kazuo Ishiguro's 1989 novel *The Remains of the Day*, begins with the breaking up of an estate. James Ivory's film from 1993 begins in the early 1950s, at a time of transition for Darlington Hall, when its former owner Lord Darlington has died and the estate has been purchased by an American Congressman. The handover is being overseen by the butler who appears to have been supplied with the house, Mr Stevens (in one of Anthony Hopkins's most celebrated performances). Early on, there's a magical double-exposed shot through a doorway: Stevens, throwing open the shutters at the far end of a room, at the still centre of a great deal of busy activity. Other staff members, seated at posts outside the door, literally fade from the frame, but Stevens remains, striding now towards the camera. Time passes and people come and go, but Stevens and his routines are constant and steadfast as he maintains a 'dignity in keeping with his position', in his own definition of a butler's role.

As we slide back in time to the 1930s, when Lord Darlington (James Fox) was ruling this particular roost, Stevens is discovered petitioning his employer for a post for his ageing father, revealing that there is a family lineage of service and butlering. Part of the first half of the film foregrounds the strange, formal, collegiate/professional relationship between Stevens and his father, and the fact that Stevens will always prioritise his service over family obligations, even when his father is clearly developing infirmity.

Like *The Shooting Party*, *The Remains of the Day* is partly about the unspoken complicity between the ruling and serving class in preserving the status quo, where duty and impeccable manners suck up any energy that might have been usefully employed in overturning it. Hopkins's flawlessly groomed appearance and finicky attention to detail is matched by the sumptuousness of the house itself, which is actually a composite of interiors from a selection of real country houses (not all of them open to the public), all accumulating to make what might be the idealised Merchant–Ivory country house.

This is Stevens's domain, and he surely knows more of the house's crannies than even his master, who is more preoccupied with encouraging private meetings with emerging English fascists and appeasers, collectively trying to heal a 'diseased England'. Several times Stevens is seen popping out of concealed doors or unexpectedly pushing open a portal hidden in a bookcase, often accompanied by a gasp of discomfiture from whoever is standing near. That is, often enough, Miss Kenton (Emma Thompson), the new housekeeper, who tries to breathe fresh air and common sense into the stuffy household, with limited success. In parallel with the machinations of Lord Darlington, the house becomes a battleground for Stevens's and Kenton's power games. The camera occasionally pokes through circular windows or keyholes, emphasising the sense of mutual suspicion and quietly guarded secrets infesting the house. While the routines of Stevens and his staff continue as they always have, no matter whether his ailing father is collapsing over the shoe-polish trolley or drooling snot into a grandee's wine glass, Lord Darlington slowly comes apart due to his misplaced alliances. The film is designed to demonstrate that order and tradition must prevail, come what may. What Stevens sees or hears is of no consequence: when the duke's godson Reginald Cardinal, an investigative journalist, attempts to pump Stevens as a source for what is being discussed at a summit, the butler explicitly holds back from expressing any opinion.

It's only later, after the war, that he is forced to confront his own responsibilities and feelings, including those for Miss Kenton, which he refused to acknowledge despite her best efforts. As in *The Go-Between*, the older man is revisiting parts of his past, that foreign country he only now begins to understand. Miss Kenton is now the married Mrs Benn, but is separated from her husband and running a guest house in the West Country. Her walk with Stevens on the pier at Clevedon is lit by neon tubes, a form of illumination far from the candlelit dinner tables of yore. 'People prefer the evening – look forward to it,' she tells him, as the pier is lit up in preparation for a night of jollity. Stevens will now depart, grabbing a tearful Mrs Benn's hand as desperately as his father's fingers once gripped his cleaning trolley, to face the evening of his own life. Under the more relaxed regime of his new American master, it's implied the but-ler might permit himself a little more lassitude. Recalling an earlier scene where Stevens set free a stray pigeon through the leaded win-dows, a final aerial helicopter shot takes us soaring over the estate, capturing a serendipitous shaft of sunlight falling on it as the clouds blow away.

■

There's a similar moment of uncalculated chiaroscuro late in *The Draughtsman's Contract* (1982), the debut feature of director Peter Greenaway. In a film whose *mise-en-scène* is largely in the open air, with a major plot point hingeing on what the weather is doing at any given moment, there's one particular scene in a field where the sun is hidden behind a cloud and the principal characters turn almost black in the shadows it throws over them. It's the crowning glory of a film that positively revels in the English climate and the colours and ambience of the landscape.

Set in 1694, *The Draughtsman's Contract* was an example of an English film boasting European art-house credentials. The acting has all the stiffness of Restoration drama, while the composition of the exterior shots is worthy of Claude Lorrain. Greenaway had worked as a film editor for television documentaries, and his own early short art films were largely 'catalogue-based' – composites of images based on systems and correspondences. In *The Draughtsman's Contract*, he applied this template to a country-house murder mystery, but one which has no Agatha Christie-style denouement.

Released in the wake of *Brideshead Revisited*, the film coincidentally shares a number of themes with that series: the uncomfortable relations between Catholicism and Protestantism; decadent and indolent lifestyles; a soundtrack of neo-Baroque music; the arrival of a self-regarding commoner–artist into an aristocratic milieu; the sexual liaisons of said incomer with the inhabitants; and the ultimate destruction of this individual. But the film is very much Greenaway's own scheme. It was filmed in summertime entirely around Groombridge Place in Kent, whose chlorophyll-rich green lawns and fields are contrasted with the crisp whites and blacks of the actors' costumes.

Before departing for Southampton, artist Mr Neville is engaged by his host, Mr Herbert, to make twelve drawings of his estate. Reluctant at first, the vain and self-regarding Neville strikes a deal with Mrs Herbert to execute the drawings, and at the same time, be allowed to have sexual relations with her at the times and places of his choosing. Neville turns out to be an artistic control freak, dictating the movements of the estate's dwellers and servants, arranging the locations and views like elements of a film set. There is a constant push and pull between the artist's point of view and the medium of the camera itself. Many shots are filmed through Neville's framing apparatus, with its grids dividing up the frame according to the rule of thirds. The actors in their exaggerated French fashions and mountainous bouffants are like statues, ordered into place or commanded to stand aside. A constant refrain of snide, backbiting dialogue provides an undercurrent as Neville sketches and screws his days away, while the aristos discuss their property, inheritances and the fortunes of their estates. 'Away from the house', says the Herberts' daughter Sarah, 'I feel I grow smaller and of less significance.' It is in this property that everything, including personal identity, is invested.

In *Remains of the Day*, Mr Stevens is an empty vessel, an all-seeing eye that affects to know nothing. The key philosophical question posed in *The Draughtsman's Contract* is: should the artist draw what he sees or what he knows? Unforeseen details insinuate themselves into Mr Neville's prospects – a pleaching ladder propped by a window, a shirt snagged on a yew – clues to a hidden narrative, in which Mr Herbert has been murdered and Neville himself is being framed for the deed. The apparent willingness of the mother (and eventually her daughter) to be seduced is part of a plot to provide an heir for the line to continue, as their preening, emasculated males cannot cut it in the bedroom.

The importance of *The Draughtsman's Contract* lies in the way it sublimates many familiar elements of the period drama into something unforgettably ravishing and strange. A 'statue' unfreezes and clambers around the portico or disguises itself against a stone wall. This voyeuristic green man/fool figure provides an untamed, freely roving foil to the restraint of the rest of the cast. By far the most vigour comes from Michael Nyman's neo-Baroque soundtrack, which pummels away in the foreground, playfully relentless and seemingly without end. When the music finally stops, an ambient birdsong track rises up that emphasises the remoteness of the rural estate.

Greenaway's experience with documentaries made him hypersensitive to the ability of film to tell the truth (or the manipulations required to make it seem to be true). *The Draughtsman's Contract* also turns on the question of to what extent the artist's productions reflect a consciousness of the truth before his eyes. Despite his insistence on nothing coming between his subjects and his own vision, Neville realises at the end that he has been blind all along, and symbolically, when he is finally confronted as planned, his accusers gouge his eyes out.

Thirty years on, the ITV series *Downton Abbey* (2010–15) reaped the rewards of the trail blazed by *Brideshead Revisited* to become the most popular international British TV series ever, at the same time placing Highclere Castle in Hampshire at number one on the

Tripadvisor stately home bucket list. The writer and creator of the
series, Julian Fellowes, has a reputation for authenticity and familiarity with the moneyed classes, but as the series (five in all) wore on,
the opportunities for dramatic tensions between upstairs and downstairs became progressively smoothed out. The Crawleys were surely
the most liberal, egalitarian aristocratic family in southern England,
helping their staff solve their problems wherever possible. A ladies'
maid raped by a passing guest? Keep her on and hang the family reputation. An Irish Republican chauffeur marrying into the family?
Great craic! Coupled with the plentiful linguistic anachronisms and
Americanisms, *Downton* was too eager to let the ruling class off the
hook. It may have attempted to give a voice to and tell the stories of
the people whose experiences are seldom told, as well as their employers, but those histories were for the most part highly improbable.

This is 1806, for heaven's sake . . .
Maria Crawford (Embeth Davidtz),
Mansfield Park (1999)

One thing *Downton Abbey* did get right: for some, life in a mansion
was, to quote Jane Austen, 'nothing more than a quick succession of
busy nothings'. The phrase crops up in one of the more successful
(for being darker) adaptations of Austen's genteel fictions. Canadian
director Patricia Rozema took on *Mansfield Park* in 1999, boosting
the lead character of Fanny Price from the priggish moral compass
of the novel to a more free-spirited and enlightened heroine. (And,
incidentally, casting Hugh Bonneville, the future Lord Crawley of
Downton, as the bumbling Mr Rushworth.)

Rozema's version – she also wrote the script – aligns with Edward
Said's commentary on the novel, where he states that 'The Bertrams
could not have been possible without the slave trade, sugar, and the

colonial planter class.'[4] This was a relatively new English commercial class, one that occupied large houses and engaged in progressive social rituals, but – Austen suggests – lacking the moral attributes that constitute a decent life. Rozema's *Mansfield Park* eviscerates the story by picking up one tiny detail from Austen's book – the information that the Bertram family's riches derive from the Antiguan slave plantations – and placing it openly in view. These indolent 'busy nothings' – the social life and balls, ladies' accomplishments and domestic improvements – are funded solely by human traffic, the horrific reality of which Fanny discovers in a sketchbook showing the brutal torture and sexual abuse perpetrated by Sir Thomas Bertram (Harold Pinter) himself.

From the early scene where Fanny as a girl sees a slave ship ('Black cargo, Miss') off the coast while travelling to Mansfield Park for the first time, to the African waiter bearing a large, corked bottle of wine in the conservatory (as well as Salif Keita's 'Slavery' playing over the closing credits), this film keeps the issue firmly in view. 'There is no shame in wealth, my dear,' her mother tells Fanny during her sabbatical in Portsmouth. 'That depends on how it is arrived at,' she replies. Sir Thomas complains about the rise of the Abolitionists – the anti-slavery movement that would throttle his livelihood and terminate the very existence of his family.

This Mansfield Park – an amalgam of locations at Kirby Hall, Northamptonshire, and Kenwood House, north London – is cold and barely furnished: uncarpeted stone floors and stairways, and limestone banisters carved into the walls. A shabby-chic Austen with grimy antlers and ram's horn trophies on the calico walls, the family viewed through the antique filter of three-hundred-year-old leaded glass, as the sisters coax a weird strain of music from a glass armonica. Sir Thomas's study is a hotchpotch of pagan effigies, tribal carved heads and an Indian tabla – the exotic spoils of colonial conquest. We never see Antigua (apart from the briefly flashed disturbing charcoal sketches), but we see everywhere, both in the set dressing and the dissolute and dysfunctional behaviour of the family and their acquaintances, the effects of this ill-gotten wealth.

Rozema and director of photography Michael Coulter capture the foxed and decaying edges of Mansfield Park, a run-down estate ripe for the calculated, cynical 'improvements' of Henry and Maria Crawford, including 'the new ruins' that a visiting *Times* journalist professes to love. In this film, the ruthless brother/sister duo are shown to be digging their claws into this failing family for their own gain and gratification (there's even a suggestion that Maria is attracted to Fanny). Several striking landscape shots lift this *Mansfield Park* above the stereotypical Regency costume extravaganza, such as the coach racing across a field with a full-size concert harp strapped to the roof, the dawn fog lingering around the topiary, and the happy lovers Fanny and Edmund walking at last arm in arm past a massive fallen tree, its sprawling roots torn up.

As a literary adaptation that engages with race, only Andrea Arnold's take on *Wuthering Heights* (2011) has gone further, by casting mixed-race actors as the boy and adult Heathcliff. It's a perfectly reasonable interpretation, given how many references there are in Emily Brontë's original novel to the character's darkness (a 'lascar', 'Gypsy', 'not a regular black'). The mysterious Heathcliff is simply brought home without warning by Mr Earnshaw, Cathy's father, after a business trip to Liverpool – one of England's chief slave trading ports at the time the story is set. Arnold's film emphasises the sensuality and physicality of the story and the relationship between Cathy and Heathcliff. Intimacy and punishment are filmed and recorded viscerally, with some of the audio reaching ASMR levels of tactility. And as in the novel, Arnold finds a part for the Yorkshire landscape, its flora and fauna and its extreme climate, in order to reflect back the characters' inner lives.

There's a brilliant photo in the National Portrait Gallery's collection in London. Winner of the 2011 National Photographic Portrait award, it shows what looks like a Victorian curate, in black garb and mutton chops, emerging from a wooden barn. Hovering in mid-air while running towards him from the left is a modern man in wellington boots, purple and green puffa jacket and beanie hat. It looks like a clash of two time-travellers, though it's not clear who has travelled to which time zone.

The photo was snapped by the actress Mia Wasikowska. The man in mid-air is the director Cary Fukunaga, the man of the cloth is actor Jamie Bell, and it was taken on the set of the 2011 film *Jane Eyre*. It's rare to see these chronological clashes that take place during the making of a period film, and Wasikowska's photo captures a wonderfully quirky and arresting moment, when industry, artifice and creative human interaction are frozen in time.

As a keen photographer, Wasikowska apparently had a special hidden pocket sewn into her costume's corsets where she could conceal a small digital camera to take candid on-set shots. Modelled on the extant portraits of Charlotte Brontë herself, with centre-parted hair and dove-grey dresses, this is a Jane Eyre whose self-will is expressed in a controlled fashion. Fukunaga's version, adapted by Moira Buffini, emphasises the Gothic atmospheres of the piece, beginning with the cruelty of Lowood, the girls' orphanage where the young Jane is sent by her callous aunt, Mrs Reed. Thornfield Hall was played by Haddon Hall in Derbyshire, a thousand-year-old castle whose cold and darkness appear to have left their mark on Wasikowska's icy performance as Jane. 'You are a ghost,' Rochester tells her, even at their passionate reunion. 'I dream.' Her last line in the film – 'Awaken, then' – is a fairy-tale ending, reversed to cast Rochester as the sleeping beauty, Jane as the magician. (And a cinematic rendering of the book's confessional ending, 'Reader, I married him.')

The darkness and cold, blue glimmer of the interiors, shot in natural light, are striking, especially when contrasted with the orange glow of the fireplaces. Occasionally, Jane's face emerges from shadows as if in some Vermeer or Joseph Wright painting. Fukunaga spoke afterwards of simply setting up his cameras inside, shining a little extra light through the windows and getting on with the takes.

Jane is frequently associated with magic; her first encounter with Mr Rochester, when he, looking like a Black Rider, is frightened off his horse, has a decidedly Tolkien-esque ring to it. Without introducing himself, he associates her with 'the imps' and says she has 'the look of another world about you', and indeed, there is something almost elvish about the way she is made up at this point. Weird intrusions into the soundtrack – the thundering of his horse's hooves, the mysterious screeches and thumps heard deep in the concealed chambers of the house, the explosion of soot firing out of the chimney breast when the child Jane is locked up as punishment, and Rochester's voice in the air calling her name at the end, when she runs away from her protectors across the moor – give off a subtle tang of the supernatural. But Fukunaga also brilliantly integrates nature into the telling: the course of Jane's stay at Thornfield is painstakingly marked by the changing seasons, and cinematographer Adriano Goldman beautifully captures the winter sun and the morning frost, the lichen-stained walled gardens, and later the edging-in of spring that coincides with the burgeoning love between Jane and Rochester.

This is a house isolated from the world by bleak moorlands and marshes, and whose fortunes are smutted with colonial misadventure – this time Rochester's clandestine marriage to Bertha Mason in Jamaica. If the revelation of Bertha's existence on Jane's wedding day feels rather rushed, her presence has been exposed several times previously in purely aural terms, with faint howls, screams and slamming doors: the house's hidden dimensions mapped in hallucinatory acoustics.

The film ends with Thornfield a charred ruin, although with the prospect that with Jane's inherited fortune, it can be reconstructed. What will become of it, and other remote houses like it, far into the future?

■

English as tuppence, changeless as canal water, nestling
in green nowhere, armoured and effete, bold flag-bearer.
Lotus the hedonist, havishambling, hermit crab tight-fist
eremite. Feudal still, reactionary . . .

    Vivian Stanshall, *Sir Henry at Rawlinson End* (1980)

Films such as the ones detailed in this chapter contain implicit criticisms of the values behind the facades of great houses, and yet paradoxically they also generate visitor numbers and boost the sense of wonder and respect for Britain's preserved heritage. In the twenty-first century, stately homes are now visitor attractions, spa hotels, adventure parks, music festival venues, wedding locales, historical museums and luxury apartments. And, of course, film sets. Roped-off dining rooms and bedrooms are no longer lived in; blue blood has relocated to the outhouse and the converted stables.

The shabby decline of the ruling class into eccentricity and borderline insanity is the subject of *Sir Henry at Rawlinson End* (Steve Roberts, 1980). This was a visualisation of the *Rawlinson End* monologues devised by Vivian Stanshall, the eccentric former vocalist of the Bonzo Dog Doo-Dah Band. Some of that group's surrealist burlesque creeps into Stanshall's scripts, which were frequently tried out during his radio sessions for John Peel in the 1970s and have been favourably compared to Dylan Thomas's *Under Milk Wood*. The lines quoted above accompany the film's first few seconds, with establishing shots of Rawlinson End (filmed, like *The Shooting Party*, around Knebworth House in Hertfordshire). The allusion to Miss Havisham of Dickens's *Great Expectations* – queen of the time-locked, sealed-up mansion – locates this in the realm of privilege gone to seed. If the Victoria Memorial outside Buckingham Palace is the omphalos of Empire, Rawlinson End lies on its stagnating fringe.

Sir Henry is a riot of a movie in many ways, a classic of English absurdism, cheerfully disobeying the rules of film-making and structure. Written during a long, boozy week at the estate of Tony

Stratton-Smith (the legendary rock impresario who owned Stanshall's record label, Charisma, and who produced this movie), the project was described by Stanshall's biographer as 'A ramshackle expedition setting out with inadequate funds and no map.'[5] Yet a plot, of sorts, underpins the chaos, although a single viewing is not really enough to unravel the spaghetti. At root, this scrawled postcard from the precipice of the English lunatic mind is a ghost story culminating in a pagan/Arthurian exorcism rite. The spirit of Humbert, Sir Henry's late brother, walks the house's upper corridors, pushing a stuffed bulldog called Gums, mounted on trolley wheels, and the ghost must be propitiated with an offering of a new pair of trousers. In a flashback, we see how Humbert lost the garment during a secret tryst with the wife of a local tradesman, when the jealous Sir Henry (a belligerently deranged performance by Trevor Howard), out on a drunken duck shoot, shot him dead in the reeds. Along the way, there are vignettes such as Sir Henry's jovial attempts to thwart two German POWs' escape plans (he keeps these 'playthings, long post-war' in a miniature detention camp); a billiard game played by a rider on a charging steed; the eternal fight against tapeworms by the charwoman; and a farcical subplot involving the vicar and the local spiv. Finally, there is the 'Blazing', a midsummer fire ritual presided over by the lord of the manor.

This is a film built from a radio work that existed entirely as verbiage and sound effects, so it's hard to follow all the Tati-esque details of the non-plot. Partly due to Stanshall's intricate imagination, partly because of Steve Roberts's inexperience as a director (this was his first feature), there are plenty of visual gags, odd but significant actions and in-jokes that are inadequately signalled or occur briefly at the edges of the frame. These include a priapic garden gnome that is swiftly castrated by Aunt Florrie's walking stick; a too-brief shot of all the shenanigans going on beneath the dining table; and a brief cameo by author Lawrence Durrell in the local pub.

Although intended to be released in black and white, a film-processing error left the final print as a sickly sepia, whose nicotine

tint only bolstered the fever-dream quality. Despite the monochrome, Howard dyed his hair red for the part of the fiery, irascible
aristocrat. The gesture made sense in the post-punk era in which
it was filmed. The veteran actor of so many patriotic war movies,
classics like *Brief Encounter* and *The Third Man*, and who at the time
was appearing in *Shillingbury Tales*, an ITV comedy set in a rural
village, plays Sir Henry as a kind of inverse Johnny Rotten, tweeds
held together with safety pins and celebrating the last days of the
British Empire with just as much nihilistic vim and vigour. In his
first scene, he is woken up in his bedroom, which is a mock-up of
a First World War trench, where he is separated from his wife by
barbed wire and sandbags. Much of his performance feeds off the
fact that the English never got over winning the war: he's forever
letting off loud reports from his shotgun or cursing the enemy. But
as in the apocalyptic black comedy *The Bed Sitting Room*, victory is
pyrrhic if all you're left with is ruins.

As well as narrating the whole nonsense, Stanshall himself pops up
in assorted tableaux as the dissolute Hubert Rawlinson, sitting dream-
ily on the banks of a river or strumming a guitar while suspended in
a hammock over a room filled with tons of oozing fruit. Stanshall's
own music was an unparochial mix of psychedelic folk, English music
hall and trad jazz, African rhythms and calypso, and these elements
sit nicely at odds with the poetic absurdity of the script. The footage
resembles salvaged reels from the 1930s, and the costumes could be
from any period from the Edwardian era to the present, but this slice
of artificially aged fruit cake remains a subversive clash between the
counter-culture and the landed gentry.

■

The house in the country, a charmed space at the world's end, is a mag-
net for British film beyond the aristocratic milieu. There's the beautifully proportioned Oxfordshire house of Stephen (Dirk Bogarde)

in Joseph Losey's *Accident* (1967), the site of a sexual power struggle between two middle-aged college dons. There's the tumbledown Lake District cottage where the two renegades of Bruce Robinson's dark 1987 comedy *Withnail & I* go 'on holiday by mistake', in the gregarious company of Uncle Monty. (Robinson's distillation of several years of his life around the turn of the 1960s and '70s echoed the dissolute, directionless youth culture depicted in the 1970 folk-horror film *Tam Lin*, in which he played a small role.) The squirmingly awkward family reunion in Joanna Hogg's *Archipelago* (2010) exposes middle-class aspiration to a form of leisure experience that is a watered-down, ersatz version of country-house living. Renting a holiday cottage on Tresco in the Isles of Scilly, brother and sister Edward and Cynthia have been brought together by their mother Patricia, who's apparently being restrained from having a nervous breakdown by the presence of a painting instructor, hired for the week to teach Patricia landscape-painting, who offers soothing yet banal encouragements. Rose, a live-in cook, has also been retained for the duration of the stay, but Edward's residual middle-class guilt over the idea of treating another human being as a servant blurs the boundaries, and his suggestion that she should be invited to join them at a celebratory meal becomes the catalyst for old resentments to boil over.

Archipelago is riddled with wormwood, undermining the foundations of the country-house drama. The occasion is ostensibly a farewell party for Edward, who's about to quit his job and embark on volunteer work in Africa, but the patrician figure is an estranged father who remains absent throughout the film, although the mother is frequently, tearfully on the phone to him, believing he will come and join the party. This is a family quietly at war with itself, each one unleashing passive-aggressive comments, each an island temporarily floating among the meagrest trappings of a civilised domestic life. An unwanted guinea fowl served at a silent, almost empty restaurant provides one of the most excruciating scenes, a bleached travesty of the traditional dining-room set piece. The ever-present backdrop of wide overcast skies, primeval geology, wind and birdsong point up the emptiness and remoteness of these characters as they fail to connect.

Perhaps the ultimate destination for the isolated-house trope – completing the trajectory from the castle to the shack – is something like *The Garden* (Derek Jarman, 1990). Jarman's film was made in Prospect Cottage, a wooden hut on the shingle beach of Dungeness on England's south coast, while the director was dying of HIV. It is a powerful soliloquy, a film about mental survival while making maximum use of the limited available resources. Shot with a Super 8 camera, with a hazy grain suggesting dwindling vision and a dying of the light, *The Garden* places us directly among the thoughts and visions of an English artist alone in his house, tending to his garden, gazing out to sea and readying himself for death.

The Garden is a personal diary, but it also exists in a liminal filmic environment that stands apart from time. In its resolutely outsider stance, especially in contrast to the traditional depiction of Britain's grand houses and of its history, it reminds us of the unofficial histories and discussions of Britishness that are closed down by the prevalence of straight historical and costume drama.

15

The Geography of Peace

Jack Hargreaves, Fyfe Robertson, Fred Dibnah, Ian Nairn,
Sir John Betjeman, British Transport Films, Humphrey
Jennings, Patrick Keiller, Chris Petit

The 1980s had its fair share of televisual moments, or days
dominated by the television. There were times when reality
took back control, such as the May Day bank holiday in 1980,
when *Rio Lobo* on BBC1 was interrupted by a live feed from a
camera pointed at the rooftop of a cream-painted townhouse
in west London. Black-clad SAS raiders were launching their
assault on the hostage-takers inside the Iranian Embassy
with smoke grenades and submachine-gun fire, with Kate
Adie providing a tense running commentary. Then there were
special days off school for royal weddings. The TV was left on
all day during the union of Princess Anne and Captain Mark
Phillips in 1973, which included hours of remarkably tedious
analysis of the footmen's livery and the history of the Queen's
carriage fleet. The 1981 wedding of Prince Charles and Lady
Diana Spencer was even more of an epic of national-holiday
pomp and circumstance – a timeline of monarchical television
that looks simultaneously back to the coronation of 1953 and
forward to Diana's unprecedented confessional interview with
Martin Bashir in a 1995 *Panorama* special.

But the Golden Yawn award for the most disappointingly
dull day of television must go to 11 October 1982. On that
day, the *Mary Rose*, a Tudor galleon that sank in the Solent
in 1545, was due to be raised in one of the most advanced
maritime recovery operations ever attempted in the UK.

The promise of the BBC's live coverage was the magical manifestation of a timber time capsule, dripping with treasures and perhaps the skeletal inmates of Davy Jones's Locker. What we got instead was hours of a static video feed of the choppy grey channel, random ships and smaller craft bobbing in the vicinity like some half-assed Dunkirk, and a cable sunk into the sea that resolutely refused to be winched up for hours on end. The operation began just after nine in the morning, but despite the near-disastrous slippage of the cable lifting the cage in which the hulk was cradled, I think I had lost all interest by elevenses. In those days there were no studio cutaways, no on-screen information tickers, no on-site reporters doing public walkabouts to relieve the boredom. The event, slowed to a crawl by mechanical and environmental setbacks, delivered very little on its original promise. The recovered archaeological glories eventually displayed in the Mary Rose Museum in Portsmouth's historic dockyards are indeed wondrous to behold, but television could not get anywhere near the heart of this event. Which suggests that, in those instances when television does attempt to look back in time and rescue antiquity, the viewer needs to be accompanied by the right kind of spirit guide.

■

Of all the BBC's inventions for television, *Antiques Roadshow* is one of the most successful. First aired in 1979, following a one-off documentary in 1977, it has survived into the twenty-first century and spawned numerous international versions all around the world. The appeal of buried treasure, both aesthetically and in terms of monetary value, is universal. The screen becomes a bell jar in which artefacts can be dredged up from the depths and put on public display, along with the family stories and anecdotes that go hand in hand with the ornaments, paintings, tea sets, timepieces and other sundry collectables and curios.

Television might be a modern technological phenomenon, but in Britain at least, it has hosted a significant strain of antiquarianism. There had been no direct television equivalent of Julian Cope's book *The Modern Antiquarian*, a fanboy survey of ancient Albion's megalithic sites (unless you count the promotional programme Cope himself made for BBC Four in 2000), until Tony Robinson – the screen archaeologist of Channel 4's *Time Team* – inaugurated his *Britain's Ancient Tracks* series in 2016. This omission is surprising, given the glut of books published on the subject during the 1970s, from John Michell's *New View Over Atlantis* to the series of books about Britain's 'secret country' of ancient stone monuments and ley lines by Colin and Janet Bord. As we have seen, it was left to the domain of children's programmes – *The Owl Service*, *Children of the Stones*, etc. – to mythologise the megalith.

But history of a more parochial kind has found its home on the small screen through a number of spirit guides who have led the cameras on a merry gambol through the highways, byways and forgotten nooks of Vanishing Britain. Jack Hargreaves, born in London in 1911, became a loamy-voiced rustic shaman bridging the modern world with the lost agrarian England of his youth. In 1963 he broadcast the first episode of *Out of Town*, a series of rural rambles that ran until 1981. Their gentle hand-held quality and Hargreaves's informed, genial presentation took viewers into 'the feeling of the old, small-farming life and the know-how of it', as he put it in his memoir, *Out of Town: A Life Relived on Television* (1987). Despite its title, Hargreaves's autobiography barely mentions television at all and, strangely, concludes in 1929 with the sentence, 'After that the world changed.'

Hargreaves regularly worked with cameraman Stan Bréhaut, and their on-the-spot relationship was key. Bréhaut's ignorance of the subject matter equated him with Hargreaves's 'Mr Average' viewer.

Covering anything from animal husbandry, sailing boats and local characters to arcane measurements, and inviting viewer feedback in identifying mysterious old farm implements, *Out of Town* was a magazine programme that – like the radio soap *The Archers* – connected Britain's distant corners to an increasingly urbanised mass audience.

Fyfe Robertson was even older than Jack Hargreaves, first drawing breath in 1902 in Edinburgh. Like Hargreaves, he worked for *Picture Post* magazine in the 1950s, before leaving to work as a news reporter for *Tonight*. I have hazy memories of watching episodes of a series in the mid-1970s called *Robbie* – which I noticed mainly because that was the name my parents used to call my junior self. Was there an old, generously bearded, wizardy uncle adrift in a rowing boat, waxing lyrical about the quiet pleasures of fishing? Was that Robertson, in a mistily recalled advert for Kraft cheese slices, calmly trimming the corners off with a penknife while waiting for the trout to bite? In his museum-focused series *Brush Off the Dust* (1964), Robertson's lanky frame might stride out in search of the real English pint or go behind the scenes at the nation's lesser-known nostalgic Aladdin's caves, like York's Castle Museum or the British Motor Museum in Warwick.

A gentleman wanderer, Robertson kept his smartly dressed dignity intact through most of his programmes. Fred Dibnah, on the other hand, would most likely have needed to literally brush the dust off his overalls by the time the cameras stopped rolling. This hyperactive professional steeplejack and steam engine enthusiast was discovered during a 1978 BBC local news report, filmed at the summit of some scaffolding while he was repairing the chimney at Bolton town hall, eventually dynamiting the whole thing with a cheerful 'Did you like that?' He proved so genial on camera that the story was expanded to a documentary, *Fred Dibnah – Steeplejack* (1979). His ability to ramble to camera while teetering hundreds of feet up on a hoist proved endearing and he became a minor celebrity, with more series such as *Fred – A Disappearing World* (1983). In the era following the Thatcher government's evisceration of trade unions and northern manufacturing, his name became inextricably brand-linked to the unearthing of the nation's labouring heritage in a string of later serials, including *Fred Dibnah's Industrial Age* (1999), *Fred Dibnah's Magnificent Monuments* (2000), *Fred Dibnah's Victorian Heroes* (2001), *Fred Dibnah's Age of Steam* (2003) and *Fred Dibnah's Made in Britain* (2005). His world was all pumping pistons and brick dust, mineshafts and collieries, chimney stacks and church spires, and he carried their engineering secrets and industrial ingenuity with him everywhere. He drove to Buckingham Palace to collect his MBE in a traction engine.

Meanwhile, there was the maverick Ian Nairn, opinionated architectural critic and author, whose finely calibrated sense of place was translated to a handful of television programmes taking him around Britain's significant sites. An opinionated contributor to Nikolaus Pevsner's 1960s handbooks on the English countryside, and the author of *Counter-Attack Against Subtopia* (1957), *Nairn's London* (1966) and *Britain's Changing Towns* (1967), Nairn fronted a variety of architectural reportage programmes and travel series in the 1960s and '70s, bringing his idiosyncratic sense of outrage to bear on everything from British heritage and suburban spread to his own purposeful journeys around Britain and beyond. In a special edition of the *Architectural Review* from 1955 entitled 'Outrage', he came out with 'the prophecy that if what is called development is allowed to multiply at the present rate, then by the end of the century Great Britain will consist of isolated oases of preserved monuments in a desert of wire, concrete roads, cosy plots and bungalows. There will be no real distinction between town and country . . . it is a morbid condition that spreads both ways from suburbia, out into the country, and back into the devitalized hearts of towns . . . subtopia is the world of universal low-density mess.' In his TV series *Nairn Across Britain* (1972), he embarked on a car journey around the nation's roads, avoiding newly laid motorways whenever he could, stopping off to reveal 'things that are just waiting, quietly, to be looked at'; to lambast a local council's demolition plans here, suggest better uses for public commons there. As a seeker of the lovely, lingering detail (but no misty-eyed nostalgist), he would acknowledge when the twentieth century actually improved on what was there before, but railed against the cold hand of brutalist town planning.[1]

Nairn, Hargreaves, Robertson, Dibnah and their ilk inhabited an age of television in which commentators could be experts without being institutionalised. Individualistic, charismatic, occasionally obstreperous and combative, their personal views aimed to speak for the entire audience, not for the sake of stirring up controversy, but to unite and mobilise opinion. It was a difficult tightrope to walk, and no one teetered more surely on the wire than Nairn's former associate at the *Architectural Review*, the venerable laureate of parochial England, Sir John Betjeman.

■

For me, the big movie of 1981 is *Raiders of the Lost Ark* – Harrison Ford's Han Solo transplanted to the daredevil world of interwar archaeology. The memory of seeing this on the big screen, though, is indivisibly linked with the short B-movie that preceded it. This was a long-forgotten custom at theatrical cinema showings up until about the late 1980s: nearly all films were coupled with a short of some kind, screened before the main feature.

For some inexplicable reason, the film accompanying *Raiders of the Lost Ark* was *Late Flowering Love* (Charles Wallace, 1981), in which a handful of John Betjeman poems, narrated by the poet himself, were set to dramatised scenarios featuring actors such as Susannah York, Eric Morecambe, Beryl Reid, John Alderton, John Le Mesurier and Jenny

Agutter. I can find little trace of it now, but in my recollection it
was the wistful, romantic side of Betjeman: poems of idealised
femininity like 'Myfanwy' and 'Late Flowering Love', the
images chocolate-boxy and soft-focus (the cinematography was
by Harry Waxman), and with a footling trad-jazz soundtrack.

So, a ticket to see *Raiders of the Lost Ark* in a British
cinema in 1981 took you on a journey from an Edwardian waif
riding a bicycle down a glowing country lane to German faces
melting at the opening of the Ark of the Covenant. What did
that do to me? I'm still not sure. But perhaps it represents
just what those of us born after the Second World War have
had to deal with.

Born in 1906, self-identifying as a 'poet and hack', Sir John Betjeman
became one of the nation's best-loved bards of the twentieth century.
Born to a wealthy Dutch family based in London, he was educated
at Oxford, where his teddy bear was immortalised as the Aloysius
cuddled by Evelyn Waugh's effete Sebastian Flyte in *Brideshead
Revisited*. The landscape, architecture and churches of Great Britain
were Betjeman's passion, and he wrote about them for the interwar
Architectural Review, as well as authoring a number of Shell guide-
books for adventurous motorists of the age. In the early 1960s, when
Betjeman was awarded the Queen's medal for poetry, he was given
licence to funnel his enthusiasms for British history and a sense of
place via the new medium of television.

He had presented a number of arts and architecture programmes
during the 1950s, and as a poet was a subject in *Monitor*'s influential series of artistic portraits, in a profile directed by Ken Russell in
1959. But with the ten-minute BBC short *John Betjeman Goes by
Train* (1961), he anointed himself king of the branch line and set the
template for at least two decades of programmes in which he acted as

the lone guardian and travel guide to a post-war Britain he intimately knew. More often than not, Betjeman would ride trains alone (aloof from the cameras), musing on the villages and sidings he passed by, occasionally alighting at a distant, abandoned halt to savour the vertigo of history. 'The past cries out to us,' he said on one occasion, 'even when we try to smother the cries.'

Where a writer like J. G. Ballard could turn the disfigured landscapes left behind after the war into dystopian imaginings of drowned worlds and tangled road wreckage, Betjeman could stand amid the bracken and rosebay of a London bomb site and fondly recall the tea rooms and tiled hotel lobbies that stood there a few years prior. In *John Betjeman Goes by Train*, which traces the short branch line from King's Lynn via Sandringham to the coast of north Norfolk, as he approaches the Hunstanton terminus he playfully imagines the train crashing into the buffers, tearing through the hotel and steaming on into the sea. In Ballard's hands this would have been an apocalyptic terminal beach; for Betjeman it was a whimsical fancy briefly entertained, then quickly dismissed.

In *Branch Line* (1963), the self-styled 'Pickwickian figure in the hat' pokes about the Somerset and Dorset Joint Railway in an attempt to 'Dream again that ambitious Victorian dream which caused this long railway still to be running through deepest, quietest, flattest, remotest, least-spoiled Somerset.' His narrations are tapestries of voiceover verse, factual fill-ins and to-camera improvisations. But he always sees with a poet's eye. Trudging through an abandoned carriage vandalised by 'Teds from Highbridge', noting the sepia prints of villages and churches still hanging on the carriage walls, Betjeman imagines the train as a vector of stories, speculating on the holidays City commuters dreamed of while sitting in these ripped-up seats.

As a TV presenter, Betjeman achieved a conversational register that chivalrously accommodated both his Oxbridge learning and his common touch. He notes the benefits of rail travel for both passengers and the environment: goods being conveyed by rail means 'the

roads are that amount clearer', and the public can see more countryside from a train window, and more easily reach the coast, than in a
car. If rail disappeared, the roads would become impossibly clogged
with traffic, he quite reasonably argues. His description of Charles
Eamer Kempe's stained glass at Sandringham church – 'unity by
inclusion' – could serve for Betjeman's own presentation. His railways and stations, even the towns and villages he visits, are largely
empty of humanity; he remains a distant observer, waiting for the
spaces to be vacated before leading the camera on. The royal station
at Wolferton, its waiting room polished and shining, is immaculate –
but where are the staff who keep it so spick and span?

It is precisely this absence that lends these films their eerie effect.
(John McGlashan, Betjeman's cameraman on the 1974 documentary
A Passion for Churches, worked on all of Lawrence Gordon Clark's
BBC Christmas ghost stories up to 1975.) The emptiness surrounding the poet feels like amnesia's encroachment; these programmes are
spells woven against forgetting. In *Branch Line* he points out failed
projects, plans that came to naught: a line to Burnham-on-Sea that
was supposed to connect to a ferry pier to transport holidaymak-
ers across the Bristol Channel to Wales; or another dockside project meant to stimulate trade; or tracks intended to connect Wales
with, eventually, the European mainland. Dreams of engineers that
hit the buffers. The 'deep, sad undertone' Betjeman detected in the
music of English church bells pervades the entire film, and the final
shot is unforgettably poignant, with the rear of the train pulling out
of Pylle Halt, leaving the track empty, abandoned to weeds, bees
and drifting birdsong.

Shortly before being appointed Poet Laureate in 1972, Betjeman
was a leading participant in one of the BBC's most ambitious and
costly projects. The corporation had arranged several hundred hours'
worth of helicopter hire, with the idea of filming Britain from the
air. Landscape was seldom filmed from aircraft on British TV, due
to prohibitive costs and logistics, but what eventually became the

thirteen-part series *Bird's-Eye View* (1969–71) made aerial footage the sole content. Writers such as Stuart Hood, Correlli Barnett and John Lloyd were commissioned to sift through hours of film, shot from the chopper in all weathers by the intrepid John Bird, and construct themed narratives out of it all with titles such as 'A Green and Pleasant Land', 'The Island Fortress' and 'John Bull's Workshop'. Narrators including Gordon Jackson, John Le Mesurier and Leo McKern purred reassuringly through the scripts.

Betjeman wrote and narrated three of the programmes, including the first, 'The Englishman's Home'. It set the tone for the remainder of the series: a dreamlike drift over familiar and strange features of the isles. 'What were they like, who dug these holes for huts?' he speculates (in iambic pentameter), as the camera skims over mysterious circular Celtic foundations on Anglesey. The helicopter transporting the camera moves in a hypnotic sweep, floating (at times more like a hot-air balloon) across fields and rolling dales, seaside resorts and country estates, occasionally descending so low as to almost knock the top off a clock tower or church steeple. There is a chronological, rather than geographical, logic to the itinerary; medieval castles, Elizabethan manors, Baroque palaces (the man who inspired Sebastian Flyte waxes lyrical about Castle Howard, afterwards used in both the film and TV adaptations of *Brideshead Revisited*), Brighton Pavilion, new towns, garden cities. 'Swanning high in a trance of freedom,'[2] as one contemporary TV critic described it, Betjeman masterfully shepherds his raptures towards a mild polemic, as the film concludes over Thamesmead in London's Docklands district, a wasteland being primed for redevelopment. Sympathising with those who have to make their lives in east London's newly erected high-rises, he tacitly criticises the planners and architects, but never patronises the people who live there. Here and in *Beside the Sea*, he championed humane, utopian, modern town planning.

Under the eye of series producer Edward Mirzoeff, all the contributors to *Bird's-Eye View* were encouraged to incorporate a little argument in order to stimulate debate about a Britain in the throes of change and a rising population. In these first two programmes, Betjeman handled the issues with finesse. In the third, 'A Land for All Seasons', he eschewed narrative altogether and compiled an anthology of English verse – his own and others' – over a montage that spun viewers through the wheel of the year. Here, with its use of patriotic verse and triumphalist orchestral music, such as Holst's 'I Vow to Thee My Country', this programme veers dangerously close to jingoistic rapture (as Betjeman would later do, in the Silver Jubilee year of 1977, in *The Queen's Realm: A Prospect of England*), but it's only at the end that it fails to resist this temptation. Much of the rest beautifully evokes the life cycles of both the landscape and the human lives that dwell within it. The godlike hovering camera catches miraculous moments that stand outside time: an old man scything upon a Welsh hill, a hare ripped apart by a pack of hounds, a huntsman unhorsed in a leap, children dancing around a spring maypole, hill runners and Cumberland wrestlers in the Lake District, a winter funeral cortège. This was pagan television showing an unbroken dream of British life.

Anticipating much later BBC series such as *Coast* and *Britain from Above*, and prefiguring the now-ubiquitous use of drone footage and 'slow TV', *Bird's-Eye View* flew ahead of the pack and created a brand-new perspective on British television, allowing viewers to lift up and away from the pale-green dot of the sceptred isle. For many, it would have justified the purchase of a new colour TV set.

■

That first *Betjeman Goes by Train* film of 1961 had been a collaboration between the BBC and British Transport Films. For picture-house audiences with ration books still in their pockets, the early British Transport Films were not touting railway tickets so much as promoting the idea that the nation was on the rails and tooting its whistle again after the devastation of war. But beyond that, they invoked the

older meaning of 'transport': to be carried away into some kind of
rapture or visionary state. From the mid-1950s the films, averaging
around eighteen minutes in length, were magic lantern slideshows
displaying the best of Britain, sometimes barely featuring any trains
at all. The railway, these films implied, constituted the country's
invisible arterial system, the most convenient chariot for passengers
to conduct their own private tours of Britain's treasury of landscape,
people and architecture. Ride about on the majestic steam engines
that Britain invented and see for yourselves that the country is in
full vigour, the seasons changing as they should, the people provided
for. Later in the unit's development, more experimental approaches
were essayed, and the films became more like illustrated lectures.
But at their best, such as *West Country Journey* (Syd Sharples, 1953),
The England of Elizabeth (John Taylor, 1957) and *The Coasts of Clyde*
(James Ritchie, 1959), classic British Transport Films were effective
rhetorical assertions of national pride that transcended their era. The
British public, living in the ruins and austerity of war's aftermath,
needed to know what they had been fighting for. With their radiant
16 mm footage, stirring music and commentaries that mixed gravitas
with light humour, they sounded a grace note of populist pomp in
reduced circumstances.

'History is not forgotten here. The Dales trap it among the hills
and fill the land with ghosts and magic from the past.' Thus runs a
typical line from *North to the Dales* (Ronald Craigen, 1962), as the
camera scans a valley of drystone walls 'draped like a net across the
landscape'. The deeper the camera ventured into the wild, the more
naturally the films came to conjure a sense of enchantment. The
combine harvesters in *The Heart of England* (Michael Clarke, 1954),
'so modern', are also 'prehistoric monsters, dragons, dinosaurs'.
Stone cottages and village high streets are described as having grown
organically out of the soil. In *East Anglian Holiday* (Michael Clarke,
1954), the flint pebbles speckling the houses were once primeval sea
sponges. This dreamy excursion from the fenland 'mountain' of Ely

Cathedral to the Norfolk Broads opens with an abstract field of waving wheat – just like *Listen to Britain* (1942) twelve years earlier, the patriotic montage by director Humphrey Jennings that helped set the template for the later shorts.

Jennings was the great visionary hope of the British documentary movement before his too-early death in 1950, after an accident in Greece. A polymath who participated in the Mass Observation project of the 1930s, assisted in the installation in London of the International Surrealist Exhibition of 1936 and compiled *Pandaemonium*, a posthumously published anthology of reactions to the arrival of the machine age, Jennings kept a steadying hand on his cameras throughout the chaos of war, documenting air raids during the Blitz (*Fires Were Started*, 1943) and, in the wordless tapestry of *Listen to Britain*, juxtaposing frantic arms manufactories and agricultural labour with rustling oaks, reassuring art and ordinary people finding solace in everyday chores and music. Children dance in a ring, nature sounds intrude on the soundtrack – then a convoy of Bren gun carriers revs down a village street of half-timbered cottages. Jennings was well matched for this unique historical moment, when the civilian home front was more involved in the war effort than at any other time in British history; yet in this pre-atomic age, the home front was still a hopeful collective effort. The sequence featuring Myra Hess performing a Mozart piano concerto for Queen Mary at the National Gallery is one of Britain's most hallowed cinematic images. The gallery's empty gilt frames and sandbags testify to masterpieces that have been squirrelled away in the face of Luftwaffe raids, but the building remains a sanctuary in the midst of the capital, culture providing unity across class and national divides. Jennings's *A Diary for Timothy* (1945), scripted by E. M. Forster, looked forward to the approaching Armistice and spoke movingly of a rebirth of the nation. War, for Jennings, transfigured and illuminated the British people and landscape as never before, and he made it his mission to capture its full dynamic range. He did so largely with images from a fixed camera (although there are instances of graceful, almost imperceptible tracking shots), observing and recording common objects or actions, and editing them to unveil 'the whole pattern that can emerge when such commonplace, significant things and people are fitted together in the right order'.[3]

Jennings's wartime films were made under the auspices of the Crown Film Unit. The ancestry of this organisation can be traced back, via the GPO Film Unit (1933), to the Empire Marketing Board Film Unit of the 1920s, which showcased the glory of British trade and industry. The latter was inaugurated in 1926, the same year John Grierson coined the word 'documentary' to describe the emergent genre of actuality film-making. With Robert Flaherty's anthropological study of Polynesian life *Moana* (1926) as a guide, Grierson's *Drifters* (1929) uncovered the lives and labour of North Sea trawlermen. Afterwards, as the EMB's producer, he assembled a crew of idealistic young film-makers, including Jennings, Basil Wright, Edgar Anstey, John Taylor, Paul Rotha, Harry Watt and Alberto Cavalcanti. When the board's film unit was broken up in 1933, the flock migrated to the new GPO Film Unit set up by the General Post Office. Like the later British Transport Films, short films such as *Coal Face* (Alberto Cavalcanti, 1935) and *Night Mail* (Harry Watt and Basil Wright, 1936), with words by W. H. Auden and music by Benjamin Britten, were more than just promotional pictures for a public service; they stepped beyond the quotidian to show how, in far-reaching ways, the entire postal infrastructure, or miners' communities, knitted the nation together and brought out the best of its organisational and social qualities. With equipment powered by generators salvaged from Barnes Wallis's R100 airship, the GPO Film Unit literally drew its energy from the fabric of British industry.

Certain names from the GPO's film crews can be traced to the British Transport Film Unit, with several of them becoming feature directors in their own right. John Taylor got into films only because Grierson had married his sister; as an assistant at the EMB he got to work on *Man of Aran* (Robert Flaherty, 1934), *Song of Ceylon* (Basil Wright, 1934) and several travel films by Cavalcanti. On the Aran Islands with Flaherty, he learned to process the film stock on site, making do with primitive facilities inside a windswept wooden hut and drying the stock with dangerous paraffin stoves. After the war, he set up Countryman Films to make nature documentaries and ended up producing *The Conquest of Everest* (George Lowe, 1953), which tracked the pioneering expedition of Sir Edmund Hillary and Tenzing Norgay, although due to weight restrictions the climbers forbade the use of a camera at the actual summit.

By the time Taylor fetched up in the British Transport Films team, the use of 16 mm cameras was ubiquitous. Portability and ease of set-up was paramount for BTF's open-air methodology. David Watkin – the young cameraman Taylor hired in 1957 to film *Holiday*, a jazzy tour of Blackpool and its seaside fun – proved adept with these cameras and was prepared to stand waist-deep in Scottish lochs to film grey seals or painstakingly manoeuvre the lighting in King's College Chapel, Cambridge, to achieve the most memorable effect. Watkin and Taylor stamped their mark all over some of the best BTF output. Like the films of Humphrey Jennings, the films are predominantly a slideshow of static scenes. *The England of Elizabeth* – in which trains make no appearance whatsoever – rousingly celebrates the age of Elizabeth Tudor through the prism of Elizabeth Windsor. In both epochs 'peace was a new thing in the land', runs the commentary, encouraging viewers to 'spur your quick fancy to jump the wide centuries'. Shakespeare's birthplace, with its humble wooden dining plates, the half-timbered mansions of the deep countryside, the naval triumphs of Sir Francis Drake and Sir Walter Raleigh and the elaborate artefacts inspired by the new trades opening up in the Orient are depicted in saturated colours, defying the conventional rendering of the 1950s as a monochrome age. The red robes of the choir of King's College, as they process through a chapel side-lit with dusty beams, are thick as oil paint. The colours blaze off the screen as if trying to melt the celluloid, as hot as the ancient fire beacon Watkin filmed at Tog Hill, near the house of Grierson himself.

David Watkin was an alchemist of the screen whose lifespan (1925–2008) formed a bridge between the first generation of leftist British documentarists and the UK cinema industry's 1980s rapprochement with Hollywood. His most famous work as director of photography came in the 1980s, with *Chariots of Fire* (Hugh Hudson, 1981), *Yentl* (Barbra Streisand, 1983), *White Nights* (Taylor Hackford, 1985) and the Academy Award-winning *Out of Africa* (Sydney Pollack, 1985), but his career stretched back to the mid-1950s, when he was attached to the British Transport Films unit under Edgar Anstey. Watkin was an old-school liberal: gay, erudite, a lover of literature and music (especially Vaughan Williams), irreverent, technically experimental, devil-may-care improvisatory and sensitive to the magical way the lens and camera mechanism traps and diffuses light. He was behind the camera on so many interesting and quirkily English films of the 1960s and '70s: *The Knack . . . and How to Get It* (Richard Lester, 1965), *Help!* (Lester, 1965) *Mademoiselle* (Tony Richardson, 1966), *How I Won the War* (Lester, 1967), *Charge of the Light Brigade* (Richardson, 1968), *The Bed Sitting Room* (Lester, 1969), *The Devils* (Ken Russell, 1971) and *The Boy Friend* (Russell, 1971), through to Lester's *Musketeers* movies, the mythic swan song *Robin and Marian* (1976) and the televisation of *Jesus of Nazareth* (Franco Zeffirelli, 1977). It was his own technical brilliance that worked out how to slow the motion of the runners in *Chariots of Fire* to such swooningly triumphal effect. A lover of the tenebrous paintings of Vermeer (whom he called 'a cameraman of sorts'[4]), he also invented a bespoke multi-bulb system for convincing night shooting.

When it came to Tony Richardson's Woodfall production *The Charge of the Light Brigade*, Watkin was aware that the Crimean War of 1853–6 overlapped with the age of the camera, which meant that photographic precedents for the era's look could be found. When he was making Transport Films, Watkin shot with a camera with brass-mounted Ross Xpress lenses (later replaced with Cooke Speed-Panchros). He realised that the Ross lenses, with their uncoated glass elements, had similar specs to those used by Roger Fenton, the Victorian photographer who documented the army camps during the original Crimean campaign. Watkin assembled a 'workable set' of such lenses by rummaging through a camera workshop in a 'Dickensian basement'[5] in Charlotte Street, Soho, and mounted them on a standard BNC Mitchell film camera. Thus, he was using a complicated hybrid vintage camera kit to shoot a movie in Panavision CinemaScope, placing a separate anamorphic filter in front of the lens to correct the picture ratio for cinema screens. 'With a Ross,' explained Watkin in his autobiography, 'there is a fraction of light that gets scattered every time it hits an element so that the image is undergoing a progressive change during its passage through the lens until it reaches the film. The result of something happening inside a lens is different altogether from the blanket effect of diffusion placed outside it; unexpected and delightful accidents happen.'[6]

Watkin, who exhibited a particular sensitivity to lighting, colour palette and the grain of a film, here took the notion of making a historical film literally to the point of shooting it through the oldest lenses he could source. Light refracts through antique glass, conferring an extra patina, a supplementary layer of historical noise, to the picture. 'Intimate contact with the tools we employ and their closeness to everyday life is something we are losing,' Watkin wrote, 'and that is a pity. Electronic image manipulation might be capable of reproducing the beauty and subtlety of the Ross lenses on *Charge of the Light Brigade* but how could anybody program it? The Ross Xpress made their own magic as they went along – it couldn't be envisaged before it happened.'[7]

My filmography, as a teenage film extra in the mid-1980s, stretches to a grand total of two pictures. My involvement was entirely due to the fact that key scenes – concert sequences requiring a large, patient audience – were shot at locations in Bristol. One of them took place at the music venue formerly known as the Colston Hall, where Bob Dylan was shooting some gig sequences for *Hearts of Fire* (Richard Marquand, 1987). A tetchy, tedious day of sitting in the auditorium, waiting to be told to stand up and rave on, was alleviated only by the appearance of Dylan himself, during an extended hold-up while some technical snag was resolved. The master sat humbly on his amp, plugged in a guitar and proceeded to busk a couple of bluesy instrumentals to an enraptured crowd. The people in the front rows caught the spotlights in their wristwatches and projected a galactic light show of flickering stars over the stage as Dylan picked out the chords. If the director had bothered to shoot the stunned applause that followed this impromptu micro-show, the film might have looked a good deal more authentic.

My Hollywood debut, though, came in 1984, when, aged fifteen, my best friend Kevin and I answered an ad in the local paper looking for people to turn up in evening dress at the Bristol Hippodrome, a large Edwardian theatre of crimson velvet seats, flaking gilt and opera glasses that you could release with a fifty-pence piece. This was for *White Nights*, a film about a Russian ballet dancer who defects from the Soviet Union to the West. The movie was mildly notorious at the time as its lead actor, Mikhail Baryshnikov, had been a dancer with the Kirov Ballet and was a real-life Russian defector.

Borrowing my father's moth-eaten dinner jacket and a starched collar that had barely seen the light of day since his graduation, we bagged seats in the middle of the front row

of the upper circle. Work as an extra involved the promise of
£20 per day, plus the inevitable overtime. At lunchtime you
stood in line for your paper bag containing sandwiches, apple,
cellophane-wrapped fruit cake and carton of Kia-Ora. The rest
of the day was spent mostly sitting still, chatting awkwardly
to those in the neighbouring seats. It was as well to bring a
book. Occasionally there was work to do. The director would
choreograph the action via megaphone; I lost count of the
number of standing ovations we delivered that day.

My teenage self would never have taken any notice of
the director of photography credit. But while I was content
enough to pocket the cash and spend it on David Bowie
albums, retrospectively I'm glad to know that for that one day
only, I must have been under the same roof as David Watkin.
White Nights was not this camera wizard's finest hour, but if
I had known in 1984 what I know now, I would have snuck
down to the Hippodrome stalls and asked him to autograph
my sandwich bag.

■

From Daniel Defoe's *Tour Through the Whole Island of Great Britain*
(1724–7) to Robert Macfarlane's *Landmarks* (2015), the literature
devoted to traversing the expanses of these small isles forms a monumental canon. The *Rural Rides* of William Cobbett ended up as
a snapshot of English radicalism in the 1820s, a volatile period in
British politics. H. V. Morton's motoring travelogues, like *In Search
of England* (1927) and *I Saw Two Englands* (1942), lovingly toured
the country's byways, vividly describing historical quirks and social
histories. Alfred Watkins's *The Old Straight Track* (1925) dowsed for
ley lines connecting Britain's downs, barrows and megaliths. Richard
Mabey's *The Unofficial Countryside* (1973) sniffed out patches of
rural ground overlooked by urban sprawl, noting the British attitude

to nature as being 'a strangely contradictory blend of romanticism and gloom'. Roger Deakin's *Waterlog* (1999) took joyous plunges in the riverscape. Twenty-first-century Britain has witnessed a positive explosion of indigenous writing that fuses nature, geography and history, from Iain Sinclair's psychogeographic *dérives* to Paul Farley's *Edgelands* (2011) and Helen Macdonald's *H is for Hawk* (2014).

Film-makers, too, have made their own private pilgrimages to the heart of the country. In 1971 Derek Jarman brought his Super 8 camera to Avebury's stone circle, capturing the megaliths lit up by golden-hour sun rays and daybreak shadows, glittering with chromatic aberrations, melting and solidifying with the passing of the daylight hours like Monet's multiple haystacks. Jarman's short silent film *Journey to Avebury* gazes as intensely on the landscape of southern England as the paintings of Eric Ravilious, making it strange, absorbed in the prehistoric mysteries the standing stones throw across the cornfields and coppices. Hallucinations produced by the lucent alchemy of sunbeam passing through vintage glass.

A similar frisson comes from a contemporaneous public information advert, issued by the Countryside Commission and often screened between longer TV programmes in the early 1970s. These were odd, evocative vignettes promoting newly designated walks and public hiking routes, each marked with the trademark acorn logo. In a three-minute film about the Ridgeway – the hundred-mile ancient track winding across southern England between Avebury and the Ivinghoe Beacon in Buckinghamshire – the present day and the pagan past merge under a solemn voiceover ('The geography . . . of peace') and the Arcadian trills of a mystic flute. Hikers are intercut with actors clad in historical costumes, on horseback or herding sheep, who fade in and out of the pathways, ghostly guardians lingering in the leys. 'Witches cast their spell over many a sleepy hamlet,' warns the narrator. We watch through ultra-wide-angle lenses, held close to the earth. This is backpacking as time travel, rambling along Albion's wyrd Stone Age pathways. These walks, the commission declared, were more than just a breath of fresh air; they were earnest acts of ancestral communion, allowing you to follow in the footsteps of the departed.

■

There was never a film called *Robinson on the Ridgeway*, but it's tempting to imagine one. The mantle of psychogeographic travelogue was taken up in the 1990s by film-maker and artist Patrick Keiller. *London* (1994) and *Robinson in Space* (1997) attempted to deconstruct urban and suburban landscapes respectively. Keiller's tripod-mounted 16 mm camera is a static eye observing selected scenes, forgotten nooks and corners, revealing the landscape's subtle transformation by capital and geopolitical realities in post-Thatcher Britain. The footage, often beautifully composed, becomes part of a meta-fiction presented by voiceover (in these two films, by the veteran Shakespearean Paul Scofield). The narration declares that these movies have been made by the mysterious Robinson and his companion/lover, the unnamed one who is speaking. *Robinson in Space* is framed as a 'peripatetic study of the problem of England' consisting of seven journeys. Keiller projects his own concerns – the distribution of goods and the corporate enclosure of land and property – through this wry fiction, which compounds the sense that we are looking through the eyes of an individual who has since disappeared. Defoe's eighteenth-century *Tour Through the Whole Island of Great Britain* is invoked as a precedent for these *dérives*, which accumulate into a barrage of images and information, encompassing horizontal movement and vertical history.

Robinson in Space mentions figures on the right – Donald Trump, John Redwood and Michael Heseltine – who would remain active more than twenty years after it appeared in cinemas. Turning his lens on Cliveden House (a shelter for aristocratic Nazis) and Oxford (Hitler's choice to be England's capital city in the event of a successful

German invasion), Keiller/Robinson archly pursues a land survey that takes in the Tolpuddle Martyrs of Dorset and a Clevedon Pier shorn of the pleasure palace Betjeman found when he steamed in with cameras in tow some decades earlier.

In the tapestry of panoramas and observations, the film's more arresting fabrications shoot past like stray Red Arrows. Richard Jefferies's *fin de siècle* eco-apocalypse novel, *After London*, is mentioned: 'They heard it on the radio and mistook it for a documentary.' Hull, it's claimed, is really England's easternmost point on the 'Dublin to Berlin motorway'. Of such utopian projections upon the fabric of Britain Keiller's fantastical stuff is woven.

The film's terminus, Blackpool, is 'the key to Robinson's utopia'. Here it's not the garish sun trap portrayed in the British Transport Film *Holiday*, but a wind-lashed promenade, its Ferris wheel hammered by grey waves. *Robinson in Space* was shot in the months before the general election that brought Tony Blair's New Labour to power, in the final phase of John Major's Conservative government, with the zombies of free-market capitalism still stalking the land. One of the film's striking theses is that despite appearances, the UK economy was not declining, but thriving. The invisibility of wealth merely skewed the picture. Trade takes place in the anonymous surroundings of container ports and goods warehouses, protected behind high-security fencing. These and other concentrations of wealth, such as suburban shopping malls, stand next door to conspicuous dilapidation. The UK may be a wealthy nation, but its riches are not trickling down to affect the visible environment.

The name 'Robinson' wanders between several linked film projects around this time. One of the big influences on film-maker Chris Petit, when he made *Radio On* in 1979, was Céline's novel *Journey to the End of the Night* (1932), whose lead character followed in the footsteps of an enigmatic character of that name. Petit later used the name Robinson for the protagonist of several of his own novels. A stronger link between the work of Keiller and Petit is the producer Keith

Griffiths, who in a career spanning fifty years has been responsible for bringing a wealth of avant-garde culture and film to the television screen. As well as documentaries on artists, film directors, animators and more, he has worked with the Brothers Quay, on Peter Strickland's psychoacoustic fantasy *Berberian Sound Studio* (2012), and on the dreamlike rural drama *Light Years* (Esther May Campbell, 2015). All of Keiller's art-house films were produced by Griffiths, as were the TV collaborations between Petit and the great literary psychogeographer of London and England, Iain Sinclair: *The Cardinal and the Corpse* (1992), *The Falconer* (1998) and *London Orbital* (2002). In the latter, Sinclair and Petit drive around the M25 motorway – an ouroboros of contemporary geographic malaise – with a dashcam picking up traces of history and signs of urban degradation.

Petit first began filming roads to nowhere in *Radio On*, an English road movie in the shadow of the famous trilogy by Wim Wenders in the mid-1970s.[8] On this quest with no grail, the notion of the road movie turns inward, as it must in Britain, its roads being in no way comparable in length to the highways and freeways of the US, nor as efficient as the autoroutes and autobahns of mainland Europe. In his drift along the A4 between London and Bristol, ostensibly in search of the murderer of his brother, Robert B. encounters various lost souls (including musician Sting as a garage attendant with troubadour aspirations). Meanwhile, the muted and stalled post-depression landscapes of southern England unspool around him. (A futurist soundtrack of middle European pop from Kraftwerk and David Bowie mocks the run-down homelands.) This portrayal of a phantom nation was echoed by Petit himself, when he suggested it should have been double-billed with Clayton's *The Innocents*, describing it as a kind of ghost story, even going so far as to call it a 'muted pagan sacrifice to that strange beast, British cinema (a post-industrial twin to *The Wicker Man*)'.[9]

Petit's later film *Content* (2010) took a more essayistic approach, combining the text of a digital correspondence between writer Ian Penman and German musician/lyricist Antye Greie with a roving camera that stalked the movements of goods from mega-container ports to giant inland warehouses. Coming as a long-delayed, melancholic coda to *Radio On*, these dreamlike visions of sinister capitalist hulks and mysterious military installations are undercut by a narration that speaks of the previous thirty years of British history as like 'reversing into a tomorrow based on a non-existent past'.

■

The work of Petit and Keiller has proved to be a vital extension of the tradition of the British travel documentary. Behind the inclusiveness of the British Transport Films and the idiosyncratic melancholia of the Betjeman-style travelogues lay a fundamental conservatism – an attitude that accepted the nation as the film-makers found it, even if there was evidence that it was changing. Petit and Keiller, taking their cue from Ian Nairn, adopted a more critical mode, questioning the ownership of land, problematising issues around private property and public access, and seeking the truth about the hidden forces that were accelerating change across the landscape. With *Robinson in Ruins* (2010), Keiller continued his investigations of the hidden movements of capital and goods and the weird mismatch between Britain's inherent wealth and the threadbare appearance of its open spaces and residential areas.

Even more than *Robinson in Space*, *Ruins* was a road movie that had run off the road. The film is composed only of static views at the places where the film-maker's journey is interrupted. The project was initiated after the stock market crash of 2008, at a time when British cinema was dominated by gangster movies and costume dramas. Keiller's opaque, peripatetic style sat uncomfortably in this company, but the film grew out of an artistic and academic research project and was allowed to develop with few limitations.

What we are seeing, the narration discloses, is the surviving footage shot by a Robinson who had been released after serving a prison sentence, 'looked for somewhere to haunt', and then made this filmic research trip, before disappearing once more. The film aligns past and present in parallel and visits significant sites of resistance and martyrdom. Freedom of movement for the population, it points out, was granted by decree in 1795 to enable workers to participate in an increasingly fluid labour market. The failed Oxfordshire rising of 1596 (which, Keiller discovers, originated close to his own home) is also roped in, as an early example of pushback against enclosure. There's a brief panorama of a copse – the location where the body of David Kelly, the UN weapons inspector who was caught in the middle of a political scandal during Blair's push for war in Iraq, was discovered. 'Possession', we're reminded, can signify both ownership and madness. In these views, the landscape is rarely innocent.

And yet, at times, it is. As if responding to its rural environment, the pace of *Ruins* is even slower and more meditative than its predecessors. There are extended close-ups of flowers, trees and crops, with the longest takes reserved for a combine harvester crawling across a field. But Keiller achieves something rare here: he offers us the real-time tedium of actual agricultural work, not the rosy view of pastoral Romanticism. This field of wheat has nothing to do with the waving fronds of a Humphrey Jennings documentary or the reapers, bathed in a painterly golden glow, of Roman Polanski's *Tess*. Instead of the dream vision of Albion, Keiller here makes a successful attempt to depict the English countryside as it exists in the twenty-first century: an outdoor food factory, with little sense of nostalgia attached. At this distance, human agriculture begins to look more like the slow spread of a biological organism such as mould or lichen.

In one of the script's many abstruse lines, we are told that Robinson was searching for landscapes that reveal the molecular basis of historical events. This may have something to do with the frequent appearance in the film of lichens growing on a motorway sign near Newbury, Berkshire (itself the site of the Speenhamland rebellion of 1795 and a fierce eco-warrior protest in the 1990s). One particular

334 THE MAGIC BOX

patch of mould, which is revisited at intervals, resembles the profile of Goethe or an eighteenth-century judge. Nearby he locates a house in which Enlightenment scientist Robert Boyle developed his theory of gases, which led to the invention of the steam engine and, consequently, the Industrial Revolution. Like an episode of James Burke's *Connections* on steroids, *Robinson in Ruins* extracts maximum signifying power from each of its carefully selected views.

The lichens and minutely observed plant life introduce a dimension of non-human intelligence, which is another of Robinson's obsessions. A white foxglove wavering in a breeze has an 'aliveness', and the lichen is credited with a kind of sentience as it assumes a human shape. Like the medieval 'possessioners' of the Yorkshire moors, who combatted enclosure by ripping up fields, hedgerows and other border markers, these natural almost-still lives slow the speed of thought down to the vegetal or geological, a natural remedy for the clean economic brainwash of zombie capitalism.

In an interview, Keiller revealed two locations he wanted to film but never managed to reach: Castle Acre Priory in Norfolk, where Roger Corman shot *The Tomb of Ligeia* in 1964, and the ruined Waverley Abbey in Surrey – used as a location in the film *28 Days Later* by Danny Boyle.[10] Cinematic dystopias are not so far from *Robinson in Ruins* as you might think. The reason given for Robinson's arrest is that he was caught snooping around RAF Spadeadam in Cumbria. This site in the north of England was a test bed for the rocket motors used in Blue Streak, the last missile defence system developed and manufactured within the UK, before being replaced in the early 1960s by the US Polaris system. In the Hammer Films version of *Quatermass 2* (1957), there was a clear signal that the alien industrial plant is located in the north of England (a road sign points towards 'Carlisle'), which betrayed an awareness of the well-guarded activities at Spadeadam. 'I imagine', Keiller speculated, 'Robinson has conflated this narrative of *Quatermass 2* with that of Blue Streak, so that he understands the UK's subservience to the US in matters of foreign policy as the result of some *Invasion of the Bodysnatchers*-style takeover by a malevolent vegetal intelligence, like that of the Quatermass story, signalled by the cancellation of the (supposedly impractical) weapons system.'[11] (A tantalising footnote: in the original BBC version of *Quatermass II*, the professor was played by one John Robinson.)

As we have seen, all three of Nigel Kneale's Quatermass stories from the 1950s dealt in different ways with the encroachment of non-human intelligences and, in *Quatermass and the Pit*, the lingering effect of prehistory. As Robinson reaches his latest version of Utopia at the end of *Robinson in Ruins*, we see two very different forms of inscription on the landscape: prehistoric rock carvings and the urban calligraphy of Newcastle's skyline. Since forging this connection with invisible ancestors and a regenerated northern powerhouse city that has become a beacon for culture in the north-east, Robinson has vanished from the screen and gallivanted off into obscurity.

16

The Ragged Fringes

Gallivant, The Moon and the Sledgehammer, Requiem for a Village, Akenfield, Sleep Furiously, Way of the Morris, Two Years at Sea, Oss Oss Old Oss, Bait

Blackpool might have been the celestial city at the end of Robinson's/ Keiller's trajectory, but for another film-maker out and about with his cameras at almost exactly the same time, it was just another baubled stop on a longer itinerary. After a decade of involvement in performance art and eccentric short folk films, Andrew Kötting finally made his first feature at the mid-point of the 1990s. *Gallivant* (1996) announced a new kind of itinerant movie: 'a sometimes spry, sometimes clumping gavotte around Britain's ragged fringes'[1] that turned the Betjemanite *dérive* inside out, replacing the informed expert travel guide with a patchwork quilt of scuffed-up thoughts and memories, serendipitous encounters and counter-intuitive escapades. It's one of the most accomplished examples of the strain of film-making we'll uncover in this chapter: a narrative documentary approach that finds the camera rambling towards the last vestiges of the British wilderness. In these films the lens seeks out neglected corners of the landscape and outsider figures that, by accident or design, have ended up on the margins.

In *Gallivant*, Kötting set out to drift clockwise around Great Britain's coastline. Along the way, he bodged a movie from a mishmash of sped-up, time-lapsed and occasionally colour-washed Super 8, 35 mm and vidcam footage. There's no goal or thesis in mind, other than it being a bonding exercise between Kötting's six-year-old daughter Eden, who has Joubert's syndrome, and his grandmother Gladys, aged eighty-four, who has never travelled beyond England's shores. With its raffish associations, a gallivant carries the promise of devil-may-care freedom of movement. That's exactly the spirit in which Kötting approaches this jaunt.

The director proposed this as a 'snapshot of Britain today (complete with its past, which is part of today)'.[2] The long perambulation around the British mainland begins and ends on the beach at Bexhill-on-Sea, with the recently restored modernist icon, the De La Warr Pavilion, as a gleaming backdrop. The clean lines of this building, full of the post-war promise of a streamlined future, is counterpointed by almost every frame of the film that ensues, which evokes a nation coming gloriously apart at the seams. Beachside bungalows, displayed as a sequence of formal stills, have had their uniform design customised, but none of the 'improvements' can disguise the fact that these are little more than human hutches. Tudorbethan filling stations with vintage Shell pumps, a privately run toilet curated as kitsch artwork and the formerly busy dock of Port Carlisle, now an assemblage of disused stone quays, are among the signs of a discombobulated society encountered by the Kötting crew.

The developing bond between Gladys and Eden as the film progresses adds a warmth and poignancy absent from the more formal cinematic geographers. Kötting seizes the opportunity to document this once-in-a-lifetime experience with gusto. Gladys's memory is fraying like the East Anglian coastline – she never appears to know where they are on the map. Eden, meanwhile, is rapidly acquiring new skills – communicating in Makaton sign language – and, in a delightful moment halfway through the film, taking her first tottering steps.

As well as bonding with these two generations of his family, Kötting also attempts to get under the skin of his homeland. In a homage to the Edwardian folk-song collectors who beat the bounds of Britain in the early twentieth century in search of the people's secret music, he asks the characters he encounters to sing folk songs by heart. The mostly tentative blurtings of 'D'Ye Ken John Peel?'

provide an aching symbol of the fractured and tenuous survival of folk song in contemporary Britain, but he does eventually manage to find a Canute-like folk accordionist on the beach at Grimsby, belting out his song as his feet are mulched into the drowning sands.

Kötting finds a new way to represent the sensation of motion through the isles. There is hyper-speed dashcam footage, churning forward through overhung lanes and swishing between sunlit paddocks. Inside the 'round Britain' narrative arc, he inserts repeated motifs of eddying and circular motion: a becalmed, single-oared rowing boat; sword-wielding morris dancers. The film even circulates around its own making: the crew frequently butt into the frame; Kötting clacks a clapperboard before tucking it into his jacket; and he and Eden lick stamps, seal a batch of finished Super 8 reels into distinctive yellow padded envelopes and post them off for processing at the Kodak labs.

The frequent recourse to herky-jerky fast-mo, and time-lapse exposures, steeps the film in a nervous, tic-ridden sense of impatience. The word 'lapse', from the Latin for 'slipping' or 'falling' – both a literal landslide and a moral decline – comes with baked-in entropy. Kötting's manic energy, which results in him spontaneously leaping fully clothed into the sea or falling off the side of his camper van and shattering his ankle, seems part of a staving-off of the impending collapse. For all its outward charm, eccentricity and make-do endurance, the sanity of the country itself hangs by a thread. Sandy cliffs, people's land and livelihoods, are literally being eaten away by the actions of the very sea that has protected the nation for a thousand years. Eerie ancestral traces remain: 'On a day like this you can almost hear the ghosts of them,' says a local man whose family used to live at Hallsands, Devon, where only one ruined stone cottage now resists the briny assault.

Kötting's journey, though, proves you don't have to venture far into the English countryside before encountering a rich inner life of myth and legend. Tall tales of Cornish giants patrol the coastal paths as surely as the outsized effigies that show up in the film when the fairy stories are retold near the rocks of Tintagel. A boom mic is suspended over a dolmen. Welsh rugby players huddle in scrums next to a megalithic circle. The pagan Jack-in-the-Green ceremony is capered out in the darkened streets of Hastings. To outside observers, Britain's folklore communicates its strange past using a kind of archaic Makaton.

The landscape out here on Albion's crumbling periphery might give the impression of a threadbare, dilapidated, jerry-built nation, but it is a wonder-filled tapestry in Eden's eyes (and, to some extent, the director's). Like the metal detectorists gliding their electronic probes over the Norfolk shingle, Kötting is a diviner of Britain's concealed treasures, sifting the myths, mysteries, characters and histories buried just under the surface of things.[3]

■

In 1969 the painter Julian Trevelyan, veteran of the English surrealist movement, former student of etching with Picasso, Miró, Ernst and Kokoschka, made the *Thames Suite*, a series of twelve woodcuts depicting the life and landscape of one of England's great rivers. That same summer his son, Philip Trevelyan, and a small film crew spent a month in a camper van in a glade outside Horsham in Sussex, near Gatwick airport and barely twenty miles from London. Trevelyan had by chance met the seventy-five-year-old Mr Page, a former RAF engineer and part-time clown, and a well-known local character who lived with his family in a woodland clearing. Trevelyan's attempt to document the Pages' peculiar little slice of the Weald, their musings on life and their pottering, rambling, smithying and musicking, became the subject of the influential *The Moon and the Sledgehammer*, released in 1971.

The Moon and the Sledgehammer occupies its own microcosmic patch of English post-industrial Sylvania – a shabby cottage, a tangle of rusting mechanical components and tools, shotguns and short stretches of rail track, a rose garden, pianos and harmoniums, vehicle wrecks and a water well. Page, the father, lords over this manor, overseeing his sons' squabbles about the size of their traction engines. He can see the moon but is far enough away that he can swing his sledgehammer if he wants to. The image captures Page's benign resistance to modernity and reinforces the age-old notion – from the legend of the sleeping King Arthur to Johnny Byron, hero of Jez Butterworth's play *Jerusalem* – that the true magical, animal spirit of ancient Britain lies dormant, tucked away and out of sight in the countryside.

Cameraman Richard Stanley made creative use of a roving wide-angle lens to scope out the property (similar to how the Avebury ring was filmed in *Children of the Stones*), as well as tight close-ups on faces, the camera tracking the body language as the protagonists riff on their philosophies, hopes and opinions. 'England ought to be run by steam,' muses Peter, anticipating the coming oil shortage, in a gently dystopian vision that could only be bred in the garden of England. 'England's all to pieces.' His younger brother Jim, who may be having an incestuous relationship with his sister Kathy, or at least stares at her like a lovestruck puppy, expertly mimics different frequencies of steam-engine noise. The Pages are Luddites, but they are machine-makers, not breakers. Peter coaxes life out of a dead steam engine, and the brothers are separately restoring a pair of Victorian traction engines. Kathy trains doves to flap their wings, plays at fleeing the nest while at the wheel of an abandoned coach, tinkles the ivories of a ruined piano. The other sister, Nancy, keeps out of sight.

There is absurdist playfulness (old 'Oily' Page dons a gas mask and pretends to be an elephant and gleefully paints his cheeks with creosote), but as the film goes on a sadness emerges, along with a degree of familial tension. The brothers critique each other's tastes, the father is unimpressed with any of his brood, the girls would rather be somewhere else entirely. Kathy complains several times that her father is trying to 'dishearten' her. This film, in which every sequence

Weird scenes in England's backwoods: *The Moon and the Sledgehammer* (1971).

is dazzlingly framed, painted in nature's colours, with humans whose bodies and skin appear to take on the olive and charcoal shades of their craft and habitat, asks you to question who, really, owns the title deeds to the 'real world'.

Earlier in the 1960s Trevelyan had made some acclaimed shorter documentaries about rural labour, focusing on pottery and lambing. After making *The Moon and the Sledgehammer* he largely abandoned film-making and repaired to a patch of Yorkshire farming country, where he learned handicrafts of his own. Completing the film appears to have given him permission to do that, and to accept the wisdoms that can be learned about nature, people and ecology from the continuous occupation of one particular spot.

The film's close-ups on the speaking faces bring us into this family's intimate space. Sometimes macro shots of insects tumbling on piano keys or bogged down in sump oil are intercut with the slow action. Occasionally as they speak, light aircraft can be heard passing overhead. All of this builds up a picture of a group of humans who have pushed the modern world as far away from their everyday lives as possible. At the end, though, they emerge exuberantly into the streets around Horsham railway station, a police escort clearing traffic so that their infernal black traction engine can thunder past – a Blakeian nightmare returned through a wormhole – on its way to some steam fair.

■

> Everywhere . . . the change from old to new involving one certainty, whatever else may be doubtful, a worsening of the aspect of the country. This is the condition of England: of England the country of order, peace and stability, the land of common sense and practicality; the country to which all eyes are turned of those whose hope is for the continuance and perfection of modern progress.[4]
> William Morris

The spirit of William Morris, the 'anti-scrape' campaigner – in other words, the spirited opponent of urban sprawl and the sacrifice of the past to the march of industry – speaks strongest through *Requiem for a Village*, the David Gladwell project released by the BFI in 1975. Gladwell was obsessed with film from an early age and produced his own experimental shorts in the late 1950s, inspired by the surrealistic European art cinema of Cocteau and the slow-motion pillow fight in Truffaut's *Zéro de conduite*. He joined the British Transport Films unit in the early 1960s and was the editor on John Schlesinger's *Terminus* (1961). He worked for the rest of the decade on sponsored documentaries with Derrick Knight and Partners, creating a filmic hymn to *The Great Steam Fair* (1964) and pictures promoting the benefits of new towns – both of which are key elements in

Requiem. He edited Lindsay Anderson's *If . . .* (1968) and *O Lucky Man!* (1973), the early Merchant–Ivory production *Bombay Talkie* (1970) and the inspirational BBC visual essay series *Ways of Seeing* with John Berger (1972).

By the mid-1970s Gladwell had secured a commission for a feature intended to be shot entirely in slow motion. Prohibited by costs and technical difficulties, just a few choice slo-mo passages remain in *Requiem for a Village*. It intensifies the sense of the past made strange, lending an enchanted, supernatural air to a blacksmith's shoeing of a horse or the casting of an iron-rimmed wooden cartwheel. The film's first shots establish the semi-detached dwellings of a new town, built opposite an old rural village across the other side of a busy dual carriageway. An old man on a bicycle pedals across the causeway, metaphorically crossing a threshold of time into another realm of crooked cottages (some derelict, others gentrified), churchyard and fields. David Fanshawe's solipsistic solo flute music calls to mind the Countryside Commission's public information films. The film details the changes threatened by the new developments – capital fluttering around the diggers like the gulls and carrion birds that surround the ploughman.

The dreaded scraper is here, a steel bulldozer in Wimpey Homes' muddied yellow livery, ready to plough up more chunks of ancient field and forest. Between its destructive horsepower and the geometric plots of newbuild semis Gladwell intercuts static shots (in rhythms later taken up in Patrick Keiller's films) of gnarled, organic forms – spalled bricks, lichen-spattered gravestones, rippling roof tiles – a quiet celebration of imperfection and the patina of age. Unlike the murderous insurrection in a film like *If . . .*, the only protest in *Requiem* comes as the old man petulantly hurls a rock at the scraper's wheels. This impotent resistance encapsulates the mood of resignation that later pervades the film: the profound and lingering melancholia for the passing of old ways of life, of memories, of entire swathes of social history, and with them an uninterrupted connection to the past. The hairline cracks of 'broken Britain' are shown already emerging here, not as the outcome of social behaviours, but as a disconnection engendered by the destructive, profit-driven activities of commercial redevelopment.

The local squire and vicar attempt to drum up a resistance movement in a church hall populated by complacent, tea-drinking pensioners. In the woods – site of romantic encounters, fairy tales, magic – trees are marked for felling. Among these branches, the old man as a young boy collected birds' eggs and learned to cast spells with frog bones. Timber was logged sustainably and in proportion to need. The camera quietly observes the elegant spectacle of genuine wheelwrights binding a cartwheel's iron rim in fire, water and steam.

Has temporality in this Suffolk village (a village that could be anywhere in southern England) been upset by the arrival of the developers? The artist Stanley Spencer once explained how he wanted to paint the living and the dead reunited in joy, people emerging from graves wearing the clothes they wore in life. In this village, memories, and the former inhabitants, refuse to stay buried. While the

Meditation on the death of the countryside or English zombie flick? The strange case of *Requiem for a Village* (1975).

old man works in the graveyard, bodies literally rise up out of their tombs, dressed in Edwardian costumes. He is reunited with his dead wife and flashes back to various key life events, such as his wedding party, where the bride's father's speech refers to the biblical, cyclic notion that we come from dust and return to dust: 'And then a little boy says, "Look under the bed, there's a lot of folks either going or coming!"' – a characteristically whimsical English joke to deal with the abyss of eternity.

In the US, movies like *The Wild One* and *Easy Rider* celebrate the motorbike as the engine of freedom. By contrast, in the UK, two wheels are bad: the roar of progress, unwelcome change, black angels heralding the collapse of society. In *Requiem*, the village's stability is already being prodded, but into its midst ride the Triumph-mounted Hell's Angels of Death – copycat bikers, perhaps, from *Psychomania* and *The Damned*, or anticipating the scooter-revving Mods of *Quadrophenia*. They rip through the country lanes, party in the churchyard and rattle the air with noise, irreverence and sexual licentiousness. There are some uncomfortable scenes of parallel rapes and sexual violations from the bucolic past and the rowdy present. A farm girl is seduced by two studs at harvest time, and a biker chick is molested (apparently willingly). In the old man's own domestic memory, his mother submits to being drunkenly humped by his father in the communal bedroom.

The film offers no easy answers to the problem of progress. Inevitably, the old man is knocked off his bike by the Hell's Angels and takes his own place in the churchyard's kingdom of the dead. The bikers and the new town appear to win their claim on the future. The village proves to be as stagnant as the new town and shopping centre.

Requiem for a Village is a strange beast: part essay film, part social history, a dreamscape documentary. It breaks the bounds of factual film-making without quite becoming entirely fiction. It is an 'essay' in the original sense of the French *essai* (a try, an attempt), marking it as truly experimental, without it veering too far into the avant-garde. With its elements of documentary, abstraction, rural fiction, soft porn and horror/zombie stylings, *Requiem for a Village*'s sheer hybridity birthed few descendants over the following decades.

■

> In the middle of the copse, the remains of a smashed television.
>
> Jez Butterworth, *Jerusalem* (2009), stage direction, Act One

Requiem can be seen as the culmination of a string of films made in the first half of the 1970s, all in various ways concerned with the precarious state of rural and community life in England. Its closest relative is *Akenfield* (Peter Brook, 1974), filmed at Charsfield in Suffolk, a short gallop from *Requiem*'s Witnesham. Based on Ronald Blythe's novel/memoir, *Akenfield* is an essay on the relationships between country and city, couched in a trans-generational fiction using local amateur participants as actors, which revels in the textures, sounds and colour palette of the East Anglian countryside. It shares a nostalgic affinity with George Ewart Evans's mid-1960s books *Ask the Fellows Who Cut the Hay* and *The Pattern Under the Plough*, wistful but unsentimental evocations of rustic life compiled from oral histories collected around Suffolk farms. Or, again, the Suffolk horse fairs, held in villages such as Barsham in the early 1970s, which recreated the flavour of medieval (via early-twentieth-century) pageants and Victorian steam fairs, with jousting, hog roasts, folk theatre and military re-enactments – portals to the imagined villein-ery of 'merrie England'.

Later films like Gideon Koppel's magnificent debut *Sleep Furiously* (2008) take a similar delight in recording life at the far reaches of rural Britain. This artistic documentary finds the Welsh village of Trefeurig – where the director's mother still lives – dealing with the impending closure of its local school. This comes on the heels of the shutdown of local public transport routes and shops. It's not a mournful movie, but its portrait of everyday life in this close community is very aware of the changes that are eating away at its former certainties. Released in the year of the great global credit crunch, it foreshadows the sharper claws of austerity that would take hold over the following decade. Still, Koppel focuses on hopeful signs – a mobile library appears, like a pedlar's caravan importing exotic goods from afar – and he peppers the narrative with arresting landscape views and even blocks of solid colour, allowing a measure of meditative space. His roving camera captures and transfigures a Welsh village at peace with itself, even as outside forces gently but irreparably nag at it. Without reaching for the soapbox, it's a stirring reminder of the otherness of life in tranquil spots away from urban centres. Aphex Twin's Satie-esque piano music provides the perfect note of bittersweet pastoralia.

Sleep Furiously benefits from Koppel's personal connection to its locale, and the same applies to *Way of the Morris* (2011), in which co-directors Tim Plester and Rob Curry attempt to strike a connection with the traditional English morris dance. Plester's father had been a long-standing member of the Adderbury morris side, and the film tracks Plester as he literally steps into his father's shoes and joins the group, learns the moves and their ritual meanings, and finds his youthful scepticism turning to understanding and acceptance. In this elegiac film that skips along the magical songlines of Oxfordshire, the morris is restored from its frequently satirised little Englander image to something mysterious and powerful, a lightning rod for communities and social history. Plester ends up travelling with the lads to France and the battlefields of the Somme, where they learn how many of their Adderbury morris ancestors died in the trenches of the First World War. Plester is young enough to be aware of all the reasons why morris dancing is mocked and misunderstood, but alert to its important place in Britain's folk history.[5]

A hermit at the edge of the world: *Two Years at Sea* (2011).

Venturing ever further towards Britain's margins and frontiers, *Two Years at Sea* (2011), by film-maker Ben Rivers, is an extended motion-picture portrait of a real-life hermit. Rivers discovered Jake Williams living in a tumbledown shooting lodge in the middle of a forest at Bogancloch, near Rhynie in Scotland. The film observes Jake's daily routines, such as washing, going to the toilet, foraging and even sleeping, as well as his more ambitious construction projects, like single-handedly hoisting an old camper van into a tree to act as a crow's nest. Like the family in *The Moon and the Sledgehammer*, Jake is a strictly analogue dweller on the threshold, living outside time, holding modern routines at bay. Since he hardly speaks in the film, we are left to infer his personal history from the artefacts, photos and clutter surrounding him. He appears to be a survivor of the Scottish alternative communities of the late 1960s and early '70s (such as the Incredible String Band's residence on the baronial estate of Lord Glenconner). At one point he puts a scratched and skipping LP of folk music on his turntable: Dave Goulder and Liz Dyer's highly collectable *The Raven and the Crow*, on the Argo label. Other times he listens to an old cassette of riveting Indian/subcontinental drone music. These ancient and ponderous rhythms penetrate deep into Jake's own daily life. He hikes through the glens, plastic canisters bumping on his back, and constructs a crude raft, which he launches onto a small loch to go fishing. Rivers lingers long on this becalmed, silent drift on the glassy lake, marvelling at the image of a life beautifully becalmed.

Like *Sleep Furiously*, Rivers's previous short film, *Ah, Liberty!* (2008), penetrated the daily experience of a way-out community – here, a group of young children on a farm in the wilderness. Detached even from the ordered life of a village, he chronicles a more random succession of human activity, where practical tasks blend into play. Rivers shot that film and *Two Years at Sea* in black and white on a vintage Bolex 16 mm camera. He hand-processed the footage, so that the flaws, white-outs as the camera is opened and grain of the older film stock could be incorporated into the texture of the film. In *Two Years at Sea*, most of the shots are static, tripod-mounted, observing Jake's life without judgement. The duration of the film encompasses a micro-life cycle, beginning as this solitary human awakes, comes to life and makes various marks on his ecological island, and ending in near darkness as he sits with his own thoughts by a crackling fire. The film observes a hermit's private utopia, which can only be attained by shutting the door on the modern world. Viewed from another angle, it might be showing us the last survivalist human on Earth.

■

There's my father in black and white, nine years old and dancing in a ring of children in a street in the middle of the tiny Cornish fishing village of Mevagissey. It's 1945, and he's in a film called *Johnny Frenchman*, set in the early years of the war – typical patriotic fare, a love story set between fishing communities on the coasts of Cornwall and Brittany. Joe and Eileen, my dad's parents, spent the last year of the war running a guest house a few miles up the road. Penarwen, with multiple bedrooms, surrounded by sprawling grounds, was absurdly cheap in the wartime housing market and was bought in a somewhat run-down state (my grandpa didn't actually want to move there at all). For a few weeks during the shooting of *Johnny Frenchman*, Penarwen was requisitioned as the hotel for the film crew, director Charles Frend and actors like Tom Walls, Patricia Roc and Françoise Rosay. Long before Mevagissey was fictionalised as Trewissick in Susan Cooper's *Dark Is Rising* trilogy, doubled as Whitby in a 1979 version of *Dracula*, and even longer before the gastropubs moved in, it was a straightforward Cornish fishing village. My granny recalled those weeks, in the dying months of the war, as a highlight of what turned out to be a relatively brief tenure of the property, the actors bringing a dash of debonair charm to the rambling Victorian residence.

Six years after, on the northern coast of Cornwall, above Mevagissey, folklorists Alan Lomax and Peter Kennedy arrived in Padstow, their car boot loaded with film equipment, and recorded the local dances, costumes and street life. The result was a magical–anthropological documentary called *Oss Oss Wee Oss* (1953). It features the 'Old Oss' of the annual Obby Oss ceremony in that village, which, with its strange black shape and snapping jaws, might be a survival of some atavistic fertility dance. The Cornish tribe here is depicted with as much fascinated distance as a Western documentary on a lost African tribe. I can sink into its high-saturation colours and smoky pub interiors and feel attuned to a vanished world, the England of my father's boyhood, where he too danced in unconscious delight on Cornwall's sunny cobbled streets.

■

'You didn't expect to see this sort of dancing in Cornwall . . .'

One of the driving forces behind the filming of *Oss Oss Wee Oss* in 1951 was its director, the celebrated American folklorist Alan Lomax. In self-imposed exile from the McCarthy anti-communist investigations, Lomax had based himself in London in 1950, from where he carried out a series of field trips around the British Isles, Europe and beyond, making recordings of regional folk musics for the Columbia record label. In the process he galvanised the British folk scene, injecting it with the spark of life and radical politics it needed before it could take flight during the 1950s. Acting as producer on the expeditions was Peter Kennedy, the British equivalent to Lomax, who played a similar role in documenting local folk music, dialects and dances. As the son of the then president of the English Folk Dance and Song Society (EFDSS), Douglas Kennedy, Peter was carrying on a family tradition.

On their way down to Cornwall, the crew, including cameraman George Pickow, stopped off for a break at Stonehenge. Having filled their lungs with the pagan air of Neolithic Albion, they drove on to Padstow and proceeded to film the revels on the eve of the May Day ceremony. Pickow used a Bolex film camera and Kodachrome stock, and in much of the film's colour sequences the Beltane fire of spring seems to almost ignite the celluloid with its brightness. Amazing tribal dances were filmed on May Day eve in the Golden Lion pub, on the last two rolls of black-and-white film Pickow managed to find at the chemist. Here, as he shot hand-held by torchlight, young men performed a vigorous shamanic dance to a demented side-drum pulse. The music is far removed from the morris: a thunderous tattoo that suggests painted skins, war dances, heels on glowing ashes. That is what makes *Oss Oss Wee Oss* so remarkable: it paints a picture of a peripheral England that's now utterly gone. Barely half a decade after the Second World War, these blue-rinsed ladies, fishermen and civic burghers are instinctively swept up in a surviving pagan rite. Historically, the community has even defended the Oss tradition against more puritanical adversity. The village greengrocer who delivers the welcome speech on May morning reminds the population that 'eighty years ago', the people had to fight the authorities who wanted to stop the Oss coming out.

It was Lomax, scribbling notes in the car on the journey, who decided on the narrative frame: the Cockney city-boy voiceover, putting questions that are answered by Cornish local Charlie Bate. Charlie, with his accordion, acts as the spirit guide to Padstow, pointing out the key facts: that some local historians believe the Oss comes from a Stone Age fertility ritual; the cutting of the green and the decking of the streets with sycamore branches; the various local characters. If Lomax's archival work was driven by his desire to sweep up whatever shards of the past remained in contemporary culture, here he found a surreal assemblage of images and actions that, even to a twenty-first-century British observer, taste exotic and uncanny. Subject matter and cinematic texture combine in a timeless fever dream.

■

'At Highclere, tourist after tourist talks about their love for British drama. Lesley, from Australia, says that she likes *Grantchester* and *Doc Martin*. Cyndi name-checks *Midsomer Murders* and *Pride and Prejudice* as favourites. Sharon, 72, and Angela, 71, neatly bobbed friends from New Jersey, say that they have planned their UK holiday around their favourite British shows: Highclere for *Downton*, Cornwall because of *Poldark*, and Scotland because of *Outlander* . . .'[6]

Film alters the landscape. Not only thanks to the filters, lighting and post-processing that tints a scene with its cinematic identity, but because it also leaves a mark on the land. Britain's costume drama exports created a market for British film tours in the 2000s. One of the most successful companies, Brit Movie Tours, founded in 2009, was conducting sixty different tours each year by 2019, taking forty-five thousand tourists on routes featured in series such as *Peaky Blinders*, *Sherlock*, *Doctor Who*, the *Harry Potter* movies and *Midsomer Murders*. 'Things that have a very quintessentially British flavour do best,' the company founder, Lewis Swan, told an interviewer. 'Tourists want to see quaint villages or something that represents the national identity.'[7] Fifty per cent of the visitors came from the US and Canada, and most of the rest were British.

Highclere Castle, a five-thousand-acre estate in Hampshire, has been one of the biggest beneficiaries of the Brit period-film boom. It had featured in various productions, including *Jeeves and Wooster* and *Eyes Wide Shut*, but by 2009 its owners were looking at a bill for repairs around the estate of some £12 million. The following year the house was cast as the principal location in *Downton Abbey*, and within two years the gigantic upturn in tourism the series had generated had effectively covered the costs.

The meaning and experience of a place can be fundamentally altered after the film crews have left. People still make pilgrimages to the blustery caravan site at Burrowhead Holiday Village, on the west coast of Scotland, to sit for a few minutes at the feet of the original wicker man – and feet are pretty much all that's left, two wooden stumps embedded in a block of concrete overlooking the black cliffs. Recalling his visit to the location decades afterwards, actor Edward Woodward said that he found the remains of a wooden cross in the ruins of a chapel, still lying undisturbed where he had chucked it after shooting a particular scene in the middle of the film.

I can't pass through the medieval village of Lavenham in Suffolk without projecting straw and sawdust onto the main square and seeing the witch-burning scenes from

Witchfinder General. Out by the Suffolk coast, the white
water tower outside Southwold and a particular beach
house at Thorpeness are inscribed with the memory of Peter
Greenaway's *Drowning by Numbers.* The first flat I bought in
London stood directly opposite an imposing Victorian pile in
Dalston where Mike Leigh shot *Naked.*

The knowledge that a piece of ground has been occupied by
the director, actors and crew, with all the attendant logistics,
problems, takes, retakes, emotion, frustration and jubilation,
casts a spell over a place. Sometimes the filming leaves an
even deeper mark. May Day revellers at the Obby Oss festival
at Padstow in Cornwall still wear hats and colourful costumes
that were used for the first time in 1951 in order to look better
on camera when Alan Lomax and Peter Kennedy came to
town. At moments like these, film records itself in the folk
memory and becomes a part of the tradition.

■

In his good-natured way, Alan Lomax touched on age-old tensions
between country and city in scripting the faux-ignorant questions
posed on the soundtrack to *Oss Oss Wee Oss.* Decades later, those
tensions were not only still in place, but even amplified after decades
of throttled local authority budgets and stalled social mobility. As the
second-poorest district in the European Union,[8] Cornwall harboured
some of the largest inequalities in the country, as well as being a
region where hardscrabble industries such as fishing and agriculture
rub up against competitive tourism and gentrification. The shabby
Mevagissey of *Johnny Frenchman* no longer exists. Its visible face is
a 'quaint fishing hamlet', while what remains of genuine industry is
almost invisible.

Just as Bill Forsyth good-humouredly explored roots and disconnection, the true meaning of wealth and the environmental cost

of capitalism in the Scottish-set *Local Hero* (1983), English director Mark Jenkin set out to explore these tensions in his first feature, *Bait* (2019). The film not only holds these ideas in play, but is shot and edited with a consciously vintage black-and-white patina that harks back to the documentaries of Robert Flaherty and John Grierson, the art films of Maya Deren and the more recent work of Andrew Kötting and Ben Rivers. It feels like a transfigured version of the kitchen-sink drama – pressing social issues refracted and made strange through the vintage lens of another dusty old Bolex. The result suggests that these problems are not just restricted to 2019, but are part of a deeper structural flaw in English society.

Most of the locations are around the village of Sennen, far down towards the jumping-off point of Land's End. The principal dramatic tension is a microcosm of the change afoot. The Leighs, a self-important middle-class family from London, have just bought the cottage, and former family home, of local fisherman Martin Ward and his brother Neil, to use and rent out as holiday accommodation.

Bait (2019), a twenty-first-century film shot on a vintage camera to timeless effect.

Martin continues his trade, while Neil has repurposed their late father's old fishing boat to take tourists on cruises. Symbolising the precarious economy, Martin catches lobsters by hanging his nets off jagged rocks, while the Leigh family stock their new fridge with wine, champagne, cream teas and supermarket cheeses. Martin still haunts the cramped seafront terrace, unable to sever his ties to the house, while sarcastically viewing the kitsch improvements made out of his old buoys, anchors and portholes.

Both parties are trying to make a living here, but the dice are weighted in favour of the incoming landlords. There's a telling exchange where the family's young tenants complain about the noise of Martin's boat engine, as if their entitlement to a peaceful lie-in trumps the local economy. The Leighs forbid Martin to use the cottage's parking space any more: the tenants have priority because 'they pay'. Money talks here, but money also walks away – Martin refers to the profits from holiday lettings being spent 'in the Maldives', rather than reinvested in the local economy. Meanwhile, the ghost of Martin's father keeps watch on the situation, keeping him company. Behind its increasingly tangled storyline, *Bait* has much to say about the mutual ignorance and hostility of town and country; about the illusions sold as part of the Airbnb package; and about the inexorable deepening of social immobility in Britain. It's another kind of requiem for a village, but also a requiem for a vanished ideal of national unity that seems impossible to resurrect.

DIVIDED KINGDOM

17

Pageants and Pandæmonium

Orlando, A Diary for Timothy, Family Portrait, 2012
Olympics Opening Ceremony, *In the Forest, Jubilee,* Philip
Donnellan, *For Memory, Living on the Edge, The Lie of the
Land, The Levelling, The Stuart Hall Project, Arcadia*

> A family with the wrong members in control – that,
> perhaps, is as near as one can come to describing England
> in a phrase.
>
> > George Orwell, 'The Lion and the Unicorn: Socialism
> > and the English Genius'

This section ventures beyond the costume drama to enquire into the strategies film-makers and television producers have used to approach *unofficial* histories, underdog vantage points and unconventional timelines. Sometimes, to tell a wider historical story, it's necessary to step off the temporal travelator and enter a more symbolic time frame.

There are many odd words in the English language whose meaning we instantly comprehend, but whose etymology remains shrouded in the fog of ages. 'Pageant' is one of those: it possibly derives from the Latin *pagina*, meaning page, or part of the script of a play; equally possible is that *pagina* once indicated some kind of movable scaffold, perhaps of the sort used in the staging of a medieval mystery play. In any case, when we think of a pageant, what comes to mind is a succession of tableaux celebrating a national story, a conveyor belt of juicy historical chunks, boiled down to their bare bones.

Since they chronicle a nation's transit through the ages, pageants are, by definition, microcosms of change. Edmund Spenser's epic

Elizabethan poem *The Faerie Queene* featured 'Mutabilitie's pageant'. Twentieth-century writers such as E. M. Forster and Virginia Woolf were also fond of the idea. Woolf's final novel, *Between the Acts* (published in 1941, months before her suicide), is entirely to do with a pageant taking place on a country estate shortly before the war. Set in June 1939, it features a lone woman, Mrs Manresa, directing the local community in a series of historical fragments from Great Britain's island story. At this muggy moment of rural stillness in the brewing storm of war, disparate folks and classes are briefly united, in the light of a shared history and telling of a national myth.

Woolf realised that the British are so attached to pageants because they are compressed journeys through time and between changes of state. Her earlier novel *Orlando: A Biography* (1928) is a trip through English history, starting in the age of Elizabeth I; the peregrinating protagonist is both temporally- and gender-fluid. Sally Potter's 1992 film adaptation starring Tilda Swinton ranges through historical periods, with gear-changes of costume and setting, and even a gender metamorphosis from male to female. The section set in 1700, in the age of William and Mary, cannot avoid paying visual homage to *The Draughtsman's Contract* in its formal compositions, colour geometrics and neoclassical music. It opens with Orlando as a male youth reading Elizabethan sonnets under a tree, and circles round to a present-day, young mother Orlando, leaning against an oak tree in a sunlit meadow. Her daughter runs around the field, playing with a hand-held video camera. 'She is no longer trapped by destiny,' speaks the voiceover, 'and ever since she let go of the past, she found her life was beginning.'

Forster's novel *Abinger Harvest* was published in 1934, with an attached script for an *Abinger Pageant*. Performed in Forster's Surrey village of Abinger, with music composed by Ralph Vaughan Williams, the real-life event featured a 'Woodman' retelling local history, from the Roman invasion to the present, and an implied future in which the local meadows and forests are bulldozed away by 'houses and bungalows, hotels, restaurants and flats, arterial roads, bypasses, petrol pumps and pylons'. Four years later, Forster staged a more ambitious pageant along similar lines: *England's Pleasant Land*, for the Dorking and Leith Preservation Society. Vaughan Williams again contributed the music, and the yarn dived deeper into the English history of resistance to enclosures and aristocratic land grabs. In the finale, Forster's stage directions called for a procession of small bungalows, traffic and litter to fill the stage, in a build-up of urban chaos and pollution.

In *England's Pleasant Land*, the country was under threat of enclosure, and the gentry/rural labourers and the past/future were set bitterly at odds. As her pageant winds down in *Between the Acts*, Woolf's Mrs Manresa puts on a record: 'The gramophone gurgled Unity – Dispersity.' What better summation could be found of the mongrel British condition? Like folk revivals, pageants grasp at national stories, even at the moment they appear to be breaking up and fading away in favour of something new. *Between the Acts* 'is a book about a continuous English way of life,' writes one commentator on the period, 'that now threatens to break apart, and it asks how it might be possible to hold the pieces together'.[1] This recognises the suspicion that Britons remain covertly at war with themselves – an adversarial society perpetually unable to resolve its squabbles.

■

How often, though, does anyone try to achieve unity across the battle lines? The form and intention of the pageant necessitates a concluding note of hope. Before and during the Second World War, Humphrey Jennings's documentaries, such as *English Harvest* (1938), *The Heart of Britain* (1941) and *This Is England* (1941), had already probed, and to an extent cemented, self-images of the nation, strengthening identity in a time of fracture and crisis. *Fires Were Started* (1943) still provides the defining filmic imagery of the

Blitz and its aftermath. *A Diary for Timothy* (1945), a sequence of vignettes of British life filmed and produced in the final year of the war, gains in poignancy precisely because of the moment in which it was made. Emerging from the long shadows of war, an exhausted population is tired but determined. The enemy is on the run, but the war is not yet won. This panoramic pageant of wartime Britain is framed as a letter to a newborn baby in a comfortably middle-class borough of Oxfordshire. The shelter, care and comfort of this infant are the recurring images, even as his father is absent fighting in the Far East. News – of breakthroughs and setbacks – arrives by wireless, telegram, letter, newspaper, idle gossip. The film revolves around many of Jennings's familiar images – of miners, farms, railways, bomb damage – and even recycles some of his famous National Gallery footage of Myra Hess playing Mozart. Jennings bears witness to the green shoots of Britain's recovery: scaffolding and land mines are removed from the beaches; a pilot downed over France regains the use of his broken leg; luxury goods tentatively return to shop windows; smiles at Christmas. E. M. Forster's script,

Rebirth of a nation: *A Diary for Timothy* (1945).

narrated by Michael Redgrave (in the solemn tone later adopted by Oliver Postgate in his voiceovers for *Ivor the Engine* and *Bagpuss*), attempts to construct a panorama of the nation this baby is born into, and finally ponders what kind of human being the child will choose to become.

Jennings made his best films in wartime. Although he is considered to have floundered during the last five years of his life, one of his final works was another cinematic pageant, *Family Portrait* (1951). In honour of the Festival of Britain, this twenty-three-minute black-and-white short was yet another precursor of the British Transport Films and the grand geographic tours of the televisual age. This time, Jennings himself wrote the script, which begins by laying out the unique properties of the island nation: its natural defences, maritime heritage, its huge variety of land structure and soil variation, all matching the diversity of the people and their spirit of enterprise. From there the edit sweeps in a broad arc from prehistoric artefacts like Avebury and the Long Man of Wilmington to the factory chimneys of London and sundry shots of 'the march of the machine' and its operators.

But neither does the film shirk from the negative fallout from Victorian progress, and from observations of English eccentricity. He appears to have understood, within the limits of the propagandistic production companies who funded his work, that Britain could never be reduced to a jingoistic, one-nation approach, and that the key to understanding the national character lies in its eternal paradox: its zeal for progress and attachment to tradition. 'We like sitting quiet at home [man asleep in sunny suburban garden] and we like pageantry [Life Guards parading outside Buckingham Palace] . . . But then, pageantry in Britain, believe it or not, isn't put on by a sinister power to impress anyone, nor just to have fun. It's part of the pattern of life.'

The pattern of life: it could almost be a manifesto for Jennings's own attempts at a total synthesis in his film-making. 'Carnival' might be too rumbustious a word, but his documentaries are certainly parades of human activity in the British Isles designed to convey a sense of nationhood across a range of locations and classes. If he had lived longer, he might have embarked upon one of the several projects he was considering before his death: his biographer Kevin Jackson records that he had made 'hundreds and hundreds of pages of notes'[2] for a twelve-part series, most likely for television, on the history of the British Empire. And he had written a detailed treatment for a film based on R. J. Cruikshank's *Roaring Century*, a history of Britain between 1846 and 1946. These billowing thought-clouds were all intended to gain an insight into the character and state of the nation. 'Not even the film could keep pace with this man who wanted, in effect, to compress the life experience of a modern renaissance into a symmetrical shape prolonged in time for less than sixty minutes,' wrote his fellow director Basil Wright in an epitaph.[3]

At the time of his death in 1950, Jennings was close to completing a book project that was even more of a montage than his films. He had collected hundreds of written eyewitness accounts of the coming of the machine in early modern Britain, which he described as 'an imaginative history of the Industrial Revolution'.[4] What this meant was a sequence of public and private texts, starting in 1660 with an extract from Milton's *Paradise Lost*, and ending with a passage from William Morris's *A Dream of John Ball*, from 1886–7. Edited by Mary-Lou Jennings and Charles Madge, the volume finally emerged in 1985 with the Miltonian title *Pandæmonium*. All the texts spanning this two-hundred-year period were chosen because they describe 'certain moments, events, clashes, ideas . . . which either in the writing or in the nature of the matter itself or both have revolutionary and symbolic and illuminatory quality . . . they are the knots in a great net of tangled time and space . . . Each', Jennings added crucially in his introduction, 'is in a particular place in an unrolling film.'

The film-maker's concept of history: frame succeeding frame as the universe unspools through the projector of time. Read as a totality,

Pandæmonium – a kind of historical retrospective Mass Observation project – is a psychic register of the effects of rapid change, when an agricultural/rural economy transitioned to an industrial/urban one, altering not just the economy, but the nation's self-image. In compiling it, and true to his socialist Crown Film Unit ideology, Jennings witnessed the undercurrents driving the transformation: the capitalisation of land, technology and the workforce.

■

A similar version of the national story underpinned what is probably the most widely viewed example of British pageantry ever seen by an international audience to date. The opening ceremony of the London Olympic Games in Stratford in 2012 was devised by a film director, Danny Boyle, and a writer, Frank Cottrell-Boyce, who had many television and film screenplays under his belt. The ceremony was a performance scaled up to the size of a stadium and tailored to the requirements of an international televised spectacle. Unusually theatrical, it paid surprising attention to detail, including small incidents and characters that would have been invisible to the stadium crowd but could be tracked with close-up, hand-held cameras.

The first part of the three-hour event was a gargantuan ensemble piece titled (with a nod to both John Milton and Humphrey Jennings) 'Pandæmonium'. In Milton's *Paradise Lost*, Pandæmonium is the region of hell where the fallen angel Mammon and his hordes mine gold and other symbols of vanity from within the bowels of the earth. The passage describing the process sounds – as Jennings remarked when he chose it as the first extract of his *Pandæmonium* book – very much like the fiery furnaces and belching factories of the coming Industrial Revolution: 'Anon out of the earth a Fabrick huge / Rose like an Exhalation, with the sound / of Dulcet Symphonies and voices sweet.' Even back in the republican 1660s, Milton could sniff the stench of Blake's dark satanic mills.

When Elgar's 'Nimrod' faded and the lights went up in the Olympic Stadium, the entire athletics field had been transformed into a stylised patch of English arable Arcadia, dotted with rustic yeomen, shepherds, milkmaids, maypoles and sheaves of corn. The television coverage intercut between the dramatic action and a film montage made earlier by Boyle. This started in the primordial ooze of the source of the Thames in Oxfordshire. The camera whizzed along the river's surface at high speed, skimming past innocent children playing, the characters from *The Wind in the Willows*, the Oxford versus Cambridge Boat Race, cricket on a Surrey village green; flew over Richmond Bridge and on into the metropolis, past Pink Floyd's barrage-balloon pig over Battersea Power Station, past the South Bank to the strains of the Sex Pistols' 'God Save the Queen' and the Clash's 'London Calling', swooping over the Docklands and its distinctive U-shaped river bend to freeze briefly on the *EastEnders* title sequence, overflying Tower Bridge and tacking north-east towards Stratford.

In the stadium, the artificial landscape-in-a-bowl comes to life. Reapers reap, farmhands tend livestock, beekeepers huff smoke at hives, youngsters skip around maypoles. All is green and white, Arcadia's natural palette. Children's choirs beam in from Northern Ireland, Scotland and Wales. 'Jerusalem' is sung, and the dark, satanic mills sprout from the earth. To one side lies a small grassy knoll, criss-crossed with pathways: Milton's 'Hill whose grisly top / Belch'd fire and rowling smoke; the rest entire / Shone with a glossy scurf, undoubted sign / That in his womb was hid metallic Ore, / The work of Sulphur.' Industrialists in top hats and tails, headed by Kenneth Branagh as Isambard Kingdom Brunel, emerge from the hill and look proudly on as the village-green paradise is paved over with factories, chimneys and machinery. Yokels and farmhands transform into factory workers and engineers; sheaves are shunted out of the way by factory engines, weaving looms and smokestacks. When Branagh recites the famous speech of Caliban from

Shakespeare's *The Tempest*, about the isle being full of noises, it's not the strange magical music of Prospero's island that's being described. This is the threshing machine of industrial Britain that eventually sent its male youth out as cannon fodder in the First World War, administered a supercharged global empire and then struggled to deal with its multicultural consequences. With its parades of infantrymen, bandsmen in *Sgt Pepper* uniforms, Chelsea Pensioners and Windrush immigrants, the Olympic performance dramatises all of this in the space of a few minutes, in a telling whose nuances were only visible to television viewers. This was the kind of overarching national story that no one seemed able to muster up in time for the Millennium Dome in 2000.

Danny Boyle's and Frank Cottrell-Boyce's Olympic Ceremony was notable, then, for not involving a historical parade of kings and queens; instead, it acknowledged the cultural and economic forces that have shaped Albion into the United Kingdom, for better and for worse. It also insisted that, like Mrs Manresa's *tableau vivant* in *Between the Acts*, pageants can be as much people's histories as official versions.

There exists a significant body of work, for both television and cinema, that reinforces the idea of the pageant/historical panorama as grass-roots or reconfigured history. Much of it consists of small-scale productions or one-time TV broadcasts. Phil Mulloy's fascinating obscurity *In the Forest* (1978) tracks the progress of a trio of peasants in a forest in England, from the feudal age to the Civil War, Industrial Revolution and the Peterloo massacre. Amid snippets of *Macbeth* and an appearance from King James I, as well as English politicians such as William Pitt and Walpole, there are discourses on the social position of the yeomanry; the new social contract proposed by Gerrard Winstanley; and the ongoing, systematic brutality of the ruling class and aristocracy towards the oppressed poor. Knights, monks, brigands, Roundheads, landowners, merchants and old John Bull himself flit through this fragmentary, black-and-white portmanteau, which admits, in one resonant line, that 'history is but a fable in which we agree to believe'.

The same year saw the release of Derek Jarman's *Jubilee* (1978), which contained the almost identical sentiment: 'History's intangible – you can weave facts any way you like.' *Jubilee* is a punk carnival of the grotesque, in which Elizabeth I is transported by her court magician John Dee to a vision of the future state of her kingdom. Jarman's England of 1977 is a wasteland of punk anomie and corporatised entertainment, symbolised by the vampiric Borgia Ginz, who now owns Buckingham Palace and has converted the royal residence into a punk-rock recording facility: 'As long as the music's loud enough,' he cackles, 'we won't hear the world falling apart!' The principal players are a commune of four female punks – a motley collection of amateur historians (Amyl Nitrate, played by Jordan, begins the film by saying, 'I will reveal to thee the shadow of this time'), artists and borderline psychopaths. Across a loose storyline of an increasingly murderous spree through the vestiges of the entertainment industry, Jarman drapes various tableaux, such as children dancing around a barbed-wire maypole; 'The Kid' (a pre-fame Adam Ant) snogging a TV screen and genuflecting before the Albert Memorial in Hyde Park; and the Virgin Queen and her entourage, guided by the magical spirit Ariel, wandering the barren streets of London and the rocky coastlines of Dorset. Unlike punk movies like Julien Temple's *Great Rock 'n' Roll Swindle*, this was a state-of-the-underground-nation movie that refused to glamorise the nihilism of punk rock. As Jarman himself once put it, 'The present dreams the past future.'[5]

■

'Will all people now arriving please make their way to the "M" of "MORNING".'

Three weeks before, the *Bristol Evening Post* had carried an advertisement asking for volunteers to take part in a

crowd filming session for the first-ever breakfast TV show on
British commercial TV. The location happens to be on a flat,
wide-open grassy plain on Durdham Downs, right next to the
Avon Gorge with its famous Clifton Suspension Bridge, and
a couple of hundred metres from the front door of my home.
Here's me on this blustery, sunny Sunday morning in January
1983, carried along in a tide of extras, approaching the plain,
which is already heaving with humanity.

The assembled flock is being shepherded into formations
that will spell out the words 'GOOD MORNING BRITAIN'
when seen from the air. Lengths of string, skewered into the
turf, trace the outlines of the letters. My mate and I have
clad ourselves in fluorescent orange anoraks, the better to
be spotted by the helicopter, which is idling its rotors over
by a small copse. As instructed by the voice over the tannoy,
we head for the 'M' of 'MORNING' and find ourselves
crushed together with others in that consonant's right-hand
downstroke.

Good Morning Britain, under the auspices of the ITV
franchise TV-am, was intended to be the first attempt at early-
morning broadcasting in the history of British television. As
it turned out, the show, originally hosted by David Frost and
Anna Ford, was just beaten to the post by the BBC's rival
Breakfast Time show. But this twin-channelled assault on
the peace and quiet of the British morning would change the
media landscape for ever, opening up more life-hours to the
thrall of the television set.

I'm not sure if I am proud of my small contribution to
this minor media revolution, but I do vividly remember the
hours standing there, as a chopper wheeled back and forth
over my head, while the producer shouted at us through his
metallic loudhailer. After the helicopter had made some low
passes over the gigantic logo, we were ordered to scatter into

a formless mass, then run back to re-form into our assigned
letters, as the cameras whirred. 'Beautiful!' rasped the
megaphone. 'The director wants you all to know he's having
orgasms up here!'

The moment is out there still, in its fuzzy YouTube version.
The final title sequence eventually also included 'Good
Morning Britain' spelled out by free-falling parachutists, by
troops on the deck of an aircraft carrier and by pigeons in
Trafalgar Square. We Bristolian pigeons, who didn't even have
the luxury of birdseed to peck at, were on screen for all of two
seconds, but the performance is positively BAFTA-worthy.

Plus, it looks sunnier than I remember it.

■

Television has entertained plenty of instances where documentary has overlapped with art film, folk archives and the spirit of
the people's pageant. You could look at the total output of director

Philip Donnellan as one example: between 1958 and 1982 he made upwards of fifty films and documentaries, many for the BBC's factual department, and frequently focused on Britain's colonial legacy, the lives of ordinary folk and the untold stories of Gypsies, soldiers and craftspeople. His debut, *Joe the Chainsmith* (1958), documented the metalworking skills of a chain-maker in the East Midlands, in order 'to capture an atmosphere and demonstrate a personality, to evoke in pictures, words and music a form of community which though it is now outdated and rapidly passing away has kept in the people who make it up many qualities: dignity, honesty and the capacity for hard work among them, which cannot always be found in the men and women of the society which is succeeding it'.[6]

In the early 1970s Donnellan televised several of the *Radio Ballads* of Ewan MacColl, Peggy Seeger and Charles Parker. These had been innovative radio collages transmitted in the late 1950s and early '60s, products of the first post-war folk revival, which was driven by the socialist clique around MacColl, A. L. Lloyd and others. The original *Radio Ballads* told stories of fishermen, coal miners, railway drivers and teenagers, in a creative mixture of field recording, interviews and specially composed folk music. Donnellan's television versions of *Shoals of Herring* (1972), *The Fight Game* (1973) and *The Big Hewer* (1974) were reboots and remixes of the original radio works, adding archive footage and newly filmed visuals to the mix, alongside some new music from MacColl. Donnellan's own political sensibility caused him to turn up the contrast on the social inequality aspects even more than the original *Radio Ballads* had done. *The Other Music* (1981) documented what was left of Britain's dwindling folk club circuit, which had to a large degree been founded by MacColl, Seeger and Lloyd in the early 1950s. In the wake of at least two separate revivals, the folk scene had at that moment hit a slump, although Donnellan makes a brave stab at celebrating British grass-roots traditional music and the folk who keep on singing it, at a cultural moment when folk became unhip and largely went to ground.

■

Television's reaction to the bite of Thatcherite monetarism in the 1980s tended towards realistic social drama, such as the works of Alan Bleasdale (e.g. *Boys from the Blackstuff*, 1982) or newsreel-based documentary (e.g. ITV's *World in Action*). Programmes like these reacted to contemporary social problems, but there was still space, occasionally, for programme-makers to step back and take the longer view in a kind of alternative pageant or 'people's history'.

Because confused BBC programme controllers buried it in day-time programming in March 1986, *For Memory* (Marc Karlin) was viewed by a small audience and is barely remembered today. Karlin, who died in 1999, was a political film-maker and television essayist who wasn't afraid to incorporate avant-garde techniques. One commentator has said, 'His rigour, his intellectualism and intolerance of anything he considered lazy or in bad faith conspired with the trend towards corporatism in television to render him and his work all but invisible.'[7] *For Memory* was begun in the mid-1970s as a film about the televisual medium, memory and cultural amnesia. With a recurring motif of a camera worming its way around the streets of a specially constructed model city (a kind of three-dimensional telegenic memory theatre), it features testimonies from historians E. P. Thompson and Cliff Williams, the anti-fascist activist Charlie Goodman and Alzheimer's disease patients whose memories are fading away. There are interviews with members of the British Army Film Unit, who talk about filming the liberation of Belsen. *For Memory* manages to comment on television's responsibility to enshrine memories – not necessarily collective or universal – as well as to critique its tendency to trivialise and whitewash fact with a fictional version of its own.

There were other wide-scope projects tackling the social cost of Thatcherism and the ripping-up of roots and memory. Broadcast on Central TV in November 1987, *Living on the Edge* (Michael Grigsby,

1987) was a documentary co-written by John Furse that was explicitly inspired by Raymond Williams's great study of the urban and rural dichotomy in British culture, *The Country and the City* (1973), and the films of Humphrey Jennings. In its nationwide survey of deprived areas and dispossessed folk, it asked what had happened to the compassionate, utopian social policies promised after the Second World War, and wondered what became of the challenge laid down at the end of *A Diary for Timothy*: 'Are you going to have greed for money and power ousting decency from the world as they have in the past? Or are you going to make the world a different place – you and all the other babies?'

It starts on the Rolfe family's Devonshire farm, where they face eviction by bailiffs. Frank Rolfe is stunned by the collapse of the farming business he has tended his whole life, now left with no profit and nothing to take away, staring at a future spent living in a modern council house. The film cuts between his plight and that of a group of young unemployed Glaswegian men, some Welsh former unionists, two generations of women in Sheffield and a young man in a bedsit who sings electronic folk songs about a collapsing Britain.

The film intercuts archive and stock footage, and audio such as Churchill's VE Day speech. His utopian post-war pledges ('to preserve and enhance the beauty of our country') are offered up as an ironic counterpoint to the precarious lives shown here. This is a labour force in a state of shock in the years immediately following the miners' strike and the break-up of union power, scrabbling to stay afloat in an economy that one interviewee describes as 'going backwards'. It's an England where the traces of old community bonds – a pub singalong that's straight out of a Terence Davies movie – are capitulating to an encroaching culture of instant gratification ('Can't Wait', screams a bus-shelter ad for French Connection).

After a six-month pre-production period in which they immersed themselves in these communities, Grigsby and Furse came up with a film that helped to give voice to the left-behind, to tell their own stories (no interlocutors or interviewers; all the quotes are taken from spontaneous conversations among the participants themselves), and thus an unofficial history accumulates. The Glasgow boys resist the mobility and freedom of movement potentially offered by the labour market; they would prefer to live and work in the area in which they grew up. At the end of the film the camera crew embarks with them on an overnight coach to London, where they are forced to go in order to find work. The Welsh unionists discuss the break-up of organised workforces and name the culprit as 'power in its raw sense. Not authority, power.' A new form of neo-liberalism is taking over Britain and the police are participating in riot drills – a country at war with itself. The film ends with a deliberate echo of the final scenes of *A Diary for Timothy*: with the birth of a baby and a mother's hopeful, loving gaze. Chancellor Nigel Lawson's budget speech of 1987 is played over the image, in which he announces tax cuts for the rich – to cheering Tory benches.

Living on the Edge is among the most powerful documentaries to get under the skin of the country. It stands alongside the likes of the *Seven Up* series (Michael Apted, tracking the lives of individuals at seven-year intervals), *The Family* (Frank Roddam, 1974), *Public School* (Roger Denton, 1980), 'The Fishing Party' (Paul Watson, 1986, part of the BBC's *40 Minutes* series) and *The Lie of the Land* (Molly Dineen, 2007). These were all actuality programmes that took the temperature of their times and accentuated notions about privilege, social mobility and the parlous state of the countryside, among other factors.

Dineen shot *The Lie of the Land* on the hoof. The portability of a hand-held video camera allows her to get her feet dirty by penetrating beyond the Tourist Board vision of rural England. She develops tentative friendships with various farmers and smallholders in Cornwall and the south-west and is given access to their scruffy farms and dilapidated slaughterhouses, and to the inner sanctums of local fox hunts. She ventures inside the daily life of remote farms, with their spattered mud and blood, piled carcasses, pheasants plucked and chucked into cramped crates.

In these muddy heartlands agriculture is in crisis, stretched to breaking point by government subsidies and European quotas. Sheep and cattle breeders pay pittances for the 'flesh run', in which healthy but unsellable animals are collected in pickup trucks and driven away to be executed. Fox-hunting is about to be banned by New Labour, and the film opens with a protest march to London by the pro-hunt Countryside Alliance. Worlds and time zones collide as a hunt careens past the futuristic space telescopes at Goonhilly. 'The land has been nationalised,' complains one farmer, who fears that as the UK imports more and more food instead of growing its own, his traditional role is pivoting towards stewardship of the land as a 'playground for people from the towns', rather than growing crops or raising livestock. Supermarkets are the new barons, whose mutual competition holds sway at the expense of local farmers and, by extension, impacts the land itself – its function and appearance. Townies take it for granted that outside the city there will always be the possibility of escape to rolling acres and green, pleasant pastures. These embittered yeomen remind them that the scenery exists for a practical purpose, and if the farms disappear, so will the very image of England. 'The country is becoming unreal,' says one.

The overcast, unsentimental landscape and the rural abjection in *The Lie of the Land* rebound in Hope Dickson Leach's feature *The Levelling* (2016). Trainee vet Clover returns to her father Aubrey's farm on the flooded Somerset levels, where her brother is to be buried after apparently shooting himself following a night of bonfire-lit revelry. This is the demoralised, subsistence-level side of farming that is rarely depicted in the long-running BBC radio drama series *The Archers*, which makes Dickson Leach's casting of David Troughton (who voices Tony Archer in the series) as Aubrey eerily apposite. The swelling rain clouds, sodden fields and muddy trackways are brilliantly captured in wide angle by Nanu Segal, while unpleasant, harsh

Agricultural abjection: *The Levelling* (2016).

noises clag the sound design. This straggling family's dysfunction is mirrored in the sight and sound of the landscape, and Aubrey's denial and rudderless leadership can be read as a microcosm of wider structural failings. Britain's national imagination might still harbour a deep dream that its pastoral paradise will one day be restored. *The Levelling* suggests the gate may have closed on that particular escape route.

■

In earlier decades questions of race, and Britain's post-colonial legacy, were less often explored or held to account on the television. The contributions of a figure like Stuart Hall to the media landscape were vital, but being spread across a myriad of brief appearances on talk shows and current-affairs debates, the complete picture was hard to assimilate. Hall was an Oxford scholar, instigator of the *New Left Review* with Raymond Williams and co-founder of the Birmingham University Centre of Cultural Studies with Richard Hoggart. But as a non-white cultural commentator holding power and prejudice to account on television as far back as the mid-1960s, Hall was a rare sight. Only in retrospect, in *The Stuart Hall Project* (John Akomfrah, 2013) – produced as both a three-screen installation and a ninety-five-minute film – can Hall's cumulative impact and contribution to the national conversation be appreciated. An immense act of retrieval, *The Stuart Hall Project*, in its documentary film version – a pageant of impressions, found footage and TV clips forming the immigrant perspective on Britishness – places Hall's message in sharp relief. His was a lifelong mission to alert the British to the fact that immigration was not a random accident, but a logical outcome of the imperial legacy that nationalists are so proud of; that immigrants from around the Commonwealth did not come from nowhere, but were a product of the British Empire, driving the profitability and global influence of the UK. In recent years, mainstream television has begun exploring the immigrant experience and black British perspectives in, for example, documentaries on the *Windrush* generation and Steve McQueen's superb drama series *Small Axe*.

Hall himself alludes, in one clip, to his own status as an immigrant, the in-between state that means it's hard for him to use the word 'we' in either the Caribbean or the UK. The idea is perhaps even more pertinent for subsequent generations of British-born, non-white children, largely raised in Britain's urban environments but struggling to integrate and find a voice. 'The question of "honoring" begins . . .' wrote Akomfrah of the un-archiving process, 'with memory, with uncovering the stems of memory, the ghosts of history, sifting through the debris and detritus of past events for traces of the phantoms . . .'[8] The procession of retrieved imagery in *The Stuart Hall Project* is a forensic act of detection, uncovering Hall's mercurial trajectory through the broadcasting and intellectual landscape of British culture in the late twentieth century. The film ends up as a pageant of all the 'unfinished conversations' Hall initiated or took part in: on anti-colonialism, the Suez crisis, the Hungarian revolution, the Vietnam War, the civil rights movement, the New Left, feminism, class politics and cultural studies.

Afterwards, Akomfrah made reference to the opening ceremony of the 2012 Olympics, which took place while he was assembling his film: 'The casting of it was inconceivable,' he wrote, 'hard to imagine that you might have such a multicultural meaning in such a national event. I think the fact that it happens is an indication of a national drift. The sense that you are part of a dialogue is much more assured than before.'[9]

∎

The 'lost Eden' narrative compressed into the Olympics opening ceremony has certainly ushered in new versions of a similar story. Bucolic black-and-white clips featuring golden post-war imagery – timbered houses, ivy-choked pubs, farm workers with big smiles, Women's Institute cycling clubs: the Stanley Baldwin/Ladybird Books/John Major mythology of England – form the opening sequence of *Arcadia* (Paul Wright, 2017). This feature-length film montage plundered the BFI's archives and a huge array of other regional videotape banks, documentaries, feature films such as *Winstanley*, *Requiem for a Village* and *Anchoress* (Chris Newby, 1993), television snippets and private videos to create a seventy-eight-minute psychoanalysis of the British rural subconscious. From its first shot – inevitably, a muddy field in England – it moves through a cyclic, seasonal structure, with chapter titles such as 'Amnesia', 'Folk', 'Utopia' and 'The Turning' marking a metamorphosis from innocence to experience, both a celebration and a warning that love of the soil can unlock darker exceptionalist or fascistic desires. 'The truth was in the soil' and 'There's nowhere like it on Earth' are two spoken quotes that leap out of the first minutes. Then falls the sickle. The strange, sometimes violent survivals of pagan ritual, such as pace-egging and cheese-rolling, the sheer weirdness of children dressed in Lincoln green, the stag antlers, Burry Men, straw bears, maypoles and May queens, fairy dancers and nudists all attest to Wright's aim of evoking 'nightmare, dream, memory, reality, all blurring together without being too clearly defined as to which is which'.[10]

The agrarian paradise of Gerrard Winstanley, as portrayed in Kevin Brownlow and Andrew Mollo's eponymous 1975 film, is a recurring motif in *Arcadia*: 'Why may we not have our heaven here?' The Diggers' self-reliant earthly Eden is appropriately juxtaposed with images from the hippie encampments and festivals of the 1960s and '70s, the ring-road acid-house parties of the late 1980s, and earlier examples of naturism and exotic folk dances, dating right back to the Edwardians. Emanating from the trance-like editing rhythm of this Blakeian accumulation of frolics, acid-house beats and anti-urban enlightenment, you sense a deep yearning in the British soul for transcendence, nature worship and the weird.

But somehow the inheritance has still not been won. 'The Turning' sequence shows how Jerusalem hasn't even been granted planning permission. The Diggers on St George's Hill were forcibly dispersed by a combination of Roundhead officials and locally hired mercenaries. A montage shows how much British current affairs television has denigrated the idea of socialism, its theories stamped upon and derided as antithetical to common sense. Private land ownership allows regulation to be suspended or ignored. Trespass laws close down access to nature – a symbolic casting-out from the Garden. The film suggests that the seventeenth-century eviction of the Diggers was merely the start of a process that is still ongoing. Machines (including the bull-dozers from David Gladwell's *Requiem for a Village*) mash up the earth, gouge out quarries; forests are set ablaze. Traditional English fox-hunting turns to savagery and Darwinian barbarism. The final 'Winter Solstice' section offers a depressing reel of urban and rural decline, poverty and recession, cattle carcasses burning during the foot-and-mouth crisis, teenage glue-sniffers, the heartsick society. *Arcadia* signs off with a natural logic – the suggestion of rebirth and new dawns – but its 'answer' to the problems thrown up – 'The past is gone, the future is unwritten' – is provisional and speculative at best. In tapping the collective unconscious in Britain's pageant of filmic memory, *Arcadia*'s poignant mudlarking churns up an unwelcome home truth: that Britain, for all its richness of history, diversity, eccentricity, memory, mythology and mutability, remains a nation with a civil war forever raging under its surface.

18

Ill Fares the Land

The Luddites, Winstanley, Comrades, The Wind That Shakes the Barley, The Massacre of Glencoe, Peterloo

> The General Enclosure Act at the beginning of the [nineteenth] century completed the triumph not only of the landlord over the peasant but of one type of civilization over another. Once more, it was the victory of Imperial Rome over the city-states of Greece.
>
> H. J. Massingham, 'Our Inheritance from the Past', in *Britain and the Beast*, 1938

The English Civil War, with its clashes of monarchists versus republicans, Catholics versus Protestants, libertarians versus Puritans, superstition versus rationalism, rich against poor, encapsulated so many of England's fault lines, and they still affect the national character. Apart from the comic black-and-white *Cardboard Cavalier* (Walter Forde, 1949), the Civil War rarely featured on British screens, until 1963, when Hammer's *The Scarlet Blade* (John Gilling, released in the US as *The Crimson Blade*) came out – a film that showed divided and conflicting loyalties within families. As we've seen, the 1960s mark the transition from theatrical, studio-bound representations to period reconstruction. Ken Hughes's epic *Cromwell* (1970) attempted the full sweep of the Civil War era, culminating in the beheading of Charles I, but featured some convincing battle scenes, even if their chronology was not always on point. More recently, television has showcased the BBC's *By the Sword Divided* (1983–5) and Channel 4's *The Devil's Whore* (2009). In terms of historical accuracy, the stakes were raised at the end of 1960s. Nineteen sixty-eight saw the foundation of the Sealed Knot, a society dedicated to recreating English Civil War skirmishes and battles in full Roundhead and Cavalier garb, with authentic pikes and muskets. Sealed Knot societies have advised and lent costumes and equipment to films ranging from *Winstanley* to *A Field in England*. But however authentically this period in English history is treated, it always opens up fundamental questions about what kind of country England should be, who owns the balance of power, who has the right to use the land or exploit it and its people. These questions, opened up in the wake of the Civil War, were intensified by the land clearances and enclosures of the century that followed, and each age has produced its own uprisings of rebellious reactionaries, protesting peacefully or violently against change, technology and exploitation.

For instance, d'ye ken Ned Ludd? Given that he often seems to be lurking just off camera in the subtext of so many British films, Ned Ludd ought perhaps to supplant John Peel and John Bull as a national mascot. Whether Ludd was a real historical figure or a mythical conflation of several leading figures in the 'Captain Swing' movement of machine-breakers in the late eighteenth and early nineteenth centuries, as the Industrial Revolution got under way, his name has passed for ever into the English language. The Luddite resistance movement launched by weavers and textile craftsmen against the Jacquard loom and other labour-saving technology that threatened to make them redundant has given rise to a commonly used expression that refers to anyone resisting the tidal wave of technological advance (or struggling to operate a TV remote). It's surprising to find, then, that the story of the Luddite movement has almost never been told on the big or small screen. There was *The Luddites*, a half-hour programme made by Thames Television, broadcast in 1988, in which director Richard Broad attempted to tell their tale as a faux-documentary inspired by *Culloden*. This dramatised the face-off, in one town, between uncaring and brutal factory owners and their employees, whose 'arcane crafts' are being rendered extinct by the workforce being sucked of necessity into the factories. The film does what it can within its short duration, but we still lack a widescreen account of this workers' uprising that combined solidarity with anti-technological sedition.

An earlier, proto-Luddite movement of English history has fared better. In *Winstanley* (1975) Kevin Brownlow and Andrew Mollo – the directing partnership responsible for *It Happened Here* – hit on a timely moment to film their living tableau of the Diggers' last stand. As a Civil War-era movie filmed in crisp black and white, it is an obvious precursor to *A Field in England*, but it is more planted in the solid loam of fact, with much of the dialogue lifted verbatim from the visionary writings of Gerrard Winstanley himself.

The shoot dovetailed with what remained in the mid-1970s of Britain's radical counter-culture. On America's West Coast, the name 'the Diggers' had been revived by the counter-cultural collective that went around idealistically handing out food to frazzled San Francisco festival-goers. By 1974–5 British hippiedom had fragmented into an underground of communes and LSD farms; of religious quackery and spiritual retreats; of free festivals and mildly miffed brigades of sit-in students.

The events enacted in *Winstanley* did, in reality, happen here (on St George's Hill at Cobham in Surrey, to be precise – currently a gated community of luxury housing). They represent the enactment of an ideal, absurd perhaps, but no less desirable. Winstanley's dream was truly revolutionary: to take back the land as a divinely ordained inheritance, to till the soil and live off the common treasury of the land as God had intended; to return the fields of England to their prelapsarian, agrarian state. To restore power to the collective and make an Eden in Albion's paradise garden.

Such essentialist altruism pops up now and again in times when idealism itself is under extreme pressure. For instance, *News from Nowhere*, the 1890 novel by William Morris, imagined Britain in a projected future where all traces of industrialisation have been destroyed by the populace and replaced with barter, craftsmanship and small-'c' communism. These values, it seems, even trickled down into the cast and crew's experience of making *Winstanley*: it was principled, sustainable film-making, avoiding much of the waste and self-indulgence of commercial pictures. 'It was an enterprise', recalled the novelist Marina Lewycka, who worked on the set and appeared in a small role, 'held together by a shared belief that commitment was more important than money, a lack of hierarchy that occasionally bordered on the anarchic, the spirit of voluntarism, good humour, camaraderie, stoicism in the face of setbacks, and a willingness to submit to the rigours of English dirt and English weather in pursuit of a higher purpose.'[1]

The battle scenes between Cavaliers and Roundheads at the beginning of the film are a masterclass in cinematic economy. Brownlow and Mollo shot the combatants – amateur members of military re-enactment societies wearing armour borrowed from the Tower of London – in tight close-ups, to avoid having to deploy large numbers of extras. The viewer is shoved face to face with the nervous soldiers and trapped between these two poles of the English schism, with their muskets, pikes and stampeding horses. In the aftermath of war, we're quickly shown the injustices that led Winstanley to seek his third way. The victorious Roundheads demand the birthright for which they believed they were fighting, but under Cromwell's protectorate, social injustices still prevailed. Organised Christianity and its preachers – like Parson Platt, who owns the land where the Diggers have settled – conspired to preserve hierarchies and foment public opinion against the pioneers. Platt practises carrot-and-stick dogma (feeding pies to his children only once they have learned to recite their abstruse scripture); another pious local noblewoman believes the Lord wanted charity to exist. In their 'battle for the whole of England', the Diggers are forced into an almost gnostic position, in which their right to use the land peacefully is a direct legacy from God, bypassing human agencies.

Cultivating Eden in Albion's paradise garden: *Winstanley* (1975).

As we've seen, there are many instances in British film where penetrating the soil releases devilish and unspeakable horrors. Winstanley,
William Everard and their huddled masses start to build their life
on St George's Hill by shoving their weight against a genuine
seventeenth-century breast plough. The methods may be crude, but
this is digging in pursuit of a new world, laying the foundations of
the kingdom of heaven, not dredging up buried nightmares. Mollo,
who first came to Brownlow's attention as an obsessive collector of
Nazi and wartime memorabilia, engaged various local history societies and even the Victoria and Albert Museum in his quest for authentic costumes and props. By harnessing the English heritage industry,
the film radiates a sense of the past, but at the same time characters
project themselves with human individuality. Tom Haydon, a pau-
per who arrives with his wife and baby, is beautifully clad in sacking
and a felt hat with a spoon tucked into its brim. Mollo even tracked
down the correct types of pig and cow, even though those breeds
were now as rare as hen's teeth.

After Winstanley's first, tempestuous encounter on the heath with Parson Platt, the wind whistling around their ears, the camera pulls back for one of this film's many broad aerial views. Numerous significant scenes and events are filmed from a distant perspective, with the human figures tiny among this wide, unspoiled yet contested landscape. When the local congregation attacks the Diggers as they are toiling on a hillside, the violence is far out of reach, as incidental as the background of a Brueghel canvas, while the soundtrack is only insouciant birdsong.

These long shots contrast with the close-up intimacy of the woodland camp site. The film immerses itself in the ambience of the quietly meditative rhythm of the Diggers' daily lives, the slow labours involved in constructing shelter and preparing food. It was shot across a whole year, so weather plays a leading role, and the changing seasons are embedded in the frames. Crops were actually planted and harvested during the shoot. *Winstanley* tries to place the viewer *in* this world, yet for all its realism and minute detail, it also has a faint, dreamlike, artificial quality to it. The editing has a strange, unfamiliar ebb and flow. This may be down to the use of so many non-professional cast members and the schoolmasterly tone in which Miles Halliwell delivers Winstanley's verbatim quotes; or to the silences on the soundtrack, which were partly forced upon it by the proximity of Heathrow airport.

Neither does the film shy away from observing how Winstanley's passive leadership left a power vacuum that was filled by the arrival of a group of Ranters, tearing up the Bible and preaching free thought and free love. Here came another casting masterstroke, with Sid Rawle as Ranter-in-chief. After smashing down the barricades at the infamous Isle of Wight Festival in 1970, Rawle became a key agitator in the early-1970s commune and free-festival scene, and a prime mover behind the Windsor Free Festival. This made him something of a hippie figurehead by the time the film was made, and the anarchic energy of him and his swivel-eyed compadres, preaching for permissiveness and the end of sin, erupts into the forest tranquillity almost as violently as the villagers' provocations. If only the Diggers could have found themselves an island, they might have walled themselves up in the kind of parallel universe Sgt Howie discovered on Summerisle in *The Wicker Man*, united in their beliefs. The reality, as Brownlow and Mollo convincingly demonstrate, is that idealism attracts opportunists, and its innocent, liberal openness is a short step away from lawless chaos. In the end, though, the anarchy is supplied by their supposedly decent neighbours as they ransack the Digger settlement one last time in a night raid. In the nocturnal firelight, silhouettes of Christian householders tussle over looted cooking pots. Winstanley's face is the picture of thwarted altruism, bewildered at how his vision could come to be so hated.

■

Buckled into the back seat of my grandfather's duck-egg-blue Triumph Herald, watching the speedometer set in its gloss walnut dashboard, I'm babbling. 'Did you see this, last night I watched that, there was this great episode where . . . and then he . . . you wouldn't believe what she . . . I love the bit where . . . will we get home in time to watch . . .?' It's the only time I remember my grandparents ever getting cross with me, because all I want to talk about is what I've seen on TV. 'Did you see . . .?' They exchange a horrified look and, as one, snap my head off.

Sometimes the television set becomes a battleground. In the early 1980s the household acquires its first home computer, thanks to my powers of persuasion (it will be an invaluable aid to my study of arithmetic): a Commodore Vic-20 with 3.5 kilobytes of RAM and eight colours. It's a cream and chocolate keyboard, but there's no dedicated screen. Instead, you plug it straight into the back of your domestic TV set.

Unfortunately, since it takes around four hours to one-finger-type the BASIC code required to make an animated '$' hop from one moving '=======' to another across a river, my mother's evening viewing time becomes somewhat contracted. It develops into a source of teenage arguments, until one fraught night it all ends with Mum in tears, and I decide it's no longer a good time to bug her with buggy software.

My granny moved in with us after my grandfather died, in a spare room converted into an elderly person's bedsit. She won't disturb anybody, she insists, settling into her new room with her three-piece suite, foldaway dining table, Grandpa's book collection, china Staffordshire dogs on guard at the gas fire and new Hitachi colour TV. No wooden cabinet for this bad boy; it commands the room in its naked state. 'You all live your lives as normal. You won't know I'm here.'

Although she will live the last years of her life with an active household around her, my granny never completely gets over the loneliness. She does the gardening and writes letters and watches more television than ever before. The screen is a comfort, as it has been for so many of the elderly and the bereaved. Now, when I'm back home on college vacation, it's her turn to try my patience with the TV babble. As a student I'm embarking on a period of many years without a TV set of my own, but it's a luxury to come home and feast on the riches that late-1980s nocturnal scheduling has to offer. The television is an alternative education, a repertory cinema showing foreign movies, Hammer horrors, literary adaptations, live music, art and science documentaries. All-night chat shows hosted by Tony Wilson of Factory Records. Life-changing stuff: an hour-long interview with Jean Genet for the BBC's *Arena*; *The Human Condition* trilogy by Masaki Kobayashi; Channel 4's 'red triangle' series of transgressive movies; *Snub* and *The Tube*; and a series of personal essays on British film by Alan Parker, Lindsay Anderson and others. Feet crooked over the arm of the easy chair, I'm soaking this stuff up like a book, long after midnight.

There are the two gentle taps on the door, and Granny's head appears. Several seconds later: 'Would you like to come in and watch that on my set?' And what that really means is, 'Please come and help me feel less alone.'

■

Winstanley's righteous followers had only the books of Genesis and the New Testament to cling to. Less than two hundred years later, the germs of the British trade union movement took shape around very tangible measures of injustice. The introductory scenes of *Comrades* (Bill Douglas, 1986), an epic but seldom-screened movie based on the lives of the Tolpuddle Martyrs, feature a band of machine-breakers in a field in England smashing the automated grain hoppers that are taking away their livelihoods. It's 1833, and laws have been passed banning all public assembly. These Luddites are beaten back by the cavalry. There's little in the remainder of Douglas's film to match this degree of brutality, but there's a more insidious hurt being perpetrated on the peasants of this Dorset village by their landowning employers.

Tolpuddle's cottages and muddy streets are barely an improvement on the Diggers' thatched hovels. Douglas brings his cameras inside these bare-walled, dilapidated homes and finds a husband and wife, both carpenters, being forced to conceal their extra work on a Sunday, necessary to fulfil an order of wooden chairs but forbidden by the church. He focuses on the warmth of the Loveless family, whose breadwinner, George, also practises lay preaching in the chapel on Sundays. A highly effective early sequence sets the high church, where the vicar speaks of the 'natural order of things' – inequity is divinely ordained – in marked contrast to the chapel. As James Hammett wrenches himself out of the pews and takes his place with the chapel brethren, competing musics enact the underlying social discord – solemn, funereal anthems laid across uplifting, polyphonic folk hymns. George's mode of address to his labouring congregation is the opposite of the vicar's: warm and inclusive; unifying, not divisive.

These working people are craftsmen and farm labourers who have not yet been required to shift from field to factory. But the power relations between them and the gentry who employ them are firmly entrenched, as witnessed on pay day. The serfs, standing nervously in line to be handed dwindling amounts of coins by their grudging masters, are pitiful to behold. Their dignity is broken and there is no form of appeal against the reduced wages. At one point we see the nobles gambling with marked cards: the deck is perpetually stacked in these cheats' favour. The proto-union meetings George convenes in an upstairs room are a form of secret society, with swearing-in rituals, a flag based on a skeleton and a bond of mutual trust.

The complete Tolpuddle Martyrs story – which ends up journeying to the far side of the planet and back, when the rebels are arrested and transported to the Australian colonies – requires a cinema's wide screen, and Douglas communicates his awareness of the medium. The director had a peculiar affinity for the history of cinema and its prehistory in the art of illusion. He amassed an enormous collection of books on the subject, and his cramped flat was a miniature museum of optical curios. Certain scenes in *Comrades* feature props from his own collection: magic lanterns, a *trompe l'œil* engraving of a skull in a print-shop window, a cavalier portrait in the mansion that alters as you move in front of it. These eerie placements contributed to the sense that a sophisticated trickery has been spun by the ruling class around the impoverished lives of the protagonists, whose self-appointed task is to penetrate the illusion and break free using their comradeship.

There is a recurring figure of fate played by Alex Norton, who begins the tale as a nomadic lanternist passing in front of the Cerne Abbas Giant hill figure on his way into Dorset. He is refused permission to project his light show at the manor house and sets up instead in the village. This primitive cinema, enthralling to the stimulus-deprived paupers, recurs via Norton's reappearances throughout the course of the film: as a purveyor of dramatic, chiaroscuro dioramas; as a silhouettist; and as a 'mad photographer' in the Australian outback, miserably failing to take a portrait of an Aborigine with his clunky apparatus. Norton's occasional glances directly into the camera exhibit the self-awareness of the film, and as he takes his final bow, staring directly at the viewer, a voiceover observes, 'It was almost as though he'd been present throughout.'

Comrades is so powerful because you realise how rare it was, in a 1980s movie, to approach the country house from the position of the people holding the begging bowl. In the parlours of Squire Frampton's house you could imagine his daughters being involved in their own Jane Austen-style romantic intrigues, but from this film's perspective, the house is an economic fortress defending itself against the poor. The paying of subsistence wages is a form of economic rather than physical brutality; only later, after the rebels are convicted and packed off on the transports to Australia, do conditions become even harsher. There they are forced into violent chain gangs, with long marches in the bush, and back-breaking labour in the service of a new, expatriate aristocracy.

With increasing ferocity from the late 1960s until well into the twenty-first century, Ken Loach directed movies focusing on the continuing plight of British citizens struggling to survive on a pittance. The savagery of the state turning its forces inward on itself and its own people also came into play as far back as his controversial 1975 BBC series *Days of Hope*, a historical journey that dealt with the fate of conscientious objectors in the First World War, the spiteful suppression of striking miners by the military in the early 1920s, and the tense yet somewhat tedious stand-off between union leaders and the Stanley Baldwin government in 1926.

The same internal conflicts ripple through Loach's *The Wind That Shakes the Barley* (2006). The foundation of the IRA and Sinn Féin in 1919–21 is clearly located here in the cruelty of the British army in Ireland, who conduct themselves like a fascist militia, with vicious beatings, executions and the burning down of ancestral homes. This army is a yelling, faceless mass whose conduct pushes the fledgling Irish Republicans inevitably onto a war footing. This is a film with very little sunlight; here the hilly landscape of County Cork is a retreat offering privacy in which the Irish rebels can rehearse military manoeuvres, as well as a conveniently out-of-the-way site for assassinations.

Loach's film was a welcome attempt to understand and empathise with the Republican cause, so often misunderstood and misrepresented in the British media, but it also pointed up how few of these flashpoint moments in the history of England's relationship with Scotland, Wales and Ireland have ever been filmed or televised.

The Massacre of Glencoe was one, a short (hour-long) film directed by Austin Campbell (to his own script) in 1971 and starring James Robertson Justice. Despite its budgetary constraints, it used the local glens and crofts to enhance the atmosphere of looming terror among the beleaguered clans. But the film remains a rarity. The Highland Clearances of 1750–1860 cry out for a serialisation or film treatment, but as yet there has been nothing, apart from a few documentaries and the 1974 TV play *The Cheviot, the Stag and the Black, Black Oil* (John Mackenzie), which joins the dots between exploitation from the mid-eighteenth century onwards to the early-1970s oil boom. Mike Leigh's *Peterloo* (2018), which set out to recreate the build-up to, and day of, the Peterloo Massacre in Manchester in 1819, feels cut from a similar cloth. Here, though, is a chance to show the brute force of the British Establishment when directed against its own people. A violently suppressed peaceful demonstration ends in a military slaughter of the innocents, conducted with a bestial fury usually reserved for foreign colonial subjects. But overall these events that have defined the Union and its discontents remain too sensitive to commit to film. These particular regions of the past are a foreign country where we do not permit ourselves the right to roam.

19

Private Dysfunctions

If . . ., O Lucky Man!, Unman, Wittering and Zigo, Scum, Kes, Scotch on the Rocks, Death Line, The Ruling Class, Pink Floyd: The Wall, Britannia Hospital

If it isn't kicking off in 1968, it's never going to kick off at all. British revolutionary zeal has been held in check since the Civil War – a miracle, given the gross inequalities and predominantly Tory governments that have ruled for generations. Empire, symbols of hard and soft power and victory in two world wars (not without cost) have mostly staved off any nationwide anti-government protests. Sometimes it feels like revolution is fomented not from the streets, but from within the Establishment itself. That's the premise of *If . . .* (1968), Lindsay Anderson's triumphant public-school movie, which enters the educational breeding grounds of Britain's brutal hierarchy.

The school depicted in *If . . .* is Cheltenham College, a typical Victorian compound (and Anderson's own alma mater): austere classrooms, wood-panelled dormitories, chapel services, cold showers. It's also a de facto prison and military barracks, with punitive regimes run by the boys themselves and an armoury for use by its cadet squad. In such a weaponised environment, is it any wonder Mick Travis (Malcolm McDowell) and his fellow pupils cast themselves as enemies of this privately educated state, papering their bedroom walls with magazine cuttings of Che Guevara, Viet Cong warriors and Mau Mau mercenaries?

If . . . brilliantly displays this hothouse of mixed messages and confusing values. Teachers have largely ceded control and the unpleasant practice of discipline to the boys themselves, while their earthly representatives – the prefects – inhabit a common room festooned with images of respectable politicians, royal personages and the House of Commons. Younger boys, meanwhile, join the rough and tumble of the school corridors armed with paperback copies of *The Penguin John Lennon*. Amid the establishing shots of school life, Travis appears with his handful of attitude. As he turns up with his trunk on his shoulder, one wag announces, 'God, it's Guy Fawkes back again!' It's not gunpowder but assault rifles that this particular heretic ends up secreting in the cellar under the school. Guido Fawkes's anti-authoritarian treason and plot is the invisible thread connecting Mick Travis with the masked vigilante of *V for Vendetta* (James McTeigue, 2005).

The pomp and circumstance of public life is repeatedly undercut by the sadism that rules the school. The boys might be belting out the noble Vaughan Williams hymn 'To Be a Pilgrim' at morning chapel, but back in his private dorm room the disaffected Travis is muttering, 'The whole world will end pretty soon. Black, brittle bodies peeling into ash.' The history teacher lectures on the perpetuation of 'evil' systems due to their inbuilt, unstoppable momentum, and the docile complicity of their citizens in the rise of fascism. In Latin class, a translation exercise reveals a scene of ancient Roman children forced to witness war atrocities 'like a young whelp or puppy'. By the end of the film, when Travis has assembled a close-knit revolutionary cadre of classmates and 'the Girl', whom he picked up in a roadside cafe, the school's young whelps and their genteel parents will be tasting hot lead blasted from the chapel roof.

As the 1968 riots in Paris and beyond had shown, you never quite knew who might be willing to drop everything and pick up a brick. Times were changing – 'You could say we are all becoming middle class,' laments the headmaster – but Anderson (and screenwriter David Sherwin) set out here to situate the heart of Britain's rot in the compressed savagery of the private education system that churns out a large proportion of the nation's cabinet ministers. Far-sightedness is bullied out of existence: Peanuts, the dorm nerd, often seen stargazing with his telescope, is ordered to 'Get it out of here.' If you treat humans like this, no matter how high up the social chain, warns the film, then don't be surprised when things turn into a massacre.

In 1973 the Mick Travis character returned as a travelling salesman in Anderson's *O Lucky Man!* Although set very much in the present day, its fragmentary form and cast of archetypal characters make it a quest movie whose disjointedness and unpredictability resemble a legendary yarn from the *Mabinogion*. Malcolm McDowell returned in a role he had actually created himself in a screenplay he developed some years earlier.

The film is divided into four 'acts' titled 'West', 'North', 'South' and, concluding in the slum districts of London, 'East End'. There's a brief black-and-white silent film prologue/nightmare in which Central American coffee pickers are roughed up by armed guards. Travis, with a drooping moustache and dark hair, is arrested after pocketing a handful of coffee beans for his own consumption and sentenced to lose his hands to the machete. The dream shuts down in mid-scream. Then we find Travis and a group of sheepish young recruits being given a tour of an English coffee factory, in preparation for their new jobs as travelling salesmen. Travis has perfected the art of presenting himself in the respectful manner the management want to see and hear, convincing the boss, Mr Duff (Arthur Lowe at his most bumptiously patrician), that he can step into the shoes of the company's former star salesman, who has mysteriously vanished on the job. Travis embarks on his journey to the north in a Ford Anglia estate loaded with coffee beans. Like a mythical hero, he encounters a motley crew of figures on the way, with varying degrees of trust-worthiness. The film's cast take on a number of roles, reinforcing the sense of a parable or mystery play being enacted.

In contrast to the thrusting ambition required of him in his employment – emblematic of an idealistic, modern Britain – Travis's picaresque wanderings bring him into contact with the left-behind regions of the late 1950s and '60s. The bed-and-breakfast where he bases himself in the north is as grotty and sinister as the Hampstead flat depicted in Michael Powell's *Peeping Tom*. His room, formerly tenanted by his vanished predecessor, contains puzzling mementoes of the latter's life, which is expanded upon by the cryptic recollection of Monty, a permanent resident in the neighbouring suite.

Music plays a key role in *O Lucky Man!*, with real-life rock star Alan Price and his band acting as a recurring chorus. Price's songs comment on and narrate the action. The band first appears in an opening credit sequence that still feels radical and has been rarely imitated. Price, at the keyboard, and his band have set up in a circle on a sound stage to perform the *O Lucky Man!* theme tune live to camera. The camera dollies around the group, revealing the rest of the crew and even director Anderson, who leaves his seat, briefly consults with Price in mid-song and swaps a sheet of lyrics for a new one he has just drafted. The fourth-wall-breaking gesture is a perfect illustration of a film production realised with serendipity and a measure of improvisation, as circumstances demand – all qualities demonstrated by the film's lead character. Anderson makes a second cameo at the end of the film, as Travis stumbles in on a film audition, where he reprises the disingenuous smile he previously turned on for his bosses. Anderson steps forward to slap him in the face with the script, like some Zen master waking his student from spiritual slumber. He later commented that the incident was based on McDowell's original audition for *If. . ..*

It's not the only slap in the face. Travis's quest is interrupted, and his fortunes reversed, by several explosive and violent incidents along the way. There's the realisation that a medical experiment he has volunteered for is actually an excuse for a crazed vivisectionist to transform him into a pig. He breaks out of the sanatorium by jumping through a glass window and is rescued by Alan Price and the boys in a tour van, along with an alluring groupie (Helen Mirren) whose multi-millionaire father eventually embroils Travis in a fraud that lands him in jail. There's the attack by a group of East End down-and-outs on the reformed Travis, fresh out of prison as a born-again humanist idiot savant. And there's the explosion in a military nuclear installation, into which he has unwittingly blundered while looking for petrol to refuel his car. Interrogated and electrocuted as a suspected spy (in scenes recalling McDowell's recent appearance in Stanley Kubrick's *A Clockwork Orange*), the torture session is interrupted by a safety alert, and Travis escapes just as the power station goes up in smoke. The transition from his staggering through drifting smoke and debris, into a sylvan wood with a running stream, and over a hill into a golden-lit rustic valley is the film's most dreamlike passage, and one that most keenly locates the narrative as a modern-day *Pilgrim's Progress*. The final credits roll over another demolition of the fourth wall, as the whole cast dance with wild abandon to Price's rocked-up version of the theme tune.

■

The young actor David Cashman appeared as a schoolboy in both *If . . .* and another of the period's films set in a disturbing public school, *Unman, Wittering and Zigo* (John Mackenzie, 1971). (Or perhaps it's the same character, transferred after the bloodbath.) In this screen adaptation of a radio play by Giles Cooper,[1] pupil power and rebellion are likewise embedded in the daily life of the remote Chantry School (motto: 'Authority is the child of obedience'). Here, like a prison where the inmates take control, the privileged pupils have banded together to force the teachers to comply with their demands. John Ebony (David Hemmings) takes up residence in a cottage near the school, a windswept institution built near a rocky Cornish shore and surrounded by antique cannons and barbed wire. Formerly an advertising executive in London, he's taken a post as relief teacher after the recent death, apparently by suicide, of another teacher, Mr Pelham. Like Sgt Howie arriving on Summerisle in *The Wicker Man*, Ebony's attempts to wrest control of his classroom, with his by-rote expressions of discipline and arbitrary punishments, are impotent. His one sympathetic colleague, the clubbable Mr Farthingale, nevertheless tries to wipe out any romanticism about the nobility of teaching when he identifies Ebony as 'a chap who rides out of the real world in search of fairy castles and finds a desolate tower at the arse end of nowhere'.

The entitled teenage princes in this desolate tower, subtle in their sneering sarcasm while playing every confrontation just inside the rules, subvert Ebony's authority as they apparently did with the late Mr Pelham, even emboldened enough to admit that they were the ones who murdered him. Ebony's complaints to the headmaster fall on deaf ears and he becomes progressively inured to the *Lord of the Flies*-style savagery, from the bullying of 'wet' Wittering to the attempted gang rape of Ebony's wife Silvia. As in *If. . .*, the boys are brutalised and defensive by nature – and by the nature of the institution.

The imbalance of power, and the brutality of the education system, has of course been a feature of British culture since Victorian novels like Dickens's *Hard Times*, Thomas Hughes's *Tom Brown's School Days* and Kipling's *Stalky & Co. If. . .* and *Unman, Wittering and Zigo* take their place in that lineage, as would *Scum* (Alan Clarke, 1977), originally a banned BBC 'Play for Today' production but later made into a feature film starring Ray Winstone and Phil Daniels (1982). Set in a bleak borstal institution, the BBC play featured a game of 'murderball' that ended with many actors and extras being taken to hospital after Clarke allowed the shoot to degenerate into a proper fight. The misery is compounded by the fact that these working-class inmates, at the other end of the social scale, are not protected by family privilege and will face a future without hope on the outside.

A similar fate awaits the young Billy Casper, the lead character in *Kes* (1969), the most lyrical of all Ken Loach's films. The expectations in Billy's Yorkshire community – his destiny – is that he will get a job 'down t'pit'. His family situation appears hopeless, but when he steals and trains a baby kestrel, the sense of liberation the bird embodies is accompanied by his improvement at school. Like Hazel's tame fox in *Gone to Earth*, Billy clings to the kestrel as a beacon of hope, while his personal circumstances go from bad to worse. Society isn't offering any friendship or advancement, so he finds solace flying free in spirit with this winged familiar. Harold McNair's soaring flute solos on John Cameron's deservedly praised soundtrack chime with the radiant open-air footage of the Yorkshire countryside shot by Chris Menges (although *Kes* was his first credit as cinematographer, Menges was Lindsay Anderson's camera operator on *If . . .*). Loach and Menges would later team up on another dissection of class and rigid hierarchy for ATV, *The Gamekeeper* (1980).

A cliché it might be, but Loach's images of the boy in the wild, on the edge of woodland, letting the bird fly free, are poetic scenes of liberation. Historically, in Britain, while hawks were always the preserve of the gentry, the kestrel was the bird of the underdog and underclass – servants, children and knaves. Billy's comprehensive education is unlikely to raise him above this level, and his dreams are buried along with his kestrel, which is killed by his brother.

These are all films steamed in the pressure cooker of a nation mired in structural inequality. If not quashed, the rebellious instinct erupts in violent opposition. Another of these was *Scotch on the Rocks* (1973), a lost BBC serial written by none other than future Thatcher cabinet minister Douglas Hurd (with Andrew Osmond) that imagined a Scottish separatist militia waging a war of independence against the British state. Its five episodes were broadcast despite fears that they would cause a spike in sympathy for the newly formed Scottish National Party. In fact, the SNP officially objected to the suggestion that their party might encourage armed insurrection, and the BBC upheld its complaint. The series was quietly laid to rest.

Death Line (Gary Sherman, 1972) is an unusual horror movie set almost entirely in the dark labyrinths of the London Underground. In these forgotten chambers, an abject, cannibalistic couple cling on to existence, occasionally hunting for human meat on lonely, deserted platforms late at night. These ghouls purport to be distantly descended from Victorian labourers lost in the system during the construction of the Tube. They stand in for all the forgotten labourers who died while building Britain's imperial power.

Rich and poor live according to different rules and expectations. Luxury apartments versus hideous, lightless tunnels full of rats, maggots and gnawed human corpses. Hugh Armstrong plays the cannibal with a degree of humanity – he loves his dying partner and decorates the bones of his victims with items of jewellery – but he is not the only character out in search of 'raw meat' (the film's American title). It starts, in fact, with a politician propositioning a woman on the platform and receiving a kick in the nuts for his pains. At all levels of life, humans can be treated as carrion.

The Ruling Class (Peter Medak), a black comedy from 1972, went all out on portraying the upper crust as demented, afflicted with a messianic belief in their own divine right to rule, and in serious need of therapy. 'Englishmen like to hear the truth about themselves,' says Peter O'Toole as Jack, the fourteenth Earl of Gurney, and while this film has not aged well, its hysteria is one more reflection of the encroaching sense of societal breakdown in the early 1970s. The murmur of male voices played over the opening credits (a similar soundtrack is audible at the start of *If. . .*) could be the subdued hubbub of any institution, whether private school, bank or Parliament. The susurration increasingly masks the insanity, megalomania and overreach at the seat of power.

As many were keen to point out, this feral instinct was seeded at an early age. In the feature film *Pink Floyd: The Wall* (Alan Parker, 1982), the song 'Another Brick in the Wall' plays out over scenes in a typical English schoolroom, the teachers heading out to class like a platoon marching into battle. A boy's private poetry writings are held up for ridicule. Then, a shift into dystopian fantasy: uniformed pupils seated at their desks are on a conveyor belt to the meat grinder. It ends with a full-on classroom riot, reminiscent of the prison skirmishes of *Scum*, as desks are smashed and set on fire and the teachers attacked. In real life, the children's choir from Islington Green School were banned from appearing on *Top of the Pops* by their head teacher, and their voicing of Pink Floyd's memorable lyrics about not needing education or thought control scandalised everyone from the Inner London Education Authority to Prime Minister Margaret Thatcher.

It's easy to forget, though, that the film opens in a sleepy English suburban garden, in 1944. The silent pram stands near the birdbath, the birdsong approaches its late-afternoon crescendo, a mother dozes in the sunlight. Parker's film was based on autobiographical recollections by Pink Floyd's founding member, Roger Waters. The film is loaded with heavy rhetorical imagery, but this scene is where the bombardment pauses for a few brief instants, a fleeting lacuna of domestic harmony in between aerial bombing raids. For the baby in the perambulator, it's a period of blissful ignorance about the fact that he has just lost a parent – his father has been killed while fighting in Italy.

In this garden, secretly, stealthily, the law of the jungle holds sway. A predatory black-and-white cat stalks a white dove. Later, 1950s schoolchildren shoot each other with imitation pistols and tommy guns in the playground. The grotesque cartoons of Gerald Scarfe animate a gigantic metropolis of tower blocks and smoke-belching factories as they trample across empty countryside. Eventually, it is the Wall itself – psychological, metaphorical, actual – that bulldozes its way through the meadows. One of the film's earliest shots shows the silhouette of a tiny boy running across a rugby field. The distant, H-shaped posts could be the first right-angled strokes of a sketch for the edifice of brick and cement that will come to eat up the entire screen and consume the consciousness of its damaged protagonist.

Pink Floyd: The Wall's idyllic opening sequence gestured towards the band's earliest incarnations in mid-1960s Cambridge, when they hitched psychedelic rock to a cocktail of innocence, interstellar travel and Edwardian whimsy. But as the product of the same group – or, at least, the same franchise – that also composed 'See Emily Play', 'Grantchester Meadows' and *The Piper at the Gates of Dawn*, the film must be considered as part of the same continuum. The lifespan of most groups associated with the golden age of British psychedelia was short. As a band, Pink Floyd survived long enough to outlive their adolescence, grow old with the century and gain a veteran's perspective upon their earlier depictions of innocent pleasures. Even in their psychedelic–pastoral heyday, those pleasures were always tempered with darker apparitions, lurking in the woods. Pink Floyd eventually broke free of the meat grinder. In the early years of the Thatcher administration, there were plenty who were still stuck on the conveyor belt.

Lindsay Anderson harnessed the hysteria much more effectively when he checked in to *Britannia Hospital* (1982). Capturing a sense of desperation in British political life, the film takes equally wicked potshots at both management and unions. Britannia Hospital – the building and institution itself – is a microcosm of the state at the dawn of the 1980s. Buffing up the careworn British pomp in time for the grand opening of a new wing by HRH the Queen Mother, besieged on all sides by protesters opposing the billeting of an exiled African dictator, there are rioters, conflicted unions, guerrilla journalists and that peculiar British combination of deference and disrespect for regulations. Decorators tasked to repaint the staircase never quite seem to get the job done; an ambulance screeches up outside the building to deliver a life-threatened elderly patient, who is transferred to a trolley by two orderlies, who then abandon their urgent duties to enjoy a regulation tea break, as the patient expires in front of us. Truculent union leaders can be bought off by the authorities with the promise of honours. By this point, Anderson's critique extended to all levels of society.

Britannia Hospital also forms the third in the sequence that began with *If . . .* and continued with *O Lucky Man!* and features many of the same actors, including the return of Malcolm McDowell. Here Mick Travis is a rogue freelance journalist attempting to break into the hospital on the day of the Queen Mother's visit to open a new experimental research wing run by the demented Professor Millar (Graham Crowden). The set is as shiny and sanitised as the Death Star's corridors, and appropriately enough, *Star Wars'* Mark Hamill has a small part in the film, playing Travis's stoned and giggly outside broadcast technician. This battle-hardened and cynical incarnation of Travis is as intrepid as the Milk Tray chocolates' SAS delivery man, shinning through a window from a window cleaner's gondola with the aid of an inside job from lover Nurse Persil. McDowell as an actor was certainly used to enduring human experiments and crank surgery, whether it was in the vivisection centre in *O Lucky Man!* (which was presided over by a lunatic doctor played, as here, by Crowden), his pinned-back eyelids in *A Clockwork Orange* or, here, knocked unconscious and spreadeagled on an operating table as a last-minute replacement subject for the professor's debut experiment. It's an undignified fate for Anderson's pilgrim/alter ego, crudely stitched together from a rattlebag of limbs and organs, who is beaten to death after trying to throttle the manic professor. There are continuities for the sharp-eyed – 'I started in coffee,' explains Travis, in a sidelong reference to his job in *O Lucky Man!* – but for Anderson, the three films were less of a causally related trilogy, more of a 'philosophical sequence'.[2]

Britannia Hospital was largely panned by critics in the early 1980s, but its grotesque caricatures serve tolerably well two decades into the twenty-first century. If its panoply of characters and its satirical depiction of the contradictions of public healthcare and private treatment, of the violent and riotous ferment just below the outward pomp and circumstance of English institutions, are viewed as a kind of cinematic Gillray cartoon, the film becomes considerably more enjoyable. 'One of the chief reasons why satire is not traditionally popular is because it is disturbing and, fundamentally, questioning,'[3] commented Anderson, who pushed the action beyond traditionally absurdist Monty Python-style humour to end up invoking blood-soaked horror, as well as a kind of affectionate takedown of the loony left. Meanwhile, as the hospital's power cuts out, the most modern, hi-tech facility ('the Rudyard Kipling Ward') stands unused due to a shortage of cleaning staff. If riot police beating up protesters to the tune of 'God Save the Queen' might seem heavy-handed, Anderson's vision (again with co-writer David Sherwin) of a future of cold-blooded technology and artificial intelligence is crudely prescient. Professor Millar's reduction of the human experience to 'Genesis' – a brain in a box with a silicon chip implant – is advertised with a line from Hamlet's 'What a piece of work is man' soliloquy. In Britain, you can sell anything by draping it with the vestments of high culture and promoting it with a posh accent. Private enterprise leads only to grotesque delusions and Frankensteinian monsters. To the moral dilemmas it raises, 'The film gives no answer,' said Anderson, 'which again goes to prove how mistaken I was in encouraging people to think.'[4]

In the decades since, *Britannia Hospital* has in some respects aged, but at the same time its relevance to the crumbling pillars of Britain's welfare state and the precarious balance between the private and public sectors has been renewed. Perhaps the most enduring image from its weird conclusion is the constant beatific smile on the face of HRH (played by lookalike Gladys Crosbie), as she is tactfully steered one step ahead of the chaotic hullabaloo gathering outside the hospital. The Establishment, ever implacable, unshakable, never to be moved.

20

Tangled Up in Time

Sapphire and Steel, Corridor of Mirrors, The Time Machine, The Ploughman's Lunch, Wetherby, The Line of Beauty, Close My Eyes

'How's the enemy?' my dad says whenever he wants to know what time it is. In 1977 I get my first digital watch; not a maths-cheating one tricked out with miniature calculator buttons, as some of my friends have, but a Casio LCD that looks chunky on my ten-year-old wrist, with a yellow button for the built-in light and a black one for reprogramming the time and date. This was advanced tech, but it had its limitations. In the autumn of 1976 I would rush to the TV set at 7.10 p.m. every Tuesday, ready to watch the American series *Gemini Man*, in which secret agent Sam Casey, after a strange and clumsily defined undersea radiation accident, can press a button on his digital watch and turn invisible (for fifteen minutes at a time). It was never really made clear how this watch could render a human being incorporeal, but it certainly made for some fun playground games.

Earlier in 1976 my favourite show had involved yet more invisibility, and my hero had been experimental scientist Daniel Westin (David McCallum) in *The Invisible Man*. This time a botched attempt to destroy his teleportation apparatus had rendered the unfortunate Westin transparent, but a plastic-surgeon friend had recreated his face in a lifelike 'Dermaplex' mask (with a matching pair of hand-like gloves), supplied a wardrobe of natty suits and sent him back to work in Pentagon-sponsored black ops. The money-shot in each episode was McCallum reaching around to the back of his neck and pulling off his own head, complete with its Byrds-style blond bob, and stripping off his clothes. Once in his invisible state, this truly was a naked civil servant.

■

> The Past is no longer an inspiration: it is a refuge.[1]
> Lindsay Anderson

As familiar things disappear, so the act of remembering becomes more urgent.

The 1980s found the past under attack. Margaret Thatcher was, in her own calamitous way, a revolutionary disguised as a conservative. Her government's policies shifted the economy from manufacturing and industry to finance, and changed the soul of Britain. During her reign, she wiped out the coal, steel and shipbuilding industries and saw the nation gaining greater influence in the EEC, while increasingly talking the country out of love with its European neighbours. In her time the gap between rich and poor opened up, intensifying divisive and corrosive social inequality. The unions, media and the left generally were accused of being 'the enemy within'. The family silver was sold: industries and services that had been run by the state since the war passed into private and sometimes foreign ownership. Thatcherism left a harder-edged nation, more focused on the bottom line.

Her Conservative philosophy was full of contradictions, looking back nostalgically to the supposedly simpler and more innocent and decent 1950s, and the imagined propriety and strict self-discipline of Victorian values, while introducing deindustrialisation policies that broke down communities and reduced trust in institutions and law and order. She fired the first rounds against perceived bias in the BBC and Channel 4, questioning their right to receive public money, in a culture war that was still raging on the Tory front lines in 2020.

Even though it deferred to history for its moral authority, this government was about New Times. The Labour opposition, symbolised by Michael Foot in his duffel coat, offered a stodgier image (in a decade when image became all important): nostalgic and backward-looking, slouching towards its Jerusalem. Driven by global communication networks, jet travel and syndicated Western popular culture, the new capitalism created an unprecedented compression of time and space. In this version of capitalism, one that exploded internationally thanks to the silicon chip, the gaze of brokers and traders turned to the VDUs attached to their computers, monitoring the upticks and downturns of daily trading. The screen thus became part of the visual mythology of capital.

The Saatchi & Saatchi PR agency sold a thrusting capitalist vision of the new Britain, but its future was pushed further out of reach. Noting the 'multiplication of museums, heritage centres and commercial attractions – calculated to give an ever more pleasing "experience" of a past that was in fact irrecoverable', the cultural critic Brian Appleyard noted that 'the emphasis on the past served both as a mask for the revolution of the present, and as a compensation for it'.[2] In practice, this meant defunct factories, mills and mines being converted into visitor centres; and National Trust and English Heritage houses that suppressed the narratives of slavery and exploitation that generated the wealth on show in these lavish properties. London and other major cities began to sprout new towers and postmodern architecture; retail and distribution retreated to the brownfields. Rapid metropolitan growth only increases the sensation of stasis in the countryside, where history slows down, the past peeps from behind the rose bushes and ghost memories lurk under the ivy. The journey from the city to the village and the surrounding countryside, while not geographically huge, is a slippage in time, provoking yearnings for a fading past.

This 1980s boom in the heritage industry ran in parallel with a spike in costume and period drama. *Brideshead Revisited* and *A Room with a View* encouraged and set the tone for what would follow. This chapter will focus on several films and TV programmes from the 1980s that expressed this temporal discomfiture, with various takes on time travel, political reality against manufactured national illusions, and the dream of living in the past as an alternative to the harsher conditions of the present.

In 1979, the year Margaret Thatcher came to power as Britain's first female prime minister, screenwriter Peter J. Hammond came up with the cult classic *Sapphire and Steel* (directed by Shaun O'Riordan) for Thames Television. One analyst has speculated on the series as a kind of metaphor for the new era of Thatcherism, and there is some mileage in that theory.[3] Thatcher's government, trumpeting monetarism and neo-liberalism, promised to accelerate out of the stagnation of the late 1970s, with its ineffective Labour government, strikes and power cuts. In *Sapphire and Steel*, the two lead characters are 'time agents', Sapphire (Joanna Lumley) and Steel (David McCallum), assigned to solve crises on Earth by a mysterious galactic authority. The duo are envoys from a cosmic nanny state, seductive authoritarians arriving in the present to pull folks' socks up and get them back on their bikes. Their chilly, sparkling, mineral/metal essence is reflected in their appearance: a blue cocktail frock and grey business suit, looking for all the world as if they have been held up on their way to Christmas drinks at the Conservative Association. Their remedies, human collateral damage and all, anticipate that infamous Tory election declaration of 1996: 'Yes it hurt. Yes it worked.'

Writer Hammond was no stranger to the more esoteric side of children's programming, having written ITV's *Ace of Wands* in the early 1970s, a fantasy tale based on magical practices and the Tarot, and contributed an episode of the supernatural series *Shadows*. But after the first six-episode 'Assignment', which revolves around two children and the disappearance of their parents from a remote house full of antiques, *Sapphire and Steel* became darker, stranger, more adult. Even in that first Assignment from 1979, though, the mood is stern and cold, with an authoritarian aura emitting especially from Steel. Their strategies for dealing with wave upon wave of problems seem baffling, their technical explanations hard to follow, and they leave a whiff of the uncanny in their slipstream.

Although Hammond claimed to be interested in the experiments with time travel imagined by H. G. Wells and J. B. Priestley, he set out to rethink the role of time as a hostile immaterial force that seeks ways to irrupt into the present. If *Sapphire and Steel* has any premise at all, it seems to be about eliminating any factors in a given setting that interfere with the linear flow of time. The house in Assignment One is home to a traditional nuclear family, decorated with antiques and curios; there is an Aga cooker in the kitchen, and the children chant old nursery rhymes at bedtime. A secret portal is embedded in these rhymes. 'Time reaches in,' as Sapphire puts it. This 'enemy' is invisible, immaterial – an eerie, creeping threat.

Nursery rhymes are a kind of folk poetry that has proved remarkably adept at preserving songs and lyrics from antiquity. Recited and handed down through generations, the songs use humans as transmission vessels to ensure their survival. In this Assignment, Time, the enemy, encourages the children to repeat certain rhymes – especially 'Goosey Goosey Gander' – which, when uttered, stretch the fabric of time thin enough to allow the past to come rampaging in. Roundhead soldiers charge through the house, threatening to hang, draw and quarter Sapphire while she is trapped in a painting. Nostalgic chants summon soldiers of anti-monarchist, republican revolution: Tory nightmares made real. At these times, when characters find themselves transplanted to parallel time zones, Steel asks them to describe features in the rooms without letting their

Envoys from a cosmic nanny state: Joanna
Lumley and David McCallum as time detectives
in *Sapphire and Steel* (1979).

gaze linger on any details. It's as if too much immersion in the past
will keep them frozen there. The Assignment ends with Time lured
into a foundation stone from 1736 and crushed. The parents return,
bedtime is resumed, the family (Thatcherism's moral bedrock) is
restored.

Who or what is this enemy, and why does it strive so hard to effect
its 'Time breaks'? The answer is never fully supplied in any of the
six Assignments, but all of Sapphire and Steel's psychic powers are
directed towards foiling their adversary. They want to restore and
impose order – a form of conservatism, yet one with no interest in
conserving nostalgic visions.

Sapphire and Steel's subsequent Assignments all feature variations on time slippages, on the dangerous persistence of memories.

In Assignment Two, the duo materialise in an abandoned railway station that is under investigation by George Tully, an aged ghost-hunter. Tully gets short shrift from Steel, who mocks his 'Stone Age' tape recorders and microphones. Sapphire and Steel's mission is to eradicate all traces of these ghosts and seal up the rents in the temporal fabric that allow them to burst through. In this episode the enemy is feeding off the lingering hatred and resentment harboured by the spirits of those who died for unjust causes during the wars. The nation's collective grief is the gateway for malevolence to leak into the world. Patches of the station diffract the past through the present: Sapphire's dress momentarily changes into an Edwardian lady's costume with a straw bonnet, and her sixth-sense antenna detects the ambience of a warm, idyllic summer's day laden with the scent of flowers; sitting on a particular chair, Steel morphs into a fighter pilot heading into a fatal crash dive. 'They attack us with their own pasts,' he muses later. Eventually, he will propitiate the enemy by sacrificing Tully.

The early 1980s also saw the more conventional approach to time travel in the 'Play for Today' *The Flipside of Dominick Hide* (Alan Gibson, 1980), in which an observer from 2130 flies back to London and sires his own great-grandfather. In *Sapphire and Steel*, Hammond deconstructed the idea of time travel and speculated that it could be more multidimensional than a linear journey forward or backward to a future or historical period. Like Dominick Hide, Assignment Three's Eldred and Rothwyn are historical researchers from the future, currently living in a self-created chrono-bubble in a metropolitan tower block. Their self-chosen Anglo-Saxon names are anachronistic because of the compression of centuries when viewed from afar. In Assignment Five, the setting is a fancy-dress party with a 1930s theme, which allows for an exploration of the classic whodunnit genre,[4] but which also asserts the privilege of the upper-middle-class partygoers, as they attempt to turn back time to avoid the death of one of their number in a fire.

The most disturbing Assignment is number four, where a face-less being called 'The Shape' uses photographs to enter the human world, import people preserved in photos into the present and freeze others in photographic scenes. This is about film as frozen time, as a visible history that can be summoned and resuscitated, but which is also a potential trap. Like *Bagpuss*, the series starts with sepia prints of children from the previous century, but then the photos empty out and the kids erupt into the present, playing in the backyard of a pawnbroker's shop. Almost every object on display is old, used or rejected, or its owner dead. As such, it is, as Steel says, a 'room full of triggers'. Again: beware of memory, nostalgia and the antique. The only remedy is to burn and destroy all existing photographs; the beings depicted in them are collateral damage. These extreme meas-ures are an inoculation against wallowing in lost times.

In televisual terms, *Sapphire and Steel* is composed of some of the most static drama ever filmed. It has none of the elements that a modern viewership would call 'entertaining', but it remains hypnotic and eerie. An entropic sense of stasis sometimes threatens to over-whelm the action, and the dialogue runs through terse, Pinter-esque iterations. Many of the shots are close-ups of faces; chiaroscuro sets alternating dark patches amid shifting pools of light; there are stair-ways and portals; time-sensitive patches where characters' costumes suddenly change; disembodied voices, unearthly music and sound effects. Each Assignment takes place in one location, and rather than emotion or interpersonal drama, it is the space, the architecture of the set and its spatial relationship to time that the characters are most preoccupied with. By the final Assignment, set entirely in a petrol station, time has all but crawled to a halt. The pair are trapped in its boundaries while 'Transient Beings' from 1925, 1948 and 1957 move through the space, including the folkish mumming 'everyman' figure of Johnny Jack.

As the series bowed out, Sapphire and Steel were left abandoned by this roadside, gazing out of a blank window. *Sapphire and Steel*'s

Gordian knot-play with the fabric of time remains one of British television's most tantalising enigmas; its small-budget production values were outplayed by its devotion to the eerie.

■

We're going to watch a video. The classroom is where I first see something taped off the telly, played on a VHS recorder that lives on an industrial metal trolley. A teacher needing to pacify the class introduced us to the BBC's *Hitchhiker's Guide to the Galaxy* in 1981, which blew my mind in five dimensions – not least because it offered the first tremor of the digital infinite, the linkage of pocketable tech with the vastness of space, and the wry characterisation of bewildered English space cadet Arthur Dent. From Peter Jones's gently enthusiastic readings of the *Guide*'s dazzlingly silly entries to the animated graphics and trickling layer of information (ideal for the age of the recorder's pause button), nothing had looked or sounded this way on TV before.

But back to the video trolley. It lived in the science block, but as far as I recall, it was only ever commandeered by the arts teachers. In French lessons, I sit through a two-hour dramatisation of Sartre's existentialist three-way *Huis clos* ('Hell is other people') with Jeanne Moreau, Cherie Lunghi and Omar Sharif. Around the same time, my English teacher draws the blinds and drops Truffaut's *Jules et Jim* on us fifth-formers, in which Moreau, in her carefree twenties, enjoys the kind of bohemian *ménage à trois* that we, in our school ties and blazers, can only dream of. This particular English teacher, nicknamed 'CJ', who dresses in body-hugging black turtlenecks and sports a wayward comb-over of grey-blue hair, is faintly intimidating but seems to hold a passport to a world of art, literature, film and culture, on the threshold of which I'm standing, intrigued. He can declaim an epic verse of Browning or talk about European cinema in a way no other teacher can be bothered to, which gives you permission to feel awe. He makes us watch his VHS of a 1970s Italian art-house film, *The Tree of Wooden Clogs*, directed by Ermanno Olmi. It's probably the first film I've watched that lasts more than three hours, and I'm lost in its nineteenth-century rhythm, its crepuscular evening scenes, and how it depicts rural life unfolding in hovels, the revolutionary stirrings and advent of communism, the mistreatment of tenant farmers by a hostile landlord. It also marks the first time I've actually had to write an essay about a film.

Unlike some teachers, CJ wasn't easy to get to know. He certainly never sought the limelight. Which is what made it so shocking when, a quarter of a century after I'd left school, he started appearing on my television screen. After his retirement, Christopher Jefferies still lived in the same flat he'd inhabited as a teacher, but he was renting out his basement to a young woman, Jo Yeates, who was found strangled to death one Christmas, and for a few days he was hung out to dry as the prime suspect. The tabloid press and media had a field day with his 'weird' appearance, bachelor status and penchant for arty movies, but he turned out to be innocent and played an articulate role in the Leveson Inquiry into press intrusion that followed the case. The writer Peter Morgan even created a TV reconstruction of Jefferies's experience (*The Lost Honour of Christopher Jefferies*, Roger Michell, ITV, 2014). Jason Watkins captured Jefferies's mannerisms and chiselled mode of speech uncannily accurately, though occasionally with slightly too much of an effeminate edge. Thanks to Jefferies I got introduced to a bunch of interesting stuff and learned it was OK to take art seriously, as well as to take time and persevere with the difficult. He was a private man who quietly found a way to share so much.

■

Sapphire and Steel weirdly foreshadowed the growing disquiet in a decade when many old certainties were being eradicated by policy decisions, as if history itself was being wiped from the photographs. Several films from the same era dealt in their own ways with new and altered relationships between country and city, metropolitan development and rural stasis, left wing and right, public and private morality, the present dreaming the past future.

Time travel of a literal sort has, of course, featured in many films and television programmes. Indeed, the notion of flipping between historical eras could be called something of an obsession in twentieth-century British stories. In *Corridor of Mirrors* (Terence Young, 1948), Paul Mangin reconstructs his London town house as a belle époque Venetian palazzo, where he and his inamorata live out a fantasy of being reincarnated historical figures. That was one way of dreaming oneself out of post-war austerity.

George Pal's 1960 version of H. G. Wells's *The Time Machine* was effective, for its time, in visualising the temporally travelling Victorian inventor, still clad in his smoking gown (a pre-echo of Arthur Dent's perennial bathrobe), sitting on his ornate, wood-and-brass steampunk contraption, throwing the control lever forward and watching the centuries rack up on the mechanical ticker. Behind him, in stop-motion, buildings rise and collapse; he jumps off in the future 1966 in the middle of a mass panic before a nuclear strike; fast-forwarding through the millennia he is encased in a lava mountain and uncovered again; until he tumbles into the future post-industrial paradise/hell of the Eloi and their monstrous masters the Morlocks.

Time travel and exchanging experiences with those who have gone before, or meeting one's ancestors in an old familiar house, were the theme of children's series such as *A Traveller in Time* (1978), *The Children of Green Knowe* (1986) and *Moondial* (1988). In addition to the story, the time-based medium of film can also suggest slippages via flashbacks, jumps between urban and rural locations, and changes of rhythm and tone. Even to watch a television programme or movie is, essentially, to embark on a form of mental time travel. In my book *Electric Eden*, I argued that the revival of folk music in Britain constituted a kind of portal to the past. An imaginary past, in many cases, but one that the folk process refines and sublimates by reviving and replaying a song or artefact over and over until it is polished down into its essential shape. At whatever historical moment a folk song is sung, it is simultaneously authentic and fake. It's a counterfeit of an artefact that has no provable origin or author, nor a definitive version. Like an oak dropping its acorns across the forest floor, each iteration is the fresh progeny of an ever-changing ancestor.

That paradox helps to explain why the idea of folk has continued to be championed, over the years, by proponents of both reaction and radicalism. Many British traditions, believed to come from ancient times, are relatively recent inventions. What could be more hale and hearty than the classic pub staple, the ploughman's lunch? Simple ingredients – wholemeal bread and cheddar cheese, salad, apple and pickled onion – representing the fruits of the pasture, furrow, orchard and dairy. Hunks of agrarian England scattered on a platter. It's a meal of convenience, not only for the putative field labourers of yore, but also for pub landlords, whose establishments, in the 1950s, couldn't stretch to running a kitchen or hiring cooks.

There's a minor cottage industry out there dedicated to uncovering the mythic origins of this popular repast. While it's impossible to pinpoint, it does appear that by the mid-1950s, the term 'ploughboy's lunch' was being bandied around the catering industry, while a 1957 edition of a British trade magazine reported on an alliance between the national Cheese Bureau and the Brewers' Company, who together hosted a London event to promote 'the traditional public house meal of bread, beer, cheese and pickles'. After the reception, 'there followed a "Ploughman's Lunch" of cottage bread, cheese, lettuce, hard-boiled eggs, cold sausages and, of course, beer'.[5] This appears to be the earliest known use of the phrase in print. A few years later, the concept was revived by the Milk Marketing Board, which was specifically trying to boost the consumption of cheese. So the familiar ploughman's really came of age in the 1960s and '70s.

As always with these 'fake authentic' products, this prompts the question, does it matter? For the novelist Ian McEwan, who scripted the 1983 film *The Ploughman's Lunch* (Richard Eyre), the question was crucial in understanding the unsavoury drift of British politics. An actual ploughman's lunch doesn't appear in the film until near the end. It's in a London pub, where two characters are taking a break from work, and when we see the plate in close-up, it's a particularly unsavoury portion: a dry white crusty roll, flimsy salad leaf, vacuum-packed lump of sweaty Cheddar and mini-cowpat of Branston pickle. It's 'a completely successful fabrication of the past', comments Matthew Fox, a silver-haired director of television adverts, to his fellow diner, the young journalist James Penfield (Jonathan Pryce). This 'traditional English fare' is an advertiser's fantasy of a changeless England. A few minutes before, we joined James in watching the director on set, filming a nostalgic advert for Ovaltine. A cosy 1930s sitting room has been created, the husband in an armchair puffing his pipe, children playing by his feet, his wife carrying in a tray of hot drinks. Eyre's camera tracks around this fictional film set, leading our eye around the back of the painted wooden flats and flimsy scenery, where studio technicians are hosing a light rain against the outside of the windows. The artifice of national mythology exposed in one single hypnotic take.

There are many forms of deception afoot in *The Ploughman's Lunch*. Penfield's work as an editor in the BBC radio newsroom has lifted him from his lower-middle-class origins to mingling with the upper echelons of the media and political Establishment. The film's first shots show the BBC's editorial office as the introduction to the day's episode of *Woman's Hour* is heard; the show's guests are all men, variously discussing an escape from a prisoner-of-war camp, the conquest of Mount Everest and how East European propagandists rewrote history. This is the early-1980s political conversation in a nutshell: the refusal of the war to die in the collective memory; the repeated celebration of national triumphs; and the co-option of both to justify dubious policies. The film joins the dots between the 1956 Suez crisis – a major post-war act of duplicity by the British government – and the dispatch of a task force to the Falkland Islands, which coincided with the making of this film. Both incidents revealed the illusions invoked when Britain continues to press its colonial claims. Political philosophy as a ploughman's lunch of historical morsels.

Penfield also rewrites his own past to suit his interests. He's an apolitical Oxford graduate who dissembles as a socialist to advance his writing career. He grudgingly visits the suburban dwelling of his aged parents, shows little sympathy for his bed-ridden mother and can't bear to sit and chat with his father. Later, he'll lie to Susan Barrington, a glamorous counterpart at ITN whom he's attempting to date, that his parents are dead. Penfield has been commissioned to write a new history of the Suez debacle, and Susan can provide access to 1956 newsreels from her archive, which are equally convincing examples of history rewritten as propaganda. It's no accident that she's called Suzie: she is Penfield's own Suez, a channel affording access to her mother, Ann Barrington, a left-wing historian who, in her Norfolk house, grants him extensive interviews that vastly expand the scope of his book. With Suzie teasingly refusing his advances, it's her mother who ends up sleeping with Penfield. Which is what eventually brings Ann's husband Matthew Fox together with Penfield over the cheese and pickle. Fox tells him he consents to the affair – after all, he's juggling a few of his own down in London. These sham marital arrangements are yet another example of this film's many duplicitous smokescreens.

Switching between the airless offices, squash courts, literary parties
and streets of London and the broad, windswept horizons of Norfolk
(even though the peace is regularly shattered by low-flying fighter
jets), the locations reflect the script's dialogue between history and the
future. 'If we leave the remembering to historians,' declares Ann at her
first meeting with Penfield, 'then the struggle is already lost. Everyone
must have a memory, everyone needs to be a historian. In this country,
for example, we are in danger of losing hard-won freedoms by dozing
off into a perpetual present.' Over dinner at the country house, she
speaks of the lost hopes and opportunities of the British state after
1945, its failure to rebuild a nation to serve all its citizens. A German
guest replies, 'The future is not ours to control.' Several times we see
old people, who would have been of fighting age during the war, still
employed and just about holding things together: a press-pool typist;
a doddering waiter handing round drinks at a book launch. Walking
out of a film at the newly completed Barbican Centre, Susan and
James disagree on everything. 'I don't like flashbacks,' she says, 'they
make me feel as if I'm holding my breath.' Left alone for a moment
with Ann's young stepson, Penfield listens as the boy rattles off a list
of English kings and queens since Henry VIII. 'You missed out the
Cromwells,' he observes, reminding the boy about England's revolutionary interregnum, but is told: 'They don't count.'

Penfield allows himself to be tossed whichever way the wind is blowing. With his fellow journalist and Oxford chum Jeremy Hancock,
he'll happily chortle at the irrelevance of modern poetry and smoke
fags in a private gym. To drive to Norfolk he wheels out his dad's old
black Jaguar, a vintage vehicle whose sumptuousness makes a mockery of the Capris and Cortinas that line the streets. Motoring down
the East Anglian A-roads reveals a classic post-war field-and-pylon
ensemble. But there is hidden disquiet in the shires, as he discovers
when he punctures a tyre and wanders through woods in search of a
fix. There he is confronted with both a massive US aerodrome and
protesters manning a Greenham Common-style peace camp.

The film's *coup de grâce* is the end sequence, in which the film crew and actors infiltrate the real-life Conservative Party conference in Brighton in October 1982. Doubling down on the political capital amassed during the Falklands campaign, Margaret Thatcher's faux-Churchillian speech talked of 'British patriotism [being] rediscovered in those spring days'. McEwan had his script written for him here, in a succession of speeches that invoked fantasies about the past while demonising socialism. With magnificent serendipity, Eyre's cameras were there to capture Environment Secretary Michael Heseltine railing against a 'professional left installed in local councils at the ratepayer's expense'. Cabinet bigwigs Kenneth Baker and Kenneth Clarke are visible in the entranceway to the Grand Hotel, and in a crowded lobby a young John Major (who would take over as PM less than a decade after the film was made) can be seen in earnest conversation over coffee. With hindsight, Major is similar to Penfield: the son of a lower-middle-class family who 'bettered himself' to escape the suburbs of Surrey. In a 1993 speech that has passed into political legend, Major set out his vision of a Britain fifty years hence. Like all the best British sci-fi, his perception of the future is actually infused with what has gone before: 'the country of long shadows on country grounds, warm beer, invincible green suburbs, dog lovers and – as George Orwell said – old maids bicycling to Holy Communion through the morning mist . . . Britain will survive unamendable in all essentials.'

This Arcadian rhapsodising, with extraordinarily specific visual details, was the tactic of an earlier Conservative prime minister, Stanley Baldwin, who in a 1924 speech invoked the medieval soundscape of the village blacksmith's anvil, the cry of a corncrake and a scythe sharpened against a whetstone.[6] *The Ploughman's Lunch* brilliantly dissevers such nostalgic conjuring tricks; its final shot is of Penfield looking anxiously at his watch, impatient for the future to begin.

War movies are a comfort zone. The snugness of cockpits and
gun turrets in Wellington bombers. Black and white, sharp
dialogue and long cross-fades between scenes: the rhythm
of a weekend afternoon. Sunday lunch is cleared away, but
the scented Bisto trail still lingers down the corridors of my
grandparents' house. The wooden doors of the cabinet are
rolled back and the magic box is aglow. Weekend afternoons,
huddled into the sofa, are a time for war stories. This is
the domain of my father and grandfather, neither of whom
actually fought in the Second World War (although my
grandpa was in the Home Guard and loves *Dad's Army*), but
both seem to know far too much about it. A nation's struggle,
an island's pride defended, etched in black and white. Battles
in forests, across exploding bridges, in dogfight-streaked
airspace. *Reach for the Sky, One of Our Aircraft Is Missing,
The Dam Busters, 633 Squadron, Mosquito Squadron, The
Battle of Britain.* And the propellers are still spinning: my
dad tunes in to the regular televised air shows, narrated by
the indomitable Raymond Baxter, with their Red Arrows
aerobatics and fly-pasts of Lancasters and Vulcans, Spitfires
and Hurricanes. Dad is obsessed with aeroplanes and is often
to be found in his workshop, gluing together various balsa-
wood, remote-controlled model aircraft. If he hadn't taken up
dentistry, he would have been a pilot. Whenever a plane on
screen is taking off, as the nose lifts Dad shouts, 'Rotate!'

There is tension on the high seas in *Battle of the River
Plate* and *Above Us the Waves*; POW derring-do in *The Great
Escape, The Wooden Horse, The Colditz Story, Tenko* and *The
Bridge Over the River Kwai*; land battles across the raging
theatres of the world's war zones – *The Longest Day, Arnhem,
Where Eagles Dare, Ice Cold in Alex, Merrill's Marauders, Von
Ryan's Express, The Steel Bayonet, The Guns of Navarone* . . .
On and on it goes, the parade of Panzer and Churchill tanks,

tommy guns, Schmeissers and '*Achtung Minen*' (never any
actual German-made movies, of course). Shared cigs and
bombed-out strongpoints. Dogfights and cat-tracks. Beamed
on television in the mid-1970s, these films were already
familiar to my father, who had watched them from the velvet
seats on their first cinematic outings. That gave him the
right to provide a running commentary and explanation, and
occasionally to pull down one of the many volumes of wartime
memoirs that lined our bookshelves. It also cemented the
institutional belief that Britain, aka England, was a worthy
victor entitled to greatest-nation status. We never quite got
over winning the war, and TV is partly responsible for keeping
the fantasy alive.

■

For some lives, beached in the mid-1980s, the future never quite
arrived. *Wetherby* (1985), written and directed by David Hare, flashes
between modern Britain and the early 1950s, in a style more redolent of a French chamber piece than a realist English movie made
at the mid-point of the Thatcher years. Set in a small market town
in the north of England, it begins and ends with two old friends,
schoolteacher Jean Travers (Vanessa Redgrave) and lawyer Stanley
Pilborough (Ian Holm), ruminating quietly in the rambling lounge
bar of a Yorkshire pub. 'We've lived in this town too long,' says Jean,
as the landlord calls, 'Time, gentlemen, please.' She and Stanley
came of age shortly after the Second World War, but the brave new
world promised in the aftermath never quite materialised. They live
quiet, uneventful lives in the shires while, somewhere distant and out
of sight, cities expand and politics becomes sour and corrupt. At the
end, Stanley describes his generation as 'prisoners of dreams'.

It's true that Jean's stone cottage does appear like a jail cell, albeit
gilded with books and spartan furniture (the portable TV is stored

behind the sofa). Her staid life is interrupted by John Morgan (Tim McInnerny), a student who gatecrashes Jean's dinner party and, the next day, blows his brains out while sitting at her kitchen table. The rest of the film deals with the expansion of dark matter in the after-shock of this event, including Jean's revived memories of a doomed teenage love affair that changed the course of the rest of her life.

Time-travelling between the past and present, the film contrasts the idealism of Jean's generation with the nihilism and apathy of today's youth. Her old friend Marcia (Judi Dench) rails against the blankness and lack of ambition in the young. A hundred thousand years of human evolution, and all they want is to get married and buy a two-up two-down. Her husband Stanley, the lawyer – 'the town's official sanctifier of greed' – has become bitter in midlife, railing against crimes hidden behind the privet hedge and against Thatcher, who's 'taking revenge on the country for some personal hurt'. Somewhere along the way, this generation unconsciously relinquished its hope.

Addressing the nation's soul in the mid-1980s, the central dilemma of this film is: to what extent are you spiritually dead? And how accurate are you at reading the future? When Jean (played as a young girl by Redgrave's daughter Joely Richardson) flashes back to her passionate affair with Jim, a young aircraft fitter in 1949, she remembers their furtive sex but also the awkward visit to his parents, who expect her to abandon her studies and settle down as a housewife, while Jim serves for several years in the Far East. Neither they nor Jim, who also expects her to put her life on hold (and who winds up dead in a Malayan gambling den), are able to correctly read where the future is heading. Jean went on to empower herself through education and is attempting to pass that inspiration on to her pupils, but at the same time she has eased herself out of history. All the while, behind all these hard choices, I can't help hearing Julie Christie's voice as Liz in *Billy Liar*, back in 1963, urging Billy to stop dithering, act on his dreams and start a new life in London. 'You buy a ticket and get on a train – that's all you have to do.' By 1985, would Liz have been throwing glamorous dinner parties in Hampstead, or was she a struggling supply teacher in Yorkshire?

McInnerny would appear as a cynical Conservative politician, Gerald Fedden, in the BBC's mini-series of Alan Hollinghurst's 1980s zeitgeist novel *The Line of Beauty* (Saul Dibb, 2006). Like a *Go-Between* or *Brideshead Revisited* for the age of the yuppie, a middle-class Oxford English graduate, Nick Guest, is embedded in the household of his upper-class student friend, with the refinement of being an overtly queer presence within the family of a Conservative minister. At times dreamy and elegiac, the series moves through its own golden arc of hedonism, sexual discovery and liberation, leading to a fall through the revelation of corruption and scandal on the part of the Tory father, and the encroachment of Aids into the gay community, leading Nick to be scapegoated for the family's collapsed reputation. But most relevant here is the fact that much of the action occurs within an insulated bubble of privilege: the Fedden family's Notting Hill townhouse, their holiday estate in France and various country manor houses. The indolent lifestyle, the trappings of fine art and the traditional dinner parties could almost be something out of a High Victorian saga, but the backdrop is the thrusting entre-preneurialism of the Thatcher years, which Nick is privy to in his day job as a hopeful screenwriter and co-founder of an art magazine. Appropriately, the film he is trying to get funded is an adaptation of Henry James's *The Spoils of Poynton*, which is itself a novel set in a house that's a time capsule, in which a widow has cocooned her-self with a sumptuous collection of fine art and antique furniture. Everybody is decadent on some level, whether it's Nick and his aes-theticism or the Establishment's hypocritical family values.

This sense of wealth providing insulation from modernity is even more pronounced in *Close My Eyes* (Stephen Poliakoff, 1991). Working at the tail end of the Thatcher years, Poliakoff (who both wrote and directed) consciously set the story amid contrasting architectural and geographic spaces. This is not only a story of brother–sister incest (between Richard, played by Clive Owen, and Natalie, played by Saskia Reeves), but of modern Britain's incestuous relationship with its own past. Even though Natalie is married to the vain, controlling financial analyst Sinclair (Alan Rickman), she continues the sibling affair over several years, though it threatens to break everyone apart. Richard works in a central London that's wracked with the constant background clang of building sites; he lives in a world of late-night snack bars, glass office blocks and cluttered desks. This introduces the ongoing paradox of 1980s conservatism: even as it claims to uphold Victorian values, capitalist growth projects (such as the London Docklands development) are destroying old buildings and monuments. When Richard travels to Surrey to visit his sister in her new marital home, it's presented as a journey back in time: a mansion and extensive gardens by the River Thames, cricket whites and picnics on rowing boats. Riches generated in the City give financiers the power to disappear from the present and construct this fantasy of a historical idyll. Even Sinclair's London apartment is enormous, and noticeably soundproofed from the noisy streets outside. He takes tea in a hotel that is decorated like an Edwardian patisserie.

The lure of the country and the escape from the urban has been a dream of romantics and revolutionaries ever since the first factories appeared on the horizon. These films confirm that this dream is still abundant, only this time it's the super-rich who also crave escape (and only they who can afford it). Nostalgia is the salve of the monetarist's conscience.

THE WEIRD OLD ALBION

21

English Magic

A Canterbury Tale, *Penda's Fen*, *Robin of Sherwood*: 'The Swords of Wayland', *Stargazy on Zummerdown*, *Detectorists*, *Britannia*, *Worzel Gummidge*

> Trim the lamp; polish the lens; draw, one by one, rare coins to the light.
>
> Geoffrey Hill, 'XIII', *Mercian Hymns* (1971)

> What have they got up there, besides trees and nightmares?
>
> *Britannia*, season one, episode one

My grandparents keep a wooden toy box in the attic: a miniature farm set, a squeaky rubber effigy of Windy Miller from *Camberwick Green*, who came out at bath-time and was renamed 'Adge' (in tribute to the lead singer of the Wurzels), a hotchpotch collection of Dinky toys, including tractors, a cream holiday coach and a replica of a dark-green 1950s BBC outside broadcast camera van. Buried underneath is a clump of educational children's magazines called *Treasure*, dating from the early 1960s, and it is in these yellowing pages, in between nature reports, 'The Wonderful Story of Britain', cartoon serialisations of *The Wind in the Willows*, magical tales of Princess Marigold and traffic-safety tips from the Tufty Club, that I discover Worzel Gummidge. The sentient scarecrow of Scatterbrook Farm leaves a trail of tattered chaos in his wake, in a rural setting that embodies all the parochial pleasures of rustic England: jumble sales, harvest festivals and farmyard scrapes.

When I first cast eyes on these pages, Jon Pertwee is the incumbent Doctor Who. After the Doctor metamorphoses into Tom Baker, Pertwee goes AWOL for a while, before re-enchanting the television screens not as a Time Lord straddling all four dimensions of the galaxy, but as the lead character in the four seasons of *Worzel Gummidge* made for Southern Television between 1979 and 1981. Swapping the sonic screwdriver for a collection of interchangeable turnip heads, and frequently expressing his partiality to a 'cup o'tea and a slice o'cake', this unexpected career development (apparently a long-held dream of Pertwee himself) raises the tantalising suggestion that the fate of former Time Lords is to reincarnate as animated bird-scarers.

The television adaptation by Keith Waterhouse and Willis Hall rewrites a few details from the original 1930s novel by Barbara Euphan Todd. Worzel's creator the Crowman, for instance, is invented for TV. He is played by Geoffrey Bayldon, who at the beginning of the decade had immortalised the wizard Catweazle, a dimension-hopping time lord from England's Dark Ages. This type of connection between parochial England and the magical–scientific capability to break through temporality opens up portholes in the space–time continuum. Catweazle, Worzel and others are lightning conductors of an innately English magic, one that reaches the kernel of an obsession with preserving the past so that its monuments and its culture may be transported deep into the future. In this vision, modernity, technology and city ways are no more than trivial ephemera, glowing briefly as fireflies, while a long-learned folklore and the wisdom of the Earth, and of England's mythological treasury, secretly and invisibly hold things together. While Arthur sleeps under Glastonbury

Tor, and the ravens strut about the Tower of London, England cannot fall. These protective forces may briefly surface into the present via a variety of means – a crack in the ground, a survivor from another age, even a scarecrow that reveals it can walk and talk. Just as a knitted tea cosy, a jar of chutney or a slice of Battenberg cake may have whole imperial histories embedded in their traditions and ingredients, what is commonly and innately understood to be 'English' often resides in the small local details that we never seem to want eradicated from our countryside.

■

What does it mean, to *haunt*, or to *be haunted*?

The word we use so freely, this word that contorts our mouth into the shape of a fearful 'Oh!', arrives in the English language out of the fog of ancient time. Birds and animals are said to haunt certain types of field and forest; that is to say, they frequent those places, they eternally cling to them and instinctively keep coming back. Like them, the ghosts we now associate with that word are not so much living in a space but eternally intruding upon it, unable to let it alone. Long before 'haunting' became affixed to the supernatural, it was about familiarity with, and return to, the habitat: the Old French *hanter* meaning 'to visit regularly, frequent'; the Norse *heimta* meaning 'bring home'; the proto-Germanic *Haimaz* (currently *Heimat*) signifying 'home, village'. This denotation from antiquity has inscribed its legacy in the English language, too, in all the place names ending in '-ham' and the word for a cluster of cottages, a 'hamlet'.

So the secret history of haunting – by phantoms that we might assume to be uncanny, unfamiliar and not of this Earth – turns out to be entwined with home and the familiar. Haunting is only horrifying if the connection with home, and everything implied within that emotive designation, has been broken: the land, history and the

ancestors that have gone before. Many ghost stories conclude by laying the ghosts to rest, exorcising the malevolent malingerers. The
ghosts are open to a peace treaty. Guardians of certain chosen places,
they serve the needs of the land – and remind those still living of
their obligations. Haunting puts the haunted back in touch with the
memories of a place that, for survival's sake, must not be forgotten.
The haunting points towards everything vital that may be buried,
physically or metaphorically, beneath our feet. A haunted place is a
conflicted place: friendly and known, and at the same time strange
and uncanny. It's a small step from the homely to the *unheimlich*.

In the ghost stories, folk-horror films and even the science-fiction
innovations of Britain, we have seen secrets hidden in the earth bursting out to unleash malevolent forces and dark, repressed memories.
This is responsible for the 'horror' in 'folk horror': an inkling that
beneath the beloved country lie forgotten nasties.

But even though it's steeped, as we've seen, in historical events
and etched with mementoes of past lives, the English landscape
remains, for many, the focus of idealism and dreams. To preserve
forests, to amble along ridgeways and riverbanks or snooze on clean
beaches is to follow ancestral trails. The mythically uncomplicated
country cottage – the rose garden, the quieter and slower pace of
life – is still a powerful influence in England's dreaming, just as it has
been for many generations. This was articulated in the preposterous,
unachievable altruism of William Morris's *News from Nowhere*, with
its yearning to revert to a pre-industrial social model where the forces
of heavy industry, urban blight and human greed are eradicated, in
favour of an organic, sustainable existence in an equal society that
loves labour for its own sake. In this view, held by so many who
have exited the city and headed for the country's internal exile, the
Industrial Revolution, technological progress and the massive growth
of cities are aberrations. As long as areas of natural beauty can be
preserved, there is always a garden awaiting our return. This hopeful
vision is based on the idea that the land and the earth itself hold

not corruption and evil, but one of the keys to national identity. The films and programmes in this chapter seek to capture this spirit of place. Characters are drawn to humours in the land under their feet. The mythical beings and spirits of old England observe human events, but stay detached from history.

Rustling leaves, waving corn stalks, a field rippled by the breeze, butterflies settling on a bloom . . . Nature-book vignettes, filmed from a static camera, crop up repeatedly as brief breathing spaces on the British screen, from Humphrey Jennings's documentaries to Patrick Keiller's travelogues and even the comedy series *Detectorists*. A breeze ruffles the surface of the frame, calming yet needling, somewhere between gentle swaying and the onset of a gale. In British film scenes like this are frequently used as an introductory establishing shot, a bookend, a frontispiece. It is picturesque but sometimes unsettling, untroubled by modernity (save for the film crew that is invisibly recording it), a seven-second establishing shot of Eden. Even in black and white, it's a scene essentially unchanged since the Norman invasion.

The undespoiled landscape of England is a salient feature of *A Canterbury Tale* (1944), one of the classic wartime movies of the Archers, aka the writing/directing duo of Michael Powell and Emeric Pressburger. Made in the summer and autumn of 1943, the film took advantage of its ample opportunities to show off the rolling expanses of rural Kent – the English county where Powell spent his childhood. As well as a kind of homecoming for the director, the film is ultimately about precisely the forces and energies – of history and individual/collective memory – that adhere people to the land and to each other.

It is not a ghost story, but it contains its fair share of phantom presences. Beginning with a reading from Chaucer, the camera observes medieval pilgrims riding along ferny lanes, joshing and sharing their stories. A hawk is briskly unhooded, revealing its hungry stare. The film appeals to its viewers: Sit up. Open your eyes. Magic is about to happen.

It's not done with any special trickery, just sharp cutting. The bird, soaring high in the clouds, white, billowy English clouds, suddenly develops stiff wings and travels at many more miles per hour. The guttural cry is now the exhaust throb of a Rolls-Royce Merlin engine as a Hurricane swoops down and dive-bombs the camera. (After the war, Powell and Pressburger will once again strafe the camera crew, this time with a Mosquito roaring past David Niven on a Devon beach in *A Matter of Life and Death*, proving that he is not dead but tangibly still on Earth.) When the plane has zoomed out of shot to protect the skies from another Luftwaffe attack, the hawker who released the bird is now wearing a Second World War military helmet with camouflage webbing. The next shot is a panoramic view of the Kentish Weald, overcast but rich in field and woodland, a Constable or Gainsborough prospect reframed for cinema. 'Though much has changed since Chaucer's day,' reads the narrator, 'another kind of pilgrim walks the way,' and a whining convoy of Bren gun carriers comes bumping along the narrow lanes.

A Canterbury Tale has been called a 'perverse Romantic pastoral',[1] a not unhelpful description of a narrative that begins with a mystery and a chaotic meeting of three strangers on a dark train platform, devolves into a rambling drift around the byways and village streets of deepest Kent, and ends up with a pilgrimage to Canterbury Cathedral, where simultaneous miracles occur that offer hope in the dark, uncertain time of war. In the dead of night, a huffing, smoky beast of a locomotive stops at Chillingbourne station, the last stop before Canterbury. Three figures alight: Alison (Sheila Sim), a London shop assistant, arriving to start work as a land girl; British soldier Peter Gibbs, part of a military build-up on the south coast; and American Bob Johnson (played by John Sweet, a real-life US sergeant who had been stationed as a clerk at General Eisenhower's London HQ). Bob's on weekend leave to meet an old services friend, but he's missed his stop. Before the trio have even left the platform, a sense of difference and mistrust has sprung up. A huffy platform

How do you mend a broken nation? The Glueman
opens up portals to the past in *A Canterbury Tale*
(1944).

guard accuses Bob of wearing his US sergeant's stripes upside down
and points out that the town was constituted four hundred years
before Columbus discovered America; furthermore, 'No young lady
must go alone at night,' he cautions Alison. 'Mr Colpeper's orders.'
Moments later, something unseen happens to Alison while the screen
is almost pitch black. When the men rush to help her, she finds a
sticky substance plastered in her hair. 'So this is England,' muses Bob
wryly. 'Never a dull moment.'

Alison is the eleventh victim of the mysterious 'Glueman', who's
been causing local consternation by ejaculating adhesive into the
topknots of village women. While it's only ever referred to as 'glue',
the film subtly reinforces the sexual undertones of these attacks in a

scene where Alison questions another victim, fellow farm worker Fee
Baker. As Fee speculates, 'Might be any one of a dozen . . . Might be a
Glue Woman,' she pops the top of a milk bottle, which spurts a jet of
cream into the air. It's one of those amazingly serendipitous moments
in Powell's movies that leave you wondering if it was planned or not,
but which leaves a lingering magic nevertheless.[2]

While Alison is conducting her enquiries around Chillingbourne,
the film's pace gears down to a meander. We have already met
Thomas Colpeper, the local magistrate, who lives with his mother
in a beautifully appointed Queen Anne mansion and keeps an office
at the town hall, sequestered behind a panelled door carved with
'1593'. Colpeper's frosty reaction to the young people's Glueman
enquiries is overtly chauvinistic. He sneers at Alison's land girl posting, showing no faith in her ability to work; and he keeps a medieval ducking stool displayed in his chambers, 'very sensibly used for
silencing talkative women'. (Sexism is everywhere. Even Peter calls
Alison 'just an objective' when he and his comrades surround her
with revving Bren gun carriers.)

But it's Colpeper who turns out to be the Glueman, and his con-
voluted motives are the key to this mystical movie's meaning. By
scaring local women into staying at home, he hopes to prevent them
from fraternising with the foreign soldiers billeted in Kent, in an
attempt to mend the broken homeland. Colpeper is a gentleman
fanatic, and at the heart of his sticky assaults lies a desire to preserve
continuity. At the same time, he is seizing the opportunity to dissem-
inate his knowledge of local history and culture to the newly arrived
captive audience of soldiers, via a series of illustrated lectures at the
town hall.

Silhouetted against a halo of white light, this patrician projection-
ist encourages the soldiers to walk the old Pilgrim's Road and remember the ancestors. (His commentary is in the style later adopted by
the narrators of the British Transport Films.) This inverted propaganda is his weird method of transcending the chaos and fog of

war and staying connected to 'knowledge of our country, and love of its beauty'. The Glueman sees himself as a missionary, pouring knowledge into people's heads. When eventually confronted by the three young 'pilgrims' in a train compartment, he likens himself to the school that parents must force their children to attend. When Gibbs, scoffing, asks who cares about these things in wartime, his answer is incontrovertible: 'Who cares about them in peacetime?' The Glueman is the ghost that haunts the green grass of home.

The real 'glue' that abounds in the film is found in the connections across space and time that are discovered, and the bonds forged as a result. Bob, who hails from Three Sisters Falls in Oregon (lying next to the Separation Creek) and 'cut his teeth on wood shavings', visits a wheelwrights' workshop and smithy, where he discovers the craftsmen treat their timber in very similar ways to his countrymen, even though they are separated by five thousand miles. In the former colonies, time has preserved customs and the lore of craft against physical distance. The scene features genuine Kentish wheelwrights whom Powell had known in his childhood, in a workshop 'sheltered from intruders by hedgerows full of honeysuckle, foxgloves and columbine . . . It was a heavenly place.'[3] At the end of the film, Bob will connect the vaulted ceiling of Canterbury Cathedral with his own grandfather's church in Oregon. Part of the film's inclusiveness consists in how it advocates for local knowledge and the stability of the heartland, while acknowledging how traditions are unable to remain contained or localised, and can spread across the world to affect distant cultures.

'When I agreed to make *A Canterbury Tale*,' wrote Powell at the end of his life, 'I expected that it would be a far more personal film than it turned out to be. I was working, creating a story in the county I was born in, the "garden of England", a chalky country of bare downs and shallow valleys, of chestnut woods and little chuckling streams, of slowly turning water and windmills, and white-capped oasthouses with the bittersweet smell of hops drying in the kiln.'[4]

He felt he had failed to portray this environment as he wished. His principal characters were outsiders in this landscape. If *A Canterbury Tale* was Powell's magic-lantern lecture, the director himself was a Glueman, putting these images out there and hoping that at least some of them would stick.[5]

This Kentish idyll looks magnificent, especially in the immersive yet wide-angle scenes of contemplation with Alison and Colpeper in a field of long grass. Alison, it turns out, is familiar with this place: she spent a romantic sojourn with her fiancé Geoffrey, a pilot subsequently killed in the war, in a caravan at a bend in the Pilgrim's Road, the spot where the cathedral towers first revealed themselves to travellers. She explains that Geoffrey dug up some Belgian coins here, which she now pledges to donate to the local museum – an incident that connects Colpeper's interest in history with her own memories of excavating the landscape. He lies back in the meadow and exercises his peculiar sixth sense for the ghosts in the grass. 'When you see the bluebells in spring and the wild thyme and the bloom in the heather, you're only seeing what *their* eyes saw,' he tells her, in a rapture that suggests the pilgrim ancestors we saw in the opening shots could have been Colpeper's own hallucinations. The continuities and unchanged features of the landscape and climate act as aural and visual stepping stones to the past: the throb of horses' hooves, the cartwheels rumbling on the track. Alison's sensibilities prove to be almost as finely calibrated to the past as his own – she too hears cantering, voices and lutes at the bend in the road.

We don't see any actual archaeology taking place in this film, but the revelation of the Glueman's identity – and more importantly, his motives – represents another form of unearthing. All three pilgrims are cut loose and in need of a blessing; they are losing touch with the nature and history that Colpeper is striving to promote. The urbane Peter prefers the valley to the mountain. Bob likes the movies. Alison was a shopgirl in the city. Colpeper's task is to distract them from trivial diversions and reglue them to what is essential, to the history that lies buried beneath their feet. Something miraculous happens to each one of them. Peter rediscovers his musical vocation. Bob receives a packet of letters from the girlfriend he thought had ditched him. Alison's miracle at the end involves 'digging up' her old caravan, which has been abandoned at the back of a vehicle repair shop. A 'Mr Portal' looks after it, and for Alison, opening the caravan's door is a gateway to blissful memories she has been forced to suppress during the war and her bereavement. She smells her lover's straw hat and twitches his old coat, releasing a flurry of moths. This is too much for her; she flees in tears, oversaturated with memory and loss. Just at that moment her fiancé's father appears in the doorway with the news that Geoffrey has been reported alive in Gibraltar. Sheila Sim's relieved face could light up an entire auditorium.

The well-being eventually restored to each of the three on their respective personal pilgrimages contains seeds of hope; a sense, as in Humphrey Jennings's contemporaneous *A Diary for Timothy*, that the tides of war are on the turn. When Peter rediscovers his passion for playing the church organ (having settled before the war for a job as a cinema organist) and plays a Bach toccata in Canterbury Cathedral, it brings to mind Jennings's footage of recitals in the National Gallery. The bend in the road is also a turning point in the conflict, and the majestic cathedral tower standing proud in the Kentish Weald gives a glimpse of steadier times ahead. The war has brought these disparate people to this rural haven and informs their motivations, behaviour and inner lives. Although there's a war on, hardly anyone in *A Canterbury Tale* talks about it. Those horrors are kept at bay, even though Kent is about as close to the European mainland – and the Nazi invasion plans – as you can get. The village kids Bob enlists in his investigations are playing innocent, *Swallows and Amazons*-style war games in rowing boats, with apples for ammo. Peter tells Bob that it's taken the war to make him realise there even is a countryside outside of London; Bob is given a deeper understanding of his ancestral connections with the Old Country.

When Alison walks through the blitzed streets of Canterbury, in some of the film's most breathtaking shots, a local woman tells her, 'You get a very good view of the Cathedral now.' In the city centre are exposed basements and rubble marking former shops and businesses. A medieval church is orthodontically braced against air raids with iron bands. Bombing has trimmed away much of the excess fat of twentieth-century life, to reveal an essence, the flames that keep burning (a painted sign standing in a building's bombed-out foundations bears the mysterious legend 'Ancient Light'). But the cathedral, this great ocean liner of the Weald, stands firm, buoyed up on Allan Gray's stirring music.[6]

As the citizens of Canterbury file into the cathedral to bless the coming invasion into France, the three pilgrims have been glued back together, while Colpeper, the actual Glueman, stands apart. Peter decided in the end not to shop him to the police, but he will do his own private penance. Behind the closing credits, we see both men *and* women emerging from one of Colpeper's lectures (Alison previously upbraided him for not inviting women in the first place). And in the last shot of all, the children have replaced their fighting with football.

A Canterbury Tale is a flawed masterpiece, and even Powell later called it 'a frail and unconvincing structure'.[7] The script is way too wordy, with pedantic, trifling gags; the acting by Sims and Sgt John Sweet stilted (Sweet later admitted he knew nothing much about acting and felt he was totally green in the role); Gray's orchestral music a little trite at times. (The pastoral, symphonic drift of Vaughan Williams or John Ireland would have made a much better complement.) These failings are countered by some ravishing panoramas of the Kentish countryside and stupendous light effects (Bob's palatial Elizabethan bedroom when he wakes up; the haloing of light around actors' profiles; the scenes shot in almost total darkness). You find yourself imagining what it might have looked like in colour, with the green and brown of the landscapes and the khaki uniforms, the nostalgic childish pleasures of the river battle and the glorious stained glass and shafts of sunlight streaming into Canterbury Cathedral. But ultimately it seems right that the movie ended up in grey monochrome, a casualty of wartime austerity (all available Technicolor film stock had been requisitioned for military training films), emphasising the stark contrasts and silhouettes of Erwin Hillier's cinematography: the village idiot in cameo against the horizon; the first glue attack in the blackout; the architectural lines of Colpeper's immaculate house and his brandishing of a scythe in his back garden. Almost every outdoor scene is shot under a white overcast sky: Hope is in the offing but not quite ready to burst through. Hillier hated photographing clear skies and was 'a bit loony about . . . clouds in the sky',[8] to Powell's consternation. Odd things occur when you least expect them, such as when Colpeper is appealing to his interrogators to examine his case from every angle before rushing to judgement, and the train passes into a tunnel and his face is blacked out. Such moments are pregnant not so much with meaning, as with transcendence.

Ultimately, *A Canterbury Tale* reminded its contemporary audience that some things last longer than war. And that an important justification for war is its role in preserving national and local continuities from destruction. It is a lecture on how to stop society's glue dissolving.

■

In a 1971 prose-poem cycle titled *Mercian Hymns*, the poet Geoffrey Hill, who died in 2016, extracted the residue of pre-Christian history from the contemporary landscape of the Midlands. Coins stamped with the visage of King Offa are trowelled up and held to the light. Gift shops sprawl across the ancient kingdom of Mercia (the Anglo-Saxon heartland that held out against the arrival of Christianity), and iron railings prop up gnarled hedgerows of yew and hawthorn. The poem feels connected to the late-1960s back-to-the-land folk revival, a psychogeographic portrait of the becalmed peripheries of

'Coiled entrenched England', where 'Tea was enjoyed, by lakesides where all might fancy carillons of real Camelot vibrating through the silent water.'[9]

Arthur and his warriors have all long since gone under the hill. But they remain strong in Britain's mythic dreamscape, commemorated by the names that still get printed on the map. Backpackers still trudge along Offa's Dyke, named after the eighth-century pagan king. Looking back to a hundred years before Offa, the most celebrated pre-Christian monarch is Penda of Mercia, who died in the mid-seventh century. But to find traces of Penda, some decoding is in order. What mystery in this land went down with him for ever? Who is the genie in our fen?

These last questions are posed in the script of *Penda's Fen*, a BBC 'Play for Today' broadcast in 1974. This ninety-minute film, written by David Rudkin and directed by Alan Clarke, stands in sharp relief as one of British TV's all-time masterpieces: an intellectually challenging examination of self-determination, national and sexual identity and political necessity, framed in one of England's most culturally resonant landscapes (the Malvern Hills) and featuring angels, demons and ghostly mentors from history made flesh.

If the alliance of Rudkin and Clarke might seem unlikely at first, it's worth bearing in mind that much of Clarke's subsequent work as a director of television drama – from *Scum* (1977) to *Made in Britain* (1983) – would, like *Penda's Fen*, deal with strong-willed individuals violently butting up against power and state institutions. It's just that, by then, Clarke had locked into an urban realist mode. Rudkin's dramaturgy inclines to the mystic-pastoral and the supernatural, even while chewing over complex problems of politics and identity. It is the urgent, fantastical vision of a William Blake or John Cowper Powys, posing moral dilemmas in a phantasmagorical form that includes angels and demons at play.

With its dualities and counterforces vying for possession of the protagonist Stephen Franklin, *Penda's Fen* is essentially an inquiry into Manichaeism in modern England. Stephen starts out as a smugly opinionated, conventionally Christian seventeen-year-old private schoolboy espousing conservative beliefs in the debating society. He's debunking newly emerging theories about the revolutionary ambitions of the historical Jesus and his contemporaries, calling a proposed TV documentary on the subject 'atheistic and subversive trash'. The weaknesses in Stephen's priggish armour soon make themselves apparent. Later, he'll discover his own father, the local parson, is the author of a manuscript on the same 'heretical' subject. Meanwhile, the arrows of his desire are attracted to the whistling milk boy and a rugger-playing classmate, and he's persecuted by his homophobic schoolmates. As he approaches his eighteenth birthday, and his parents discuss a secret they pledged to reveal to him on that date, his emerging sexuality provides him with an insight that permits a critique of the school as an institution, its militarism, its injustices, its expectations of blind adherence to Christian norms and conventions. As in *If . . .* and *Unman, Wittering and Zigo*, the school stands in for the state. Loyalty to school equates to patriotism in the world outside. The very first lines in *Penda's Fen*, as the camera takes in the hushed countryside and hills of the Malverns, are spoken in Stephen's voice: 'Oh my country . . . I am one of your sons . . . but how shall I show my love?' It's one of several questions the play poses: how to find a way to express and live through patriotism, while rejecting its negative, divisive aspects?

'When the chips are down, *Penda's Fen* is just about somebody who has to kick things over, has to become free,'[10] Rudkin once commented. The tools for realising this freedom are latent in this charged landscape. 'Balance of mind' might be the motto inscribed on his headmaster's lectern, but the Greek inscription Stephen keeps returning to is painted around the skylight: 'Discover thyself'. Stephen listens obsessively to his LPs of Elgar's *Dream of Gerontius*, a visionary choral work about the transition of a soul in the afterlife, undergoing trials in order to be forged strong enough to withstand the terror and

shock of meeting God and enduring Purgatory.[11] The music forms a
parallel text to the action: Stephen himself undergoes ordeals, including a persecution at school in which he has pink ribbons tied into his
hair (a mockery of Christ's crown of thorns), his rejection by Joel the
milkman, and a revelatory subterranean meeting with a wheelchair-
bound Sir Edward Elgar. In *Gerontius*, the Soul at one point wakes up
in a timeless, placeless state, in the presence of a guardian angel, and
one of the most striking scenes in *Penda's Fen* features Stephen sitting
by a mirror-calm river, with a golden angel standing at his shoulder.
Maintaining the 'reality' of this scene was crucial to Rudkin, who
overrode the film editor's scepticism to insist that the angel's 'endors-
ing presence'[12] be portrayed as a concrete, physical actuality, via a
reflection in the water, not as a projection of his mind's eye. The same
applies to the (less convincing) apparition of a demonic mannequin
at the end of Stephen's bed. These visitations are not directed only
towards Stephen. Some fiery force of retribution is abroad in the
fields, and it scorches a local partygoer who ventures out of his car in
the middle of the night.

Enraptured by the power of Elgar's music, Stephen realises his
bedroom overlooks the same Malvern Hills that inspired the composer's aural evocations of divine judgement, angels and demons.
The postcard-perfect prospects montaged in the opening minutes,
as static and composed as the frames of a Patrick Keiller movie,
are triggers of dissonance, revelation and transformation. Lured
down a tunnel, he finds Elgar alone in a wheelchair,[13] who partially
demystifies his creative process, as well as whispering in Stephen's
ear the long-sought solution to his *Enigma Variations*. It's a concealed but well-known tune that overlays perfectly with Elgar's score
if you play it, as Stephen does, in your head while the composer
hums the *Enigma* theme. *Penda's Fen* offers a similar conundrum:
you need to perceive the unseen counterpoint that hovers over the
visible landscape; reveal the archetypes inscribed in invisible ink on
the fields and slopes; read the messages hiding in plain sight. The

message-bearer will turn out to be what his father calls 'The old man-god, unchanging, ever changing . . . by whom this earth is haunted ever since the first beat of the heart of man.'

Rudkin was present on set for most of the shoot in the summer of 1973, and a key moment was the recreation of a genuine experience his wife had. She had found the local road to the village of Pinvin blocked with a bright-red diversion sign, only the name had apparently been misspelled 'Pinfin'. In the film, Stephen at first remonstrates with the eerily mute sign-painter, then looks 'Pinfin' up in his father's encyclopaedia of place names and discovers that it is a corruption of 'Pendefen', which indicates that this patch of open country was once Penda's Fen.

From here, he wanders into a vision of a half-timbered Elizabethan house and its enclosed garden, with yellow-clad folk gaily queuing up to have their hands chopped off. In Rudkin's image of homogenous, sheep-like religion, Stephen is beckoned by a religious couple towards a society of uniformity, willing sacrifice and fake 'light'. This is a religion that dangles illusions like a halo over a hypocritical culture, one that his father debunks in the manuscript 'The Buried Jesus' that Stephen discovers in his study. Jesus, in the new view, was the revolutionary, but his modern worshippers have become complacent.

Stephen receives enlightenment from another revolutionary closer to home. Mr Arne, the outspoken local radical who enjoys an unexpected affinity with Stephen's father, and his wife tend to their garden like a couple of Diggers. Arne castigates the 'manipulators and fixers and psychopaths' who run the country, and the large corporations, which waste taxpayers' money on 'deliriums and fantasies'. Ahead of his time, Arne is an ecological radical whose ire is closely bound up with the abuse of the Earth: industrial spread and profit-oriented agriculture will 'hand on nothing but dust to the children of tomorrow'. Later, speaking with Stephen's father, he comes out with conspiracy theories about a top-secret installation which, he speculates,

is due to be constructed beneath Penda's Fen. Modernity, steered by
the man-made forces of Mammon, will literally be injected intraven-
ously into the soil. Stephen's father observes that similar sacrilege
has been enacted at 'such haunted sites' all over the world, like the
nuclear testing site at Los Alamos, once a holy ground for Native
American tribes. The visions that appear to Stephen, and the destructive force that commits one youth to a hospital burns unit, appear to
be the Earth in revolt against encroaching defilement.

Directly after Stephen is seen gazing up at the inscription 'Discover
thyself', he breaks his first barrier. Skiving off his cadet drill, he
marches past the 'Road Closed' sign onto the fen. Hauled before
his superiors after this transgression, he is asked, 'What are you,
Franklin?' 'A non-cooperative, sir,' he dutifully replies. The teacher's
name for those who don't toe the line is 'sixth-form revenants'. The
anarchic forces that are concentrated in the character of Stephen are
thus condemned as ghosts by the authority figures who seek to annul
their power. But Stephen is learning to focus his own powers. He
recounts his dream to another teacher: how he saw a demon sitting
on the roof of the church and turned him into an angel by force of
will. The church spire has already been described as a spiritual aerial
attracting Manichean energies to the village.

These energies, linked to anarchy and impurity, are unleashed
by the end of the film, summoned up and invoked by King Penda
himself, enthroned at the top of a ridge overlooking Stephen's
homeland. Stephen is a crucible of transition from conservatism,
small-mindedness, elitism and lack of self-knowledge to openness,
inclusivity, strangeness. On his eighteenth birthday he receives the
long-buried news about his own provenance: that his mother and
father in fact adopted him from non-English birth parents. 'Like the
English language,' they tell him, 'you have foreign parents too.' In
the final hilltop vision, he is again approached by the pair of moral
guardians, or traditional English parents, summoning him to their
cult of purity. 'I am nothing pure,' he counters. 'My race is mixed.

My sex is mixed. I am womankind man. Light with darkness. Mixed! Mixed . . .'

Rejecting these siren calls, Stephen is confronted with the commanding presence of Penda, whose words – 'The deep, dark flame must never die . . . Child, be strange, dark, true and impure' – seem to be influenced by the way Geoffrey Hill imagines Offa's diction in *Mercian Hymns*: 'Not strangeness, but strange likeness. Obstinate, outclassed forefathers, I too concede, I am your staggeringly-gifted child.'

Written and filmed around the same time as the release of *The Wicker Man, Penda's Fen* is an alternative take on the concept of pagan Britain's potential to transform society at the level of the individual. As Stephen's father explains on one of their enlightening walks in the rosy sunset, the original meaning of pagan is 'belonging to the village'. He and Arne are concerned with the imperative to 'revolt from the monolith: return to the village'. This is the struggle embodied in the figure of King Penda, 'the last of his kind, last pagan king of England, fighting his last battle against the new machine [Christianity]' – a conflict dating from before the Norman yoke, and therefore central to the English experience. The disobedience instilled in Stephen can contribute to the coming new original sin or, as Arne puts it, 'some new experiment in human living be[ing] born'.

'To some extent,' writes Marina Warner, 'contemporary conditions have returned us to pre-modern psychology: for Lucretius, a dream, a thought, a hallucination, could affect the experience of reality.'[14] Warner goes on to quote the poet Wallace Stevens: 'The imagination is the power that enables us to perceive the normal in the abnormal, the opposite of chaos in chaos.' *Penda's Fen* exults in these dualities and double visions. The flame still flickers in the fen.[15]

■

David Rudkin conceived a stage play in 2008, *Merlin Unchained*, in which the necromancer from Arthurian legend summons his mental and magical powers in the present day for one final task. The twisting path to the matter of Britain inevitably ends up under the ramparts of Camelot. The sleeping King Arthur, whose remains are reputedly buried beneath Glastonbury Tor and whose signature is inscribed in the architectural ruins of Cornwall and the mountains of North Wales, is the backstop of the English psyche. A mythic insurance policy against the nation's ruin.

Arthur, Guinevere and the Knights of the Round Table have maintained a presence in British art, music, literature and film for centuries, in countless iterations. In the cinema, two key 1970s Arthurian epics were actually French: Robert Bresson's earnest, gravitas-laden *Lancelot du Lac* (1974) and Eric Rohmer's *Perceval le Gallois* (1978). By the mid-1970s British movie budgets were depleted, and it showed in the output. *Gawain and the Green Knight*, released in 1973, with a screenplay also by David Rudkin, was a psychedelic fantasy based on one of the oldest epic poems in Middle English. Murray Head, with a flowing rock-star coiffure, goes head to head with a gigantic green knight who wants to cut off his . . . well, head. A film such as this was clearly the last straw for the Monty Python team, whose Terry Jones happened to be a scholar of medieval history. *Monty Python and the Holy Grail* (1975), with its Knights Who Say 'Ni', the anarcho-syndicalist commune of articulate, mudlark peasants and a 'dynamite' rabbit, tugged hard against the ropes of convention in medieval film, stretching them to Brechtian breaking point at the end, when the illusion finally collapses, a police car arrives to round up the miscreants and the whole thing unravels into a public-order offence perpetrated by some breakaway faction from the Sealed Knot. Undaunted, John Boorman polished up the breastplates one more time for the gleaming *Excalibur* (1981).

We've already seen that the BBC TV serial *The Changes* explained its anti-technology meltdown in Arthurian terms. Shortly afterwards, Trevor Ray and Jeremy Burnham, the same team responsible for *Children of the Stones*, came up with *The Raven* (1977) for ATV. Phil

Daniels was the youthful star, a rough-and-ready borstal inmate let out on parole (in the same year, Daniels played 'Richards' in Alan Clarke's banned TV play *Scum*) who assists an archaeologist in excavating a string of caverns, whose carvings and buried objects have fired up the professor to believe that they point to the historical truth of King Arthur. The quest is further complicated by a plan to store nuclear waste in the caves – an early eco-warrior theme, with a faint pre-echo of *Edge of Darkness*. In 1989 King Arthur collided with that other immortal saviour of Britain in peril, Doctor Who (the Sylvester McCoy incarnation), in a series entitled *Battlefield*. The series compresses the *Doctor Who* universe into the landscape of legend: Arthurian characters like Morgaine, Mordred and the King himself (or his corpse) appear; there are scenes at the mythical Lake Vortigern; and the sword of Excalibur is discovered in an underground spaceship. The Doctor himself is recast as a time-travelling Merlin.

These are just a handful of examples of the survival of the King Arthur legends in popular film and television. Arthur can be sliced so many ways on screen, from the earthy, realist HTV series *Arthur of the Britons* (1972–3), which is played more like a Wild Wessex western among warring Celtic clans, to the BBC's 2008 *Merlin*, an acclaimed five-season serial whose grand-scale power jostles, spectacular magic and dragon's cave mark it as a pre-*Game of Thrones* epic.

In the clash of clans depicted in *Arthur of the Britons*, the competition lay in which band of brigands were to be considered as outlaws and which held the magical 'X' factor that would win them power over the people. In English lore, the other great folkloric figure remains the subversive Green Man of Sherwood Forest, Robin Hood. That great redistributor of wealth has also cropped up time and again in film and television. In the Monty Python spin-off *Time Bandits* (Terry Gilliam, 1981), a macabre, absurd and nihilistic shaggy-dog story about a young boy and a group of time-travelling dwarves, John Cleese plays Hood as an immaculately turned out and cleanly laundered prep-school housemaster leading a bunch of merry hooligans. Three years later, in the HTV Saturday teatime series *Robin of Sherwood* (1984–6), Michael Praed was similarly scrubbed up and styled, looking like a rugged session guitarist for T'Pau who had stepped back into the Domesday Book era. The three series of *Robin of Sherwood* were created by Richard Carpenter – a more sophisticated undertaking than his earlier show, *Catweazle*. Filmed in sylvan locations around Bristol and Avon, with a pervasive wild-bird soundtrack, Robin of Loxley's band of merry men were pagan wood dwellers, an arboreal commando hit squad taking on the Norman despots and protecting peasants' rights against baronial tyranny. The forests and villages were muddy and real, but Robin also prays to and is occasionally visited by Herne the Hunter, another incarnation of the horned god Cernunnos, who provides spiritual counselling in his hour of need. The 1980s were not kind to folk musicians, so long after the golden age of the late-1960s and early-'70s progressive folk movement, but *Robin of Sherwood*'s musical accompaniment provided a rare instance of a folk group resonating in the mainstream – although Irish band Clannad had to incorporate a bank of twinkly synthesizers and voice processors in order to secure their BAFTA-winning soundtrack.

Of all the episodes in *Robin of Sherwood*'s three seasons, it's worth returning to the two-parter in season two, 'The Swords of Wayland'. Here the Robin story cleaves closest to Hammer Films territory, merging the usual derring-do with satanic cults and demonic apparitions. Abbess Morgwyn of Ravenscar is a nun whose order is secretly devoted to worshipping Lucifer, a sideline she runs from the crypt, where she burns an eternal flame surrounded by six of the seven swords of Wayland, each with its own magical name. Her henchmen are a troop of Nazgûl-like riders who, clad in red cloaks, they and their horses wearing demonic masks, terrorise the neighbouring villages. These scenes are shot with a hallucinatory, slow-motion beauty, with red filters, mist and eerie half-speed sound. Even though these thugs can eventually be shot down and unmasked, the black magic in this story remains real; Morgwyn eventually casts a spell on Robin's men, cursing them with smoky zombie-eyes and turning them against their leader and Marian.

Robin's band defends the villagers of 'Uffcombe-on-the-Rock' (filmed at Black Rock Quarry in Portishead, revisiting a location used in 'The Slaves' episode of *Arthur of the Britons*) against the demon riders' terror attacks. Turns out it's Robin himself who owns the missing sword, 'Albion', and Morgwyn is determined to add it to her collection. The resulting rites are pure Hammer, bundled with the naked fire dance from *The Wicker Man*. For good measure, a memorable scene from *Time Bandits* is invoked when the Merry Men are held captive in a wooden cage suspended in mid-air over a black emptiness.

Tradition demands that the hero escapes, and after a protracted sword fight around the stone altar, all is well. Six of the swords of Wayland are cast into the purging flames, but Robin is reunited with his stolen blade. As the village elder says, 'Albion is in good hands.' As for *Robin of Sherwood*, Praed would be killed off and replaced with the blond Jason Connery for the third and final series, but by then the franchise had passed its peak. There's only so many ways you can rob the rich to feed the poor before the forest spreads its tanglewood canopy over your memory.

■

Long, long before I make a living from writing, I have my first piece published on television. Not 'about' television, but actually *on* the telly. In the 1980s there is this secret dimension to the box. To unlock it you press a special key on the remote: a button embossed with a screen-shaped rectangle containing three horizontal lines. With one press, you make the jump to televisual hyperspace, otherwise known as Teletext.

The BBC's Ceefax and ITV/Channel 4's Oracle services are blunted-edge technology, marginally more thrilling than the test card, but with the internet some years away, they offer the next best source of information. You type in a three-digit page number from a menu list, put the kettle on and, on a good day, just three cups of tea later, the numbers might have ticked through to Football Scores on page 340. On a bad day they get stuck for ages on one digit or irritatingly hop over your choice, so that you have to wait for the count to trickle all the way around to 999 and back again.

When you do finally land on your designated page, you're confronted by chunky fonts and crude blocks that made Minecraft look like high-end CGI. In case you haven't read a newspaper, watched the *News at Ten* or listened to the radio in a while, there are News stories and Sports reports. The Weather forecasts read like retrospectives. You wouldn't want to rely on the Traffic updates. Instead of checking the TV Listings, you might as well just watch programmes in real time. For kids, there are Games, Quizzes and all-purpose Fun. When reading an article in Teletext, you're told how many pages it includes, but Sod's Law says you'll land on page '2/3', so you have to wait two minutes for it to scroll to '3/3', and then another two before actually reading the opening paragraphs.

After devouring the weekly music papers in print, I dial up Oracle's 'Blue Suede Views' pages, a veritable pixellated paradise of pop titbits. Launched in 1983 and edited by one Julian Newby, this is the hippest hangout on Teletext, updated daily with reviews of records, videos, films and gigs, plus news, viewers' letters, competitions and computer-graphic portraits of artists like Prince and Kate Bush. (In its charming, clumsy way, it's a foretaste of a website, before anyone has an inkling that such a thing could exist.)

I start going to my first gigs in 1984. At the end of that year I sit down with a biro and a pad of A4 and write up a side on Echo and the Bunnymen (Bristol Colston Hall, 9 October 1984) and another on Sade (Bristol Colston Hall, 29 October 1984), fold them up, stick them in an envelope and address them to Julian Newby. A couple of weeks later, there they are, typed in and lightly edited, in the Live section of 'Blue Suede Views'. No feedback, not a phone call or a letter of acknowledgement from Julian, and of course, no fee. But my work is out there, and that's reward enough. I am a published writer, and my words are on TV.

■

There is no end to the great game of imagining alternative Englands. Projections into the future are frequently indivisible from a nostalgic return to something older. Beyond William Morris's *News from Nowhere*, Rupert Thomson's 2005 novel *Divided Kingdom* geographically carved up a dystopian Britain into four distinct competing regions, with their own hard borders, and redistributed its population according to four 'humours', or temperaments. Somewhere between those two fictional speculative futures lies *Stargazy on Zummerdown*, a BBC television play from 1978 that peers two hundred years into the future and scries a 'Free Albion' that has survived war and violent social upheaval to connect with its parochial, agrarian past.

The opening shots establish a visual identity that looks mostly like portraits from Edwardian England, with bonnets and horse brasses, plus a few nods to laughably imagined future technology (giant mobile phones with extended antennae; videophones with sepia screens; a farmer leading a shire horse, chanting along to a networked religious ceremony via walkie-talkie). The aesthetic – what remains after two centuries of religious conflict and civil war – is country-pub rustic, perhaps the writer John Fletcher's ideal of the essence of the

English lifestyle. Fletcher was a professional historian rather than a full-time screenwriter, with a special interest in the English Civil War and its revolutionary dissidents. Produced in the afterglow of the previous year's patriotic Jubilee love-in, *Stargazy on Zummerdown* enacts a theatrical pageant of the commonweal.

'We value our humanity, not like the industrialists of the twentieth century,' says main character Ruth Baxter, played by Toni Arthur, whose background as a former folk singer, a researcher into the songs and lore of English pagan witchcraft and a presenter on the children's programmes *Play School* and *Playaway* ideally matched her to the role.[16] During the 'Stargazy' ceremony, she sings Richard Thompson's 1972 song 'The New St George', a post-industrial folk song that appeals equally to the workers of the factory and of the forge: a burlesque for the age of electric folk.

The Stargazy is an annual fete-cum-trade negotiation held on the summer solstice between the 'Aggros' (agricultural labourers) and the 'Toonies' (urban industrial workers) to thrash out the terms of trade. This kingdom of New Albion is divided along sharp fault lines. The Aggros and their 'New Harmony' party personify the roughshod country folk, while the Toonies are relics of the urban managerial class. This is a televisual mummers' play, a self-consciously theatrical enactment of an Anglo-Saxon constitution in which Albion's social inequities have been codified as a series of ritual games and folk customs. The previous two centuries have witnessed a massacre on Salisbury Plain during the Reformation of England and a Reformed Celtic Church, whose druidic priesthood now practises paganism and sun worship as the official religion, while preaching a Blakeian vision of the microcosm and macrocosm. Like the cathedral builders of the Middle Ages, the former manufacturing powerhouse of Sheffield is currently harnessed in the construction of a starship for space exploration, perhaps for a new generation of star-bound founding fathers.

Ruth runs a homespun astronomical observatory from a farmhouse where hens run unchecked and the telescope is an obsolete three-hundred-year-old brass model. She is given the most poetic lines, waxing rhapsodically about the 'poppy-scented blackness' of the galaxy she observes through her telescope and comparing mankind's festive rituals to the emergence of dragonflies from a black swamp. 'Man is part of the mighty process by which matter realises itself,' she observes. Aggros and Toonies recognise that they coexist in a mutually interdependent ecosystem. The towns provide and maintain the technology and engineering that allow the farmers to work the land; they in turn provide food for the towns and improvised craft workshops that now abound in the back gardens of Stoke-on-Trent, Birmingham and Wolverhampton.

Connecting earthiness with the galactic (Astro-Saxon?), the play has an ecological consciousness. As they 'niggle and haggle tonight', Father Cuchlain reminds the assembly of the colossal energy the sun has so far expended so that they can carry on their parochial existence on Earth. The duration of the negotiations will last as long as one candle burns, equivalent to one kilowatt of energy burned back into the atmosphere. This society has learned from its past mistakes and sustainably aligned itself with the cycles of nature.

The Stargazy is a series of folkish competitive sports, morris dancing and ritualised combat: a scrap between morris dancers, a choleric duel of insults and an onion-eating competition between two old men. Like many televised dramas of the 1970s, it's excessively wordy and wears its arguments way too heavily. At one point Ruth's fiancé, historian Sidney, delivers a firebrand staring-to-camera lecture on the history of social enslavement, oppression and revolution, the collapse of Marxism and capitalism. But *Stargazy* is, at root, an essay on the English condition, and on humanity's place in nature, wrapped up in the formal structure of a play. Like William Morris, it posits an unachievably idealistic future.

This new-age Anglicana ends with the festive alchemical wedding of Sidney and Ruth, the marriage of town and country. Their union resolves differences; the sun comes up, the world briefly seems to open its arms. Horizons have narrowed, but Sidney is obsessed with wandering the world. Forget the starship – exotic destinations like Derby, Wolverhampton and Sheffield are new planets waiting to be explored. In a supremely curious twist that occurs while the credits are rolling, the BBC cameras pull back to reveal the studio and its technical staff.

■

Until the starship is constructed, there remains a comparatively vast expanse of space to recolonise in the neighbourhood. For Lance and Andy, the lead characters in the three BBC series of *Detectorists* (2015–18), the abandoned pastures and untilled fields of eastern England are unknown regions stuffed with potential, and a potential pot of gold at the end of the rainbow.

Detectorists, a very English endeavour in its gentle pacing, self-deprecating humour and subtle ecological undertow, went on to achieve popularity on international TV networks. Written and directed by Mackenzie Crook, who also takes a leading role as metal-detecting hobbyist Andy Stone, the series successfully combines midlife-crisis comedy with more profound undercurrents of English history, mythology and the relationship with the landscape.

Following his coming of age in the BBC comedy series *The Office*, Crook emerged as a central figure in several British television productions that explored the matter of Britain from a variety of angles, including *Britannia* (Sky Atlantic, 2018–19) and *Worzel Gummidge* (BBC, 2019–20). A self-confessed nature lover who purchased eight acres of hornbeam, oak and sweet chestnut forest in Essex, Crook's creative career appears to have gathered momentum after his involvement in *Jerusalem*, a theatre play by Jez Butterworth that premiered in 2009 and ran in the West End and Broadway over the next decade. *Jerusalem*, surprisingly, is yet to be adapted for the big or small screen, but it provided some core members of the *Detectorists* cast, such as

Gerard Horan and Aimee-Ffion Edwards. *Jerusalem*'s Rooster Byron is a mythic John Bull, a larger-than-life Pied Piper for the rave generation who combines Blake's electric energy with anti-authoritarian earthiness. Living rough in a clearing in a Wiltshire forest, he is an alcohol-fuelled Peter Pan, gathering lost boys and girls around his static caravan. In the greenwood, he maintains a connection with the wilder impulses, a deep-rooted English rebel consciousness.

In *Detectorists*, the rebel yell has been shushed to a whisper: the members of the Danebury Metal Detecting Club channel their differences into a hobby which is pursued solo or in pairs. The 'finds table' in their village hall meetings is more of a Round Table: the club is a Camelot for scavengers on a quest to uncover the grail of a Saxon hoard or Roman burial. The enthusiasts brandish their metal detectors like magic swords and operate according to a self-imposed chivalric code. Andy's long-suffering girlfriend Becky wryly compares him to Lord Carnarvon and Howard Carter, in a lineage of great English archaeologists and antiquarians, but this noble pursuit has now shrunk to digging ring-pulls, Matchbox cars and a *Jim'll Fix It* badge out of the ground.

What Crook achieves so well here is to keep a seam of English magic running in the background. 'I've done some plays before', he told an interviewer, 'which are steeped in the folklore of British ancestry and the British landscape in particular. I've always loved where I live and that makes me feel a lot more deeply about England and its place and also my place in it. So that was a big inspiration – and East Anglia, and that part of Suffolk especially, really captures that sort of mythology, as well as being full of ancient history and archaeology.'[17] Although set in Essex (the unseen market-town Britain of crystal/New Age shops, second-hand book shops and pubs), most of the series was filmed in Suffolk, amid its trove of rolling meadows, hedgerows and wide-open skies. The hobby is 'our escape from the rude world, from the madding crowd', says Lance (Toby Jones), and it's not only Thomas Hardy who is invoked. Many shots are filmed with the camera placed at ground level, reminiscent of the ploughing scenes way back in *The Blood on Satan's Claw*.

In the last shot of season one, Lance dusts off a Shandy Bass ring-pull, while the camera dives under the soil strata to reveal a buried Saxon lord's jewellery and armour beneath his feet. Season two opens with a medieval monk running away from four horsemen (a homage, surely, to the riders of *Robin of Sherwood*'s 'Swords of Wayland') and burying an ornamental cross saved from his chapel next to a standing stone. In time-lapse we watch the wooden staff rot away, leaving just the jewelled head, then the camera surfaces through layers of sediment to open air, birdsong and an overhead shot of Andy and Lance in the field, with 'coils to the soil' next to the stone, which has now fallen on its side. At the end of this series, on the same spot, Lance experiences an eerie aural hallucination of the horses. 'Metal-detecting is the closest you'll get to time travel,' he muses in a later episode. Detectorists fulfil a different function from archaeologists: 'We unearth the scattered memories, mine for stories, fill in the personality.'

The third series introduces more explicitly ecological themes, with land and trees threatened by a proposed solar farm, and capitalist developers destroying a Roman mosaic in their eagerness to build an office block. While temping as a roadside weed sprayer, Andy saves a hedgehog from being run over, and when he carries it into the safety of a nearby wood, he discovers the dreamy Tatterdown Cottage, which will eventually become his and Becky's idyllic home. Karma is the thread running through this final series, as old rivalries are patched up, the DMDC members enjoy a perfect day of communal detecting, and a magpie's nest in the ancient oak tree finally delivers its jackpot of gold coins. Sometimes, the grail is above head height, not underfoot.

For his role as Veran, the druid chieftain, in *Britannia*, Crook had to endure heavy layers of latex. The series, which has run for two seasons at the time of writing, was conceived by Jez Butterworth and his

brother Tom and imagined Britain at the time of the Roman invasion in 43 CE. This sometimes uneven mix of drama, violence and
absurdist comedy plunges into the strangeness of pagan Britain and
its tribes as they encounter the Imperium. Including British folk rock
and psychedelic music on the soundtrack – Fairport Convention,
Donovan, the Pretty Things and Cream, among others – is a masterstroke. Not intended as serious historical revisionism, this is a fantasy
that takes advantage of the lack of a historical record of the period.
Pitting exotic, drug-addled, shamanic natives against the rigid lines
and institutional brutality of the Romans, *Britannia* transposes the
dynamic of *Jerusalem* to ancient history.

■

With his matted hair and necklace of ivy leaves, Jack Woodwose
(Michael Palin) could have been a straggler from the set of *Britannia*.
Instead, he appears in Mackenzie Crook's 2019 *Worzel Gummidge*
reboot. As the creator of Worzel and his scarecrow compadres, the
character of Jack replaced the 'Crowman' of the earlier 1970s series,
with added gravitas. Woodwose is simultaneously a dreadlocked
vagrant odd-job man and a cunning Jack-in-the-Green, mythic
guardian of Albion's sceptred isle.

This version of Worzel expresses concerns about the tangible
effects of climate change on the countryside. The leaves are not turning and the blackberries have not ripened. Crook's Worzel comes
with a shaggy turnip head and is clad in a mangy British Grenadier's
tunic from the late 1700s, harking back to the age of antiquarianism and the origins of folklore studies, the first gatherings of folk
songs and the popularity of broadsides. Farmer Braithwaite is also
troubled by the weather conditions: if he can't get the harvest in,
he'll lose the farm. Broadcast in two episodes over Christmas 2019,
Worzel Gummidge manages to cram in the 'farmers' ruin' scenario
familiar from *The Lie of the Land* and *The Levelling*, environmental

consciousness ('We're stuck in midsummer and nothing's moving on' sounds like a line from *Sapphire and Steel*) and a tart selection of acoustic folk music by the Unthanks. The second episode, 'The Green Man', incorporates homages to the biker gangs of *Psychomania* and *Requiem for a Village*, with its pumpkin-headed, leather-jacketed 'Trubbelmaker' crow-scarers, as well as to an infamous 1970s Public Information Film called *Apaches*, when the young boy John is sent to fetch something from the precarious barn loft – "Course it's safe – mind the scythes . . .'

The scarecrows are embodiments of that peculiar English dichotomy: the parallel conservatism and radicalism that surround the countryside, folklore and tradition. Worzel's pre-technological mindset paradoxically helps the children to become re-enchanted with their natural surroundings (he clumsily breaks their mobile phone, forcing them into other outdoor activities). What sets him apart from the rest of the scarecrow community is his eagerness to push against the grain of tradition. He questions the notion of doing things just because they've always been done that way, citing as an example the banning of fox-hunting. The scarecrow and its role in farming represent continuity and protection; it's an anthropomorphic tool that acts as a human interface between agriculture and the wild. Sitting on a ring of ancient stones on a hillside, Woodwose reminds Worzel that he's a 'guardian of the levels, sentinel of the seasons', intended to be his eyes and ears in the field, keeping watch for changes and disturbances in the natural order. In effect, Worzel is a television antenna, transmitting a real-time feed to Woodwose's Gaian control centre.

Back in the year before the declaration of the Second World War upended even more of Britain's old ways, the writer H. J. Massingham wrote of how 'The village itself . . . was not so much a casual cluster of natives and immigrants . . . as a single farm cultivated in partnership and by a group whose interests, activities, privileges, and obligations were enjoyed and respected by the shareholders of the whole community.'[18] Out in Scatterbrook, far from the city's electrickery, here we are again, returned to what *Penda's Fen* reminded us was the pagan village, the village that raises the child (enacted here in the comeuppance of the bullying Trubbelmakers), the countryside whose topography is the visible result of humans and nature working in harmony. As the drone camera rises up for the last time over Worzel and Woodwose, away stretches the heartland, the homeland, the land of illusions, the land of lost content, the haunted *heim*. Where sleeping kings and ancient lights are ghosts in the slipstream, seeking a wavelength, seeking the aerial that will channel them back into the ground.

22

Closedown

From the outside, Matt's Gallery looks more like a semi-detached house than an art space. After a long bus ride and a walk through the low-rise estates of Bermondsey in south London, I push open a door that leads directly off the street. The exhibition space occupies what was once a Victorian sitting room. Through the house, in a cramped backyard, are waste bins, a small garden and a lunch area. On this particular day in October 2019, the gallery is running a show called *Ghost/TV*, which consists of a single plinth on which a cathode-ray television set has been mounted at head height.

The television screen is displaying a video piece titled *Running on Empty*, which is a ten-minute film of another television. Susan Hiller, the artist responsible, became somewhat obsessed with television towards the end of her life (she died in January 2019). She previously exhibited *Channels*, consisting of one hundred and six television sets, each showing a report of a near-death experience. *Running on Empty* is scaled right back to a single screen in her workshop, intimate and private. The TV set she filmed – probably a late-1980s or early-'90s model, with a black frame and glass screen curved like an aerodynamic wing – was itself close to death. Like so many electronic products, its built-in obsolescence is part of the spec.

Hiller decided to make a video portrait of this particular machine because in its death throes it appeared to exhibit weird signs of sentience. It produced outlandish colour balance, shifting grain and occasional shimmer effects that would have been impossible for a human twiddling its knobs to recreate. It appeared to react when a hand drew near or touched it. Its digital clock was engaged in a perpetual countdown, skipping numbers like a dicky heart. Hiller's attention had been drawn to this particular set when, in its Teletext-style system font, it had started intermittently displaying random, vaguely threatening messages. 'Fuck.Video.You.' 'I WHO WANTS TO LIVE FOREVER.' Whatever soul remained in these fritzing valves was huffing out its last gasp.

I sat for around an hour in the company of Hiller's piece, watching it loop around again and again. Television as a medium has become increasingly attention-grabbing. There are anecdotal accounts of commissioning editors insisting on a new plot development every three minutes, otherwise a script goes out the window. Certainly, as television has become the source millions turn to for long-form episodic narratives (where they might formerly have reached for a novel), the medium has had to focus on story and forward drive over ambience and atmosphere. Put another way, atmosphere has been reduced to a familiar set of signs and gestures. Every single Scandinavian noir thriller, for instance, seems to contain an oblig- atory sequence in which the female detective enters a dark, dank basement, alone, brandishing a pistol and a torch. And yet it was Scandinavia – Norway in particular – that introduced the concept of 'slow TV': real-time, unedited streams from a camera mounted on the front of a train or a fjord cruise ship, or footage of someone expertly constructing a pile of firewood. At such moments, TV slows down, but still it never stops. There is never a blank screen, nor even a snowstorm, when you turn it on. The television has become part of the digital data flow and the never-ending conversation of social media. The mobile phone has, to all intents and purposes, become a TV that fits in your pocket.

Almost every work of cinema and television discussed in these pages is viewable in some form today, having survived the earlier culls of the 1960s and '70s. For all sorts of reasons, economic or cultural, much television output was deemed unworthy of being retained for posterity, and technicians erased or recorded over existing videotapes. The British film industry abounds with stories about unwanted foot- age being dumped or destroyed, including the persistent legend of the lost *Wicker Man* reels that a British Lion employee accidentally added to a pile that was to be carted off for use as landfill under the M3 motorway. Domestic video recorders have at least allowed material from the late 1970s onwards to reappear on YouTube or bootleg DVDs. As for the rest, it will likely remain forever lost, living on in rumour, its memory imprinted only in TV listings. Like Susan Hiller's ghost TV, the secret history of television will fizzle and decompose into electrical dust.

Before we switch off, there's one final paradox to consider. Even though television is a technology of the air, of aerials and etheric transmission, of distant seeing and remote viewing, we still refer to scheduled networks as 'terrestrial television'. In other words, we use the Latin word for 'earth'. 'Channels' were originally physical conduits, either naturally occurring or excavated by human ingenuity. The language that first sprung up around television was rooted in the ground. Television was bonded to the earth, while fed through the antenna mounted on your roof – a perch for crows and other winged signal-disruptors; one metal tree in a forest of aerial dreamcatchers. An alchemical chamber of earth, air and fire in the valves.

Nowadays, the television never sleeps; it has unlocked itself from the planet's circadian rhythm. As the name suggests, 'streaming' TV offers a never-ending trickle of data and entertainment. When I was a child, the TV went to sleep, and I longed to reach the age when I would be allowed to stay awake until that magical moment – usually sometime between midnight and 1 a.m. – described in the TV schedule as 'Closedown'. You imagined the night technicians at the BBC and ITV, yawning in their beige overalls, flicking switches and levers to the 'off' position, and the power shutting down with a gigantic sigh.

In the last year or so of writing this book, I heard a great deal of public debate about the role of television, the difficulty faced by terrestrial channels forced into competition with global streaming giants, the migration of advertising revenues to social media platforms, et cetera. In the wake of the political coverage of major events such as general elections, Brexit and the 2020 coronavirus outbreak, public trust in the impartiality of television channels, especially their news reporting departments, took a significant hit. During the lockdown of spring 2020, Netflix announced that its subscription base had reached 182 million – nearly 23 per cent up on previous years.

Where once there was a box, there is now a flat screen harbouring digital chips that contain multiple boxes. Those streaming services, with their virtual 'box sets', create a demand for grand narratives, topical documentaries and dramatised actuality. There is a place for on-demand viewing, but it should not be a case of either/or. Netflix and its ilk are transnational entertainment hubs that spread content on a subscription basis, but they don't generate news, don't cover current affairs, don't have continuity announcements, satirical quizzes, sports results or game shows. They don't have Comic Relief or any other fundraising strategies, they can't help track down criminals, and they don't host the Open University. They don't reveal the winning lottery numbers. They don't hang spaghetti on trees for April Fools' Day. They don't track the seasons or keep an eye on nature unfolding, like *Springwatch* or *Countryfile*. Most importantly, they can't react to rolling news, don't transmit the daily goings-on in Parliament or Congress, and are not equipped to hold a nation together in times of uncertainty or crisis. No newsflash will interrupt an on-demand episode.

I can't help feeling that culling Britain's terrestrial television – for example, reducing the influence of the BBC by removing the licence fee, as was proposed in Conservative government reviews after the 2019 election – would remove a vital backbone of British cultural life. Much of the output I have discussed in *The Magic Box* would never have made it past the proposal stage in a meeting with the commissioning editors of a global streaming service. Too quirky, too local, too slow, too dry, too difficult, too weird. If the television I grew up with had been driven solely by commercial interests and algorithmic recommendations, my life and my consciousness would not have been exposed to so much that I now look back on with fondness and wonder. And some that I recall as if in a mist, a half-remembered dream. Perhaps it was a rare winter night when, via some parenting loophole, I may indeed have stayed up, huddled in a dressing gown, skin warmed by the three-bar fire and its fibreglass coals as, outside the window, a November gale howls through the holly. The screen turns green as grass. Green with pinpricks of white, circulating, spilling in and out of their enclosures, the stragglers rounded up by an agile black-and-white dot that resolves into a panting sheepdog, alert to Cumbrian and Pennine dialects and their age-old commands of 'Come by 'ere,' 'Away to me' and 'That'll do' . . . Rounding up the sheep, darting back for the strays and shepherding them home to the pen. *One Man and His Dog* was, for much of the 1970s and '80s, transmitted shortly before the box shut down for the night. Whatever other crisis or drama had gone on that day, here was the television returning everything back to its right place, reconnecting with immemorial rural traditions and shutting the gate. Even if it couldn't brew your nightcap, at least television could help you count sheep.

The screen contracts to a pale white dot. The soundtrack is a high-frequency whine that continues through the night. Time, in the televisual dimension, has come to a stop. Until, with the dawn, the band strikes up, the clock appears on its sky of blue, the seconds pluck off like berries from the branch, and the spirits in the magic box blink awake.

Notes

INTRODUCTION: THE TEST CARD

1 For years I never knew what this monster movie could be. Then one night at the very end of the 1990s, at a techno party in a Cologne warehouse, I saw the same film projected onto a bare concrete wall behind the DJs: a Ray Harryhausen stop-motion special called *20 Million Miles to Earth*.

2 To take three examples: Ruth Inglis, *The Window in the Corner* (London: Peter Owen, 2003); Stuart Jeffries, *Mrs. Slocombe's Pussy: Growing Up in Front of the Telly* (London: Flamingo, 2008); Brian Viner, *Nice to See It, to See It, Nice* (London: Simon & Schuster, 2010).

1 TWO GREAT LEAPS FORWARD (1953 AND 1963)

1 *Daily Mail* review of the 1937 coronation day coverage, quoted in Bruce Norman, *Here's Looking at You: The Story of British Television 1908–39* (London: BBC Books, 1984), p. 194.

2 Philip Hope-Wallace, quoted in Asa Briggs, *The BBC: The First Fifty Years* (Oxford: Oxford University Press, 1985), p. 275.

3 Briggs, p. 275.

4 The American director John Carpenter made a later adaptation in 1995.

5 A brief scene in the Indian embassy, with a portrait of Mahatma Gandhi hanging on the wall, is prophetic: Briley would later win an Oscar for his screenplay for Richard Attenborough's *Gandhi* (1982).

6 http://www.bbc.co.uk/archive/doctorwho/6406.shtml.

7 Cecil Webber, BBC internal memo to Donald Wilson, 29 March 1963. Found at http://www.doctorwhonews.net/2013/03/unearthly-series-origins-tv-legend-8-260313040017.html.

8 Benjamin Cook, 'Chaos and Creation in the Junkyard', in *Doctor Who Magazine Special Edition: In Their Own Words* (Panini Comics, 12 January 2006).

9 Webber, memo to Donald Wilson.

10 Tony Richardson, *Long Distance Runner* (London: Faber and Faber, 1993), p. 126.

11 Richardson, *Long Distance Runner*, p. 130.

12 Richardson, *Long Distance Runner*, p. 134.

2 THE CREEPING MENACE

1 As an interesting aside, Gordon Flemyng's son Jason Flemyng starred

as Professor Quatermass in the BBC's live remake of *The Quatermass
Experiment* in 2005.

3 THIS NATION'S UNDERMIND

1 *Theatre Facts* #4 (November–January 1975).

2 Andy Beckett, *When the Lights Went Out: Britain in the Seventies*
(London: Faber and Faber, 2009), p. 376.

3 Quoted in Victoria Hainworth, *1990* preview, *Radio Times* 2810 (15
September 1977).

4 THE BOMB WILL KEEP US TOGETHER

1 Rosalie Horner, *Inside BBC Television: A Year Behind the Camera* (Exeter:
Webb and Bower, 1983).

2 John Darragh, *The Real Camelot: Paganism and the Arthurian Romances*
(London: Thames & Hudson, 1981).

5 RETURN TO THE RURAL

1 Adam Scovell, *Folk Horror: Hours Dreadful and Things Strange* (Leighton
Buzzard: Auteur, 2017).

2 M. J. Simpson, '*The Blood on Satan's Claw*: One Scary Skin Flick', in
Fangoria #230 (March 2004).

3 Caroline Tisdall, 'Freudulent' (review of a Henry Fuseli exhibition),
Guardian, 19 February 1975. There are earlier examples of the phrase
'folk horror', although these are highly sporadic, decades before the
context arose for its more pointed usage in the twenty-first century. The
earliest I have located is a reference to 'the old folk horror of mothers'
[*sic*] smothering their babies in bed' in a medical text by Roy Graham
Hoskins, *The Tides of Life: The Endocrine Glands in Bodily Adjustment*
(New York: W. W. Norton & Co., 1933). Closer to the subject at hand,
in a discussion of Gottfried August Bürger, the German Romantic poet
whose ballad *Lenore* (1774) was a popular eerie folk tale of its time,
featuring an undead knight who prefigures the vampire archetype, a
contributor to a Chicago-based academic publication referred to 'the
ballad, derived first from Bürger, with its freightage of superstition and
folk horror' (*English Journal*, Vol. 25, January 1936 (Chicago: University
of Chicago Press, 1936)). In an appreciation of Robert Louis Stevenson
in a 1945 edition of cultural magazine *Our Time*, a journalist cited 'that
tour de force of folk-horror, *Thrawn Janet*'.

4 Peter Hutchings, 'Uncanny Landscapes in British Film and Television', in
Visual Culture in Britain (winter 2004).

6 FATE THE FIRST: EVIL HERITAGE

1 *Kizzy* (BBC, 1976) was an adaptation of Rumer Godden's novel *The Diddakoi*.

2 Michael Reeves, 'Alan Bennett's Views' (letter), *The Listener*, 30 May 1968.

3 Ken Russell, *A British Picture: An Autobiography* (London: William Heinemann, 1989).

4 Ibid.

5 The sequence where Crossley demonstrates his shout was filmed on Saunton Sands in Devon, the same location used by Powell and Pressburger for the moment when David Niven's pilot crash-lands in *A Matter of Life and Death*.

7 FATE THE SECOND: THE GHOULS ARE AMONG US

1 Quoted in Bryan Senn, *'Twice the Thrills! Twice the Chills!' Horror and Science Fiction Double Features, 1955–1974* (Jefferson, NC: McFarland & Company, Inc., 2019).

2 The conflation of witchcraft, ancient curses and motorbikes on country backroads would also form the content of Robert Westall's novel *The Devil on the Road* (1978).

8 FATE THE THIRD: PAGANS RULE OK!

1 These brief early scenes are interesting in themselves as they include black fellow teachers, allies of Gwen, not representations of the Other, also quitting under the onslaught. Director Cyril Frankel's previously best-known achievement in film had been *Man of Africa* (1953), which again pioneered the use of non-white actors as believable individuals in a British film.

2 Alan Garner, 'The Beauty Things', in *The Voice That Thunders* (London: Harvill Press, 1997), p. 202.

3 Ibid.

4 Due to an industrial dispute, *The Owl Service* was shown in black and white in 1969, but retransmitted in colour later in the 1970s.

5 Alan Garner, 'Inner Time', in *The Voice That Thunders* (London: Harvill Press, 2010), p. 111.

6 Quoted in Stephen McKay, '*The Owl Service*: The Legend Unravelled' (sleeve note), *The Owl Service* DVD (Network DVD, 2008).

7 Quoted in Stephen McKay, '*The Owl Service*: The Legend Unravelled'.

8 Ibid.

9 Edward Woodward, Introduction to Allan Brown, *Inside* The Wicker Man: *How Not to Make a Cult Classic* (Edinburgh: Polygon/Birlinn, 2012).

10 Anthony Shaffer, interviewed in *The Wicker Man Enigma* (David Gregory, 2001), a special feature included on *The Wicker Man (Director's Cut)* DVD (Studio Canal, 2002).

11 Philip French, *Kill List* review in the *Guardian* (4 September 2011). https://www.theguardian.com/film/2011/sep/04/kill-list-review.

12 Ben Wheatley interview, https://www.youtube.com/ watch?v=ndB7uVZfjt0.

9 SPOOKS AND STONES
1 Marina Warner, 'Film: Nice Life, an Extra's', in *Phantasmagoria* (Oxford: Oxford University Press, 2006), p. 326. Quote is from Tony Oursler, *The Influence Machine*.

2 Angela Carter, 'And Things That Go Bump in the Night', *Radio Times*, 20 December 1975. Quoted in *Ghost Stories: Classic Adaptations from the BBC* (BFI DVD booklet, 2012).

3 Alfred Dinsdale, *Television: Seeing by Wireless* (London: Sir Isaac Pitman & Sons, Ltd, 1926).

4 William Morris, 'Innate Socialism' (lecture), 1878, collected in Asa Briggs (Ed.), *William Morris: Selected Writings and Designs* (Harmondsworth: Pelican, 1962).

5 DeWitt Bodeen, 'Val Lewton', in *Films in Review*, XIV, no. 4 (April 1963), pp. 210–15.

6 Dominic Sandbrook, *State of Emergency: Britain 1970–74* (London: Penguin, 2011).

10 GHOSTS OF CHRISTMAS PAST
1 Simon Farquhar, 'Lawrence Gordon Clark's *The Signalman*' (sleeve note), in *Ghost Stories: Classic Adaptations from the BBC* (BFI DVD, 2012).

2 Quoted in the documentary *M. R. James: Ghost Writer* (BBC, 2013).

3 M. R. James, Introduction to V. H. Collins (Ed.), *Ghosts and Marvels: A Selection of Uncanny Tales from Daniel Defoe to Algernon Blackwood* (Oxford: Oxford University Press, 1924).

4 As I argue in *Electric Eden: Unearthing Britain's Visionary Music* (London: Faber and Faber, 2010), Chapter 14.

5 The quotes from Lawrence Gordon Clark are taken from a filmed introduction included in the box set *Ghost Stories for Christmas* (BFI DVD, 2013).

13 FLICKERS IN THE GRATE
1 Brendan Carlin and Mark Hookham, 'Culture Secretary Oliver Dowden

Demands Netflix Make It Clear *The Crown* Is "Fiction" Over Fears Viewers May Mistake It for Fact', *Mail on Sunday*, 28 November 2020. https://www.dailymail.co.uk/news/article-8996921/Culture-Secretary-Oliver-Dowden-demands-Netflix-make-clear-Crown-fiction.html.

2 In another connection with the folk-rock scene, three years later Hemmings bankrolled Mellow Candle's *Swaddling Songs*, an Irish acid-folk record latterly heralded as a cult classic.

3 Sands Films has supplied costumes and period details for, among others, *Wolf Hall*, *The Young Victoria*, *Topsy-Turvy*, *Mr Turner*, *The Woman in White* and *Jonathan Strange & Mr Norrell*.

4 David Troughton, who plays one of the two brothers in 'A Tragedy of Two Ambitions', later appeared in the BBC post-apocalypse horror *Survivors* (1975), and went on to play Tony Archer in the long-running radio drama *The Archers*, as well as appearing in the bleak rural drama *The Levelling* (2016).

14 BLEAK HOUSES

1 Chris Buckley and Karoline Kan, 'Rich Chinese, Inspired by "Downton", Fuel Demand for Butlers', in *New York Times* (14 January 2017). https://www.nytimes.com/2017/01/14/world/asia/rich-chinese-inspired-by-downton-fuel-demand-for-butlers.html.

2 Adrian Tinniswood, *The Long Weekend: Life in the English Country House Between the Wars* (London: Jonathan Cape, 2016).

3 There's a story that the book's author, L. P. Hartley, once put a spell on film producer Alex Korda, who bought the film rights in the 1950s but later claimed he never intended to make the film, only sell the rights at a profit. 'I was so annoyed when I heard of this', Hartley reportedly said, 'that I put a curse on him and he died, almost the next morning.' Nancy Banks-Smith, 'Take Three on *The Go-Between*', *Guardian* (16 March 1971).

4 Edward Said, *Culture and Imperialism* (London: Vintage, 1994), p. 155.

5 Lucian Randall, *Ginger Geezer: The Life of Vivian Stanshall* (London: Fourth Estate, 2010).

15 THE GEOGRAPHY OF PEACE

1 British electronica/dance band Saint Etienne became the unlikely inheritors of Ian Nairn's exploratory spirit. *Finisterre* (Paul Kelly and Kieran Evans, 2002), a film released alongside their album of the same name, was a homage to Geoffrey Fletcher's 1967 book *The London Nobody Knows*, and their 2005 film *What Have You Done Today Mervyn*

Day? (Paul Kelly) left central London to explore the Lower Lea Valley, later to become the site of the London 2012 Olympics. Another English group exploring geography and the national film archive was British Sea Power, who collaborated with director Penny Woodcock on *From the Sea to the Land Beyond* (2012).

2 Maurice Wiggin in the *Sunday Times* (25 April 1972). Quoted in Mark Tewdwr-Jones, *Urban Reflections: Narratives of Place, Planning and Change* (Bristol: Policy Press, 2011), p. 204.

3 Lindsay Anderson, article in *Sight & Sound* (spring 1954), reprinted as 'Only Connect', sleeve notes to *The Humphrey Jennings Collection* (Film First DVD, 2005).

4 David Watkin, *Why Is There Only One Word for Thesaurus?* (Brighton: Trouser Press, 1998).

5 Ibid.

6 Ibid.

7 Ibid.

8 *Alice in the Cities* (1974), *The Wrong Move* (1975) and *Kings of the Road* (1976).

9 Chris Petit, 'Dancing along on the Céline', sleeve note, *Radio On* booklet (BFI DVD, 2008).

10 Leo Goldsmith, 'Space Exploration: Patrick Keiller on Landscape Cinema and the Problem of Dwelling', in *Moving Image Source* (18 January 2012). www.movingimagesource.us/articles/space-exploration-20120118.

11 Ibid.

16 THE RAGGED FRINGES

1 Iain Sinclair, 'Big Granny and Little Eden' (sleeve notes), *Gallivant* (BFI DVD, 2013).

2 Andrew Kötting, Film Notes in *Gallivant* (BFI DVD, 2013).

3 In his later films, Andrew Kötting attempted more wayward travelogues, this time on a swan-shaped pedalo (*Swandown*, 2012), and returned a magical container to a beach on the island of Harris (*The Whalebone Box*, 2020), accompanied in both by psychogeographical author Iain Sinclair, daughter Eden and others.

4 William Morris, 'Art and Socialism' (lecture, 1884), reprinted in A. L. Morton (Ed.), *The Political Writings of William Morris* (London: Lawrence & Wishart, 1984).

5 Shirley and Dolly Collins's 1969 album *Anthems in Eden* – which makes a brief appearance in the film – makes similar connections between folk

music, rural village populations and the culling of the First World War. Plester and Curry went on to make an excellent documentary on Shirley Collins and her decisive role in the British folk revival: *The Ballad of Shirley Collins* (2017).

6 Kate Lloyd, 'The "Downton Abbey" Economy: How One Costume Drama Reinvented British TV'. https://www.theringer.com/tv/2019/ 9/17/20868367/downton-abbey-movie-tourism-influence-british-tv.

7 Ibid.

8 As of 2018. See http://epp.eurostat.ec.europa.eu/cache/ITY_PUBLIC/1-27022014-AP/EN/1-27022014-AP-EN.PDF.

17 PAGEANTS AND PANDÆMONIUM

1 Alexandra Harris, *Romantic Moderns: English Writers, Artists and the Imagination from Virginia Woolf to John Piper* (London: Thames & Hudson, 2010), p. 109.

2 Kevin Jackson, sleeve note, *The Complete Humphrey Jennings Volume 3* (BFI DVD, 2013).

3 Basil Wright, *Sight and Sound*, December 1951. Reprinted in a booklet accompanying *The Humphrey Jennings Collection Volume 3* (BFI DVD, 2013).

4 Humphrey Jennings, *Pandæmonium: The Coming of the Machine as Seen by Contemporary Observers*, Eds Mary-Lou Jennings and Charles Madge (London: André Deutsch, 1985).

5 Derek Jarman, *Kicking the Pricks* (London: Vintage, 1996).

6 From BBC Written Archives, Caversham, File #T32/835/1.

7 John Wyver, 'Mainstream Approaches and Alternative Forms', in *Vision On: Film, Television and the Arts in Britain* (London: Wallflower Press, 2007), p. 180.

8 John Akomfrah, 'Director's Statement' (sleeve note), *The Stuart Hall Project* (BFI DVD, 2013).

9 Quoted in 'Towards a Curiosity in the Image', John Akomfrah in conversation with Georgia Korossi (sleeve note), *The Stuart Hall Project* (BFI DVD, 2013).

10 Paul Wright, 'Ghosts Summoned from the Land', interview on *Arcadia* website. https://www.arcadia.film/ghosts-summoned/.

18 ILL FARES THE LAND

1 Marina Lewycka, 'Working on *Winstanley*' (sleeve note), *Winstanley* (BFI DVD, 2012).

19 PRIVATE DYSFUNCTIONS
1 Giles Cooper also wrote the 'lost' ITV speculative history drama *The Other Man* (1964), referred to in Chapter 3 of this book.
2 Lindsay Anderson, 'Notes for a Preface', in *Never Apologise: The Collected Writings* (London: Plexus Publishing, 2004).
3 Ibid.
4 Ibid.

20 TANGLED UP IN TIME
1 Lindsay Anderson, in M. L. Jennings (Ed.), *Humphrey Jennings: Film Maker, Painter, Poet* (London: BFI, 1982), p. 59.
2 Brian Appleyard, *Culture & Consensus: England, Art and Politics Since 1940* (London: Methuen, 1995), p. 265.
3 Peter Wright, 'Echoes of Discontent: Conservative Politics and *Sapphire and Steel*', in John R. Cook and Peter Wright (Eds), *British Science Fiction Television* (London: I. B. Tauris, 2006).
4 This episode was the only one not written by Peter J. Hammond.
5 *A Monthly Bulletin*, June 1957. Quoted at http://zythophile. co.uk/2007/07/16/the-ploughmans-lunch-guilty-or-innocent/.
6 From a speech at the annual dinner of the Royal Society of St George (6 May 1924). Quoted in Stanley Baldwin, *On England, and Other Addresses* (London: Philip Allan & Co, 1926).

21 ENGLISH MAGIC
1 Graham Fuller, 'A Canterbury Tale' (review), in *Film Comment*, 13 March 1995, p. 33.
2 Betty Jardine, who played Fee Baker, died the year after *A Canterbury Tale* was released. She was married to Wilfred Bion (1897–1979), an internationally renowned psychoanalyst, which may or may not be relevant to this scene.
3 Michael Powell, *A Life in Movies* (London: Methuen, 1987), pp. 446–7.
4 Michael Powell, *Million Dollar Movie* (London: Heinemann, 1992), p. 67.
5 Powell's autobiography mentions that while shooting *A Canterbury Tale*, he was reading Esmé Wingfield-Stratford's 1920s *History of British Civilisation*.
6 Soundtrack composer Allan Gray was a Polish expatriate who had changed his name from Józef Żmigrod.
7 Powell, *A Life in Movies*, p. 447.
8 Powell, *A Life in Movies*, p. 443.

9 Geoffrey Hill, 'XX', *Mercian Hymns*, in *Collected Poems* (London: Penguin, 1985).

10 Richard Kelly (Ed.), *Alan Clarke* (London: Faber and Faber, 1998), p. 70.

11 Stephen's copy of the LP box set of *The Dream of Gerontius* is the Decca recording conducted by Benjamin Britten, whose front cover art is the most transcendent of all – a divine hand appearing through a crack in the clouds.

12 Sukhdev Sandhu (Ed.), *The Edge Is Where the Centre Is* (New York: Texte und Töne, 2015).

13 An encounter that recalls another televised meeting between an ageing, wheelchair-bound English composer and his younger amanuensis: Ken Russell's *Delius: Song of Summer* (1968).

14 Marina Warner, *Phantasmagoria: Spirit Visions, Metaphors, and Media into the Twenty-First Century* (Oxford: Oxford University Press, 2006), pp. 19–20.

15 Broadcast just the once in 1974, and eventually repeated as part of a David Rose selection on Channel 4 in 1991, *Penda's Fen* remained a lost TV cult item until its resurrection on YouTube and then on a BFI DVD in 2017. It remains one of the masterpieces of post-war television, perhaps too mature for the medium, but an enduring essay on nation, ideology and the spirit of place. Because it was so seldom viewed, very little has been made since then that resembles it. Only the video accompanying Kate Bush's song 'Cloudbusting' (1985) has, intentionally or not, a very similar look, as well as a sexually ambiguous role for Bush as a boy, with a father–mentor (Donald Sutherland) completing his magnum opus – a Wilhelm Reich-like orgone accumulator/rain-making engine. The scenes on the weather-beaten hilltop (Uffington) are shot from markedly similar angles as in *Penda's Fen*, and the sense of personal triumph over darker, repressive forces resembles it in tone.

16 For more on Toni Arthur's role in the folk revival, see the chapter 'We Put Our Magick on You' in Rob Young, *Electric Eden: Unearthing Britain's Visionary Music* (London: Faber and Faber, 2010).

17 David Burr, 'Out of Left Field' (blog article, 20 July 2018). https://davidburr.co.uk/out-of-left-field/.

18 H. J. Massingham, 'Our Inheritance from the Past', in Clough Williams-Ellis (Ed.), *Britain and the Beast* (London: Readers Union/J. M. Dent & Sons), 1938.

Bibliography

Anderson, Lindsay, *Never Apologise: The Collected Writings* (London: Plexus Publishing, 2004)

Ashby, Justine and Higson, Andrew (Eds), *British Cinema, Past and Present* (London: Routledge, 2000)

Barr, Charles (Ed.), *All Our Yesterdays: 90 Years of British Cinema* (London: BFI, 1986)

Beckett, Andy, *When the Lights Went Out: Britain in the Seventies* (London: Faber and Faber, 2009)

Bell, James (Ed.), *Gothic: The Dark Heart of Film* (London: BFI, 2013)

Bracewell, Michael, 'Method Acting in Birmingham, London & Coventry', in *England Is Mine: Pop Life in Albion from Wilde to Goldie* (London: Flamingo, 1997)

Briggs, Asa, *The BBC: The First Fifty Years* (Oxford: Oxford University Press, 1985)

Brosnan, John, *The Primal Screen: A History of Science Fiction Film* (London: Orbit, 1991)

Brown, Allan, *Inside* The Wicker Man*: How Not to Make a Cult Classic* (Edinburgh: Polygon/Birlinn, 2012)

Brownlow, Kevin, *How It Happened Here* (London: UKA Press, 1968/2007)

—— Winstanley*: Warts and All* (London: UKA Press, 2009)

Bussell, Jan, *The Art of Television* (London: Faber and Faber, 1952)

Butterworth, Jez, *Jerusalem* (London: Nick Hern Books, 2009)

Christie, Ian, *Arrows of Desire: The Films of Michael Powell and Emeric Pressburger* (London: Faber and Faber, 1994)

Clarke, Peter, *Hope and Glory: Britain 1900–2000* (London: Penguin, 1996/2004)

Cook, John R. and Wright, Peter (Eds), *British Science Fiction Television: A Hitchhiker's Guide* (London: I. B. Tauris, 2006)

Durgnat, Raymond, *A Mirror for England: British Movies from Austerity to Affluence* (London: Palgrave Macmillan/BFI Silver, 2011)

Farley, Paul, *Distant Voices, Still Lives* (London: BFI Modern Classics, 2006)

Fisher, Mark, *The Weird and the Eerie* (London: Repeater, 2016)

Garner, Alan, *The Owl Service* (London: Collins, 1967/1973)

—— *The Voice That Thunders* (London: Harvill Press, 1997)

Halligan, Benjamin, *Michael Reeves* (Manchester: Manchester University Press, 2003)

Hamilton, John, *Beasts in the Cellar: The Exploitation Film Career of Tony Tenser* (Godalming: FAB Press, 2005)

Hewison, Robert, *Culture and Consensus: England, Art and Politics Since 1940* (London: Methuen, 1995)

Hill, Geoffrey, *Mercian Hymns*, in *Collected Poems* (London: Penguin, 1985)

Horner, Rosalie, *Inside BBC Television: A Year Behind the Camera* (Exeter: Webb & Bower, 1983)

Hutchings, Peter, *Terence Fisher* (Manchester: Manchester University Press, 2001)

James, M. R., *Ghost Stories of an Antiquary* (Harmondsworth: Penguin, 1904/1976)

Jarman, Derek, *Modern Nature* (London: Vintage, 1992)

Jennings, Humphrey, *Pandaemonium: The Coming of the Machine as Seen by Contemporary Observers*, edited by Mary Lou Jennings and Charles Madge (London: André Deutsch, 1985)

Keighren, Innes M. and Norcup, Joanne (Eds), *Landscapes of Detectorists* (Axminster: Uniformbooks, 2020)

Keiller, Patrick, *The View from the Train: Cities and Other Landscapes* (London: Verso, 2013)

Kelly, Richard T. (Ed.), *Alan Clarke* (London: Faber and Faber, 1998)

Kinsey, Wayne, *Hammer Films: The Bray Studios Years* (Richmond: Reynolds & Hearn, 2002)

Lee, Christopher, *Lord of Misrule: The Autobiography* (London: Orion, 2007)

Matless, David (Ed.), *Landscape and Englishness* (London: Reaction Books, 1998)

Murphy, Robert (Ed.), *The British Cinema Book* (London: British Film Institute, 1999)

Murray, Andy, *Into the Unknown: The Fantastic Life of Nigel Kneale* (London: Headpress, 2006)

Newman, Kim, Quatermass and the Pit (London: Palgrave Macmillan/BFI, 2014)

Pirie, David, *A New Heritage of Horror: The English Gothic Cinema* (London: I. B. Tauris, 2009)

Powell, Michael, *A Life in Movies* (London: Methuen, 1987)

—— *Million-Dollar Movie* (London: Heinemann, 1992)

Randall, Lucian, *Ginger Geezer: The Life of Vivian Stanshall* (London: Fourth Estate, 2010)

Rigby, Jonathan, *English Gothic: A Century of Horror Cinema* (Richmond: Reynolds & Hearn, 2002)

Russell, Ken, *A British Picture: An Autobiography* (London: Heinemann, 1989)

Sandbrook, Dominic, *State of Emergency: Britain 1970–74* (London: Penguin, 2011)

—— *The Great British Dream Factory: The Strange History of Our National Imagination* (London: Penguin, 2016)

Sandhu, Sukhdev (Ed.), *The Edge Is Where the Centre Is* (New York: Texte und Töne, 2015)

Scovell, Adam, *Folk Horror: Hours Dreadful and Things Strange* (Leighton Buzzard: Auteur, 2017)

Sinclair, Iain, 'Cinema Purgatorio', in *Lights Out for the Territory* (London: Granta, 1997)

Sinker, Mark, *If . . .* (London: BFI Film Classics, 2004)

Sinyard, Neil, *Jack Clayton* (Manchester: Manchester University Press, 2000)

Strong, Roy, *Visions of England* (London: Bodley Head, 2011)

Taylor, Don, *Days of Vision – Working with David Mercer: Television Drama Then and Now* (London: Methuen, 1990)

Tinniswood, Adrian, *The Long Weekend: Life in the English Country House Between the Wars* (London: Jonathan Cape, 2016)

Vincendeau, Ginette (Ed.), *Film/Literature/Heritage: A* Sight and Sound *Reader* (London: BFI, 2001)

Walker, Alexander, *Hollywood England: The British Film Industry in the Sixties* (London: Orion, 1974/2005)

—— *National Heroes: British Cinema in the Seventies and Eighties* (London: Orion, 1985/2005)

Warner, Marina, *Phantasmagoria: Spirit Visions, Metaphors, and Media into the Twenty-First Century* (Oxford: Oxford University Press, 2006)

Watkin, David, *Why Is There Only One Word for Thesaurus? Being an Autobiography of David Watkin* (Brighton: Trouser Press, 1998)

Waugh, Evelyn, *Brideshead Revisited* (London: Penguin, 1945/2000)

Williams, Raymond, *The Country and the City* (St Albans: Paladin, 1975)

—— *Television: Technology and Cultural Form* (London: Fontana, 1974)

Wymer, Rowland, *Derek Jarman* (Manchester: Manchester University Press, 2005)

Wyndham, John, *The Midwich Cuckoos* (Harmondsworth: Penguin, 1957)

Wyver, John (Ed.), *Vision On: Film, Television and the Arts in Britain* (London: Wallflower Press, 2007)

Acknowledgements

Assembling *The Magic Box* has taken a good ten years and many hundreds of hours of viewing. It began as a companion to my book *Electric Eden*, but many more channels opened up during the writing than I had originally foreseen. Almost everyone I spoke to about the book gave me a recommendation for something to watch, which meant the rabbit warren got deeper and deeper. Meanwhile, more and more obscure films and programmes were being reissued, and new work was being produced with visual and thematic connections to the vintage material. All of which means that this book's long development has made it richer – although, for the same reasons, it will probably never quite feel finished.

Immense thanks to Lee Brackstone for accepting the first, rough-cut proposal and for his ongoing enthusiastic support and encouragement. I'm sorry he isn't still at Faber to see it get published. Thanks also to my former agent, Hannah Westland, and to my current one, Sam Copeland, at Rogers, Coleridge & White.

The superbly detailed readings by my editor Alexa von Hirschberg pushed me towards improving the first drafts in countless ways. Ian Bahrami did his usual stellar copy-editing. Dan Papps, Seán Hayes, Kate Ward, Mo Hafeez and the rest of the brilliant team at Faber & Faber were a joy to work with. My special gratitude to picture researcher Amanda Russell, who dug deep for buried treasure.

Thanks to everyone who has commissioned me to write on film and television, inspired me with conversations and ideas, recommended stuff to watch or sat with me in a cinema or in front of the telly. They include Upekha Bandaranayake, James Bell, Ina Blom, Michael Bonner, Kevin Brice, Jeremy Deller, Michel Faber, Will Fowler, Kim Hiorthøy, Julian House, Jim Jupp, Stuart Maconie, David Mitchell, Mark Pilkington, Vic Pratt, Jude Rodgers, Sukhdev Sandhu, David Solomons and Jonny Trunk. Gratitude also to the late Mark Fisher.

For supplying material, including films, DVDs, photos and information, my thanks to Tom Abell at Peccadillo Pictures (*The Levelling*), Nick Alexander (for the clock graphic on the first page), Kate Byers at Early Day Films (*Bait*), Steve Chibnall (Hammer Films Archive), Katy MacMillan (*The Moon and the Sledgehammer*), Jill Reading and Espen Bale at the BFI, Ben Rivers, Jonathan Russell at Rubicon Films (*The Droving*) and M. J. Simpson.

Thanks to my grandparents Joe and Eileen Young for the original magic box; to my parents, Rod and Viv Young, for letting me stay up late.

To Anne Hilde, thanks for all the episodes we've shared. To Axel and Mathilde, the blessings of Penda: 'Child be strange, dark, true, impure and dissonant. Cherish our flame!'

Picture Credits

Index

Titles of works relate to films unless otherwise indicated. Page numbers in italics relate to illustrations. Footnotes are denoted with the relevant chapter number in parentheses, e.g. 467n1(2).